The Definitive Guide to Grails 2

Jeff Scott Brown
Graeme Rocher

The Definitive Guide to Grails 2

ISBN-13 (pbk): 978-1-4302-4377-9

ISBN-13 (electronic): 978-1-4302-4378-6

President and Publisher: Paul Manning
Lead Editor: Douglas Pundick
Technical Reviewer: Graeme Rocher
Editorial Board: Steve Anglin, Ewan Buckingham, Gary Cornell, Louise Corrigan, Morgan Ertel, Jonathan Gennick, Jonathan Hassell, Robert Hutchinson, Michelle Lowman, James Markham, Matthew Moodie, Jeff Olson, Jeffrey Pepper, Douglas Pundick, Ben Renow-Clarke, Dominic Shakeshaft, Gwenan Spearing, Matt Wade, Tom Welsh
Coordinating Editor: Katie Sullivan
Copy Editor: Thomas McCarthy
Compositor: Bytheway Publishing Services
Indexer: SPi Global
Artist: SPi Global
Cover Designer: Anna Ishchenko

Distributed to the book trade worldwide by Springer Science+Business Media New York, 233 Spring Street, 6th Floor, New York, NY 10013. Phone 1-800-SPRINGER, fax (201) 348-4505, e-mail orders-ny@springer-sbm.com, or visit www.springeronline.com.

For information on translations, please e-mail rights@apress.com, or visit www.apress.com.

Apress and friends of ED books may be purchased in bulk for academic, corporate, or promotional use. eBook versions and licenses are also available for most titles. For more information, reference our Special Bulk Sales–eBook Licensing web page at www.apress.com/bulk-sales.

Any source code or other supplementary materials referenced by the author in this text is available to readers at www.apress.com. For detailed information about how to locate your book's source code, go to www.apress.com/source-code.

To Mom.
Thanks for everything.

—Jeff Scott Brown

To Birjinia.
Thanks for being you. Maite zaitut.

—Graeme Rocher

Contents at a Glance

Contents

About the Author

 **Jeff Scott Brown** is an engineer at SpringSource, where he works as a member of the Groovy and Grails development team. Jeff, a technologist for nearly 20 years, has been a member of the Grails team since the framework's very early days. Earlier he was part of G2One, the Groovy/Grails company that eventually became part of SpringSource.

About the Technical Reviewer

 **Graeme Rocher**, a software engineer, a consultant, and an expert in dynamic language, serves as head of Grails Development at SpringSource (www. springsource.com). Graeme is the project lead of the open source Grails web application framework (http://grails.org) and a coauthor of *The Definitive Guide to Grails* (Apress). With Jeff Scott Brown, he is also an author of the present book.

Acknowledgments

First of all, I am grateful to my lovely wife, Betsy, and our boys, Jake and Zack, for all of their support. Without them, none of what I get to do would be possible. Thank you!

To Graeme I have to say a giant thank-you as well. He and I have worked together on the Grails technology for quite a few years, and that experience has been invaluable. I hope we continue enjoying accomplishments together for a very long time.

Thanks, too, to the whole Groovy and Grails team at SpringSource. I have never worked with a smarter group of people or a group that made work seem so much like pleasure.

Thanks as well to the whole Apress team for their support in completing this project. I appreciate their patience and their willingness to help me get this thing done. In particular, thanks to Katie Sullivan, Douglas Pundick, and Steve Anglin for seeing this project through to the end.

Last but not least, I have to extend a big thank-you to Damien Vitrac for contributing some fantastic CSS work to the sample application for this book. The thing looks so much nicer because of his contributions. Well done!

—Jeff Scott Brown

Writing a book is no small task. It requires hours of dedication every day—valuable time stripped away from loved ones. For this alone I thank my wife, Birjinia, whose patience and support drive me to achieve more. Also, thanks to my kids, Alex and Lexeia, who showed remarkable restraint when tempted to wrestle me away from the computer. You guys rock.

To the Grails team at SpringSource, you are a really special group. It continues to be a privilege to work with you all. I count myself extremely lucky to work in the Open Source sector, where cutting-edge innovation and technology leadership are daily occurrences. There is a very special kind of enjoyment that comes from working with such a talented team of innovators.

Thanks to the team at Apress for getting the book done. It is not easy managing all the moving pieces that go into the making of a great technical book. Kudos.

—Graeme Rocher

CHAPTER 1

■ ■ ■

The Essence of Grails

Simplicity is the ultimate sophistication.

—Leonardo da Vinci

To understand Grails, you first need to understand its goal: to dramatically simplify enterprise Java web development. To take web development to the next level of abstraction. To tap into what has been accessible to developers on other platforms for years. To have all this while still retaining the flexibility to drop down into the underlying technologies and utilize their richness and maturity. Simply put, we Java developers want to "have our cake and eat it, too."

Have you faced the pain of dealing with multiple crippling XML configuration files and an agonizing build system where testing a single change takes minutes instead of seconds? Grails brings back the fun of development on the Java platform, removing barriers and exposing users to APIs that enable them to focus purely on the business problem at hand. No configuration, zero overhead, immediate turnaround.

You might be wondering how you can achieve this remarkable feat. Grails embraces concepts such as Convention over Configuration (CoC), Don't Repeat Yourself (DRY), and sensible defaults that are enabled through the terse Groovy language and an array of domain-specific languages (DSLs) that make your life easier.

As a budding Grails developer, you might think you're cheating somehow, that you should be experiencing more pain. After all, you can't squash a two-hour gym workout into twenty minutes, can you? There must be payback somewhere, maybe in extra pounds?

As a developer you have the assurance that you are standing on the shoulders of giants with the technologies that underpin Grails: Spring, Hibernate, and of course, the Java platform. Grails takes the best of such dynamic language frameworks as Ruby on Rails, Django, and TurboGears and brings them to a Java Virtual Machine (JVM) near you.

This chapter is going to introduce the framework at the highest level and provide some essentials for getting started. All of the concepts introduced here will be explained in detail later in the book.

Simplicity and Power

A factor that clearly sets Grails apart from its competitors is evident in the design choices made during its development. By not reinventing the wheel, and by leveraging tried and trusted frameworks such as Spring and Hibernate, Grails can deliver features that make your life easier without sacrificing robustness.

Grails is powered by some of the most popular open source technologies in their respective categories:

- *Hibernate*: The de facto standard for object-relational mapping (ORM) in the Java world.

- *Spring*: The hugely popular open source Inversion of Control (IoC) container and wrapper framework for Java.

- *SiteMesh*: A robust and stable layout-rendering framework.

- *Tomcat*: A proven, embeddable servlet container.

- *H2*: A pure Java Relational Database Management System (RDBMS) implementation.

The concepts of ORM and IoC might seem a little alien to some readers. ORM simply serves as a way to map objects from the object-oriented world onto tables in a relational database. ORM provides an additional abstraction above SQL, allowing developers to think about their domain model instead of getting wrapped up in reams of SQL.

IoC provides a way of "wiring" together objects so that their dependencies are available at runtime. As an example, an object that performs persistence might require access to a data source. IoC relieves the developer of the responsibility of obtaining a reference to the data source. But don't get too wrapped up in these concepts for the moment, as their usage will become clear later in the book.

You benefit from Grails because it wraps these frameworks by introducing another layer of abstraction via the Groovy language. You, as a developer, will not know that you are building a Spring and Hibernate application. Certainly, you won't need to touch a single line of Hibernate or Spring XML, but it is there at your fingertips if you need it. Figure 1-1 illustrates how Grails relates to these frameworks and the enterprise Java stack.

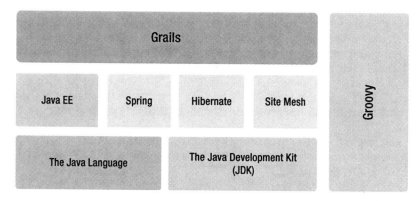

Figure 1-1. *The Grails stack*

Grails, the Platform

When approaching Grails, you might suddenly experience a deep inhalation of breath followed by an outcry of "not another web framework!?" That's understandable, given the dozens of web frameworks that exist for Java. But Grails is different and in a good way. Grails is a full-stack environment, not just a web framework. It is a *platform* with ambitious aims to handle everything from the view layer down to your persistence concerns.

In addition, through its plug-ins system (covered in Chapter 12), Grails aims to provide solutions to an extended set of problems that might not be covered out of the box. With Grails you can accomplish searching, job scheduling, enterprise messaging and remoting, and more.

The sheer breadth of Grails's coverage might conjure up unknown horrors and nightmarish thoughts of configuration, configuration, configuration. However, even in its plug-ins, Grails embraces Convention over Configuration and sensible defaults to minimize the work required to get up and running.

We encourage you to think of Grails as not just another web framework but as the *platform* upon which to build your next web 2.0 phenomenon.

Living in the Java Ecosystem

As well as leveraging Java frameworks that you know and love, Grails gives you a platform that allows you to take full advantage of Java and the JVM—thanks to Groovy. No other dynamic language on the JVM integrates with Java like Groovy. Groovy is designed to work seamlessly with Java at every level. Starting with syntax, the similarities continue as follows:

- The Groovy grammar is derived from the Java 5 grammar, making most valid Java code also valid Groovy code.

- Groovy shares the same underlying APIs as Java, so your trusty javadocs are still valid!

- Groovy objects are Java objects. This has powerful implications that might not be immediately apparent. For example, a Groovy object can implement Java.io. Serializable and be sent over Remote Method Invocation (RMI) or clustered using session-replication tools.

- Through Groovy's joint compiler you can have circular references between Groovy and Java without running into compilation issues.

- With Groovy you can easily use the same profiling tools, the same monitoring tools, and all existing and future Java technologies.

Groovy's ability to integrate seamlessly with Java, along with its Java-like syntax, is the number-one reason why its conception generated so much hype. Here was a language with capabilities similar to those of languages such as Ruby and Smalltalk running directly in the JVM. The potential is obvious, and the ability to intermingle Java code with dynamic Groovy code is huge. In addition, Groovy allows mixing of static types and dynamic types, combining the safety of static typing with the power and flexibility to use dynamic typing where necessary.

This level of Java integration is what drives Groovy's continued popularity, particularly in the world of web applications. Across different programming platforms, varying idioms essentially express the same concept. In the Java world there are servlets, filters, tag libraries, and JavaServer Pages (JSP). Moving to a new platform requires relearning all of these concepts and their equivalent APIs or idioms—easy for some, a challenge for others. Not that learning new things is bad, but a cost is attached to knowledge gain in the real world, a cost that can present a major stumbling block in the adoption of any new technology that deviates from the standards or conventions defined within the Java platform and the enterprise.

In addition, Java has standards for deployment, management, security, naming, and more. The goal of Grails is to create a platform with the essence of frameworks like Rails or Django or CakePHP, but one that embraces the mature environment of Java Enterprise Edition (Java EE) and its associated APIs.

Grails is, however, a technology that speaks for itself: the moment you experience using it, a little light bulb will go on inside your head. So without delay, let's get moving with the example application that will flow throughout the course of this book.

The gTunes example will guide you through the development of a music store similar to those provided by Apple, Amazon, and Napster. An application of this nature opens up a wide variety of interesting possibilities, from e-commerce to RESTful APIs and RSS or Atom feeds. We hope it will provide a broad understanding of Grails and its feature set.

Installing and Configuring Grails

Installing Grails is almost as simple as using it, but there is at least one prerequisite to take into account. Grails requires a valid installation of the Java SDK 1.6 or above, which, of course, can be obtained from Oracle: http://www.oracle.com/technetwork/java/javase/.

After installing the Java SDK, set the JAVA_HOME environment variable to the location where it is installed and add the JAVA_HOME/bin directory to the PATH variables.

■ **Note**   If you are working on Mac OS X, you already have Java installed! However, you still need to set JAVA_HOME in your ~/.profile file.

To test your installation, open up a command prompt and type java –version:

```
$java -version
```

You should see output similar to Listing 1-1.

Listing 1-1. Running the Java Executable

```
java version "1.6.0_29"
Java(TM) SE Runtime Environment (build 1.6.0_29-b11-402-11D50b)
Java HotSpot(TM) 64-Bit Server VM (build 20.4-b02-402, mixed mode)
```

As is typical with many other Java frameworks, including Apache Tomcat and Apache Ant, the installation process involves following a few simple steps. Download and unzip Grails from http://grails.org, create a GRAILS_HOME variable that points to the location where you installed Grails, and add the GRAILS_HOME/bin directory to your PATH variable.

To validate your installation, open a command window and type the command grails -version:

```
$ grails -version
```

If you have successfully installed Grails, the command will output the usage help shown in Listing 1-2.

Listing 1-2. Running the Grails Executable

```
Grails version: 2.1.0
```

Typing grails help will display more usage information, including a list of available commands. If more information about a particular command is needed, you can append the command name to the help command. For example, if you want to know more about the create-app command, simply type grails help create-app:

```
$ grails help create-app
```

Listing 1-3 provides an example of the typical output.

Listing 1-3. Getting Help on a Command

```
grails create-app -- Creates a Grails application for the given name
```

Usage (optionals in square brackets):

```
create-app [--inplace] [NAME]
```

where

```
--inplace  = Creates the project in the current directory rather than
             creating a new directory.
NAME       = The name of the project. If not provided, this command will
             ask you for the name.
```

The Grails command-line interface is built on another Groovy-based project called Gant (http://gant.codehaus.org/), which wraps the ever-popular Apache Ant (http://ant.apache.org/) build system. Gant allows seamless mixing of Ant targets and Groovy code.

We'll discuss the Grails command line further in Chapter 12.

Creating Your First Application

In this section you're going to create your first Grails application, which will include a simple controller. Here are the steps you'll take to achieve this:

1. Run the command grails create-app gTunes to create the application (with "gTunes" being the application's name).

2. Navigate into the gTunes directory by issuing the command cd gtunes.

3. Create a storefront controller with the command grails create-controller store.

4. Write some code to display a welcome message to the user.

5. Test your code and run the tests with grails test-app.

6. Run the application with grails run-app.

Step 1: Creating the Application

Sound easy? It is, and your first port of call is the create-app command; you managed to extract some help with it in the previous section. To run the command, simply type grails create-app and hit Enter in the command window:

```
$ grails create-app
```

Grails will automatically prompt you for a project name, as presented in Listing 1-4. When this happens, type gTunes and hit Enter. As an alternative, use the command grails create-app gTunes, in which case Grails takes the appropriate action automatically.

Listing 1-4. Creating an Application with the create-app Command

```
Environment set to development . . .
Application name not specified. Please enter: gTunes
```

Upon completion, the command will have created the gTunes Grails application and the necessary directory structure. The next step is to navigate to the newly created application in the command window using the shell command:

```
cd gTunes
```

At this point you have a clean slate—a newly created Grails application—with the default settings in place. A screenshot of the structure of a Grails application appears in Figure 1-2.

We will delve deeper into the structure of a Grails application and the roles of the various files and directories as we progress through the book. Notice, however, how Grails contains directories for controllers, domain objects (models), and views.

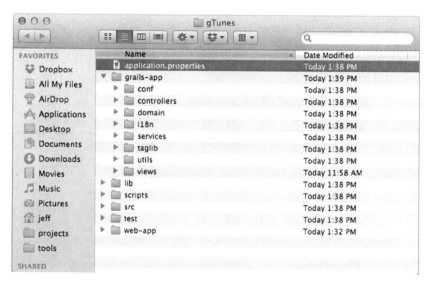

Figure 1-2. The gTunes application structure

Step 2: Creating a Controller

Grails is an MVC[1] framework, which means it has models, views, and controllers to separate concerns cleanly. Controllers, which are central to a Grails application, can easily marshal requests, deliver responses, and delegate to views. Because the gTunes application centers on the concept of a music store, we'll show how to create a "store" controller.

To help along the way, Grails features an array of helper commands for creating classes that "fit" into the various slots in a Grails application. For example, for controllers there is the `create-controller` command, which will do nicely. But using these commands is not mandatory. As you grow more familiar with the different concepts in Grails, you can just as easily create a controller class using your favorite text editor or integrated development environment (IDE).

---

1   The Model-View-Controller (MVC) pattern is a common pattern found in many web frameworks designed to separate user interface and business logic. See Wikipedia, "Model-view-controller," http://en.wikipedia.org/wiki/Model-view-controller, 2003.

Nevertheless, let's get going with the `create-controller` command, which, as with `create-app`, takes an argument where you can specify the name of the controller you wish to create. Simply type `grails create-controller store`:

```
$ grails create-controller store
```

Now sit back while Grails does the rest (see Listing 1-5).

Listing 1-5. *Creating a Controller with the create-controller Command*

```
| Created file grails-app/controllers/gtunes/StoreController.groovy
| Created file grails-app/views/store
| Created file test/unit/gtunes/StoreControllerTests.groovy
```

Once the `create-controller` command has finished running, Grails will have created, not one, but two classes for you: a new controller called `StoreController` within the `grails-app/` controllers directory and an associated test case in the `test/unit` directory. Since a package name was not specified on the command line, Grails defaults to creating artifacts in a package name that matches the application name. Figure 1-3 shows the newly created controller nesting nicely in the appropriate directory.

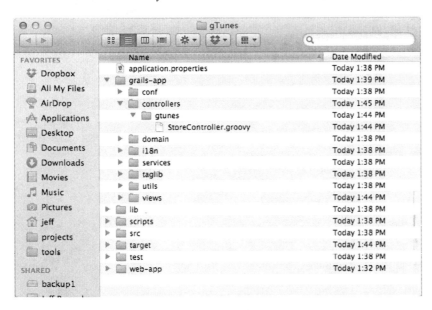

Figure 1-3. *The newly created StoreController*

Due to Groovy's dynamic nature, you should aim for a high level of test coverage[2] in any Grails project (Grails assumes you'll need a test if you're writing a controller). Dynamic languages such as Groovy, Ruby, and Python do not give nearly as much compile-time assistance as a statically typed language such as Java. Some errors that you might expect to be caught at compile time are actually left to runtime, including method resolution. Sadly, the comfort of the compiler often encourages Java developers to forget about testing altogether. Needless to say, the compiler is not a substitute for a good suite of unit tests, and what you lose in compile-time assistance you gain in expressivity.

2　Code coverage is a measure used in software testing. It describes the degree to which the source code of a program has been tested.

Throughout this book we will demonstrate automated-testing techniques that make the most of Grails's testing support.

Step 3: Printing a Message

Let's return to the StoreController. By default, Grails will create the controller and give it a single action called index. The index action is, by convention, the default action in the controller. Listing 1-6 shows the StoreController containing the default index action.

Listing 1-6. The Default index Action

```
package gtunes
class StoreController {
    def index() {}
}
```

The index action doesn't seem to be doing much, but by convention its declaration instructs Grails to try to render a view called grails-app/views/store/index.gsp automatically. Views are the subject of Chapter 5, so for the sake of simplicity we're going to try something less ambitious instead.

Grails controllers come with a number of implicit methods, which we'll cover in Chapter 4. One of these is render, a multipurpose method that, among other things, can render a simple textual response. Listing 1-7 shows how to print a simple response: "Welcome to the gTunes store!"

Listing 1-7. Printing a Message Using the render Method

```
package gtunes
class StoreController {
    def index() {
        render 'Welcome to the gTunes store!'
    }
}
```

Step 4: Testing the Code

The preceding code is simple enough, but even the simplest code shouldn't go untested. Open the StoreControllerTests test suite that was generated earlier inside the test/unit directory. Listing 1-8 shows the contents of the StoreControllerTests suite.

Listing 1-8. The Generated StoreControllerTests Test Suite

```
package gtunes

import grails.test.mixin.*
import org.junit.*

/**
 * See the API for {@link grails.test.mixin.web.ControllerUnitTestMixin} for usage instructions
 */
@TestFor(StoreController)
class StoreControllerTests {
```

```
    void testSomething() {
        fail "Implement me"
    }
}
```

Grails separates tests into "unit" and "integration" tests. Integration tests bootstrap the whole environment, including the database; hence, they tend to run more slowly. In addition, integration tests are typically designed to test the interaction of a number of classes and therefore require a more complete application before you can run them.

Unit tests, on the other hand, are fast-running tests, but they require extensive use of mocks and stubs. Stubs are classes used in testing that mimic the real behavior of methods by returning arbitrary hard-coded values. Mocks essentially do the same thing but exhibit a bit more intelligence by having "expectations." For example, a mock can specify that it "expects" a given method to be invoked at least once—even ten times if required. As we progress through the book, the difference between unit tests and integration tests will become clearer.

To test the StoreController in its current state, assert the value of the response that was sent to the user. A simple way of doing this appears in Listing 1-9.

Listing 1-9. Testing the StoreController's Index Action

```
package gtunes

import grails.test.mixin.*
import org.junit.*

/**
 * See the API for {@link grails.test.mixin.web.ControllerUnitTestMixin} for usage instructions
 */
@TestFor(StoreController)
class StoreControllerTests {

    void testSomething() {
        controller.index()
        assert 'Welcome to the gTunes store!' == response.text
    }
}
```

What we're doing here is using the built-in testing capabilities of Grails to evaluate the content of the response object. During a test run, Grails magically transforms the regular servlet HttpServletResponse object into a Grails MockHttpServletResponse, which has helper properties, such as text, that enable you to evaluate what happened as the result of a call to the render method.

Nevertheless, don't get too hung up about the ins and outs of using this code just yet. The whole book will be littered with examples; they will gradually ease you into becoming proficient at testing with Grails.

Step 5: Running the Tests

To run the tests and verify that everything works as expected, you can use the grails test-app command. The test-app command will execute all the tests in the application and output the results to the test/reports directory. In addition, you can run only StoreControllerTests by issuing the command grails test-app StoreController. Listing 1-10 shows some typical output that results when the grails test-app command is run.

Listing 1-10. Running Tests with grails test-app

```
| Completed 1 unit test, 0 failed in 1107ms
| Tests PASSED - view reports in target/test-reports
```

If you want to review the reports, you'll find XML, HTML, and plain-text reports in the test/reports directory. Figure 1-4 shows what the generated HTML reports look like in a browser—they're definitely easier on the eye than the XML equivalent!

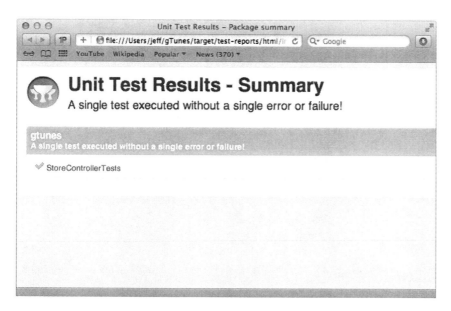

Figure 1-4. Generated HTML test reports

Step 6: Running the Application

Now that you've tested your code, the final step is to see it in action. Do this using the grails run-app command, which will start up a locally running Grails server on port 8080 by default.

Get Grails going by typing grails run-app into the command prompt:

```
$ grails run-app
```

You'll notice that Grails will start up and inform you of a URL you can use to access the Grails instance (see Listing 1-11).

Listing 1-11. Running an Application with run-app

```
...
| Server running. Browse to http://localhost:8080/gTunes
```

If you get a bind error, such as the following one, it probably resulted from a port conflict: "Server failed to start: java.net.BindException: Address already in use".

This error typically occurs if you already have another container, such as Apache Tomcat (http://tomcat.apache.org), running on port 8080. You can work around this issue by running Grails on a different port by passing the server.port argument and specifying an alternative value:

```
grails -Dserver.port=8087 run-app
```

In the preceding case, Grails will start up on port 8087 as expected. Barring any port conflicts, you should have Grails up and running and ready to serve requests at this point. Open your favorite browser and navigate to the URL prompted by the Grails run-app command shown in Listing 1-11. You'll be presented with the Grails welcome page that looks something like Figure 1-5.

The welcome screen is (by default) rendered by a Groovy Server Pages (GSP) file located at web-app/index.gsp, but you can fully customize the location of this file through URL mappings (discussed in Chapter 6).

As Figure 1-5 shows, the StoreController you created earlier is one of those listed as available. Clicking the StoreController link results in printing the "Welcome to the gTunes store!" message you implemented earlier (see Figure 1-6).

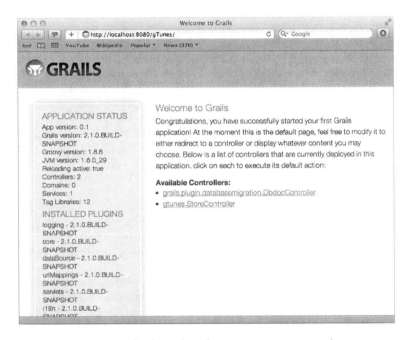

Figure 1-5. *The standard Grails welcome page*

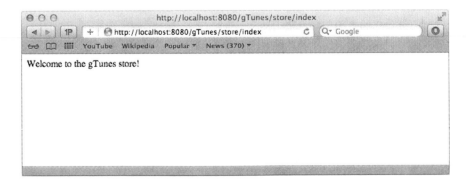

Figure 1-6. *StoreController prints a message.*

Grails Interactive Mode

So far all of the Grails commands that we have seen have been executed by running grails and passing a command name as an argument, for example, grails create-domain-class. When a command is executed like this, several things have to happen. The grails command first starts up the JVM, the Groovy runtime environment has to be initialized, and a certain amount of the Grails runtime environment has to be initialized. All of that has to happen before the command can actually be executed and all of that "warming up" takes time. The amount of time will, of course, vary depending on your hardware. Grails "interactive mode" can be a big help here. To start interactive mode, enter the grails command with no arguments. See Listing 1-12.

Listing 1-12. Starting Interactive Mode

```
$ grails
grails>
```

As long as you are in the interactive mode, any grails command that could have been executed on the command line may be executed. The syntax is exactly the same as it would be on the command line, except that there is no need to prefix every command with "grails". For example, on the command line you might type something like "grails create-domain-class com.gtunes.Store" but in interactive mode you would type the shorter "create-domain-class com.gtunes.Store" as shown in Listing 1-13.

Listing 1-13. Creating a Domain Class in Interactive Mode

```
$ grails
grails> create-domain-class com.gtunes.Store
| Created file grails-app/domain/com/gtunes/Store.groovy
| Created file test/unit/com/gtunes/StoreTests.groovy
grails>
```

Notice that running this command in interactive mode is considerably quicker than running the same command from the command line.

Since pressing the up arrow will cycle through recently executed commands, it's really quick and easy to execute similar commands one after the other. As an example, after executing "create-domain-class com.gtunes.Store", press the up arrow to recall that command and then backspace over "Store" to replace it with "Song" in order to quickly execute "create-domain-class com.gtunes.Song".

Another great productivity boost provided by interactive mode is intuitive tab completion. While in interactive mode, type "cre" followed by pressing Tab, and interactive mode will show all the available commands that start with "cre", as shown in Listing 1-14.

Listing 1-14. Tab Completion in Interactive Mode

```
grails> create-

create-controller          create-domain-class          create-filters             create-
hibernate-cfg-xml       create-integration-test    create-plugin             create-
scaffold-controller     create-script              create-service
create-tag-lib             create-unit-test              create-web-xml-config
grails> create-
```

Now that the interactive mode has completed the "cre" command as far as it can—that is, to "create-"—you can type "d" and press Tab again, at which point the interactive mode will complete the command to "create-domain-class", since that is the only available command starting with "create-d". This same style of autocompletion works for all available commands. Further, some commands that accept arguments also support autocompletion. For example, if you press Tab after "generate-all", since the generate-all command accepts a domain-class name as an argument, the console will show all of the domain classes that are available in the application. This makes it very easy to fill the argument in without typing the full class name. You need to type only enough of the domain-class name to make it unique; the interactive mode can complete the rest.

Interactive mode can help quickly open certain kinds of reports. After generating a domain class or any other artifact, run "test-app unit:" from within interactive mode to run all of the unit tests. The test results will be generated below the project root at target/test-reports/html/index.html. In order to open that report in your default web browser from within interactive mode, use the open command, as shown in Listing 1-15:

Listing 1-15. Opening Unit Test Report in Interactive Mode

```
grails> open target/test-reports/html/index.html
grails>
```

Note that tab completion may be used to help complete the path to the HTML file.

It turns out that the open command knows where to find the test report; so a simpler way to open the report is shown in Listing 1-16.

Listing 1-16. Opening Unit Test Report by Name in Interactive Mode

```
grails> open test-report
grails>
```

The way to exit the interactive mode is to enter "exit" at the interactive mode prompt. An exception to this occurs if the application is currently running, as it would be after executing "run-app" from the console. In such a case the exit command will exit the application but leave you in interactive mode. At that point you could execute "exit" again to leave interactive mode altogether.

If you are only going to execute a single command, then interactive mode isn't going to be of much use. Interactive mode really benefits the more typical workflow situation where numerous Grails commands are executed over a period of time. You may want to run the tests, view the reports, make some code changes and continue iterating through that loop. You may want to generate several domain classes at once, fill in some of their details, and then generate corresponding controllers and views. Anytime you are going to be executing more than one or two Grails commands during a work session, interactive mode is probably going to be a big help. While doing real development, executing those commands from interactive mode will save you a lot of time.

Interactive mode provides a lot of developer productivity. Getting used to using it will make many development tasks much easier to manage and quicker to execute.

Summary

Success! You have your first Grails application up and running. In this chapter you've taken the first steps toward learning Grails by setting up and configuring your Grails installation. In addition, you've created your first Grails application, along with a basic controller.

Now it is time to see what else Grails does to kick-start your project development. In the chapters that follow, we'll look at some Create, Read, Update, Delete (CRUD) generation facilities, by means of which Grails allows you to flesh out prototype applications in no time.

■ ■ ■

CHAPTER 2

Getting Started with Grails

In Chapter 1, you got your first introduction to the Grails framework and a feel for the basic command-line interface while creating the basis for the gTunes application. This chapter is going to build on that foundation by showing how you can use the Grails scaffolding feature to quickly build a prototype application that can generate simple CRUD (Create, Read, Update, Delete) interfaces.

Then comes an explanation of some of the basic concepts within the Grails ecosystem, including environments, data sources, and deployment. Get ready—this is an action-packed chapter with loads of information!

What Is Scaffolding?

Scaffolding is a Grails feature that allows you to quickly generate CRUD interfaces for an existing domain. It offers several benefits, the most significant of which is that it serves as a superb learning tool, allowing you to relate how the Grails controller and view layers interact with the domain model that you created.

You should note, however, that Grails is not just a CRUD framework. And scaffolding, although a useful feature in your repertoire, is not the main benefit of Grails. If you're looking for a framework that provides purely CRUD-oriented features, better options are at your disposal.

As with a lot of Grails features, scaffolding is best demonstrated visually, so let's plunge right in and see what can be done.

Creating a Domain

Grails's domain classes serve as the heart of your application and business-model concepts. If you were constructing a bookstore application, for example, you would be thinking about books, authors, and publishers. With gTunes you have albums, artists, songs, and other things in mind.

The most significant attribute that differentiates domain classes from other artifacts within a Grails application is that they are persistent and that Grails automatically maps each domain class onto a physical table in the configured database. (There will be more about how to change the database setup later in the chapter.)

The act of mapping classes onto a relational database layer is also known as object-relational mapping (ORM). The Grails ORM layer, called GORM, is built on the ever-popular Hibernate library (http://www.hibernate.org).

Domain classes reside snugly in the grails-app/domain directory. You create a domain class by using either the create-domain-class command from within interactive mode or your favorite IDE or text editor.

Type the helper command shown in Listing 2-1 into a command window from the root of the gTunes project.

Listing 2-1. Creating the Song Domain Class

```
grails> create-domain-class com.gtunes.Song
| Created file grails-app/domain/com/gtunes/Song.groovy
| Created file test/unit/com/gtunes/SongTests.groovy
grails>
```

Listing 2-1 shows that you'll be using a package to hold your domain classes. Groovy follows exactly the same packaging rules as Java, and as with Java, it is good practice to use packages. You might not see the benefit of packages in the beginning, but as your application grows and you begin taking advantage of Grails plug-ins and integrating more Java code, you will appreciate the organization that they provide (for more about plug-ins, see Chapter 13).

Once the command in Listing 2-1 completes, the result will be a new Song domain class located in the grails-app/domain/com/gtunes directory, as dictated by the package prefix specified. Figure 2-1 shows the newly created structure and the Song.groovy file containing the domain class definition.

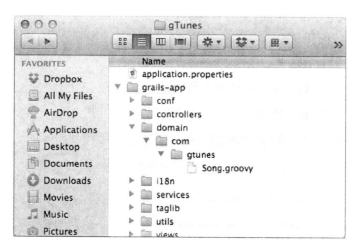

Figure 2-1. The Song domain class and the Song.groovy file

Currently, the Song domain isn't doing a great deal; it's simply a blank class definition, as shown in Listing 2-2.

Listing 2-2. The Song Domain Class

```
package com.gtunes
class Song {
    static constraints = {
    }
}
```

At this point, you should think about what aspects make up a "Song". A Song typically has a title and an artist, among other things. If you really want to go overboard, you could model your Song domain class on all the fields you can populate in an MP3 file's ID3 tag. But in this case keep it simple: add only the two previously mentioned properties, as shown in Listing 2-3.

Listing 2-3. Adding Properties to the Song Domain Class

```
package com.gtunes
class Song {
    String title
    String artist

    static constraints = {
        title blank: false
        artist blank: false
    }
}
```

That was simple enough, and the class doesn't look much different from your typical Groovy bean (see the Appendix for information about Groovy beans). GORM essentially maps the class name onto the table name and each property onto a separate column in the database, with their types relating to SQL types. Don't get too hung up on this now; we'll be digging more deeply into domain classes and GORM in Chapters 3 and 10. Also, the code in the constraints block will be discussed in more detail in Chapter 9. For the moment, let's move on to seeing the application in action.

Introducing Dynamic Scaffolding

Scaffolding comes in two flavors: dynamic (or runtime) and static (or template-driven). First, we'll look at dynamic scaffolding, where a CRUD application's controller logic and views are generated at runtime. Dynamic scaffolding does not involve boilerplate code or templates; it uses advanced techniques such as reflection and Groovy's metaprogramming capabilities to achieve its goals. However, before you can dynamically scaffold your Song class, you need a controller.

You had a brief introduction to creating controllers in Chapter 1, and the controller code necessary to enable scaffolding is minimal. Create the scaffolded controller for the Song class either manually or via the command line, as shown in Listing 2-4.

Listing 2-4. Creating the SongController

```
grails> create-scaffold-controller com.gtunes.Song
| Created file grails-app/controllers/com/gtunes/SongController.groovy
| Created file grails-app/views/song
| Created file test/unit/com/gtunes/SongControllerTests.groovy
grails>
```

Again, you should use the package prefix with the create-controller command, which will create the SongController within the grails-app/controllers/com/gtunes directory (see Figure 2-2).

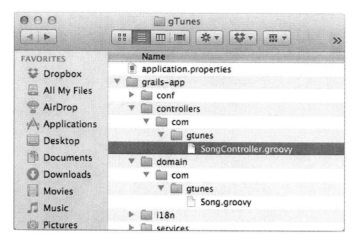

Figure 2-2. *Locating the SongController in the directory*

To enable dynamic scaffolding, the SongController defines a scaffold property with a value of true, as shown in Listing 2-5.

Listing 2-5. *Enabling Dynamic Scaffolding*

```
package com.gtunes
class SongController {
    static scaffold = true
}
```

▨ **Note** Groovy automatically resolves class names, such as Song in Listing 2-5, to the java.lang.Class instance without requiring the .class suffix. In other words Song = Song.class.

With that done, simply start up Grails with the grails run-app command, open a browser, and navigate to the gTunes application at the usual link: http://localhost:8080/gTunes.

The Grails welcome page, first demonstrated in Chapter 1, will show the SongController instance in the list of available controllers, as well as the usual comforting welcome message. Click the SongController link to pull up a page listing all the Song objects (there may be none, of course), as depicted in Figure 2-3.

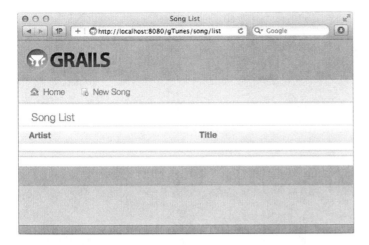

Figure 2-3. *The Song List page*

Without breaking a sweat and in a grand total of three lines of code (excluding the package declaration), you have managed to create a useful CRUD interface, one that lets you create and fully manage the Song instances within the gTunes application. Each of the components of CRUD (Create, Read, Update and Delete) is described in the rest of this section.

The Create Operation

The magic doesn't end here. By clicking the "New Song" link at the top of the screen, you can create new songs. While generating the views, Grails does its best to guess what type of field is required to edit a property's value. For example, if Grails finds a String, it will create a text field; if it finds a java.util.Date, it will render drop-down boxes that allow you to select the date and time. Figure 2-4 shows an example of what the generated song-creation interface looks like.

The Grails built-in validation mechanism, called constraints, can also affect how the interface is rendered, including the order in which fields are displayed and the type of field that is rendered. Try clicking the "Create" button; you'll get a validation error stating that the duration must be specified, as pictured in Figure 2-5. The validation messages hook into Grails's internationalization support (often referred to with the abbreviation i18n). But for now, all you need to know is that Grails is pulling these messages from the properties files within the grails-app/i18n directory. (Constraints will be discussed in Chapter 3 and internationalization in Chapter 8.)

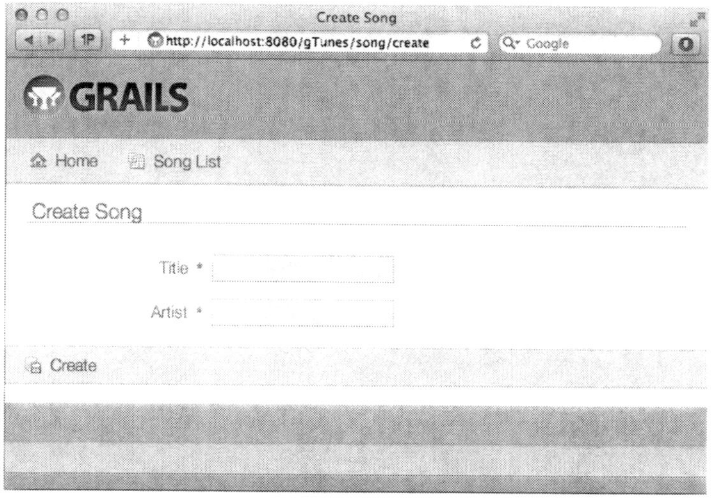

Figure 2-4. *The Create Song page*

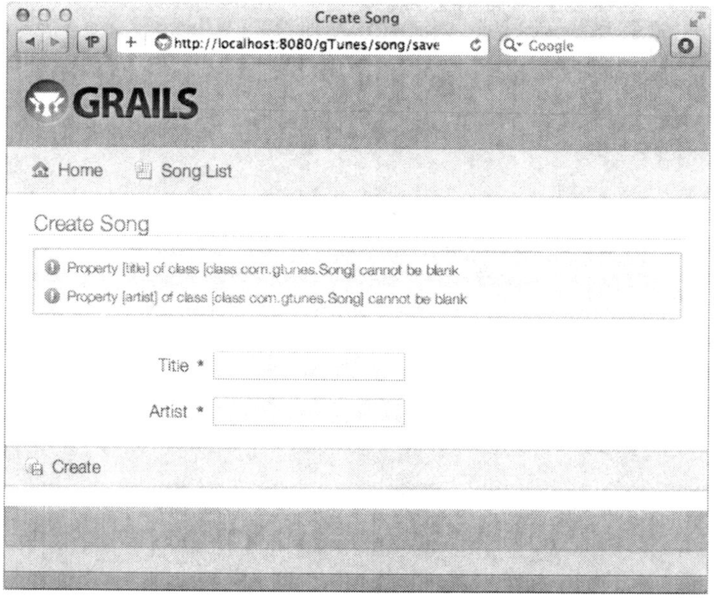

Figure 2-5. *How Grails handles validation*

You could customize the message at this point, but for now the defaults will do. Now let's try to create a song with some valid data. Specifically, try to enter these values into the provided fields:

Artist: Soundgarden
Title: Mailman

Now click the "Create" button and move on to the next section of the chapter.

The Read Operation

Grails has obeyed instructions and duly created a new Song instance with the necessary data in the database. It then redirects you to the "Show Song" screen, where you can view and admire a rendered view of the Song instance you just created.

Additionally, as pictured in Figure 2-6, the "Show Song" screen provides two buttons to let you edit or delete the Song instance from the database.

Figure 2-6. *The Show Song screen*

Currently, you're dealing with a trivial domain model with only a single Song domain class to account for. However, another attribute of domain classes is that they typically have multiple relationships: one-to-many, one-to-one, and so on. If you think about a Song for a moment, it is typically part of a collection of Songs within an album. Let's create an Album domain class to model this using the grails create-domain-class command, as shown in Listing 2-6.

Listing 2-6. *Creating the Album Domain Class*

```
grails> create-domain-class com.gtunes.Album
| Created file grails-app/domain/com/gtunes/Album.groovy
| Created file test/unit/com/gtunes/AlbumTests.groovy
grails>
```

An Album has attributes of its own, including a title, but it also contains many songs. Listing 2-7 shows how to set up a one-to-many relationship between Album and Song using the hasMany static property of domain classes. The hasMany property is assigned a Groovy map where the key is the relationship name and the value is the class, in this case Song, to which the association relates.

Listing 2-7. *Defining a One-to-Many Relationship*

```
package com.gtunes
class Album {
    String title
```

```
    static hasMany = [songs:Song]
}
```

The preceding association is unidirectional. In other words, only the Album class knows about the association, while the Song class remains blissfully unaware of it. To make the association bidirectional, modify the Song class to include an Album local property, as shown in Listing 2-8. Now Album and Song have a bidirectional, one-to-many association.

Listing 2-8. *Making the Relationship Bidirectional*

```
package com.gtunes
class Song {
    String title
    String artist
    Album album
}
```

In Chapter 3, we'll delve into other kinds of relationships and how they map onto the underlying database. For now, let's create another scaffolded controller that can deal with the creation of Album instances. Use the grails create-controller command and add the static scaffold = true property to the class definition (see Listing 2-9).

Listing 2-9. *Scaffolding the Album Class*

```
package com.gtunes
class AlbumController {
    static scaffold = true
}
```

Now if you return to your browser and refresh the Song list, you'll notice that the Song you entered previously has mysteriously vanished. The reason for this is quite simple: By default, Grails is running with an in-memory database, and updating domain classes creates a new instance of it. You might find this useful for testing, but you can configure a different database if you require a less volatile storage mechanism (we'll discuss that later in this chapter).

More significant, however, is the fact that on the welcome page we have an additional AlbumController. Click the AlbumController link, followed by the "New Album" button. Enter a title for the Album—here it's "Soundgarden"—and click the "Create" button to see your newly created Album displayed (see Figure 2-7).

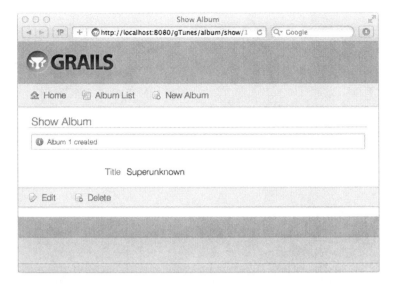

Figure 2-7. The Show Album screen

You'll also notice that the Album has a blank Songs field. Let's fix that next.

The Update Operation

You can perform updates by clicking the "Edit" button. In this case, you want to add a Song, so click the "Add Song" link to see the "Create Song" interface. This time, you'll get a useful drop-down box that lets you select which Album the Song should be part of (as shown in Figure 2-8). You'll notice that scaffolding's default behavior is simply to call toString() on each element in the drop-down list. The default toString() that Grails provides uses the class name and instance id, which is not the most pleasant thing to present to a user. You can override this behavior by implementing your own toString() method inside the Album class.

Next, populate the fields as described in the "The Create Operation" section and click the "Create" button. You'll notice that the "Show Song" screen provides a link back to the Album; clicking the link shows the Album with the newly created Song instance appearing in the list of songs (see Figure 2-9). Grails's scaffolding, although not exuding genius, is clever enough to figure out what a one-to-many relationship is and how to manage it accordingly.

Figure 2-8. The Create Song screen

Figure 2-9. Show Album screen with a list of songs

The Delete Operation

Finally, to complete the CRUD acronym, you can delete a particular Song or Album by clicking the "Delete" button. Grails is kind enough to inquire whether you are completely sure that you'd like to proceed with such a destructive operation.

This completes the tour of the dynamic-scaffolding capabilities of Grails; in the next section you'll see how to get access to the underlying controller and view the code that goes into these CRUD interfaces.

Static Scaffolding

Dynamic scaffolding can serve a number of purposes, from creating administration interfaces to providing the basis of a real application. However, it often becomes useful to take customization to a new level, particularly in terms of views. Fortunately, Grails provides the ability to take a domain class and generate a controller and associated views from the command line through the following targets:

- grails generate-controller: Generates a controller for the specified domain class.

- grails generate-views: Generates views for the specified domain class.

- grails generate-all: Generates both a controller and associated views.

Called "static" or "template-driven" scaffolding, this approach offers benefits beyond simple code generation. Notably, it provides an excellent learning tool to help you familiarize yourself with the Grails framework and how everything fits together.

You've already created a domain model that relates specifically to the problem you're attempting to solve. Now you can generate code that relates to your domain. Let's start by looking at how to generate a controller.

Generating a Controller

To generate a controller that implements the CRUD functionality mentioned in the section about dynamic scaffolding, take advantage of the grails generate-controller command. Like the other generate commands, generate-controller takes a domain-class name as its first argument. For example, Listing 2-10 shows how to use the generate-controller command to output a new controller from the Album class.

Listing 2-10. Outputting a New Controller

```
grails> generate-controller com.gtunes.Album
| Generating controller for domain class com.gtunes.Album
> File /grails-app/controllers/com/gtunes/AlbumController.groovy already exists.
Overwrite?[y,n,a] y
> File /test/unit/com/gtunes/AlbumControllerTests.groovy already exists. Overwrite?[y,n,a] y
| Finished generation for domain class com.gtunes.Album
grails>
```

Notice that, because the AlbumController class already exists, the generate-controller command will ask whether you want to overwrite the existing controller. Entering the value "y" for "yes" followed by hitting Enter will complete the process.

At this point, you should probably examine the contents of this mysterious controller to see how many thousands of code lines have been generated. If you're coming from a traditional Java web-development background, you might expect to implement a few different classes. For example, you would likely need a controller that calls a business interface, which in turn invokes a Data Access Object (DAO) that actually performs the CRUD operations.

Surely the DAO will contain mountains of ORM framework code and maybe a few lines of Java Database Connectivity (JDBC) mixed in for good measure. Surprisingly—or not, depending on your perspective—the code is extremely concise, well under 100 lines. That's still not quite short enough to list in full here, but we will step through each action in the generated controller to understand what it is doing.

The index action is the default; it is executed if no action is specified in the controller Uniform Resource Identifier (URI). It simply redirects to the list action, passing any parameters along with it (see Listing 2-11).

Listing 2-11. The index Action

```
def index() {
    redirect(action: "list", params: params)
}
```

The list action provides a list of all albums, as shown in Listing 2-12. It delegates to the static list method of the Album class to obtain a java.util.List of Album instances. It then places the list of Album instances into a Groovy map literal (a java.util.LinkedHashMap under the covers), which is then returned as the "model" from the controller to the view. (You'll begin to understand more about models and how they relate to views in Chapters 4 and 5.)

Listing 2-12. The list Action

```
def list() {
    params.max = Math.min(params.max ? params.int('max') : 10, 100)
    [albumInstanceList: Album.list(params), albumInstanceTotal: Album.count()]
}
```

But hold on a second. Before we get ahead of ourselves, have you noticed that you haven't actually written a static list method in the Album class? At this point, you will start to see the power of GORM. GORM automatically provides a whole array of methods on every domain class you write through Groovy's metaprogramming capabilities, one of which is the list method. By looking through this scaffolded code, you will get a preview of the capabilities GORM has to offer.

For example, the show action, shown in Listing 2-13, takes the id parameter from the params object and passes it to the get method of the Album class. The get method, automatically provided by GORM, allows the lookup of domain instances using their database identifiers. The result of the get method is placed inside a model ready for display, as shown in Listing 2-13.

Listing 2-13. The show Action

```
def show() {
    def albumInstance = Album.get(params.id)
    if (!albumInstance) {
        flash.message = message(code: 'default.not.found.message', args: [message(code:
'album.label', default: 'Album'), params.id])
        redirect(action: "list")
        return
    }

    [albumInstance: albumInstance]
}
```

Notice how, in Listing 2-13, if the Album instance does not exist, the code places a message inside the flash object, which is rendered in the view. The flash object is a great temporary storage for messages (or message codes if you're using i18n). It will be discussed in more detail in Chapter 4.

The action that handles deletion of albums is aptly named the delete action. It retrieves an Album for the specified id parameter and, if it exists, deletes it and redirects it to the list action (Listing 2-14).

Listing 2-14. The delete Action

```
def delete() {
    def albumInstance = Album.get(params.id)
    if (!albumInstance) {
        flash.message = message(code: 'default.not.found.message', args: [message(code:
'album.label', default: 'Album'), params.id])
        redirect(action: "list")
        return
    }

    try {
        albumInstance.delete(flush: true)
                flash.message = message(code: 'default.deleted.message', args: [message(code:
'album.label', default: 'Album'), params.id])
        redirect(action: "list")
    }
    catch (DataIntegrityViolationException e) {
                flash.message = message(code: 'default.not.deleted.message', args:
[message(code: 'album.label', default: 'Album'), params.id])
        redirect(action: "show", id: params.id)
    }
}
```

While similar to the show action, which simply displays an Album's property values, the edit action delegates to an edit view, which will render fields to edit the Album's properties (see Listing 2-15).

Listing 2-15. The edit Action

```
def edit() {
    def albumInstance = Album.get(params.id)
    if (!albumInstance) {
        flash.message = message(code: 'default.not.found.message', args: [message(code:
'album.label', default: 'Album'), params.id])
        redirect(action: "list")
        return
    }

    [albumInstance: albumInstance]
}
```

You might be wondering at this point how Grails decides which view to display, given that the code for the edit and show actions are almost identical. The answer lies in the power of convention. Grails derives the appropriate view name from the controller and action names. In this case, since there are a controller called AlbumController and an action called edit, Grails will look for a view at the location grails-app/views/album/edit.gsp with the album directory inferred from the controller name and the edit.gsp file taken from the action name. Simple, really.

For updating there is the update action, which again makes use of the static get method to obtain a reference to the Album instance. The magical expression album.properties = params automatically binds the request's parameters onto the properties of the Album instance. Save the Album instance by calling the save() method. If the save succeeds, an HTTP redirect is issued back to the user; otherwise, the edit view is rendered again. The full code is shown in Listing 2-16.

Listing 2-16. The update Action

```
def update() {
    def albumInstance = Album.get(params.id)
    if (!albumInstance) {
        flash.message = message(code: 'default.not.found.message', args: [message(code:
'album.label', default: 'Album'), params.id])
        redirect(action: "list")
        return
    }

    if (params.version) {
        def version = params.version.toLong()
        if (albumInstance.version > version) {
            albumInstance.errors.rejectValue("version",
                    "default.optimistic.locking.failure",
                    [message(code: 'album.label', default: 'Album')] as Object[],
                    "Another user has updated this Album while you were editing")
            render(view: "edit", model: [albumInstance: albumInstance])
            return
        }
    }

    albumInstance.properties = params

    if (!albumInstance.save(flush: true)) {
        render(view: "edit", model: [albumInstance: albumInstance])
        return
    }

    flash.message = message(code: 'default.updated.message', args: [message(code: 'album.
label', default: 'Album'), albumInstance.id])
    redirect(action: "show", id: albumInstance.id)
}
```

To facilitate the creation of new Albums, the create action delegates to the create view. The create view, like the edit view, displays appropriate editing fields. Note how the create action inserts a new Album into the model to ensure that field values are populated from request parameters (Listing 2-17).

Listing 2-17. The create Action

```
def create() {
    [albumInstance: new Album(params)]
}
```

Finally, the save action will attempt to create a new Album instance and save it to the database (see Listing 2-18).

Listing 2-18. The save Action

```
def save() {
    def albumInstance = new Album(params)
    if (!albumInstance.save(flush: true)) {
```

```
        render(view: "create", model: [albumInstance: albumInstance])
        return
    }

    flash.message = message(code: 'default.created.message', args: [message(code: 'album.
label', default: 'Album'), albumInstance.id])
        redirect(action: "show", id: albumInstance.id)
    }
```

In both the save and update actions, you alternate between using the redirect and render methods. These will be cover in depth in Chapter 4, but briefly, the redirect method issues an HTTP redirect that creates an entirely new request to a different action, while the render method renders a selected view to the response of the current request.

Clearly, this has been only a brief overview of the various CRUD operations and what they do, without elaboration on a lot of the magic that is going on here. There is, however, method in the madness. The nitty-gritty details of controllers and how they work will surface in Chapter 4. For the moment, however, let's try out the newly generated controller by running the gTunes application once again via the grails run-app target.

Once the server has loaded, navigate your browser to the AlbumController at the address http://localhost:8080/gTunes/album. What happens? Well, not a great deal, actually. The result is a page-not-found (404) error because the generated controller is not using dynamic scaffolding. Dynamic scaffolding renders the views at runtime, but here there is just a plain old controller—there's nothing special about it, and there are no views.

▨ **Note**   Set the scaffold property to the Album class, and the views will be generated with each action overridden.

Generating the Views

It would be nice to have some views for your actions to delegate to. Fortunately, you can generate them with the grails generate-views command, which is executed according to the same process described in the section "Generating a Controller" (see Listing 2-19).

Listing 2-19. Generating Views

```
grails> generate-views com.gtunes.Album
| Finished generation for domain class com.gtunes.Album
grails>
```

Figure 2-10. *The generated scaffolding views*

The resulting output from the command window will resemble Figure 2-10.
All in all, you can generate four views:

- `list.gsp`: Used by the `list` action to display a list of `Album` instances.

- `show.gsp`: Used by the `show` action to display an individual `Album` instance.

- `edit.gsp`: Used by the `edit` action to edit a `Album` instance's properties.

- `create.gsp`: Used by the `create` action to create a new `Album` instance.

- `_form.gsp`: Used by the `create` and `edit` views.

▪ **Note** All the views use the main layout found at `grails-app/views/layouts/main.gsp`. This includes the placement of title, logo, and any included style sheets. Layouts are discussed in detail in Chapter 5.

You now have a controller and views to perform CRUD. So what have you achieved beyond what you saw in dynamic scaffolding? Well, nothing yet. The power of command-line scaffolding is that it gives you a starting point to build your application. Having started with nothing, you now have a controller in which to place your own custom business logic. You have views, which you can customize to your heart's content. And you accomplished all this while writing minimal code. Most developers are on a constant mission to write less code, and scaffolding proves a useful tool toward achieving this goal.

With the `AlbumController` and associated views in place, delete the existing `SongController` and repeat the steps in Listings 2-10 and 2-19 to generate a controller and views for the Song domain class. You're going to need the generated code as you build on the basic CRUD functionality in later chapters.

In the meantime, let's move on to understanding more of what's necessary to kick-start Grails development, beginning with environments.

Being Environmentally Friendly

It's typical in any web-application production team to have a development configuration for the application that can be configured to work with a locally installed database. This configuration sometimes even differs from developer to developer, depending on the specific desktop configurations.

In addition, QA staff who test the work produced by developers have separate machines configured in a way similar to the production environment. Thus, there are two environments so far: the development configuration and the test configuration. The third is the production configuration, which is needed when the system goes live.

This scenario is ubiquitous across pretty much every development project, with each development team spinning custom automated-build solutions via Ant or another custom-build system, instead of getting the solution from the framework itself.

Grails supports the concept of *development*, *test*, and *production* environments by default and will configure itself accordingly when executed. Some of this is done completely transparently to the developer. For example, autoreloading is enabled when Grails is configured in development mode but disabled when it's in production mode (to increase performance and minimize any security risk, however small).

Executing Grails under different environments is remarkably simple. For instance, the following command will run a Grails application with the production settings:

```
$ grails prod run-app
```

If you recall the output of the grails help command, you will remember that the basic usage of the grails command is as follows:

```
Usage (optionals marked with *):
grails  [environment]* [target]   [arguments]*
```

In other words, the first optional token after the grails executable is the environment, and three built-in options ship with Grails:

- *prod*: The production environment settings. Grails executes in the most efficient manner possible, against all configured production settings.

- *test*: The test environment settings. Grails executes in the most efficient manner possible, against all configured test settings.

- *dev*: The development environment settings. Grails is run in development mode with tools and behavior (such as hot reloading) enabled to optimize developer productivity.

Of course, Grails is not limited to just three environments. You can specify a custom environment by passing in a system property called grails.env to the grails command. For example:

```
grails -Dgrails.env=myenvironment test-app
```

Here you execute the Grails test cases using an environment called myenvironment. All this environment switching may be handy, but what does it mean in practical terms? For one thing, it allows you to configure different databases for different environments, as you'll see in the next section.

Configuring Data Sources

Armed with your newly acquired knowledge of environments and how to switch between them, you'll see the implications when you start configuring data sources. What initial configuration steps are required to get a Grails application up and running? None. That's right; you don't have to configure a thing.

Even configuring the data source is optional. If you don't configure it, Grails will start up with an in-memory H2 database. This is highly advantageous to begin with, particularly in terms of testing, because you can start an application with a fresh set of data on each load.

However, since it is a pretty common requirement, let's delve into data sources because you'll certainly need to configure them; plus, they'll help you develop your knowledge of environments.

The DataSource.groovy File

When you create a Grails application, Grails automatically provides a `grails-app/conf/DataSource.groovy` file that contains configuration for each environment (see Figure 2-11). You might find this convenient, because it means most of the work is done for you, but you might prefer to use another database, such as MySQL, rather than the provided H2 database.

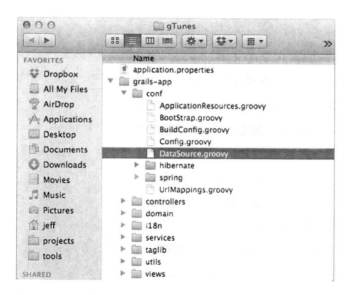

Figure 2-11. *The DataSource.groovy file*

Defining a data source is one area where the strength of the Java platform becomes apparent. Java's database connectivity technology, JDBC, is extremely mature, with drivers available for pretty much every database on the market. In fact, if a database provider does not deliver high-quality, stable JDBC drivers, its product is unlikely to be taken seriously in the marketplace.

A data-source definition is translated into a `javax.sql.DataSource` instance that supplies JDBC `Connection` objects. If you've used JDBC before, the process will be familiar, with the first step ensuring that the driver classes, normally packaged within a JAR archive, are available on the classpath.

The `DataSource.groovy` file contains some common configuration setup at the top of the data-source definition, an example of which is presented in Listing 2-20.

Listing 2-20. Common Data-Source Configuration

```
dataSource {
    pooled = true
    driverClassName = "org.h2.Driver"
    username = "sa"
    password = ""
}
```

The snippet indicates that by default you want a pooled data source using the H2 driver with a username of "sa" and a blank password. You could apply defaults to several other settings. Here's a list of the settings that the DataSource.groovy file provides:

- driverClassName: This is the class name of the JDBC driver.

- username: This is the username used to establish a JDBC connection.

- password: This is the password used to establish a JDBC connection.

- url: This is the JDBC URL of the database.

- dbCreate: This specifies whether to autogenerate the database from the domain model.

- pooled: This specifies whether to use a pool of connections (it defaults to true).

- conf igClass: This is the class that you use to configure Hibernate.

- logSql: This setting enables SQL logging.

- dialect: This is a string or class that represents the Hibernate dialect used to communicate with the database.

In addition to the standard properties described here, additional driver specific properties may be configured by defining a properties block as part of the dataSource configuration, as shown in Listing 2-21.

Listing 2-21. Configuring Additional Data-Source Properties

```
environments {
    production {
        dataSource {
            dbCreate = "update"
            url = "jdbc:h2:prodDb;MVCC=TRUE;LOCK_TIMEOUT=10000"
            pooled = true
            properties {
                maxActive = -1
                minEvictableIdleTimeMillis=1800000
                timeBetweenEvictionRunsMillis=1800000
                numTestsPerEvictionRun=3
                testOnBorrow=true
                testWhileIdle=true
                testOnReturn=true
                validationQuery="SELECT 1"
            }
        }
    }
```

```
        }
    }
```

Now comes the interesting bit. Following the global dataSource block, you'll see environment-specific settings for each known environment: development, test, and production. Listing 2-22 presents a shortened example of the environment-specific configuration.

Listing 2-22. Environment-Specific Data-Source Configuration

```
environments {
    development {
        dataSource {
            dbCreate = "create-drop" // one of 'create', 'create-drop', 'update', 'validate', ''
            url = "jdbc:h2:mem:devDb;MVCC=TRUE"
        }
    }
}
```

Notice that, by default, the development environment is configured to use an in-memory H2, with the URL of the database being jdbc:h2:mem:devDb;MVCC=TRUE;LOCK_TIMEOUT=10000". Also note the dbCreate setting, which allows you to configure how the database is autocreated.

■ **Note** Hibernate users will be familiar with the possible values because dbCreate relates directly to the hibernate.hbm2ddl.auto property.

The dbCreate setting of the development environment is configured as create-drop, which drops the database schema and re-creates it every time the Grails server is restarted. This setting can prove useful for testing because you start off with a clean set of data each time. The available settings for the dbCreate property are as follows:

- create-drop: Drops and re-creates the database schema on each application load.

- create: Creates the database on application load.

- update: Creates and/or attempts an update to existing tables on application load.

- [blank]: Does nothing.

The production and test environments both use update for dbCreate so that existing tables are, not dropped, but created or updated automatically. You might find it necessary in some production environments to create your database schema manually. Or maybe creating your database schema is your DBA's responsibility. If either is the case, simply remove the dbCreate property altogether, and Grails will do nothing, leaving this task in your hands or your colleague's.

Configuring a MySQL Database

Building on the knowledge you've gained in the previous section about configuring an alternative database, you're now going to learn how to set up MySQL with Grails. You're going to configure Grails to use MySQL within the production environment; to achieve this, you need to tell Grails how to communicate with MySQL. You're using JDBC, so this requires a suitable driver. You can download drivers from the MySQL web site, http://www.mysql.com.

In this book's examples, we'll be using version 5.1.6 of MySQL Connector/J. To configure the driver, edit the grails-app/conf/BuildConfig.groovy file shown in Figure 2-12.

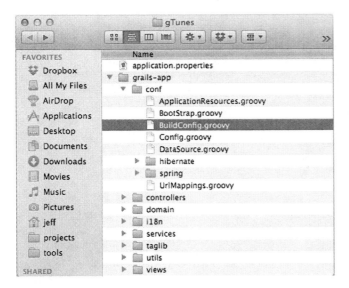

Figure 2-12. *BuildConfig.groovy*

Edit the BuildConfig.groovy file to include the Connector/J as a declared dependency. Dependency Management will be covered in more detail later. For now, include something like this in BuildConfig. groovy:

Listing 2-23. *The Connector/J Dependency*

```
grails.project.dependency.resolution = {
    …
dependencies {
        // specify dependencies here under either 'build',
        // 'compile', 'runtime', 'test' or 'provided' scopes eg.

        runtime 'mysql:mysql-connector-java:5.1.19'
    }
}
```

With the driver in place, the next thing to do is configure the Grails dataSource to use the settings defined by the driver's documentation. This is common practice with JDBC (and equivalent technologies on other platforms) and essentially requires the following information:

- the driver class name
- the URL of the database
- the username to log in with
- the password for the username

Currently the production dataSource is configured to use an H2 database that persists to a file. Listing 2-24 shows the production dataSource configuration.

Listing 2-24. The Production Data-Source Configuration

```
production {
    dataSource {
        dbCreate = "update"
        url = "jdbc:h2:prodDb;MVCC=TRUE"
        pooled = true
        properties {
            maxActive = -1
            minEvictableIdleTimeMillis=1800000
            timeBetweenEvictionRunsMillis=1800000
            numTestsPerEvictionRun=3
            testOnBorrow=true
            testWhileIdle=true
            testOnReturn=true
            validationQuery="SELECT 1"
        }
    }
}
```

Notice that the remaining settings (username, password, driverClassName, and so on) are inherited from the global configuration, as shown in Listing 2-20. To configure MySQL correctly, you need to override a few of those defaults as well as change the database URL. Listing 2-25 presents an example of a typical MySQL setup.

Listing 2-25. MySQL Data-Source Configuration

```
production {
    dataSource {
        dbCreate = "update"
        url = "jdbc:mysql://localhost/gTunes"
        driverClassName = "com.mysql.jdbc.Driver"
        username = "root"
        password = ""
        pooled = true
        properties {
            maxActive = -1
            minEvictableIdleTimeMillis=1800000
            timeBetweenEvictionRunsMillis=1800000
            numTestsPerEvictionRun=3
            testOnBorrow=true
            testWhileIdle=true
            testOnReturn=true
            validationQuery="SELECT 1"
        }
    }
}
```

This setup assumes a MySQL server is running on the local machine, which has been set up with a blank root user password. Of course, a real production environment might have the database on a different machine and almost certainly with a more secure set of permissions. Also, note that you must specify the name of the MySQL driver using the driverClassName setting.

Configuring a JNDI Data Source

Another common way to set up a production data source in Grails is to use a container-provided Java Naming and Directory Interface (JNDI) data source. This kind of setup is typical in corporate environments where the configuration of a data source is not up to you but to the deployment team or network administrators.

Configuring a JNDI data source in Grails couldn't be simpler; specifying the JNDI name is the only requirement. Listing 2-26 shows a typical JNDI setup.

Listing 2-26. JNDI Data-Source Configuration

```
production {
    dataSource {
        jndiName = "java:comp/env/jdbc/gTunesDB"
    }
}
```

Of course, this assumes that the work has been done to configure the deployment environment to supply the JNDI data source correctly. Configuring JNDI resources is typically container-specific, and we recommend that you review the documentation supplied with your container (such as Apache Tomcat) for instructions.

Supported Databases

Because Grails leverages Hibernate, it supports every database that Hibernate supports. And because Hibernate has become a de facto standard, it has been tried and tested against many different databases and versions.

As it stands, the core Hibernate team performs regular integration tests against the following database products:

- DB2 9.7
- Microsoft SQL Server 2008
- MySQL 5.1, 5.5
- Oracle 11g, 11g RAC
- PostgreSQL 8.4, 9.1
- Sybase ASE 15.5 (jConnect 6.0)

In addition, although not included in the Hibernate QA team's testing processes, these database products come with community-led support:

- Apache Derby
- HP NonStop SQL/MX 2.0
- Firebird 1.5 with JayBird 1.01
- FrontBase
- Informix
- Ingres

- InterBase 6.0.1

- Mckoi SQL

- PointBase Embedded 4.3

- Progress 9

- Microsoft Access 95, 97, 2000, XP, 2002, and 2003

- Corel Paradox 3.0, 3.5, 4.x, 5.x, and 7.x to 11.x

- a number of generic file formats including flat text, CSV, TSV, and fixed-length and variable-length binary files

- XBase (any dBASE; Visual dBASE; SIx Driver; SoftC; CodeBase; Clipper; FoxBase; FoxPro; Visual Fox Pro 3.0, 5.0, 7.0, 8.0, 9.0, and 10.0; xHarbour; Halcyon; Apollo; GoldMine; or Borland Database Engine—compatible [BDE-compatible] database)

- Microsoft Excel 5.0, 95, 97, 98, 2000, 2001, 2002, 2003, and 2004

A few, mostly older, database products that don't support JDBC metadata (which allows a database to expose information about itself) require you to specify the Hibernate dialect explicitly, using the `dialect` property of the data-source definition. You can find available dialects in the `org.hibernate.dialect` package. There'll be more to learn about data-source definitions in future chapters, including Chapter 12. For now, since we have readied our application for the production environment, let's move on to the next step: deployment.

Deploying the Application

When you execute a Grails application using the `run-app` command, Grails configures the application to be reloaded upon changes at runtime, allowing quick iterative development. This configuration does, however, affect your application's performance. The `run-app` command is thus best suited for development only. For deployment onto a production system, use a packaged Web Application Archive (WAR) file. Doing this follows Java's mature deployment strategy and the separation of roles between developers and administrators.

As a significant added bonus, Grails's compliance with the WAR format means that IT production teams don't need to learn any new skills. The same application servers, hardware, profiling, and monitoring tools that are used with today's Java applications work with Grails, too.

Deployment with run-war

If you are satisfied with the built-in Tomcat container as a deployment environment, you can quickly deploy your application by setting up Grails on your production environment and then checking out your Grails application from the version-control system you have locally. Once you've done this, simply type

```
Grails> run-war
```

This command packages up Grails as a WAR file and then runs Tomcat using the packaged WAR on port 8080. If you wish to change the port, you can follow the instructions in the "Step 6: Running the Application" section of Chapter 1.

Deployment with a WAR file

The run-war command is convenient, but you might want more control over your deployment environment, or you might want to deploy onto another container, such as Apache Tomcat or BEA WebLogic, instead of Tomcat.

What you need in these cases is a WAR file. The WAR file is the standardized mechanism for deployment in the Java world. Every Java EE–compliant web container supports the format. But some older containers might have quirks, so check out the http://grails.org/Deployment page on the wiki for helpful info on container-specific issues.

To create a WAR archive, use Grails' war command:

```
grails> war
| Done creating WAR target/gtunes-0.1.war
grails>
```

By default, if no environment is specified, Grails assumes use of the production environment for a WAR file. However, as with other commands, you can change the environment if needed. For example:

```
$ grails> test war
```

Once you've run the command, a brand-new WAR file appears in the root of your project directory (see Figure 2-13).

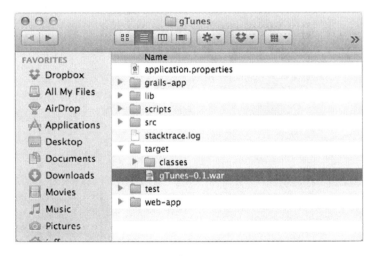

Figure 2-13. *The gTunes WAR file*

If the root directory is not a convenient location for the WAR file, you can always change it by specifying the target WAR location as the last argument to the war command:

```
$ grails test war /path/to/deploy/gTunes.war
```

With the WAR file created, you just need to follow your container's deployment instructions (which might be as simple as dropping the file into a particular directory), and you're done. Notice how the WAR file includes a version number? Grails features built-in support for application versioning. You'll learn more about versioning and deployment in Chapter 11.

Summary

Wow, that was a lot of ground to cover. You generated a simple CRUD interface, configured a different data source, and produced a WAR file ready for deployment. You learned some of the basics about how controllers work in Grails and previewed what is to come with GORM, Grails's object-relational mapping layer.

You also played with the Grails support for running different environments and configured a MySQL database for production. All of this should have provide a solid grounding in the basics of working with Grails. However, so far we've only touched on concepts such as domain classes, controllers, and views without going into much detail. This is about to change, as we plunge head first into the gory details of what makes Grails tick.

Starting with Chapter 3, we'll begin the in-depth tour of the concepts in Grails. As we do that, we'll begin to build out the gTunes application and transform it from the prototype it is now into a full-fledged, functional application.

■ ■ ■

Understanding Domain Classes

Object-oriented (OO) applications almost always involve a domain model representing the business entities that the application deals with. The gTunes application will include a number of domain classes, including Artist, Album, and Song. Each of these domain classes has properties associated with it. You must map those properties to a database in order to persist instances of those classes.

Developers of object-oriented applications face some difficult problems in mapping objects to a relational database. This is not because relational databases are especially difficult to work with; the trouble is that you encounter an "impedance mismatch"[1] between the object-oriented domain model and a relational database's table-centric view of data.

■ **Note**   As the great majority of Grails applications are built on top of relational databases, this book is going to focus on that approach. Note that Grails supports a growing number of datastores, including a number of nonrelational datastores, including MongoDB, Redis, and Cassandra.

Fortunately, Grails does most of the hard work for you. It's significantly simpler to write the domain model for a Grails application than for many other frameworks. This chapter will look at the fundamentals of a Grails domain model. Chapter 10 will cover more advanced features of the GORM technology.

Persisting Fields to the Database

By default, all the fields in a domain class are persisted to the database. For simple field types such as Strings and Integers, each field in the class will map to a column in the database. Complex properties might require multiple tables to persist all the data. The Song class from Chapter 2 contains two String properties. The table in the database will contain a separate column for each of those properties.

In MySql, that database table will look something like Listing 3-1.

---

[1]   Scott W. Ambler, "The Object-Relational Impedance Mismatch," http://www.agiledata.org/essays/impedanceMismatch.html, 2006.

Listing 3-1. The Song Table

+	+	+	+	+	+	+
I Field	I Type	I Null	I Key	I Default	I Extra	I
+	+	+	+	+	+	+
I id	I bigint(20)	I NO	I PRI	I NULL	I auto_increment I	
I version	I bigint(20)	I NO	I	I NULL	I	I
I artist	I varchar(255)	I NO	I	I NULL	I	I
I title	I varchar(255)	I NO	I	I NULL	I	I
+	+	+	+	+	+	+

Notice that the table includes a column for each of the properties in the domain class, an id column, and a version column. The id is a unique identifier for a row, and Grails uses the version column to implement optimistic locking2.

Listing 3-1 shows the default mapping for a MySQL database. Grails provides a powerful DSL for expressing how a domain model maps to the database. Details about the mapping DSL appear later, in the "Customizing Your Database Mapping" section.

Validating Domain Classes

You'll probably encounter business rules that constrain the valid values of a particular property in a domain class. For example, a Person must never have an age that is less than zero. A credit card number must adhere to an expected pattern. Rules like these should be expressed clearly and in only one place. Luckily, Grails provides a powerful mechanism for expressing these rules.

A Grails domain class can express domain constraints simply by defining a public static property, constraints, that has a closure as a value. Listing 3-2 shows a version of the Song class that has several constraints defined.

Listing 3-2. The Song Domain Class

```
class Song {
    String title
    String artist
    Integer duration

    static constraints = {
        title(blank: false)
        artist(blank: false)
        duration(min: 1)
    }
}
```

The Song class in Listing 3-2 defines constraints for each of its persistent properties. The title and artist properties cannot be blank. The duration property must have a minimum value of 1. When constraints are defined, not every property necessarily needs to be constrained. The constraints closure can include constraints for a subset of properties in the class.

---

2 Wikipedia, "Optimistic concurrency control," http://en.wikipedia.org/wiki/Optimistic_concurrency_control.

The validators used in Listing 3-2 are blank and min. Grails ships with a lot of standard validators that cover common scenarios (see Table 3-1).

Table 3-1. Standard Validators in Grails

Name	Example	Description
blank	login(blank:false)	Set to false if a string value cannot be blank
creditCard	cardNumber(creditCard:true)	Set to true if the value must be a credit-card number
email	homeEmail(email:true)	Set to true if the value must be an e-mail address
inList	login(inList:['Joe', 'Fred'])	Value must be contained within the given list
min	duration(min:1)	Sets the minimum value
mnSizei	children(minSize:5)	Sets the minimum size of a collection or number property
matches	login(matches:/[a-zA-Z]/)	Matches the supplied regular expression
max	age(max:99)	Sets the maximum value
maxSize	children(maxSize:25)	Sets the maximum size of a collection or number property
notEqual	login(notEqual:'Bob')	Must not equal the specified value
nullable	age(nullable:false)	Set to false if the property value cannot be null
range	age(range:16..59)	Set to a Groovy range of valid values
scale	salary(scale:2)	Set to the desired scale for floating-point numbers
size	children(size:5..15)	Uses a range to restrict the size of a collection or number
unique	login(unique:true)	Set to true if the property must be unique
url	homePage(url:true)	Set to true if a string value is a URL address

The constraints block in a domain class will help prevent invalid data from being saved to the database. The save() method on a domain object will automatically validate against the constraints before data are written to the database. Data are not written to the database if validation fails. If validation fails, the save() method returns null. If validation passes, then the object is saved to the database, and the save() method returns a reference to the object saved. Listing 3-3 demonstrates how code can react to the return value of the save() method.

Listing 3-3. Validating a Song Object

```
// -68 is an invalid duration
def song = new Song(title:'The Rover',
                    artist:'Led Zeppelin',
                    duration:-68)
if(song.save()) {
    println "Song was created!"
} else {
    song.errors.allErrors.each { println it.defaultMessage }
}
```

An alternative approach is to invoke the save method with a failOnError parameter set to true, which will cause the save() method to throw a grails.validation.ValidationException if validation fails. That would look like song.save(failOnError: true).

An interesting aspect of Listing 3-3 is the use of the errors property on domain classes. This property is an instance of the Spring Framework's org.springframework.validation.Errors interface, which allows advanced querying of validation errors. In Listing 3-3, when validation fails, the code generates a list of all the errors that occurred and prints them to stdout.

Some of the more useful methods in the Spring Errors interface are shown in Listing 3-4.

Listing 3-4. Methods in the Spring Errors Interface

```
package org.springframework.validation

interface Errors {
    List getAllErrors();
    int getErrorCount();
    FieldError getFieldError(String fieldName);
    int getFieldErrorCount();
    List getFieldErrors(String fieldName);
    Object getObjectName();
    boolean hasErrors();
    boolean hasFieldErrors(String fieldName);
    // ... remaining methods
}
```

Occasionally you'll find it useful to make changes to the domain model before committing to the save() method. For such a case, Grails provides a validate() method, which returns a Boolean value to indicate whether validation was successful. The semantics are exactly the same as in the example with the save() method, except that the validate() method doesn't attempt to save the instance to the database.

If validation fails, the application might want to make changes to the state of the domain object and make another attempt at validation. All domain objects have a method called clearErrors(), which clears any errors left over from a previous validation attempt. Listing 3-5 demonstrates how code might react to the return value of the validate() method.

Listing 3-5. Validating a Song Object, Revisited

```
def song = new Song(title:'The Rover',
                    duration:339)
if(!song.validate()) {
    song.clearErrors()
    song.artist = 'Led Zeppelin'
    song.validate()
}
```

Using Custom Validators

Grails provides a wide array of built-in validators to handle common scenarios. However, it is impossible to foresee every feasible domain model and every specific kind of validation that an application might need. Fortunately, Grails provides a mechanism that allows an application to express arbitrary validation rules (see Listing 3-6).

Listing 3-6. Constraining the Password Property in the User Domain Class

```
class User {
    static constraints = {
        password(unique:true, length:5..15, validator:{val, obj ->
            if(val?.equalsIgnoreCase(obj.firstName)) {
                return false
            }
        })
    }
}
```

The validator in Listing 3-6 will fail if the password is equal to the firstName property of the User class. The validator closure should return false if validation fails; otherwise it should return true. The first argument passed to the closure is the value of the property to be validated. The second argument passed to the closure is the object being validated. This second argument is often useful if validation requires the inspection of the object's other properties, as in Listing 3-6.

In addition, when false is returned from a custom validator, an error code such as user.password. validator.error is produced. However, you can specify a custom error code by returning a string.

```
if(val?.equalsIgnoreCase(obj.firstName)) {
    return "password.cannot.be.firstname"
}
```

In this example, you can trigger a validation error simply by returning a string with the value password.cannot.be.firstname. You'll learn more about error codes and how they relate to other parts of the application in later chapters. For now, let's move on to the topic of transient properties.

Understanding Transient Properties

By default, every property in a domain class is persisted to the database. For most properties, this is the right thing to do. However, occasionally a domain class will define properties that do not need to be persisted. Grails provides a simple mechanism for specifying which properties in a domain class should not be persisted. This mechanism is to define a public static property, transients, and assign to that property a value that is a list of strings. Those strings represent the names of the class's properties, which should be treated as transient and not saved to the database (see Listing 3-7).

Listing 3-7. A Transient Property in the Company Domain Class

```
class Company {
    String name
    Integer numberOfEmployees
    BigDecimal salaryPaidYTD

    static transients = ['salaryPaidYTD']
}
```

In Listing 3-7, the salaryPaidYTD property has been flagged as transient and will not be saved to the database. Note that the default generated schema for this domain class—the company table—does not contain a column for the salaryPaidYTD property (see Listing 3-8).

Listing 3-8. The Company Table

Field	Type	Null	Key	Default	Extra	
id	bigint(20)	NO	PRI	NULL	auto_increment	
version	bigint(20)	NO		NULL		
name	varchar(255)	NO		NULL		
number_of_employees	int(11)	NO		NULL		

Not all persistent properties necessarily correspond to a field in a domain class. For example, if a domain class has a method called getName() and a method called setName(), then that domain class has a persistent property called name. It doesn't matter that the class doesn't have a field called "name." Grails will handle that situation by creating the appropriate column in the database to store the value of the name property. But you can use the transients property to tell Grails not to do that if the property really should not be persisted, as in Listing 3-9.

Listing 3-9. A Transient Property in the Company Domain Class

```
class Company {
    BigDecimal cash
    BigDecimal receivables
    BigDecimal capital

    BigDecimal getNetWorth() {
        cash + receivables + capital
    }

    static transients = ['netWorth']
}
```

Another approach for managing the netWorth property is to define it as a derived property. Derived properties are read-only persistent properties whose values are derived by the database at the time of retrieval. Because the values are derived, there is no corresponding column in the database to store the value. Instead, a formula in the form of an SQL expression, which represents how the database should derive the value, must be provided. In the case of the netWorth property, the value could be derived in the database by adding the values of the CASH, RECEIVABLES, and CAPITAL columns in the table. Listing 3-10 shows what this would look like.

Listing 3-10. *A Derived Property in the Company Domain Class*

```
class Company {
    BigDecimal cash
    BigDecimal receivables
    BigDecimal capital
    BigDecimal netWorth

    static mapping = {
        netWorth formula: 'CASH + RECEIVABLES + CAPITAL'
    }
}
```

Note that the formula expressed there is SQL that must be understandable by the database. It is not code that will be parsed and executed in the application. It will be executed in the database, and SQL is not necessarily portable across relational databases. Defining derived properties, such as this one, means potentially giving up some database portability. For many applications that will not be a problem, but it is something to be aware of when the decision is made to use a derived property.

Customizing Your Database Mapping

As you've seen, Grails does a good job of mapping your domain model to a relational database without requiring any kind of mapping file. Many developer productivity gains that Grails offers arise from its Convention over Configuration (CoC) features. Whenever the conventions preferred by Grails are inconsistent with your requirements, Grails provides a simple way for you to work with those scenarios. The custom database mapping DSL in Grails falls in this category.

Grails provides an ORM DSL for expressing your domain mapping to help you deal with scenarios in which the Grails defaults will not work for you. A common use case for taking advantage of the ORM DSL is one where a Grails application is being developed on top of an existing schema that is not entirely compatible with the default domain-class mappings of Grails.

Consider a simple Person class (see Listing 3-11).

Listing 3-11. *The Person Domain Class*

```
class Person {
    String firstName
    String lastName
    Integer age
}
```

The default mapping in MySQL for that class will correspond to a schema that looks like Listing 3-12.

Listing 3-12. The Default Person Table

Field	Type	Null	Key	Default	Extra
id	bigint(20)	NO	PRI	NULL	auto_increment
version	bigint(20)	NO		NULL	
age	int(11)	NO		NULL	
first_name	varchar(255	NO		NULL	
last_name	varchar(255	NO		NULL	

That works perfectly if you have a greenfield application that doesn't need to map to an existing schema. If the application does need to map to an existing schema, the schema will probably not match up exactly with the Grails defaults. Imagine that a schema does exist and that it looks something like Listing 3-13.

Listing 3-13. A Legacy Table Containing Person Data

Field	Type	Null	Key	Default	Extra
person_id	bigint(20)	NO	PRI	NULL	auto_increment
person_age	int(11)	NO		NULL	
person_first_name	varchar(255)	NO		NULL	
person_last_name	varchar(255)	NO		NULL	

Notice that the table contains no version column and all the column names are prefixed with person_. You'll find it straightforward to map to a schema like that using the Grails ORM DSL. But to take advantage of the ORM DSL, your domain class must declare a public property called mapping and assign a closure to the property (see Listing 3-14).

Listing 3-14. Custom Mapping for the Person Domain Class

```
class Person {
    String firstName
    String lastName
    Integer age

    static mapping = {
        id column:'person_id'
        firstName column:'person_first_name'
        lastName column:'person_last_name'
```

```
        age column:'person_age'
        version false
    }
}
```

The example in Listing 3-13 defines column names for each of the properties and turns off the `version` property, which Grails uses for optimistic locking. (Optimistic locking is discussed in more detail in Chapter 9.) These are just a couple of the features that the ORM DSL supports.

The default table name for persisting instances of a Grails domain class is the name of the domain class. `Person` objects are stored in a `person` table and `Company` objects are stored in a `company` table. If `Person` objects need to be stored in a `people` table, the ORM DSL allows that. Listing 3-15 includes the necessary mapping code to store `Person` instances in the `people` table.

Listing 3-15. A Custom Table Mapping for the Person Domain Class

```
class Person {
    String firstName
    String lastName
    Integer age

    static mapping = {
        table 'people'
    }
}
```

We'll cover custom database mapping in more detail in Chapter 9.

Building Relationships

Typically an application is not made up of a bunch of disconnected domain classes. More often, domain classes have relationships to one another. Of course, not every domain class has a direct relationship with every other domain class, but it is not common for a domain class to exist in total isolation from any other domain class.

Grails provides support for several types of relationships between domain classes. In a one-to-one relationship (the simplest type), each member of the relationship has a reference to the other. The relationship represented in Listing 3-16 is a bidirectional relationship.

Listing 3-16. A One-to-One Relationship Between a Car and an Engine

```
class Car {
    Engine engine
}

class Engine {
    Car car
}
```

In this model, clearly a Car has one Engine and an Engine has one Car. The entities are peers in the relationship; there is no real "owner." Depending on application requirements, this might not be exactly what you want. Often a relationship like this really does have an owning side. Perhaps an Engine belongs to a Car, but a Car does not belong to an Engine. Grails provides a mechanism for expressing a relationship like that, and Listing 3-17 demonstrates how to specify its owning side.

Listing 3-17. An Engine Belongs to a Car

```
class Car {
    Engine engine
}

class Engine {
    static belongsTo = [car:Car]
}
```

The value of the belongsTo property in the Engine class is a Map. The key in this map is "car", and the value associated with that key is the Car class. This property tells Grails that the Car is the owning side of this relationship and that an Engine "belongs to" its owning Car. The key in the map can be named anything—the name does not need to be the same as the owning-class name. However, naming the key that way almost always makes sense. That key represents the name of a property that will be added to the Engine class, as well as representing the reference back to the owner. The Engine class in Listing 3-16 has a property, car, of type Car. When the Car and Engine classes are mapped to the relational database, there will be a foreign key in the CAR table that references the primary key in the ENGINE table. There may be cases where it is desirable to have the foreign key go in the other direction. That is, you may want to have a foreign key in the ENGINE table that references the primary key in the CAR table. The way to do that is to define a hasOne property in the Car class, as shown in Listing 3-18.

Listing 3-18. A Car hasOne Engine

```
class Car {
    static hasOne = [engine: Engine]
}
```

You might encounter situations where a relationship needs an owning side, but the owned side of the relationship does not need a reference back to its owner. Grails supports this type of relationship using the same belongsTo property, except that the value is a Class reference instead of a Map. With the approach used in Listing 3-19, the Engine still belongs to its owning Car, but the Engine has no reference back to its Car.

Listing 3-19. An Engine Belongs to a Car but Has No Reference to Its Owner

```
class Engine {
    static belongsTo = Car
}
```

One of the implications of having the belongsTo property in place is that Grails will impose cascaded deletes. Grails knows that an Engine "belongs to" its owning Car, so any time a Car is deleted from the database, its Engine will be deleted as well.

One-to-many relationships are equally simple to represent in Grails domain classes. Our gTunes application will require several one-to-many relationships, including the relationship between an Artist and its Albums and between an Album and its Songs. You might say that an artist has many albums and an album has many songs. That "has many" relationship is expressed in a domain class with the hasMany property (see Listing 3-20).

Listing 3-20. The hasMany Property

```
class Artist {
    String name

    static hasMany = [albums:Album]
}
class Album {
    String title

    static hasMany = [songs:Song]
    static belongsTo = [artist:Artist]
}

class Song {
    String title
    Integer duration

    static belongsTo = Album
}
```

In Listing 3-20, an Artist has many Albums, and an Album belongs to its owning Artist. An Album also has a reference back to its owning Artist. An Album has many Songs, and a Song belongs to its owning Album. However, a Song does not have a reference back to its owning Album.

The value of the hasMany property needs to be a Map. The keys in the map represent the names of collection properties that will be added to the domain class, and the values associated with the keys represent the types of objects that will be stored in the collection property. The Artist class has a domain property, albums, that will be a collection of Album objects. The default collection type that Grails will use is a java.util.Set, which is an unordered collection. Where this is the desired behavior, you don't need to declare the property explicitly. Grails will inject the property for you. If you need the collection to be a List or a SortedSet, you must explicitly declare the property with the appropriate type, as shown in Listing 3-21.

Listing 3-21. The Album Class Has a SortedSet of Song Objects

```
class Album {
    String title

    static hasMany = [songs:Song]
    static belongsTo = [artist:Artist]

    SortedSet songs
}
```

■ **Note** For this to work, the Song class must implement the Comparable interface. This requirement isn't specific to Grails; it's how standard SortedSet collections work in Java.

A Set is a collection of unique objects, duplicates are not allowed. A List is ordered. Hibernate has to manage all of that ordering and uniqueness, which can be expensive in terms of performance. For example, if an Album is updated with a new Song and the Song instances are being stored in a Set, Hibernate has to go look at all of the Song instances that are associated with this Album so it can figure out if the new one violates uniqueness. In this particular case the problem may not be terribly significant because an Album isn't going to have really large numbers of Songs associated with it. For relationships where the collection might have a large number of elements, the problem gets more significant. To help manage situations like these the relationship could use a Hibernate Bag. A Bag does not have to impose uniqueness and does not have to maintain order so manipulating the contents of a Bag involve potentially significantly fewer interactions with the database. The way to take advantage of a Bag is to explicitly declare the collection type as shown above in Listing 3-19 but use java.util.Collection as the declared type of the collection.

A domain class might represent the owning side of numerous one-to-many relationships. The Map associated with the hasMany property might have any number of entries in it, each entry representing another one-to-many-relationship. For example, if an Artist has many Albums but also has many Instruments, you could represent that by adding another entry to the hasMany property in the Artist class, as shown in Listing 3-22.

Listing 3-22. Multiple Entries in the hasMany Map

```
class Artist {
    String name

    static hasMany = [albums:Album, instruments:Instrument]
}
```

As stated earlier, the belongsTo property in the child class expresses that the child belongs to the owner; if the owner is ever deleted, the children should be deleted as well. By default, Grails will configure a cascading policy of all for this relationship. Cascading policy options are all, merge, save-update, delete, lock, refresh, evict, replicate, and all-delete-orphan (only for one-to-many relationships). Listing 3-23 demonstrates how to set the cascading policy for Songs that belong to an Album.

Listing 3-23. Customizing Cascade Behavior

```
class Album {
    String title

    static hasMany = [songs:Song]
    static belongsTo = [artist:Artist]

    static mapping = {
        songs cascade: 'delete'
    }
}
```

For information on and documentation of the Hibernate cascade policies, see http://docs.jboss.org/hibernate/core/3.6/reference/en-US/html/objectstate.html#objectstate-transitive.

Extending Classes with Inheritance

Grails domain classes can extend other Grails domain classes. This inheritance tree might be arbitrarily deep, but a good domain model will seldom involve more than one or two levels of inheritance.

The syntax for declaring that a Grails domain class extends from another domain class is standard Groovy inheritance syntax, as shown in Listing 3-24.

Listing 3-24. Extending the Person Class

```
class Person {
    String firstName
    String lastName
    Integer age
}

class Employee extends Person {
    String employeeNumber
    String companyName
}

class Player extends Person {
    String teamName
}
```

How should these classes map to the database? Should there be separate tables for each of these domain classes? Should there be one table for all types of Person objects? Grails provides support for both of those solutions. If all Person objects—including Players and Employees—are to be stored in the same table, this approach is known as a table-per-hierarchy mapping. That is, a table will be created for each inheritance hierarchy (see Listing 3-25). Grails imposes table-per-hierarchy mapping as the default for an inheritance relationship.

Listing 3-25. The Person Table Representing a Table-per-Hierarchy Mapping

Field	Type	Null	Key	Default	Extra	
id	bigint(20)	NO	PRI	NULL	auto_increment	
version	bigint(20)	NO		NULL		
age	int(11)	NO		NULL		
first_name	varchar(255)	NO		NULL		
last_name	varchar(255)	NO		NULL		
class	varchar(255)	NO		NULL		
company_name	varchar(255)	YES		NULL		
employee_number	varchar(255)	YES		NULL		
team_name	varchar(255)	YES		NULL		

Notice that Listing 3-25 includes columns for all the attributes in the Person class, along with columns for all the attributes in all the subclasses. In addition, the table includes a discriminator column, called class. Because this table will house all kinds of Person objects, the discriminator column is required to represent the specific type of Person represented in any given row. The application should never need to interrogate this column directly, but the column is critical for Grails to do its work. The default value for the discriminator column is the name of the class. The discriminator value may be customized in the mapping block, as shown in Listing 3-26.

Listing 3-26. Specifying a Value for the Discriminator Column

```
class Employee extends Person {
    String employeeNumber
    String companyName

    static mapping = {
        // the value of the discriminator column for
        //Employee instances should be 'working people'
        discriminator 'working people'
    }
}
```

The example there invokes the discriminator method and passes a string as an argument. The string represents a value for the discriminator for all rows that represent Person objects. There are several other discriminator properties that may be configured (see Table 3-2).

Table 3-2. Discriminator Properties

Name	Description
value	The value to use for the discriminator
column	The name of the column for storing the discriminator
formula	An SQL expression that is executed to evaluate the type of the class
type	The Hibernate type

The way to configure multiple properties for the discriminator is to pass named arguments to the discriminator method in the mapping block, as shown in Listing 3-27.

Listing 3-27. Specifying Multiple Values for the Discriminator Column

```
class Employee extends Person {
    String employeeNumber
    String companyName

    static mapping = {
        discriminator value: '42', type: 'integer'
    }
}
```

See http://docs.jboss.org/hibernate/orm/3.6/reference/en-US/html/mapping.html#d0e6906 for documentation and information about Hibernate discriminators.

The other type of inheritance mapping is known as table-per-subclass (see Listing 3-28).

Listing 3-28. *Table-per-Subclass Mapping*

```
class Person {
    String firstName
    String lastName
    Integer age

    static mapping = {
        tablePerHierarchy false
    }
}
```

Table-per-subclass mapping results in a separate table for each subclass in an inheritance hierarchy (see Listing 3-29). To take advantage of a table-per-subclass mapping, the parent class must use the ORM DSL to turn off the default table-per-hierarchy mapping.

Listing 3-29. *The Person, Employee, and Player Tables with Table-per-Subclass Mapping*

Field	Type	Null	Key	Default	Extra	
id	bigint(20)	NO	PRI	NULL	auto_increment	
version	bigint(20)	NO		NULL		
age	int(11)	NO		NULL		
first_name	varchar(255)	NO		NULL		
last_name	varchar(255)	NO		NULL		

Field	Type	Null	Key	Default	Extra	
id	bigint(20)	NO	PRI	NULL		
company_name	varchar(255)	YES		NULL		
employee_number	varchar(255)	YES		NULL		

Field	Type	Null	Key	Default	Extra	
id	bigint(20)	NO	PRI	NULL		
team_name	varchar(255)	YES		NULL		

Which of these mappings should you use? The answer depends on several factors. One of the consequences of the table-per-hierarchy approach is that none of the subclasses can have nonnullable properties. Because no joins are being executed, however, queries will perform better, because all the subclasses share a table that includes columns for all properties in all subclasses. When a Player is saved to the person table, the company_name column will be left null, because players don't have a company name. Likewise, when an Employee is saved to the player table, the team_name column will be left null. One of the consequences of using the table-per-subclass approach is that you must pay a performance penalty when retrieving instances of the subclasses, because database joins must be executed to pull together all the data necessary to construct an instance.

Grails lets you choose the approach that makes the most sense for your application. Consider your application requirements and typical query use cases. These should help you decide which mapping strategy is right for any particular inheritance relationship. Note that you don't need to apply the same mapping strategy across the entire application. There's nothing wrong with implementing one inheritance relationship using table-per-subclass mapping (because you must support nonnullable properties) and implementing some other unrelated inheritance relationship using table-per-hierarchy mapping for performance reasons.

Grails does support abstract classes in the inheritance hierarchy of persistent classes. The support for dealing with abstract persistent classes is quite intuitive. For example, if Car and Truck are classes that each extend the Vehicle class and the Vehicle class is abstract, you may query for all Vehicles; the results would include Car and Truck instances.

Embedding Objects

Grails supports the notion of composition—think of it as a stronger form of relationship. With that kind of relationship, it often makes sense to embed the "child" inline, where the "parent" is stored. Consider a simple relationship between a Car and an Engine. If that relationship were implemented with composition, the Engine would really be contained in the Car as far as persistence is concerned. That is, there will be one table that will contain columns for all of the persistent properties in the Car class, as well as all of the persistent properties of the Engine that belongs to a Car. Retrieving a Car and its Engine would not involve joins across multiple tables, since all of the information would be stored in the same table. A consequence of that is that if a Car is deleted, its Engine is deleted with it (see Listing 3-30).

Listing 3-30. A Composition Relationship Between the Car and Engine Domain Classes

```
class Car {
    String make
    String model
    Engine engine
}

class Engine {
    String manufacturer
    Integer numberOfCylinders
}
```

Normally Car objects and Engine objects are stored in separate tables; you would use a foreign key to relate the tables to each other (see Listings 3-31 and 3-32).

Listing 3-31. The Car Table

Field	Type	Null	Key	Default	Extra	
id	bigint(20)	NO	PRI	NULL	auto_increment	
version	bigint(20)	NO		NULL		
engine_id	bigint(20)	NO	MUL	NULL		
make	varchar(255)	NO		NULL		
model	varchar(255)	NO		NULL		

Listing 3-32. The Engine Table

Field	Type	Null	Key	Default	Extra	
id	bigint(20)	NO	PRI	NULL	auto_increment	
version	bigint(20)	NO		NULL		
manufacturer	varchar(255)	NO		NULL		
number_of_cylinders	int(11)	NO		NULL		

To treat the relationship between those classes as composition, the Car class must instruct Grails to "embed" the Engine in the Car. You do this by defining a public static property, embedded, in the Car class and assign that property a list of strings that contains the names of all the embedded properties (see Listing 3-33).

Listing 3-33. Embedding the Engine in a Car

```
class Car {
    String make
    String model
    Engine engine
    static embedded = ['engine']
}
```

With that embedded property in place, Grails knows that the Engine property of a Car object should be embedded in the same table with the Car object. The car table will now look like Listing 3-34.

■ **Note** Embedding properties is particularly useful in the MongoDB implementation of GORM, as it is very common to nest documents within documents in MongoDB.

Listing 3-34. The Car Table with the Engine Attributes Embedded

Field	Type	Null	Key	Default	Extra	
id	bigint(20)	NO	PRI	NULL	auto_increment	
version	bigint(20)	NO		NULL		
engine_manufacturer	varchar(255)	NO		NULL		
engine_number_of_cylinders	int(11)	NO		NULL		
make	varchar(255)	NO		NULL		
model	varchar(255)	NO		NULL		

Testing Domain Classes

Automated tests can be an important part of building complex applications and confirming that the system behaves as intended. In particular, testing is an important part of building complex systems with a dynamic language like Groovy. With dynamic languages, developers don't get the same kinds of feedback from the compiler that they might get if they were working with Java or another statically typed language.

For example, in Java if you make a typo in a method invocation, the compiler will let you know that you have made the mistake. The compiler cannot flag that same error when you use Groovy, because of the language's dynamic nature and its runtime. With Groovy, many things are not known until runtime. You must execute the code to learn whether it's correct. Executing the code from automated tests is an excellent way to ensure that the code is doing what it is supposed to do.

Grails offers first-class support for testing many aspects of your application. This section will look at testing domain classes.

Grails directly supports two kinds of tests: unit tests and integration tests. Unit tests reside at the top of the project in the test/unit/ directory, and integration tests reside in the test/integration/ directory. You must understand the difference between unit tests and integration tests. Many dynamic things happen when a Grails application starts up. One of the things Grails does at startup is augment domain classes with a lot of dynamic methods, including validate() and save(). When you run integration tests, all of that dynamic behavior is available, so a test can invoke the validate() or save() method on a domain object, even though these methods do not appear in the domain-class source code.

When you run unit tests, however, that full dynamic environment is not fired up, and so methods such as validate() and save() are not available. Starting up the whole dynamic environment comes at a cost. For this reason, you should run tests that rely on the full Grails runtime environment only as integration tests.

That said, Grails provides advanced capabilities that let you unit-test a lot of dynamic behavior in domain classes and other artifacts. If you create a domain class using the create-domain-class command, Grails will create a unit test automatically. If you execute grails create-domain-class com.gtunes.Song, Grails will create grails-app/domain/com/gtunes/Song.groovy and test/unit/com/gtunes/SongTests.groovy. Grails is encouraging you to do the right thing—to write tests for your domain classes. If you don't use the create-domain-class command to create your domain class, you can create the test on your own (see Listing 3-35). Make sure to put the test in the appropriate directory.

Listing 3-35. The Unit Test for the Song Class, Generated Automatically

```
package com.gtunes

import grails.test.mixin.*
import org.junit.*

/**
 * See the API for {@link grails.test.mixin.domain.DomainClassUnitTestMixin} for usage
instructions
 */
@TestFor(Song)
class SongTests {

    void testSomething() {
        fail "Implement me"
    }
}
```

As you can see from Listing 3-35, the default unit test template applies the @TestFor annotation to the test class and provides the Song class as the value for the annotation. This tells the testing framework that this test is a test for the Song class. This is an important step; it is necessary in order for the testing framework to rig up a lot of the dynamic behavior associated with the Song domain class. Grails unit tests run with a robust in-memory GORM implementation backed by a ConcurrentHashMap, not a real database. This in-memory implementation supports the majority of the GORM API, with the exception of string-based queries. Testing string-based queries cannot be done in a unit test and must be covered with an integration test or a functional test. Aside from string-based queries, most of your GORM interactions can be tested in a unit test. The unit testing environment has a lower startup cost since it uses only a ConcurrentHashMap for the store. Integration tests rely on a real database and will have additional associated runtime overhead.

To run the test, invoke the test-app Grails command from the command line. The test-app command will run all the unit tests and integration tests that are part of the project. To run only the unit tests, run a command like "test-app unit:". Likewise, "test-app integration:" will run only the integration tests.

The test-app target will not only run the tests but also generate a report, including the status of all the tests that were run. This report is a standard JUnit test report, which Java developers know very well. An HTML version of the report will be generated under the project root at http://test/reports/html/index.html.

The Song class in the gTunes application has title and duration properties (see Listing 3-36).

Listing 3-36. The Song Domain Class

```
package com.gtunes

class Song {
    String title
    String artist
    Integer duration
}
```

The application should consider a nonpositive duration to be an invalid value. The type of the property is java.lang.Integer, whose valid values include the full range of values in a 32-bit signed int, including zero and a lot of negative numbers. The application should include a unit test like that shown in Listing 3-37, which asserts that the system will not accept nonpositive durations.

Listing 3-37. The Song Unit Test

```
package com.gtunes

import grails.test.mixin.*
import org.junit.*

/**
 * See the API for {@link grails.test.mixin.domain.DomainClassUnitTestMixin} for usage
instructions
 */
@TestFor(Song)
class SongTests {

    void testMinimumDuration() {

        // set the Song class up for constraints testing . . .
        mockForConstraintsTests Song

        // create a new Song
        def song = new Song(title: 'Some Title',
                             artist: 'Some Artist',
                             duration: 0)
        // make sure that validation fails . . .
        assert !song.validate()

        // make sure that the 'min' constraint failed . . .
        assert 'min' == song.errors['duration']

    }
}
```

Notice the call to the `mockForConstraintsTests(Class)` method in Listing 3-36, which provides a mock implementation of the validate() method on the Song domain class. Executing grails `test-app` Song will run the test. The test (see Listing 3-38) should fail initially because it contains no code specifying that 0 is an invalid value for the duration property.

Listing 3-38. Test Output for SongTests

```
$ grails test-app unit:
| Running 1 unit test... 1 of 1
| Failure:  testMinimumDuration(com.gtunes.SongTests)
|  Assertion failed:

assert 'min' == song.errors['duration']
              |  |    |     |
              |  |    |     null
              |  |    org.codehaus.groovy.grails.plugins.testing.GrailsMockErrors: 0 errors
              |  com.gtunes.Song : null
              false


    at com.gtunes.SongTests.testMinimumDuration(SongTests.groovy:23)
| Completed 1 unit test, 1 failed in 826ms
| Tests FAILED  - view reports in /projects/gtunes/target/test-reports
```

Starting with a failing test like this subscribes to the ideas of test-driven development (TDD). The test represents required behavior, and it will "drive" the implementation to satisfy the requirement.

Adding a simple domain constraint to the Song class, as shown in Listing 3-39, should satisfy the test.

Listing 3-39. The Song Domain Class with a Constraint

```
package com.gtunes

class Song {

    String title
    String artist
    Integer duration

    static constraints = {
        duration min: 1
    }
}
```

With that constraint in place, the unit test should pass. The domain class is written to satisfy the requirements expressed in the test. Specifically, the domain class considers any nonpositive value for duration to be invalid.

More details on how to unit-test domain classes will be provided in Chapter 4, where domain class behavior can be tested within the context of testing controller actions.

Summary

This chapter, which introduced the fundamentals of Grails domain classes, covered quite a bit of ground. Grails provides slick solutions to common problems like validating domain classes and mapping to a relational database. The GORM technology is responsible for much of that capability. GORM will be explored in more detail in Chapter 9.

CHAPTER 4

■ ■ ■

Understanding Controllers

A Grails controller is a class that is responsible for handling requests coming in to the application. The controller receives a request, potentially does some work with the request, and finally decides what should happen next. What happens next might include the following:

- executing another controller action (possibly but not necessarily in the same controller)

- rendering a view

- rendering information directly to the response

A controller is prototyped by default, meaning that a new instance is created for each request, so developers don't need to be as cautious about maintaining thread-safe code in a singleton controller. The controller's scope may be defined by using a static property in the controller named scope and assigning that property a value of "singleton" or "session". To change the default scope for all controllers in an application, define a property in grails-app/conf/Config.groovy named grails.controller.defaultScope and assign it a value of "singleton" or "session".

Think of controllers as the orchestrators of a Grails application. They provide the main entry point for any Grails application by coordinating incoming requests, delegating them to services or domain classes for business logic, and rendering views.

Let's look at the basics of how to create a controller before moving on to such meatier subjects as data binding and command objects.

Defining Controllers

A controller is a class defined under the grails-app/controllers directory. The class name must end with "Controller" by convention. Controllers do not need to extend any special base class or implement any special interfaces.

Listing 4-1 shows a typical controller, one residing at the location grails-app/controllers/ SampleController.groovy; it defines an action called index. The index action renders a simple textual response.

Listing 4-1. The SampleController Class

```
class SampleController {

  def index() {
    render 'You accessed the Sample controller...'
  }
}
```

With this controller in place, a request to /sample/index will result in the String "You accessed the Sample controller" being rendered back to the browser. You can see that actions, like the index action, are defined as methods in a controller. A controller can define any number of actions, as shown in Listing 4-2.

Listing 4-2. Defining Multiple Actions

```
class SampleController {
  def first() {  ...   }
  def second() {  ...   }
  def third() {  ...   }
  def fourth() {  ...   }
}
```

In Chapter 6, you will learn about the powerful URL-mapping support that Grails provides. By default, URLs are mapped to controller actions by way of a convention. The first part of the URL represents which controller to access, and the second part of the URL represents which action should be executed. For example, /sample/first will execute the first action in the SampleController. Likewise, /sample/second will execute the second action in the SampleController.

Setting the Default Action

You don't necessarily need to specify the action to execute in the URL. If no action is specified, Grails will execute the default action in the specified controller. You can identify the default action using the following rules (see Listing 4-3):

- If the controller defines only one action, it becomes the default action.

- If the controller defines an action called index, it becomes the default action.

- If the controller defines a property called defaultAction, its value is the name of the default action.

Listing 4-3. The Default Action

```
// Here the 'list' action is the default as there is only one action defined
class SampleController {
    def list() {}
}
// In this example 'index' is the default by convention
class SampleController {
    def list() {}
    def index() {}
}
```

```
// Here 'list' is explicitly set as the default
class SampleController {
    static defaultAction = 'list'
    def list() {}
    def index() {}
}
```

Logging

Logging, an important aspect of any application, allows the application to report textual information about what is going on inside it. Various logging solutions exist on the Java platform, including third-party logging solutions as well as the standard logging API introduced in Java 1.4. You face a certain amount of complexity in configuring logging for an application.

Often, application developers will avoid this complexity by avoiding logging altogether. They opt instead for simply printing messages using System.out.println and System.err.println. For a variety of reasons, this is really not a good idea.

Fortunately, Grails tackles much of the complexity involved with setting up logging. A log property, which is injected into every controller, is an instance of org.apache.commons.logging.Log. You don't need to write any code to initialize the log property because the framework handles that. Listing 4-4 documents the org.apache.commons.logging.Log API.

Listing 4-4. The org.apache.commons.logging.Log Interface

```
public interface Log {
public void debug(Object msg);
public void debug(Object msg, Throwable t);
public void error(Object msg);
public void error(Object msg, Throwable t);
public void fatal(Object msg);
public void fatal(Object msg, Throwable t);
public void info(Object msg);
public void info(Object msg, Throwable t);
public void trace(Object msg);
public void trace(Object msg, Throwable t);
public void warn(Object msg);
public void warn(Object msg, Throwable t);
public boolean isDebugEnabled();
public boolean isErrorEnabled();
public boolean isFatalEnabled();
public boolean isInfoEnabled();
public boolean isTraceEnabled();
public boolean isWarnEnabled();
}
```

The log property that is injected into a controller can be used from any controller action or any method within the controller (see Listing 4-5).

Listing 4-5. Using the log Property

```
class SampleController {
  def index() {
    log.info('In the index action...')
    // ...
  }
}
```

Logging Exceptions

Groovy translates all exceptions into runtime exceptions, so Groovy code is never forced to catch an exception. This differs from what Java developers are used to. In any case, even though an application is never forced to catch an exception, it makes sense to catch an exception in a lot of scenarios. In Groovy, the details for how to catch an exception are exactly the same as in Java. There is no special Groovy syntax for handling exceptions.

When an exception is caught in a controller, you'll almost always want to log details about the exception using the log property (see Listing 4-6).

Listing 4-6. Logging an Exception

```
class SampleController {
  def index() {
    try {
      // do something that might throw an exception
    } catch (Exception e) {
      log.error ('some message goes here', e)
    }
  }
}
```

Accessing Request Attributes

Java servlet developers will recognize components such as HttpServletRequest, HttpServletResponse, HttpSession, ServletContext, and others. These are all standard players in the servlet space. The Grails framework differs greatly from your standard servlet-based web frameworks, of course. However, Grails is built on top of those same servlet APIs. Table 4-1 contains a list of standard attributes that are automatically injected into Grails controllers.

Table 4-1. Standard Request Attributes

Attribute	Description
actionName	The name of the currently executing action
actionUri	The relative URI of the executing action
controllerName	The name of the currently executing controller
controllerUri	The URI of executing controller
flash	The object for working with flash scope
log	An org.apache.commons.logging.Log instance

params	A map of request parameters
request	The HttpServletRequest object
response	The HttpServletResponse object
session	The HttpSession object
servletContext	The ServletContext object

Many of the previously listed attributes are standard servlet API objects, whose documentation you can find on Oracle's Java technology web site, http://www.oracle.com/technetwork/java/. It is, however, interesting to observe how working with a Grails controller differs from working with these objects.

A common way to interact with the request, for example, is to retrieve or set a request attribute. The session and servlet context also have attributes that you can set or retrieve. Grails unifies these by overriding the dot and subscript operators. Table 4-2 shows the difference between accessing request, session, and servlet context attributes in regular Java servlets and accessing them in Grails controllers.

Table 4-2. *Differences Between Request Attributes in Java Servlets and Grails Controllers*

Java Servlet	Grails Controller
request.getAttribute("myAttr");	request.myAttr
request.setAttribute("myAttr", "myValue");	request.myAttr = "myValue"
session.getAttribute("mAttr");	session.myAttr
session.setAttribute("myAttr", "myValue"");	session.myAttr = "myValue"
servletContext.getAttribute("mAttr");	servletContext.myAttr
servletContext.setAttribute("myAttr", "myValue"");	servletContext.myAttr = "myValue"

Of course, if you are accustomed to writing code like that in the left column of the table, you can continue to do so. Grails just makes it a little bit easier.

Using Controller Scopes

You can choose from a number of scopes when developing controllers. The following list defines all the scopes available in order of their longevity

- request: Objects placed into the request are kept for the duration of the currently executing request.

- flash: Objects placed into flash are kept for the duration of the current request and the next request only.

- session: Objects placed into the session are kept until the user session is invalidated, either manually or through expiration.

- servletContext: Objects placed into the servletContext are shared across the entire application and kept for the lifetime of the application.

As you can see, each scope is unique and provides very different semantics. In an ideal world, sticking to request scope allows you to maintain a completely stateless application. In terms of scalability, this has significant advantages, as you do not need to consider issues such as replication of session state and session affinity.

However, you can certainly scale stateful applications that use flash and session scope with container-provided replication services or distributed data grids. The advantage of session scope is that it allows you to associate data on the server with individual clients. This typically works using cookies to associate individual users with their sessions.

- Finally, the servletContext is a rarely used scope that allows you to share state across the entire application. Although this can prove useful, you should exercise caution when using the servletContext because objects placed within it will not be garbage-collected unless the application explicitly removes them. Also, access to the servletContext object is not synchronized, so you need to do manual synchronization if you plan to read and write objects from the servletContext object, as shown in Listing 4-7.

Listing 4-7. Synchronized Access to the servletContext

```
def index() {
    synchronized(servletContext) {
            def myValue = servletContext.myAttr
            servletContext.myAttr = "changed"
            render myValue
    }
}
```

Of course, writing code like this will result in a serious bottleneck in your application, which leads us to the best-practice usage of the servletContext object: in general, if you really need to use the servletContext, you should prepopulate it with any values you need at startup and then read those values only at runtime. This allows you to access the servletContext in an unsynchronized manner.

Understanding Flash Scope

The flash object is a map, accessible in the same way as the params object, the fundamental difference being that key/value pairs stored in the flash object are stored in flash scope. What is flash scope? It's best explained with the problem it solves.

A common usage pattern in web applications is to do some processing and then redirect the request to another controller, servlet, or whatever. This is not an issue in itself, except what happens when the request is redirected? Redirecting the request essentially creates a brand-new request, wiping out all previous data that might have resided in the request attributes. The target of the redirect often needs this data, but unfortunately, the target action is out of luck. Some have worked around this issue by storing this information in the session instead.

This is all fine and good, but the problem with the session is that developers often forget to clear out this temporarily stored data, which places the burden on the developer to explicitly manage this state. Figure 4-1 illustrates this problem in action.

The first request that comes in sets an attribute on the request called message. It then redirects the request by sending a redirect response back to the client. This creates a brand-new request instance, which is sent to the controller. Sadly, the message attribute is lost and evaluates to null.

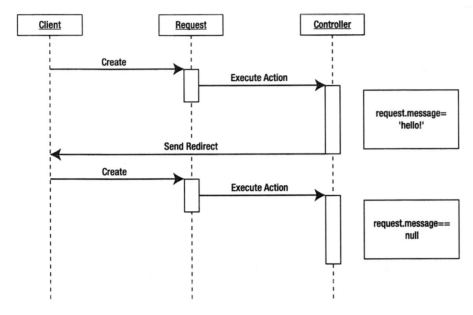

Figure 4-1. *Request attributes and redirects*

To get around this little annoyance, the flash object stores its values for the next request—and the next request only—after which they automatically vanish. This feature manages the burden of this kind of use case for you. It's another small but significant feature that allows you to focus on the problem at hand instead of the surrounding issues.

One of the more common use cases for flash scope is to store a message that will display when some form of validation fails. Listing 4-8 demonstrates how to store a hypothetical message in the flash object so it's available for the next request.

Listing 4-8. *Storing a Message in Flash Scope*

```
flash.message = 'I am available next time you request me!'
```

Remember that the flash object implements java.util.Map, so all the regular methods of this class are also available. Figure 4-2 shows how flash scope solves the aforementioned problem. Here, on the first request, you store a message variable to the flash object and then redirect the request. When the new request comes in, you can access this message; no problem. The message variable will then automatically be removed for the next request that comes in.

■ **Note**   The flash object does still use the HttpSession instance internally to store itself, so if you require any kind of session affinity or clustering, remember that it applies to the flash object, too.

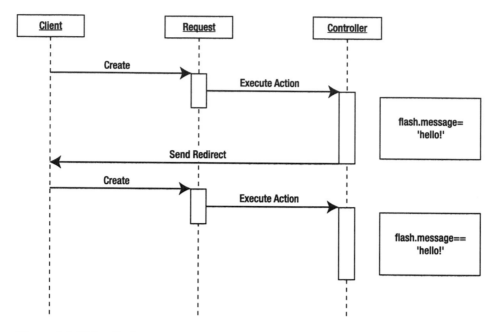

Figure 4-2. *Using flash scope*

Accessing Request Parameters

A controller action is often given input that will affect the behavior of the controller. For example, if a user submits a form that he or she has filled out, all the form's field names and values will be available to the controller in the form of request parameters. The standard servlet API provides an API for accessing request parameters. Listing 4-9 shows how a controller might retrieve the userName request parameter.

Listing 4-9. *Request Parameters via Standard Servlet API*

```
def userName = request.getParameter('userName')
log.info("User Name: ${userName}")
```

One of the dynamic properties injected into a Grails controller is a property called params. This params property is a map of request parameters. Listing 4-10 shows how a controller might retrieve the userName request parameter using the params property.

Listing 4-10. *Request Parameters via params Property*

```
def userName = params.userName
log.info("User Name: ${userName}")
```

Request Parameter Type Conversions

Incoming request parameters are typically strings. If a controller action wants to accept a request parameter named counter and use it to control how many times some operation may be executed, the code might look something like Listing 4-11.

Listing 4-11. Request Parameter Type Conversion

```
def index() {
    // since params.counter is a string, it must be converted to an int if
    // the application intends to use the value as a number
    def counter = params.counter.toInteger()
    // …
}
```

Grails provides convenience methods for doing this type of conversion on request parameters. Those methods are available on the params object and have names that correspond to all eight of the primitive types defined by Java (Boolean, byte, char, short, int, long, float, and double). The methods each accept one or two arguments. The first argument is the name of the request parameter that is to be converted, and the optional second argument is a default value that will be returned if a corresponding request parameter cannot be found or if an error occurs during the conversion. Listing 4-12 demonstrates using the int convenience method.

Listing 4-12. Using the int Type of Conversion Method

```
def index() {
    def counter = params.int('counter')
    // …
}
```

Another type of converting method is named list. The list method is useful when dealing with multiple request parameters of the same name. The list method will return a list containing all of the values associated with the specified request parameter name, as shown in Listing 4-13.

Listing 4-13. Using The list Type Conversion Method

```
def index() {
    for (name in params.list('name') {
        // do something with name
    }
}
```

If a controller action accepts parameters of simple types, including the eight primitive types, their corresponding type wrappers, and java.lang.String, then Grails will automatically attempt the corresponding type of conversion and pass the resulting value into the controller action as a method argument. The two controller actions defined in Listing 4-14 accomplish the same thing.

Listing 4-14. Binding Request Parameters to Method Arguments

```
def firstAction() {
    def counter = params.int('counter')
    def name = params.name
    // …
}
def secondAction(int counter, String name) {
    // there is no need to interact with the params object as
    // the request parameters have been bound to the counter
    // and name method arguments
}
```

By default the method argument name will correspond to a request parameter name. If for some reason the request parameter and the method argument need to have different names, then the grails. web.RequestParameter annotation may be used to be explicit about which request parameter should be bound to a particular method argument, as shown in Listing 4-15.

Listing 4-15. The RequestParameter Annotation

```
import grails.web.RequestParameter

class AdminController {

    // mainNumber will be initialized with the value
    // of params.accountNumber
    // accountType will be initialized with params.int('accountType')
    def action(@RequestParameter('accountNumber') String mainNumber,
            int accountType) {
        //
    }
}
```

Whether you are using the RequestParameter annotation or associating method arguments with request parameters by convention, if a corresponding request parameter does not exist or a conversion error occurs for method action arguments, then the default value for the corresponding type will be passed in as the argument value. For Booleans this is false, for all of the other seven primitive types this is zero (0), and for all reference types this is null. Controllers have an errors property that may contain errors related to type conversions of request parameters. Listing 4-16 shows how a controller might interact with the errors property.

Listing 4-16. A Controller's errors Property

```
class AdminController {

  def action(String accountNumber, int accountType) {
   if(accountNumber == null && errors.hasErrors()) {
     def accountNumberError = errors.getFieldError( accountNumber')
       if(accountNumberError != null) {
         // accountNumberError is an instance of
         // org.springframework.validation.FieldError
         // ...
     }
    }
   }
  }
}
```

Rendering Text

In its most basic form, you can use the render method from a controller to output text to the response. Listing 4-17 demonstrates how to render a simple string to the response.

Listing 4-17. Rendering a Simple String

```
render 'this text will be rendered back as part of the response'
```

Optionally, you can specify the contentType:

```
render text:'<album>Revolver</album>', contentType:'text/xml'
```

The most common use of the render method is to render a GSP view or a GSP template. We'll cover GSP in detail in Chapter 5.

Redirecting a Request

Often a controller action will need to redirect control to another controller action. This is a common thing for a controller action to do, so Grails provides a simple technique to manage redirecting to another controller action.

Grails provides all controllers with a redirect method that accepts a map as an argument. The map should contain all the information that Grails needs to carry out the redirect, including the name of the action to redirect to. In addition, the map can contain the name of the controller to redirect to.

Specifying the controller is required only if the request is being redirected to an action defined in a controller other than the current controller. Listing 4-18 shows a standard redirect from the first action to the second action within the sample controller.

Listing 4-18. A Simple Redirect

```
class SampleController {
  def first() {
    // redirect to the "second" action...
    redirect action: "second"
  }
  def second() {
    // ...
  }
}
```

If the redirect is bound for an action in another controller, you must specify the name of the other controller. Listing 4-19 demonstrates how to redirect to an action in another controller.

Listing 4-19. Redirecting to an Action in Another Controller

```
class SampleController {
  def first() {
    // redirect to the 'list' action in the 'store' controller...
    redirect action: "list", controller: "store"
  }
}
```

Although the previous examples are pretty trivial, the redirect method is pretty flexible. Table 4-3 shows the different arguments that the redirect method accepts.

Table 4-3. Redirect Arguments

Argument Name	Description
action	The name of or a reference to the action to redirect to
controller	The name of the controller to redirect to
id	The id parameter to pass in the redirect
params	A map of parameters to pass
uri	A relative URI to redirect to
url	An absolute URL to redirect to

As you can see, the redirect method allows you to effectively pass control from one action to the next. However, often you simply want to formulate some data to be rendered by a view. In the next couple of sections, we'll take a look at how to achieve this.

Creating a Model

One of the most fundamental activities carried out in a controller is gathering data that will be rendered in the view. A controller can gather data directly or delegate to Grails services or other components to gather the data. However the controller gathers the data, the data are typically made available to the view in the form of a map that the controller action returns. When a controller action returns a map, that map represents data that the view can reference. Listing 4-20 displays the show action of the SongController.

Listing 4-20. Returning a Map of Data to Be Rendered by the View

```
class SongController {
    def show() {
        [ song: Song.get(params.id) ]
    }
}
```

Remember that return statements are optional in Groovy. Because the last expression evaluated in the show action is a map, the map is the return value from this action. This map contains data that will be passed in to the view to be rendered. In Listing 4-14, the sole key in the map is song and the value associated with that key is a Song object retrieved from the database based on the id request parameter.

Now the view can reference this song. Whereas this map contains only a single entry, a map returned from a controller action can include as many entries as is appropriate. Every entry represents an object that the view can reference.

Rendering a View

The subject of views in Grails is so important that an entire chapter (Chapter 5) is dedicated to it. But for now, you need to understand how Grails goes about view selection from a controller's point of view. First, let's look at the default view-selection strategy.

Finding the Default View

As you saw in Listing 4-15, the SongController has a single action, called show. The show action returns a model containing a single key, called song, which references an instance of the Song domain class. However, nowhere in the code can you see any reference to the view that will be used to deal with the rendering part of this action.

That's perfectly understandable, because we haven't explicitly told Grails what view to render. To mitigate this problem, Grails makes that decision for you based on the conventions in the application. In the case of the show action, Grails will look for a view at the location grails-app/views/song/show.gsp. The name of the view is taken from the name of the action, while the name of the parent directory is taken from the controller name. Simple, really.

But what if you want to display a completely different view? The ever-flexible render method comes to the rescue again.

Selecting a Custom View

To tell Grails to render a custom view, you can use the render method's view argument, as shown in Listing 4-21.

Listing 4-21. Rendering a Custom View

```
class SongController {
    def show() {
        render view: "display", model: [ song: Song.get(params.id) ]
    }
}
```

Notice how you can use the model argument to pass in the model rather than the return value of the action. In the example in Listing 4-21, we're asking Grails to render a view called display. In this case, Grails assumes you mean a view at the location grails-app/views/song/display.gsp. Notice how the view is automatically scoped with the grails-app/views/song directory.

If the view you want to render is in another, possibly shared, directory, you can specify an absolute path to the view:

```
render view:"/common/song", model:[song: Song.get(params.id) ]
```

By starting with a / character, you can reference any view within the grails-app/views directory. In the previous example, Grails will try to render a view at the location grails-app/views/common/song.gsp.

Rendering Templates

In addition to views, Grails supports the notion of templates—small snippets of view code that other views can include. We'll be covering templates in more detail in Chapter 5, but for now, just know that you can render a template from a controller using the render method:

```
render template: "/common/song", model: [song: Song.get(params.id) ]
```

In this case, Grails will try to render a template at the location grails-app/views/common/_song.gsp. Notice how, unlike views, the name of the template starts with an underscore by convention.

Performing Data Binding

Often a controller action will need to create new domain objects and populate the properties of the instance with values received as request parameters. Consider the Album domain class, which has properties such as genre and title. If a request is made to the save action in the AlbumController, the controller action could create a new Album and save it using a technique like that shown in Listing 4-22.

Listing 4-22. Populating an Album with Request Parameters

```
class AlbumController {
    def save() {
        def album = new Album()
        album.genre = params.genre
        album.title = params.title
        album.save()
    }
}
```

The approach in Listing 4-22 assigns values to domain properties based on corresponding request parameters. It might work for simple models with a small number of properties, but as your domain model grows in complexity, this code gets longer and more tedious. Fortunately, the Grails framework provides some slick options for binding request parameters to a domain object.

Remember that the params object in your controller is a map of name/value pairs. You can pass maps to a domain class's constructor to initialize all the domain class's properties with the corresponding request parameters. Listing 4-23 shows a better approach to creating and populating an Album object.

Listing 4-23. Populating an Album by Passing params to the Constructor

```
class AlbumController {
    def save() {
        def album = new Album(params)
        album.save()
    }
}
```

▨ **Caution** The default data binding mechanism will bind all properties that are not static, not transient, and not dynamically typed. The features detailed so far can leave your web application open to URL attacks due to the automatic setting of properties from request parameters. This is a common issue among frameworks that perform such conversion (including Ruby on Rails, Spring MVC, WebWork, and others). If you are developing a web application with heightened security in mind, you should use fine-grained control over data binding through bindable constraint and/or the bindData method (each described later), along with stricter validation.

As you can see, this is a much cleaner approach and scales better as the number of properties in a domain class grows.

Occasionally, setting properties on a domain object that has already been constructed can prove useful. For example, you retrieve a domain object from the database and then need to update it with values passed to the controller as request parameters. In a case like this, passing a map of parameters to the domain-class constructor will not help, because the object already exists. Grails provides yet another slick solution here. You can use a domain class's `properties` property in conjunction with request parameters to update an existing object, as shown in Listing 4-24.

Listing 4-24. *Updating an Existing Object with Request Parameters*

```
class AlbumController {
    def update() {
        def album = Album.get(params.id)
        album.properties = params
        album.save()
    }
}
```

Whenever your application accepts user input, there is a chance that said input might not be what your application requires. You've already seen in Chapter 3 how to define custom-validation constraints on domain classes; now you'll begin to understand how you can use data binding in combination with these constraints to validate incoming data.

Validating Incoming Data

The mechanics of the data-binding and data-validation process in Grails has two phases. First, let's revisit the following line of code:

```
album.properties = params
```

At this point, Grails will attempt to bind any incoming request parameters onto the properties of the instance. Groovy is a strongly typed language, and all parameters arrive as strings, so some type conversion might be necessary.

Underneath the surface, Grails uses Spring's data-binding capabilities to convert request parameters to the target type if necessary. During this process, a type-conversion error can occur if, for example, converting the `String` representation of a number to a `java.lang.Integer` is impossible. If an error occurs, Grails automatically sets the persistent instance to read-only so it cannot persist unless you yourself explicitly make it persist (refer to Chapter 10 for more information on automatic dirty checking).

If all is well, the second phase of validation commences. At this point, you validate the persistent instance against its defined constraints, using either the `validate()` method or the `save()` method, as described in Chapter 3:

```
album.validate()
```

Grails will validate each property of the `Album` instance and populate the `Errors` object with any validation errors that might have occurred. This brings us nicely into a discussion of the Errors API.

The Errors API and Controllers

The mechanics of Grails' validation mechanism is built entirely on Spring's `org.springframework.validation` package. As discussed in Chapter 3, whenever you validate a domain instance, a Spring `org.springspringframework.validation.Errors` object is created and associated with the instance.

From a controller's point of view, when you have a domain object in an invalid state—typically due to invalid user input that changes an instance using data binding—you need to use branching logic to handle the validation error.

Listing 4-25 shows an example of how to use data binding to update an `Album` instance and validate its state.

Listing 4-25. Dealing with Validation Errors

```
def save() {
    def album = Album.get(params.id)
    album.properties = params
    if(album.save()) {
        redirect action: "show", id: album.id
    } else {
        render view: "edit", model: [album:album]
    }
}
```

Notice how in Listing 4-20 you can call the save() method, which triggers validation, and send the user back to the edit view if a validation error occurs. When a user enters invalid data, the errors property on the Album will be an Errors object containing one or more validation errors.

You can programmatically decipher these errors by iterating over them:

```
album.errors.allErrors.each { println it.code }
```

If you merely want to check whether an instance has any errors, you can call the hasErrors() method on the instance:

```
if(album.hasErrors()) println "Something went wrong!"
```

In the view, you can render these using the <g:renderErrors> tag:

```
<g:renderErrors bean="${album}" />
```

You'll be learning more about handling errors in the view through the course of the book, but as you can see, it's frequently the controller's job to coordinate errors that occur and ensure the user enters valid data.

Data Binding to Multiple Domain Objects

In the examples of data binding you've seen so far, the assumption has been that you wish to bind parameters to a single domain instance. However, you might encounter a scenario in which you must create several domain instances.

Consider, for example, the creation of Artist instances in the gTunes application. The application might require that an Artist can exist only if he or she has released at least one Album. In this case, it makes sense to create both the Artist and the first Album simultaneously.

To understand data binding when dealing with multiple domain instances, you first need to understand how parameters are submitted from forms. Consider, for example, the case of updating an Album and the line

```
album.properties = params
```

In this case, the expectation is that parameters are not namespaced in any way. In other words, to update the title property of the Album instance, you can provide an HTML input such as the following:

```
<input type="text" name="title" />
```

Notice how the name of the <input> matches the property name. This clearly would not work in the case of multiple domain classes, because you might have two different domain classes that have a property called title. You can get around this problem namespacing any parameters passed using a dot:

```
<input type="text" name="album.title" />
<input type="text" name="artist.name" />
...
```

Now create and bind both `Album` and `Artist` instances by referring to them within the `params` object by their respective namespaces:

```
def album = new Album( params["album"] )
def artist = new Artist( params["artist"] )
```

Data Binding with the bindData Method

The data-binding techniques you have seen so far are automatic and handled implicitly by Grails. However, in some circumstances you might need to exercise greater control over the data-binding process or bind data to objects other than domain classes. To help tackle this issue, Grails provides a `bindData` method that takes the object to bind the data to and a `java.util.Map`.

The map should contain keys that match the property names of the target properties within the passed object. As an example, if you wanted to ensure only the `title` property was bound to an `Album` instance, you could use the code shown in Listing 4-26.

Listing 4-26. *Using the bindData Method*

```
class AlbumController {
    def save() {
        def album = Album.get(params.id)
        bindData(album, params, [include:"title"])
        // ...
    }
}
```

Notice how in Listing 4-26 you can pass the `Album` instance as the first argument, and the parameters to bind to the instance as the second argument. The final argument is a map specifying that you wish to include only the `title` property in the data-binding process. You could change the key within the map to exclude if you wished to bind all properties *except* the title property.

Finally, as you saw in the previous section, you can bind to multiple domain instances using the default data-binding mechanism in Grails. You can do this with the `bindData` method too, using the last argument that specifies the prefix to filter by.

```
bindData(album, params, [include:"title"], "album")
```

In this example, the prefix `album` is passed as the last argument, making the `bindData` method bind all parameters that begin with the `album` prefix.

Data Binding and Associations

The final topic to consider when doing data binding is how it relates to associations. The easiest case to understand is many-to-one and one-to-one associations. For example, consider the `artist` property of the `Album` class, which is a many-to-one association, as shown in Listing 4-27.

Listing 4-27. The artist Association of the Album Class

```
class Album {
    Artist artist
    // ...
}
```

You need to consider two cases when working with a many-to-one association like this. The first involves creating new instances. Suppose you create a new Album instance using this code:

```
def album    = new Album(params)
```

In this case, if any parameters reference the artist association, such as artist.name, a new Artist instance will be automatically instantiated and assigned to the Album instance. The names of the properties to set are taken from the value of the right side of the dot in the request-parameter name. With artist.name, the property to set is name. To further clarify, the following <input> tag shows an example of a form field that will populate the artist association of the Album class:

```
<input type="text" name="artist.name" />
```

The second scenario occurs when you are assigning an existing instance of an association (an existing Artist, for example) or modifying an association. To do this, you need to pass the association's identifier using a request parameter with the .id suffix. For example, you can use the following <input> to specify the Artist that should be associated with an existing or new Album:

```
<input type="text" name="artist.id" value="1" />
```

With single-ended associations out of the way, let's consider associations that contain multiple objects. For example, an Album has many Song instances in its songs associations. What if you wanted to provide a form that enabled you to create an Album and its associated songs? To enable this, you can use subscript-style references to populate or update multiple Song instances:

```
<input type="text" name="songs[0].title" value="The Bucket" />
<input type="text" name="songs[1].title" value="Milk" />
```

Note that the default collection type for association in Grails is a java.util.Set, so unless you change the default to java.util.List, the order of entries will not be retained because Set types have no concept of order. If you want to create a new Album instance and populate the songs association with an existing collection of songs, then you can just specify their identifiers using the .id suffix:

```
<input type="text" name="songs[0].id" value="23" />
<input type="text" name="songs[1].id" value="47" />
```

The Bindable Constraint

As mentioned earlier, the default data binding mechanism will bind all properties which are not static, not transient and not dynamically typed. The bindData method allows white lists and black lists to be provided to gain more control over which properties are assigned values during data binding. An additional technique supported by the framework is to be explicit about which properties are bindable in a declarative way. Having done that, whenever data binding is carried out without supplying a white list or a black list, only properties configured to be bindable will be assigned values during data binding. Listing 4-28 demonstrates the syntax for expressing the bindability of individual properties.

Listing 4-28. The bindable Constraint

```
class User {
    /* userName and salary would be bindable by default */
    String userName
    BigDecimal salary

    /* group and numberOfActiveGroups would not be bindable by default */
    def group
    transient int numberOfActiveGroups

    static constraints = {
        salary bindable: false
        group bindable: true
    }
}
```

If an instance of the User class defined in Listing 4-28 were created and data binding was carried out with something like user.properties = params, only the userName and group properties would be subject to data binding. Normally the salary property would be subject to data binding, but expressing bindable: false for the property in the constraints block tells the framework otherwise. The salary property would not be subject to data binding because bindable: false is expressed for that property in the constraints block. The numberOfActiveGroups property would not be subject to data binding because it is transient.

Working with Command Objects

Sometimes a particular action doesn't require the involvement of a domain class but still requires the validation of user input. In this case, you might want to consider using a command object. A command object is a class that has all the data-binding and data-validation capabilities of a domain class but is not persistent. In other words, you can define constraints of a command object and validate them just like a domain class.

Defining Command Objects

A command object requires the definition of class, just as with any other object. You can define command classes in the grails-app/controllers directory or even in the same file as a controller. Unlike Java, Groovy supports the notion of multiple class definitions per file, which is quite handy if you plan to use a particular command object only for the controller you're working with.

For example, you could define an AlbumCreateCommand that encapsulates the validation and creation of new Album instances before they are saved. Listing 4-29 presents such an example.

Listing 4-29. An Example Command Object Definition

```
class AlbumCreateCommand {
    String artist
    String title
    List songs = []
    List durations = []
```

```
    static constraints = {
        artist blank:false
        title blank:false
        songs minSize:1, validator:{ val, obj ->
            if(val.size() != obj.durations.size())
                return "songs.durations.not.equal.size"
        }
    }

    Album createAlbum() {
        def artist = Artist.findByName(artist) ?: new Artist(name:artist)
        def album = new Album(title:title)
        songs.eachWithIndex { songTitle, i ->
            album.addToSongs(title:songTitle, duration:durations[i])
        }
        return album
    }
}
```

In Listing 4-29, you can see a command-object definition that is designed to capture everything necessary to subsequently create a valid Album instance. Notice how you can define constraints on a command object, just as in a domain class. The createAlbum() method, which is optional, is interesting because it shows how you can use command objects as factories that take a valid set of data and construct your domain instances. In the next section, you'll see how to take advantage of the command object in Listing 4-29.

Using Command Objects

In order to use a command object, you need to specify the command as the first argument in a controller action. For example, to use AlbumCreateCommand, you need to have a save action, such as the one shown in Listing 4-30.

Listing 4-30. Using a Command Object

```
class AlbumController {
    def save(AlbumCreateCommand cmd) {
        // ...
    }
}
```

You need to explicitly define the command object using its type definition as the first argument to the action. Here's what happens next: when a request comes in, Grails will automatically create a new instance, bind the incoming request parameters to the properties of the instance, and pass it to you as the first argument.

Providing the request parameters to a command like this is pretty trivial. Listing 4-31 shows an example form.

Listing 4-31. Providing a Form to Populate the Data

```
<g:form url="[controller: 'album', action: 'save'] ">
    Title: <input type="text" name="title" /> <br>
    Artist: <input type="text" name="artist" /> <br>
```

```
Song 1: <input type="text" name="songs[0]" /> <br>
Song 2: <input type="text" name="songs[1]" /> <br>
    ...
</g:form>
```

You'll probably want to make the input of the songs dynamic using some JavaScript; nevertheless, you can see the concept in Listing 4-31. Once you've given the user the ability to enter data and you're capturing said data using the command object, all you need to do is validate it. Not all command objects are validateable. In order for a command object to be validateable, the source code for the command object class must be defined in the same source file as a controller that uses the command object, or the command object class must be marked with the grails.validation.Validateable annotation. Note that the grails.validation.Validateable annotation is not only for command object classes but may be applied to any Groovy class that should have validation behavior associated with it. Listing 4-32 shows how the save action's logic might look with the command object in use.

Listing 4-32. Using the Command Object for Validation

```
def save(AlbumCreateCommand cmd) {
    if(cmd.validate()) {
        def album = cmd.createAlbum()
        album.save()
        redirect(action:"show", id:album.id)
    }
    else {
        render(view:"create", model:[cmd:cmd])
    }
}
```

As you can see, it's now the command object that is ensuring the validity of the request, and we're using it as a factory to construct a perfectly valid Album instance. As with domain classes, command objects have an Errors object, so you can use the <g:renderErrors> tag to display validation errors to the user.

```
<g:renderErrors bean="{cmd}" />
```

Imposing HTTP Method Restrictions

Often a web application needs to impose restrictions on which HTTP request methods are allowed for a specific controller action. For example, it is generally considered a bad idea for a controller action to carry out any destructive operation in response to an HTTP GET. Such operations should be limited to HTTP POST and DELETE.

Implementing an Imperative Solution

One approach to dealing with this concern is for a controller action to inspect the request method and prevent certain actions from being carried out in response to an inappropriate HTTP request method. Listing 4-33 shows a simple imperative approach to the problem.

Listing 4-33. Inspecting the HTTP Request Method in a Controller Action

```
class SongController {
  def delete() {
    if(request.method == "GET") {
      // do not delete in response to a GET request
      // redirect to the list action
      redirect action: "list"
    } else {
      // carry out the delete here...
    }
  }
}
```

While this approach is fairly straightforward and does get the job done, it's a tedious solution to the problem. In a real-world application, this same logic would appear in many controller actions.

Taking Advantage of a Declarative Syntax

A better solution to limiting actions to certain HTTP request methods is to take advantage of a simple declarative syntax that expresses which HTTP request methods are valid for a particular controller action. Grails supports an approach like this through the optional allowedMethods property in a controller.

The allowedMethods property expresses which HTTP request methods are valid for any particular controller action. By default, all HTTP request methods are considered valid for any particular controller action. If you want an action to be accessible through specific request methods only, then you should include the action in the allowedMethods property.

You should assign the allowedMethods property a value that is a map. The keys in the map should be the names of actions that you want restricted. The value(s) associated with the keys should be a string representing a specific request method or a list of strings representing all allowed methods for that particular action. Listing 4-34 shows an example.

Listing 4-34. Restricting Access to Controller Actions Using the allowedMethods Property

```
class SomeController {
    // action1 may be invoked via a POST
    // action2 has no restrictions
    // action3 may be invoked via a POST or DELETE
    static allowedMethods = [action1: 'POST', action3: ['POST', 'DELETE']]
    def action1() { ... }
    def action2() { ... }
    def action3() { ... }
}
```

If the rules expressed in the allowedMethods property are violated, the framework will deny the request and return a 405 error code, which the HTTP specification defines as "Method Not Allowed."

Controller IO

As you've learned so far, controllers can control request flow through redirects and rendering views. In addition to this, controllers might need to read and write binary input to and from the client. In this section, we'll look at how to read data, including file uploads, and how to write binary responses to the client.

Handling File Uploads

One of the more common use cases when developing web applications is to allow the user to upload a local file to the server using a multipart request. This is where the solid Grails foundation of Spring MVC starts to shine through.

Spring has excellent support for handling file uploads via an extension to the servlet API's HttpServletRequest interface called org.springframework.web.multipart.MultipartHttpServletRequest, the definition of which is in Listing 4-35.

Listing 4-35. The org.springframework.web.multipart.MultipartHttpServletRequest Interface

```
interface MultipartHttpServletRequest extends HttpServletRequest {
        public MultipartFile getFile(String name);
        public Map getFileMap();
        public Iterator getFileNames();
}
```

As you can see, the MultipartHttpServletRequest interface simply extends the default HttpServletRequest interface to provide useful methods to work with files in the request.

Working with Multipart Requests

Essentially, whenever a multipart request is detected, a request object that implements the MultipartHttpServletRequest interface is present in the controller instance. This provides access to the methods seen in Listing 4-35 to access files uploaded in a multipart request. Listing 4-36 also shows how you can define a multipart form using the <g:uploadForm> tag.

Listing 4-36. An Example Upload Form

```
<g:uploadForm action="upload">
      <input type="file" name="myFile" />
      <input type="submit" value="Upload! " />
</g:uploadForm>
```

The important bits are highlighted in bold, but an upload form essentially requires two things:

- A <form> tag with the enctype attribute set to the value multipart/form-data. The <g:uploadForm> in Listing 4-36 does this for you automatically.

- An <input> tag whose type attribute is set to the value file.

In the previous case, the name of the file input is myFile; this is crucial because it's the named reference that you work with when using the getFile method of the MultipartHttpServletRequest interface. For example, the code within an upload action will retrieve the uploaded file from the request (see Listing 4-37).

Listing 4-37. Retrieving the Uploaded File

```
def upload() {
    def file = request.getFile('myFile')
    // do something with the file
}
```

Note that the getFile method does not return a java.io.File. Instead, it returns an instance of org.springframework.web.multipart.MultipartFile, the interface detailed in Listing 4-38. If the file is not found in the request, the getFile method will return null.

Listing 4-38. The org.springframework.web.multipart.MultipartFile Interface

```
interface MultipartFile {
    public byte[] getBytes();
    public String getContentType();
    public java.io.InputStream getInputStream();
    public String getName();
    public String getOriginalFilename();
    public long getSize();
    public boolean isEmpty();
    public void transferTo(java.io.File dest);
}
```

Many useful methods are defined in the MultipartFile interface. Potential use cases include the following:

- Use the getSize() method to allow uploads only of certain file sizes.

- Reject empty files using the isEmpty() method.

- Read the file as a Java.io.InputStream using the getInputStream() method.

- Allow only certain file types to be uploaded using the getContentType() method.

- Transfer the file onto the server using the transferTo(dest) method.

As an example, the code in Listing 4-39 will upload a file to the server if it's not empty and if it's fewer than 1,024 bytes in size.

Listing 4-39. File Uploads in Action

```
def upload() {
    def file = request.getFile('myFile')
    if(file && !file.empty && file.size < 1024)  {
        file.transferTo( new File( "/local/server/path/${file.name}" ) )
    }
}
```

Working directly with a MultipartHttpServletRequest instance is one way to manage file uploads, but frequently you need to read the contents of a file. In the next section, we'll look at how Grails makes this easier through data binding.

Uploads and Data Binding

In the "Performing Data Binding" section, you saw how Grails handles automatic type conversion from strings to other common Java types. What we didn't discuss is how this capability extends to file uploads. Grails, through Spring MVC, will automatically bind files uploaded to properties of domain-class instances based on the following rules:

- If the target property is a byte [ ], the file's bytes will be bound.
- If the target property is a String, the file's contents as a string will be bound.

Suppose you want to allow users of the gTunes application to upload album art for each album. By adding a new property to the Album domain class called art of type byte[], you automatically have the capability to save the image data to the database, as shown in Listing 4-40.

Listing 4-40. Adding the art Property

```
class Album{
    byte[] art
    // ...
}
```

To bind an uploaded file, you simply need to add an art upload field that matches the art property name to a <g:uploadForm> tag.

```
<input type="file" name="art" />
```

The following line automatically handles binding the file to the Album:

```
def user = new Album( params )
```

Grails will automatically recognize the request as being multipart, retrieve the file, and bind the bytes that make up the file to the art byte array property of the Album class. This capability also extends to usage in conjunction with the properties property and bindData method discussed previously.

Reading the Request InputStream

If you want to get the text contained within the request body, you can use the inputStream property of the request object, as shown in Listing 4-41.

Listing 4-41. Reading the Request Body

```
def readText() {
    def text = request.inputStream.text
    render "You sent $text"
}
```

Writing a Binary Response

You can send a binary response to the client using standard servlet API calls, such as the example in Listing 4-42, which uses the HttpServletResponse object to output binary data to the response in the form of a ZIP file.

Listing 4-42. Writing Binary Data to the Response

```
def createZip() {
    byte[] zip = ... // create the zip from some source
    render file: zip
}
```

The code uses the `response` object's `outputStream` property in conjunction with Groovy's overloaded left shift `<<` operator, which is present in a number of objects that output or append to something such as `java.io.Writer` and `java.lang.StringBuffer`, to name just a couple.

Using Simple Interceptors

Frequently, it is useful to catch the flow of method execution by intercepting calls to certain methods. This concept is the foundation of aspect-oriented programming (AOP), which allows the definition of "pointcuts" (execution points) to be intercepted. You can then modify the intercepted execution through the use of *before*, *after*, and *around* "advice."

As the names suggest, *before* advice in AOP is code that can be executed before an intercepted method call; *after* advice is code that can be executed after an intercepted method call. *Around* advice is code that can replace the method call entirely. AOP's great strength is providing support for implementing cross-cutting concerns.

The example frequently used for this concept is the logging of method calls. Although the interception mechanism in Grails by no means provides the same power and flexibility in terms of what pointcuts can be intercepted, it does fulfill the basic need of intercepting calls to actions on controllers.

Additionally, interceptors are useful if they apply only to a single controller. If your requirement spans multiple controllers, you're better off having a look at filters (a topic covered in Chapter 14). With interceptors you can either intercept all actions or provide more fine-grained control by specifying which actions should be intercepted. Let's look at a few examples, starting with *before* interceptors.

Before Advice

Luckily, as with the rest of Grails, there is no hefty XML configuration or annotation trickery required, thanks to Convention over Configuration. All it takes to define a *before* interceptor is to create a closure property named `beforeInterceptor` within the target controller, as shown in Listing 4-43.

Listing 4-43. A beforeInterceptor

```
def beforeInterceptor = {
    log.trace("Executing action $actionName with params $params")
}
```

Listing 4-43 uses the `log` object to output tracing information before any action within the defining controller is executed. This example applies to every action defined in the controller. However, you can apply more fine-grained control using interception conditions.

As an example, say you wanted to trace each time a user views an `Album` and each user's country of residence. You could define a `beforeInterceptor` as shown in Listing 4-44.

Listing 4-44. Using Interception Conditions

```
class AlbumController {
    private trackCountry = {
        def country = request.locale.country
        def album = Album.get(params.id)
        new AlbumVisit(country:country, album:album).save()
    }
    def beforeInterceptor = [action: trackCountry, only: 'show']
}
```

As you can see from Listing 4-44, you can define a beforeInterceptor using a map literal. The action key defines the code that should execute. In this case, we're using an only condition, which means that the interceptor applies only to the show action. You could change this to an except condition, in which case the interceptor would apply to all actions *except* the show action.

Finally, a beforeInterceptor can also halt execution of an action by returning false. For example, if you want to allow only U.S. visitors to your site, you could send a 403 forbidden HTTP code if the user hails from outside the United States (see Listing 4-45).

Listing 4-45. Halting Execution with a beforeInterceptor

```
class AlbumController {
    def beforeInterceptor = {
        if(request.locale != Locale.US) {
            response.sendError 403
            return false
        }
    }
}
```

After Advice

After advice is defined using the unsurprisingly named afterInterceptor property that again takes a closure. The first argument passed to the closure is the resulting model from the action, as shown in Listing 4-46.

Listing 4-46. An afterInterceptor Example

```
def afterInterceptor = { model ->
    log.trace("Executed $actionName which resulted in model: $model")
}
```

Again, in this rather trivial example, the logging mechanism traces any action that executes.

Testing Controllers

Grails uses mixins to provide special behavior for unit testing controllers. As an example, the AlbumController class as it stands has no test coverage. If the controller were created with the create-controller command, a unit test would have been created at the same time. If not, to create a test for this controller, you need create a new test class. The default unit test that would have been generated by the create-controller command is shown in Listing 4-47.

Listing 4-47. Controller Unit Test Template

```
package com.gtunes

import grails.test.mixin.*
import org.junit.*

@TestFor(AlbumController)
class AlbumControllerTests {

    void testSomething() {
        fail "Implement me"
    }
}
```

Let us consider a simple controller action that we want to test. Listing 4-48 shows a list action in the AlbumController which returns a model that includes a list of all of the albums in the database.

Listing 4-48. A Simple Controller Action

```
package com.gtunes

class AlbumController {

    def list() {
        [albumList: Album.list()]
    }
}
```

A unit test that attempts to execute that action and verify that the model contains the expected information might look like the code in Listing 4-49.

Listing 4-49. A Simple Controller Unit Test

```
package com.gtunes

import grails.test.mixin.*

@TestFor(AlbumController)
class AlbumControllerTests {

    void testListAction() {
        def model = controller.list()
        // make assertions about the model
    }
}
```

Attempting to run that test will lead to an error, as shown in Listing 4-50.

Listing 4-50. Controller Unit Test Failure

```
grails> test-app unit:
| Running 1 unit test... 1 of 1
| Failure:  testListAction(com.gtunes.AlbumControllerTests)
|  groovy.lang.MissingMethodException: No signature of method: com.gtunes.Album.list() is
applicable for argument types: () values: []
| Completed 1 unit test, 1 failed in 200ms
| Tests FAILED  - view reports in target/test-reports
grails>
```

The problem with the test here is that the list action in the `AlbumController` is invoking the `Album.list()` method, which isn't available in our unit testing environment. Fortunately, the framework makes it very easy to mock the entire GORM API so a unit test like this one can be carried out. One way to do this is to use the `@Mock` annotation with a domain class argument. This instructs the framework to add the GORM API to this domain class and provides a full in-memory implementation of GORM, which allows the full GORM API to function without the need for a real database to be created. All of that is accounted for in the more complete unit shown in listing 4-51.

Listing 4-51. Updated AlbumControllerUnitTests

```
package com.gtunes

import grails.test.mixin.*
import grails.test.mixin.domain.*

@TestFor(AlbumController)
@Mock(Album)
class AlbumControllerTests {

    void testListAction() {
        new Album(title: 'Trilogy').save()
        new Album(title: 'Tarkus').save()

        def model = controller.list()
        assert model.albumList?.size() == 2
    }
}
```

In Listing 4-51, we're testing the returned model, but some controller actions write directly to the response or issue a redirect rather than return a value. To test an action that writes to the response, you can use the response object of the controller, which is an instance of the `org.codehaus.groovy.grails.plugins.testing.GrailsMockHttpServletResponse` class, which indirectly extends the `org.springframework.mock.web.MockHttpServletResponse` class and provides additional utility methods.

Several useful methods in the `MockHttpServletResponse` class allow you to inspect the state of the current response. In particular, the `getText()` method provides access to what is currently written into the response as a string. For example, if you have an action that renders some text to the response, you could test it as shown in Listing 4-52.

Listing 4-52. Testing the Contents of the Response

```
void testIndex() {
    controller.index()
    assert 'Welcome to the gTunes store!' == response.text
}
```

Controllers in Action

In this section, you'll learn how to build a simple login and registration system using Grails controllers. In Chapter 12, we'll be refactoring this system to use one of the more generic Grails security plugins, but for the moment it will serve as a useful starting point.

One of the first things to consider when developing any site is the site's point of entry. At the moment, you've just created a bunch of scaffolded pages, but now it's time to think about the real application for the first time, starting with the home page.

Creating the gTunes Home Page

The gTunes application is a music store where users can log in, browse the available music, and purchase music that they can then play. First, you need to establish a home page. You already have a `StoreController`, so you can use that as the controller that deals with the home page. To make sure visitors get routed to this controller, you can modify the `grails-app/conf/ UrlMappings.groovy` file to map visitors to the root of the application to this controller (see Listing 4-53).

Listing 4-53. Routing Users to the Root of the Application to the StoreController

```
class UrlMappings {
    static mappings = {
        "/"(controller:"store")
    }
}
```

Notice how you can use a forward slash to tell Grails to map any request to the root of the application to the `StoreController`. As you can see from the mapping, it is not mapping onto any particular action in `StoreController`, which will trigger the default action. The default action is the `index` action, which currently writes out a simple-text response. You need to change the `index` action so view delegation kicks in.

```
def index() {}
```

Now instead of returning a text response, the `index` action delegates to the `grails-app/ views/store/index.gsp` view, which you can use to render the home page. We'll start with something simple that shows just a welcome message; we can expand on this later. Listing 4-54 shows the markup code involved.

Listing 4-54. The gTunes Home Page

```
<html>
    <head>
        <meta http-equiv="Content-type" content="text/html; charset=utf-8">
        <meta name="layout" content="main">
        <title>gTunes Store</title>
```

```
        </head>
    <body id="body">
        <h1>Your online music store and storage service!</h1>
        <p>Manage your own library, browse music and purchase new tracks as they
           become available</p>
                </body>
</html>
```

The next step is to consider how to enable users to register, login, and logout. Before you can do that, you need to define the notion of a user within the gTunes application. Let's do that in the next section.

Adding the User Domain Class

To model users, you'll need to create a User domain class that contains personal information such as first name and last name, as well as the login and password for each user. To do so, you can use the create-domain-class command:

```
grails create-domain-class com.gtunes.User
```

This will create a new domain class at the location grails-app/domain/com/gtunes/User.groovy. With that done, you need to populate the User domain class with a few properties, as shown in Listing 4-55.

Listing 4-55. The User Domain Class

```
package com.gtunes
class User {
    String login
    String password
    String firstName
    String lastName
    static hasMany = [purchasedSongs:Song]
}
```

As you can see, the code in Listing 4-56 captures only the basics about users, but you could easily expand this information to include an address, contact number, and so on. One property to note is the purchasedSongs association, which will hold references to all the Songs a User buys once you have implemented music purchasing.

However, before we get too far ahead of ourselves, let's add a few constraints to ensure domain instances stay in a valid state (see Listing 4-56).

Listing 4-56. Applying Constraints to the User Class

```
class User {
    ...
    static constraints = {
        login blank:false, size:5..15,matches:/[\S]+/, unique:true
        password blank:false, size:5..15,matches:/[\S]+/
        firstName blank:false
        lastName blank:false
    }
}
```

With these constraints in place, you can ensure that a user cannot enter blank values or values that don't fall within the necessary size constraints. Also, note the usage of the unique constraint, which ensures that the login property is unique to each user. We'll revisit this in more detail later; for now, let's focus on login and registration.

Adding a Login Form

Because you already have a home page, it might make sense to add the login form there. But further down the line, you'll want to allow users to browse the gTunes music catalog anonymously, so users should be able to login from anywhere. With this in mind, you need to add a login form to the grails-app/views/layouts/main.gsp layout so that it's available on every page.

Listing 4-57 shows the GSP code to do so. Note how you can check whether a user already exists in the session object and display a welcome box or login form, accordingly.

Listing 4-57. Adding the Login Form Everywhere

```
<div id="loginBox" class="loginBox">
  <g:if test="${session?.user}">
    <div style="margin-top:20px">
      <div style="float:right;">
        <a href="#">Profile</a> | <g:link controller="user"
                                    action="logout">Logout</g:link><br>
      </div>
      Welcome back
      <span id="userFirstName">
        ${session?.user?.firstName}!
      </span><br><br>

      You have purchased (${session.user.purchasedSongs?.size() ?: 0}) songs.<br>
    </div>
  </g:if>
  <g:else>
    <g:form
      name="loginForm"
      url="[controller:'user',action:'login']">
      <div>Username:</div>
      <g:textField name="login"
                   value="${fieldValue(bean:loginCmd, field:'login')}">
      </g:textField>
      <div>Password:</div>
      <g:passwordField name="password"></g:passwordField>
      <br/>
      <input  type="image"
          src="${createLinkTo(dir:'images', file:'login-button.gif')}"
          name="loginButton" id="loginButton" border="0"></input>
    </g:form>
    <g:renderErrors bean="${loginCmd}"></g:renderErrors>
  </g:else>
</div>
```

In addition to providing a login box, you need to provide a link that allows a user to register. Once logged in, the user will be able to click through the store to browse and click a "My Music" link to view music already purchased. These links won't display when the user isn't logged in, so instead you can use the screen real estate for a prominent link to the registration page. Listing 4-58 shows the registration link added to the main.gsp layout.

Listing 4-58. Adding a Link to the Registration Page

```
<div id="navPane">
  <g:if test="${session.user}">
    <ul>
      <li><g:link controller="user"
                  action="music">My Music</g:link></li>
      <li><g:link controller="store"
                  action="shop">The Store</g:link></li>
    </ul>
  </g:if>
  <g:else>
    <div id="registerPane">
      Need an account?
        <g:link controller="user"
                action="register">Signup now</g:link>
      to start your own personal Music collection!
    </div>
  </g:else>
</div>
```

After getting the web designers involved and making a few Cascading Style Sheets (CSS) tweaks, the home page has gone from zero to something a little more respectable (see Figure 4-3).

Figure 4-3. The gTunes home page

Implementing Registration

Before users can actually log in, they need to register with the site. You'll need to run the create-controller command to create a controller that will handle the site's login and registration logic.

```
grails> create-controller com.gtunes.User
| Created file grails-app/controllers/com/gtunes/UserController.groovy
| Created file grails-app/views/user
| Created file test/unit/com/gtunes/UserControllerTests.groovy
grails>
```

Once complete, the command will create a controller at the location grails-app/controllers/com / gtunes/UserController.groovy. Open up this controller and add a register action, as shown in Listing 4-59.

Listing 4-59. Adding a register Action

```
class UserController {
    def register() {}
}
```

As you can see from the example, the register action currently does nothing beyond delegating to a view. Nevertheless, it gives you the opportunity to craft a registration form. Listing 4-60 shows the shortened code from the grails-app/views/user/register.gsp view that will render the form.

Listing 4-60. The register View

```
<body id="body">
  <h1>Registration</h1>
  <p>Complete the form below to create an account!</p>
  <g:hasErrors bean="${user}">
    <div class="errors">
      <g:renderErrors bean="${user}"></g:renderErrors>
    </div>
  </g:hasErrors>

  <g:form action="register" name="registerForm">
    <div class="formField">
      <label for="login">Login:</label>
      <g:textField name="login" value="${user?.login}"></g:textField>
    </div>
    <div class="formField">
      <label for="password">Password:</label>
      <g:passwordField name="password" value="${user?.password}"></g:passwordField>
    </div>
    <div class="formField">
      <label for="confirm">Confirm Password:</label>
      <g:passwordField name="confirm" value="${params?.confirm}"></g:passwordField>
    </div>
    <div class="formField">
      <label for="firstName">First Name:</label>
      <g:textField name="firstName" value="${user?.firstName}"></g:textField>
    </div>
```

```
    <div class="formField">
      <label for="lastName">Last Name:</label>
      <g:textField name="lastName" value="${user?.lastName}"></g:textField>
    </div>
    <g:submitButton class="formButton" name="register" value="Register"></g:submitButton>
  </g:form>
</body>
```

The rendered registration form will look like the screenshot in Figure 4-4.

As you can see from Figure 4-4, you can also provide a confirm-password field to prevent users from entering passwords incorrectly. With that done, let's consider the controller logic. To implement registration, you can take advantage of the data-binding capabilities of Grails to bind incoming request parameters to a new user instance. At this point, validation takes over, and the rest comes down to a little branching logic. Listing 4-61 shows the completed register action.

Figure 4-4. The Registration Screen

Listing 4-61. Implementing the register Action

```
def register() {
  if(request.method == 'POST') {
    def u = new User()
    u.properties['login', 'password', 'firstName', 'lastName'] = params
    if(u.password != params.confirm) {
      u.errors.rejectValue("password", "user.password.dontmatch")
      return [user:u]
```

```
    } else if(u.save()) {
      session.user = u
      redirect controller:"store"
    } else {
      return [user:u]
    }
  }
}
```

Many of the key concepts you've learned throughout the course of this chapter have been put to use in Listing 4-61, including a few new ones. Let's step through the code to see what's going on. First the code checks that the incoming request is a POST request, because doing all this processing is pointless unless a form is submitted.

```
                if(request.method == 'POST') {
```

Then data binding takes over, as it binds the incoming request parameters to the User instance.

```
                def u = new User(params)
```

Then the code confirms whether the user has entered the correct password twice. If not, the password is rejected altogether.

```
    if(u.password != params.confirm) {
        u.errors.rejectValue("password", "user.password.dontmatch")
      return [user:u]
    }
```

Notice how calling the rejectValue method of the org.springframework.validation.Errors interface accomplishes this. The rejectValue method accepts two arguments: the name of the field to reject and an error code to use. The code in Listing 4-61 uses the string user.password.dontmatch as the error code, which will appear when the <g:renderErrors> tag kicks in to display the errors. If you want to provide a better error message, you can open up the grails-app/i18n/messages.properties file and add a message like this:

```
user.password.dontmatch=The passwords specified don't match
```

Here's one final thing to note: directly after the call to rejectValue, a model from the controller action is returned, which triggers the rendering register.gsp so it can display the error.

You will notice that the code attempts to persist the user by calling the save() method. If the attempt is successful, the user is redirected back to the StoreController.

```
    else if(u.save()) {
        session.user = u
        redirect controller:"store"
    }
```

Finally, if a validation error does occur as a result of calling save(), then a simple model is returned from the register action so that the register view can render the errors:

```
                return [user:u]
```

Testing the Registration Code

Now let's consider how to test the action using the unit testing techniques you learned about earlier. When you ran the create-controller command, a new unit test for the UserController was created for you in the test/unit directory.

Now write a test for the case in which a user enters passwords that don't match. Listing 4-62 shows the testPasswordsDontMatch case that checks whether a password mismatch triggers a validation error.

Listing 4-62. The testPasswordsDoNotMatch Test Case

```
void testPasswordsDoNotMatch() {
  request.method = 'POST'

  params.login = 'henry'
  params.password = 'password'
  params.confirm = 'wrongPassword'
  params.firstName = 'Henry'
  params.lastName = 'Rollins'

  def model = controller.register()
  def user = model.user

  assert user.hasErrors()
  assert 'user.password.dontmatch' ==
        user.errors['password'].code
}
```

Notice how the testPasswordsMatch test case populates the mockParams object with two passwords that differ. Then you have a call to the register action, which should reject the new User instance with a user.password.dontmatch error code. The last line of the test asserts that this is the case by inspecting the errors object on the User instance:

```
assert 'user.password.dontmatch' ==
      user.errors['password'].code
```

The next scenario to consider is when a user enters invalid data into the registration form. You might need multiple tests that check for different kinds of data entered. Remember, you can never write too many tests! As an example of one potential scenario, Listing 4-63 shows a test that checks whether the user enters blank data or no data.

Listing 4-63. The testRegistrationFailed Test

```
void testRegistrationFailed() {
  request.method = 'POST'

  params.login = ''

  def model = controller.register()
  def user = model.user

  assert user.hasErrors()
  assert session.user == null
  assert 'blank' == user.errors['login'].code
```

```
    assert 'nullable' == user.errors['firstName'].code
    assert 'nullable' == user.errors['lastName'].code
}
```

Once again, you can see the use of the errors object to inspect that the appropriate constraints have been violated. Finally, you need to ensure two things to test a successful registration:

- The User instance has been placed in the session object.

- The request has been redirected appropriately.

Listing 4-64 shows an example of a test case that tests a successful user registration.

Listing 4-64. Testing Successful Registration

```
void testRegistrationSuccess() {
  request.method = 'POST'

  params.login = 'henry'
  params.password = 'password'
  params.confirm = 'password'
  params.firstName = 'Henry'
  params.lastName = 'Rollins'

  controller.register()

  assert '/store' == response.redirectedUrl
  assert session.user != null
}
```

With the tests written, let's now consider how to allow users to log in to the gTunes application.

Allowing Users to Log In

Since you've already added the login form, all you need to do is implement the controller logic. A login process is a good candidate for a command object because it involves capturing information—the login and password—without needing to actually persist the data.

In this example you're going to create a LoginCommand that encapsulates the login logic, leaving the controller action to do the simple stuff. Listing 4-65 shows the code for the LoginCommand class, which is defined in the same file as the UserController class.

Listing 4-65. The LoginCommand

```
class LoginCommand {
  String login
  String password
  private u
  User getUser() {
                if(!u && login) {
                  u = User.findByLogin(login, [fetch:[purchasedSongs:'join']])
                }
                return u
  }
```

```
static constraints = {
            login blank:false, validator:{ val, obj ->
                if(!obj.user)
                    return "user.not.found"
            }
        password blank:false, validator:{ val, obj ->
                if(obj.user && obj.user.password != val)
                    return "user.password.invalid"
            }
    }
}
```

The LoginCommand defines two properties that capture request parameters called login and password. The main logic of the code, however, is in the constraints definition. First, the blank constraint ensures that the login and/or password cannot be left blank. Second, a custom validator on the login parameter checks whether the user exists:

```
login blank:false, validator:{ val, cmd ->
    if(!cmd.user)
        return "user.not.found"
}
```

The custom validator constraint takes a closure that receives two arguments: the value and the LoginCommand instance. The code within the closure calls the getUser() method of the LoginCommand to check whether the user exists. If the user doesn't exist, the code returns an error code—"user.not.found"— that signifies an error has occurred.

On the password parameter, another custom validator constraint checks whether the user has specified the correct password:

```
password blank:false, validator:{ val, cmd ->
    if(cmd.user && cmd.user.password != val) return "user.password.invalid" }
```

Here the validator again uses the getUser() method of the LoginCommand to compare the password of the actual User instance with the value of the password property held by the LoginCommand. If the password is not correct, an error code is returned, triggering an error. You can add appropriate messages for each of the custom errors returned by the LoginCommand by adding them to the grails-app/i18n/messages. properties file:

```
user.not.found=User not found
user.password.invalid=Incorrect password
```

With that done, it's time to put the LoginCommand to use by implementing the login action in the UserController. Listing 4-66 shows the code for the login action.

Listing 4-66. The login Action

```
def login(LoginCommand cmd) {
  if(request.method == 'POST') {
    if(!cmd.hasErrors()) {
      session.user = cmd.getUser()
      redirect controller:'store'
    } else {
      render view:'/store/index', model:[loginCmd:cmd]
    }
```

```
    } else {
      render view:'/store/index'
    }
}
```

With the command object in place, the controller simply needs to do is what it does best: issue redirects and render views. Again, like the `register` action, login processing kicks in only when a POST request is received. Then if the command object has no errors, the user is placed into the session and the request is redirected to the `StoreController`.

Testing the Login Process

Testing the `login` action differs slightly from testing the `register` action due to the involvement of the command object. Let's look at a few scenarios that need to be tested. First, you need to test the case when a user is not found (see Listing 4-67).

Listing 4-67. *The testLoginUserNotFound Test Case*

```
void testLoginUserNotFound() {
    request.method = 'POST'

    params.login = 'frank'
    params.password = 'hotrats'

    controller.login()
    def cmd = model.loginCmd

    assert cmd.hasErrors()
    assert 'user.not.found' == cmd.errors['login'].code
    assert session.user == null
    assert '/store/index' == view
}
```

You can the inspect the command for errors, as demonstrated by the following two lines from Listing 4-59:

```
    assert cmd.hasErrors()
    assert 'user.not.found' == cmd.errors['login'].code
```

The next scenario to test is when a user enters an incorrect password. Listing 4-68 shows the `testLoginPasswordInvalid` test case that demonstrates how to do this.

Listing 4-68. *The testLoginPasswordInvalid Test Case*

```
void testLoginFailurePasswordInvalid() {
    request.method = 'POST'

    def u = new User(login: 'maynard',
                     firstName: 'Maynard',
                     lastName: 'Keenan',
                     password: 'undertow').save()
    assert u != null
```

```
        params.login = 'maynard'
        params.password = 'lateralus'

        controller.login()
        def cmd = model.loginCmd

        assert cmd.hasErrors()
        assert 'user.password.invalid' ==
                cmd.errors['password'].code
        assert session.user == null
        assert '/store/index' == view
}
```

The last test to write is one that tests a successful login. Listing 4-69 shows how to do this.

Listing 4-69. *The testLoginSuccess Test Case*

```
void testLoginSuccess() {
    request.method = 'POST'

    def u = new User(login: 'maynard',
                     firstName: 'Maynard',
                     lastName: 'Keenan',
                     password: 'undertow').save()
    assert u != null

    params.login = 'maynard'
    params.password = 'undertow'

    controller.login()

    assert session.user != null
    assert '/store' == response.redirectedUrl
}
```

Summary

And with that, you've implemented the login and registration process for the gTunes application. We'll present throughout the book many more examples of using controllers, but in this chapter you've obtained a strong grounding in the core concepts that apply to controllers. From data binding and validation to command objects, the Grails controller mechanism offers you a lot of tools. To fully see how everything fits together, you'll need a strong understanding of the Grails view technology—Groovy Server Pages (GSP). In the next chapter, we'll take a much closer look at GSP and what it has to offer, with its dynamic tag libraries and templating mechanisms.

CHAPTER 5

■ ■ ■

Understanding Views

The topic of view technologies for web applications in the open source world appears to be rather popular, at least if the seemingly endless number of them available for Java is any indication. There always seems to be a newer, better one to learn if you grow tired of the incumbent JSP. JSP, however, remains the most popular view technology produced by Sun to compete with Microsoft's Active Server Pages (ASP). JSP has become the industry standard, and there is a high level of developer knowledge surrounding JSP.

JSP allows developers to mix a traditional markup language such as HTML with bits of Java code (called *scriptlets*) to produce dynamic output. On the downside, this facility is extremely open to abuse; therefore, there are custom tag libraries that add the ability to abstract logic from a JSP page via tags. JSP has been augmented with two missing ingredients, the JSP Standard Tag Library (JSTL) and an expression language (EL), to bring it up to speed with some of its open source competitors.

Given JSP's maturity, robustness, and familiarity within the industry, why on earth, then, would anyone need yet another view technology for Grails with Groovy Server Pages (GSP)? The answer lies with the Groovy runtime environment.

- To fully take advantage of Grails, the view technology requires knowledge of Groovy's runtime environment and associated dynamic method dispatching.

- Groovy provides a far more powerful expression language, including GPath expressions, Groovy bean notation, and overrideable operators.

- Other Groovy features—such as regular expression support, GStrings, and an expressive syntax for maps and lists—make it perfect for a view technology.

Of course, for any new view technology, it is important not to fall into the same traps that JSP fell into in its early iterations. Mixing scriptlets and markup code is recognized as a bad thing, and to this end, GSP provides a mechanism for creating custom tags, just as JSP does, but without sacrificing any agility.

The Basics

Having been exposed to GSP at various points throughout the book, you may already be verging on the expert level. Still, discussing GSP's basics could prove invaluable to helping you fully grasp all the concepts within it.

It is important to note that GSP is actually remarkably similar to JSP, and you will know from experience that, with JSP, a number of objects are simply *available* by default. These include the request, response, and session objects—the same ones you saw in Chapter 4. If you recall, that particular discussion mentioned that a few additional objects, including flash, are available to controllers. You'll be pleased to know these can also be accessed from GSP views, as can an additional out attribute, which is a java.io. Writer instance representing the response output. Table 5-1 describes the GSP attributes available.

Table 5-1. GSP Attributes

Attribute	Description
application	The ServletContext instance
flash	The flash object for working with flash scope, as discussed in Chapter 7
out	The response Writer instance
params	A map of request parameters
request	The HttpServletRequest instance
response	The HttpServletResponse instance
session	The HttpSession instance

You already know how to get to these from controllers, but what about in views? Unsurprisingly, GSP supports the same constructs available in JSP, as well as a few additional ones. The next few examples may start to look a little like a JSP 101 tutorial, but don't be confused—you're definitely dealing with Groovy, not Java.

Understanding the Model

One of the fundamental activities in any MVC pattern, such as that which Grails employs, is to pass information (the model) to the view for rendering. In Chapter 4 you saw this in action, but just to recap, Listing 5-1 shows an example of how you can achieve this in Grails.

Listing 5-1. Creating the Model

```
package package com.gtunes
class StoreController {

    def shop() {
        def genreList =
            new DetachedCriteria(Album).distinct('genre').list()
        [genres:genreList.sort()]
    }
}
```

In Listing 5-1 (the shop action of the StoreController), the result is a map with one element, the key for which is a string with the value genres. This key (and its value) is then placed in a GSP model (or *binding*, for those more familiar with Groovy lingo), which makes it accessible as a variable, in the same way as the page attributes in Table 5-1 were.

In the following sections, you will see examples of a genres variable being referenced. Just remember that this variable didn't appear by magic. As in the listing, it is passed to the view in code via the controller.

Page Directives

GSP supports a limited subset of the page directives available in JSP. A *page directive* is an instruction appearing at the top of a GSP that performs an action that the page relies on. As an example, it could set the content type, perform an import, or set a page property, one that could even be container-specific.

One of the more useful of these is the contentType directive, which allows you to set the content type of the response. This is useful in that it allows you to use GSP to output formats other than HTML markup, including XML or plain text. In use, the directive is identical to JSP, with the directive appearing at the top of the page and starting with <%@.

Listing 5-2 sets the content type to text/xml, which allows you to output XML. This can be useful when working with Ajax and similar technologies.

Listing 5-2. *The contentType Page Directive*

```
<%@ page contentType="text/xml; charset=UTF-8" %>
```

Another page directive available is the import directive, which is analogous to the import statement in a Java or Groovy class. However, because Groovy imports many classes by default and Grails encourages an MVC architecture, where much of the logic should be placed in a controller and not the view, use of import is not very common. Nevertheless, Listing 5-3 shows an example of importing the Time class from the java.sql.* package.

Listing 5-3. *The import Page Directive*

```
<%@ page import="java.sql.Time" %>
```

■ **Note**   Groovy imports the java.lang, java.util, java.io, java.net, groovy.lang, and groovy.util packages by default.

Groovy Scriptlets

GSP tries to stay as true to JSP as possible, and therefore it supports traditional JSP scriptlet blocks using the <%...%> syntax. Essentially, as soon as you type the opening <% declaration, you have entered the world of Groovy and can type whatever Groovy code you so choose up until the closing %> declaration.

What this means is that you can use scriptlets to perform loops and logical if statements merely by combining scriptlet declarations, as shown in Listing 5-4.

Listing 5-4. *Scriptlets in Action*

```
<html>
    <body>
      <% 3.times { %>
        <p>I'm printed three times!</p>
      <% } %>
    </body>
</html>
```

Note that scriptlets are available more to align the syntax with JSP. In practice, they are discouraged in favor of GSP tags, which you will see in the "Built-in Grails Tags" section.

Although the previous syntax allows arbitrary code to be inserted between the opening and closing declarations, it doesn't actually explicitly output anything when inside the scriptlet block. In other words, as with the previous example, you have to use a closing %> bracket to close the scriptlet expression in order to define what you want repeated three times. You can, however, use the out attribute mentioned earlier to output to this response:

```
<% out << "print me!" %>
```

The previous code will print the text "print me!" to the response using the out attribute. As you can imagine, having these out << statements all over the place can get a little tedious, so GSP supports another syntax inherited from JSP through the <%=...%> statement (note the equal sign directly after the opening declaration). Essentially, the following example is equivalent to what you saw in the previous code:

```
<%= "print me!" %>
```

Here the = sign after the opening scriptlet bracket ensures that the result of whatever follows is printed to the response. The response in general is a mix of markup and code that results in some text being sent to the browser or client. Now that you've seen GSP's similarities with JSP, let's look at a feature you won't find in JSP: the embedded GString.

GSP As GStrings

Since the introduction of JSTL, the use of scriptlets and declarations such as those shown in the previous section has been looked down on a bit. Instead, there is an expression language in JSP that can be used in combination with the <c:out> standard tag to output values, as shown in Listing 5-5.

Listing 5-5. JSP c:out Tag

```
<%-- Output the album title --%>
<p><c:out value="${album.title}" /></p>
```

■ **Tip** The previous JSP example uses the syntax <%--...--%> for comments that should not be present in the rendered response. These comments are also supported in GSP using the same syntax.

In addition to the previous rather verbose tag, you would also need to import the tag library, which contains the <c:out> tag using a page directive at the top of the JSP. All this amounts to a lot of effort just to use a tag that lets you render values to the response. Luckily, with GSP it is a little bit simpler, because of its support for embedded GString values:

```
<p>${album.title}</p>
```

A GSP, if you think about it, is essentially one big GString, thus allowing the same ${...} expressions nested within it as found in JSP. The expressions allowed within a GString are not, thankfully, limited to simply referencing properties. The full capability Groovy offers in terms of navigating object graphs is at your fingertips, which often becomes useful when iterating, as the next section will show.

Built-in Grails Tags

GSP has a number of built-in tags for performing basic operations; they include looping, switching, and using logical if statements. In general, because they promote a cleaner separation of concerns and allow you to create well-formed markup, tags are preferable to embedding scriptlets. Each GSP tag requires the prefix g: before the tag name so that it is recognized as a GSP tag. Unlike JSP, which requires directives to import tag libraries, no additional page directive is needed.

■ **Note**   GSP also supports JSP custom tag libraries, which can be imported with the standard JSP taglib directive.

In the next few sections, you'll see the tags that are built in to Grails. These tags are there by default and require no extra work by the developer.

Setting Variables with Tags

Occasionally, it is useful to set the value of a variable or define a new variable within the scope (commonly referred to as the *page context*) of a GSP. Both use cases can be achieved via the <g:set> tag, which will set or define a variable in the page context regardless of whether it already exists. The <g:set> tag takes two attributes: the var attribute, which defines the name of the variable to set, and a value attribute, which is generally an expression:

```
<g:set var="albumTitle" value="${album.title}" />
```

By default, variables set with <g:set> are assumed to be within the page scope. What is more, you can set a variable in the session scope simply by using the scope attribute:

```
<g:set scope="session" var="user" value="${user}"  />
```

In addition to the session scope, a number of others are available.

- application: Stores variables for the scope of the whole application

- session: Stores variables for the scope of the user session

- flash: Stores variables for the current request and the next request only

- request: Stores variables for the scope of the current request

- page: Stores variables for the scope of the rendering page

Another fairly basic requirement, along with setting variables, is the ability to conditionally display information. In the next section, you'll see how you can achieve this.

Logical Tags

As previously mentioned, it is often useful to display information based on a condition. At the most basic level, it is useful to have basic programming constructs such as if and else in the view to facilitate this. GSP has the aptly named <g:if>, <g:elseif>, and <g:else> tags that, as with any regular programming construct, are used in conjunction with one another to conditionally display output.

The <g:if> and <g: elseif> tags take an attribute, called test, whose value can be in expression language (that is, statements surrounded by ${..}), as shown in Listing 5-6.

Listing 5-6. *Usage of Logical Blocks*

```
<g:if test="${album?.year < 1980 && album?.genre == 'Rock'}">
        Classic rock
</g:if>
<g:elseif test="${album?.year >= 1980 && album?.genre == 'Rock'}">
        Modern Rock
</g:elseif>
<g:else>
        Other
</g:else>
```

An interesting aspect of the previous code is the use of Groovy's safe dereference operator, ?.. The operator really comes into its own when used in views, because it is often useful to navigate an object graph and display information only if all elements navigated through don't evaluate to null. If you look at the views generated during scaffolding, you will observe a lot of this in action. Yet another useful feature of the method is that it allows the optional execution of methods. For example, you may for some reason want the title of the album in uppercase, in which case you would use an expression like the following:

```
${album.title.toUpperCase()}
```

Unfortunately, if either the album or title of the album in the previous code is null, a horrid NullPointerException will be thrown. To circumvent this, the safe dereference operator comes to the rescue:

```
${album?.title?.toUpperCase()}
```

Here the toUpperCase method is executed *only* if it can be reached; otherwise, the entire expression evaluates to null. This is useful because null in GSP results in an empty string being printed to the response.

That's it for now on logical tags, although you will see their use popping up throughout the book.

Iterative Tags

Iterating over collections of objects is one of the more common tasks when working with any view technology, GSP being no exception. Again, scriptlets *could* be used to achieve iteration, but why? You have GSP tags, which allow for a much cleaner transition between code and markup.

The first tag we'll cover is the <g:each> tag, which is essentially the tag equivalent of the Groovy each method and in fact simply delegates to this method internally, as shown in Listing 5-7.

Listing 5-7. *Iterating with <g:each>*

```
<g:each in="${album.songs?}">
  <span class="tag">${it.title}</span>
</g:each>
```

▓ **Tip** You can also use the safe dereference operator at the end of expressions (see the previous section). It will not iterate if the songs property is null.

Like its closely related JSTL cousin, the <g:each> tag allows the option of specifying the name of the object within the current iteration. The name of the object, as with closures, defaults to an argument called it, as shown in Listing 5-7. When using nested tags, however, it is good practice to name the variable being iterated over, which you can do with the var attribute, as shown in Listing 5-8.

Listing 5-8. *Iterating with <g:each> and a Named Variable*

```
<g:each var="song" in="${album.songs?}">
  <span class="song">${song.title}</span>
</g:each>
```

GSP tags are, at root, just closures, and in Groovy the variable it refers to the default argument of the *innermost* closure. If you use the <g:each> tag without declaring a var attribute and try to reference the default it variable within a nested GSP tag, this will result in evaluating it to the *current* innermost tag and not the surrounding <g:each> tag. By naming the variable used by <g:each> using the var attribute, you circumvent this conflict and any similar ones. If you remember that GSP tags are closures, you will have no trouble at all adapting to the mind-set. The next iterative tag GSP provides is the <g:while> tag, which behaves like the traditional while loop by waiting for the expression specified within the test attribute to evaluate to false. As with any while loop, the condition should always end up evaluating to false at some point; otherwise, you will find yourself in a never-ending loop. Listing 5-9 shows an example that loops while the variable i is greater than zero.

Listing 5-9. *The <g:while> Tag*

```
<g:set var="i" expr="${album.songs?.size()}" />
<g:while test="${i > 0}">
    <g:set var="i" expr="${i-1}" />
</g:while>
```

Here, you get the total number of songs from the album and store them in the variable i. You then start a <g:while> loop that will decrement the i variable on each iteration. The loop will continue until i reaches zero. The loop is equivalent to the following Groovy code:

```
while(i > 0) i=i-1
```

Using <g:each> and <g:while> is not the only way to loop over a collection. In the next section, you'll see constructs that provide the powerful combination of filtering and iteration.

Filtering and Iteration

Some of the new methods that accept closures in Groovy provide the powerful ability to filter and search collections (such as collect, findAll, and grep). It would be a shame if that power couldn't be extended into GSP tags. Fear not—there are tag equivalents of these three that allow some pretty powerful filtering capabilities.

The collect Tag

The <g:collect> tag allows you to iterate over and collect properties of objects within a collection. Say, for example, you want the titles of all albums; you can achieve this simply with <g:collect>, as Listing 5-10 shows.

Listing 5-10. Using <g:collect> to Collect Values

```
<ol>
<g:collect in="${albums}" expr="${it.title}">
   <li>${it}</li>
</g:collect>
</ol>
```

In the previous example, an HTML list of album titles is created by passing a collection of albums to the in attribute via the ${...} syntax. The second attribute, the expr attribute, contains an expression that is used to specify what should be collected (in this case the title property). Again, use the default it argument within the expression just as you would in a closure. In fact, the previous code is equivalent to the scriptlet code in Listing 5-11.

Listing 5-11. Equivalent Scriptlet Using a Closure

```
<ol>
  <% albums.collect{ it.title }.each { %>
     <li>${it}</li>
  <%}%>
</ol>
```

As you can see, the expression equates to what is found within the curly braces of the collect closure. Whatever you place in there can also be placed inside the expr attribute.

Of course, you can also do this with a GPath expression. Recall what you learned about GPath: if you reference the title property and use the dereference operator on a *list* of albums, a list of titles is produced, as Listing 5-12 shows.

Listing 5-12. Using GPath to Iterate over Album Titles

```
<ol>
   <g:each in="${albums.title}" >
      <li>${it}</li>
   </g:each>
</ol>
```

The <g:collect> tag does, however, give you another option and allows the logic within the expr attribute to be in your control.

The findAll Tag

Collecting properties from a collection via the object graph is handy, but sometimes you want to iterate over only those values that meet certain criteria. This is often achieved by iterating over all elements and having nested if statements. However, using <g:findAll>, as shown in Listing 5-13, is far more elegant.

Listing 5-13. Using <g:findAll> to Locate Specific Elements

```
<g:findAll in="${albums}" expr="${it.songs?.title.contains('Love')}">
  <li>${it.title}</li>
</g:findAll>
```

This example is another interesting demonstration of the power of GPath, Groovy's expression language. The expression in bold references the default argument it, which is the current Album instance being iterated over, and then uses GPath to retrieve a collection of all the names of the songs.

The songs property, too, is itself a collection (a java.util.Set, to be specific) and does not have a title property, but GPath recognizes that the reference to the title property is an attempt to retrieve a collection of name properties from the contained elements within the songs property.

Since the result is a collection, you can invoke the regular JDK contains method to look up all albums that have the word *Love* in their title. The result, far more readable than a bunch of nested if statements, is another case where you can see how a Groovy view technology like GSP makes a remarkable amount of sense.

You've seen quite a few options for performing different kinds of logical statements and iteration. Controlling the logical flow of a view is not, however, the only task you have when writing the view. One common activity is linking controllers and actions, which you will look at next. But before that, there is something important to note. This marks the end of the built-in tags. The tags you've seen so far are internally handled and optimized by GSP. The next section shifts the focus to Grails dynamic tags and how they differ from the built-in tags.

Grails Dynamic Tags

Dynamic tags in Grails are those provided through classes called *tag libraries*, which can be found within the grails-app/taglib directory of any Grails project. Grails provides a number of tag libraries out of the box that you will see in the next few sections. Then creating your own tag libraries will be explored.

First, you need to understand what makes dynamic tags different from other tags—that is, besides the fact that they are provided by these libraries. Fundamentally, they can be used just as any other tag is. For example, you can use the <g:link> tag like the built-in tags you saw previously without requiring any import directive.

More interestingly, dynamic tags can also be invoked as methods from scriptlets and GString expressions. Why is this useful? To maintain a clean syntax and valid XML, it is best to avoid nesting tags within tag attributes. In JSP you often see code like that in Listing 5-14, code that can be difficult to read and is not well-formed markup.

Listing 5-14. Unattractive JSP Example

```
<a href="<c:out value="${application.contextPath}" />/show.jsp">A dynamic link</a>
```

Clearly, because of GSP's rather JSP-like nature, this problem could have been inherited if it were not for the dynamic nature of Groovy. So how would you invoke a GSP tag as a method call? Observe the example in Listing 5-15.

Listing 5-15. An Example of a GSP Tag as a Method Call

```
<!-- With a regular tag -->
<a href="<g:createLink action="list" />">A dynamic link</a>
<!-- As a method call -->
<a href="${createLink(action:'list')}">A dynamic link</a>
```

The two previous examples produce the same result. They call a tag called createLink, which creates a link to the list action. The second example, notably cleaner, produces well-formed markup. In addition, the body of the tag can be provided as the last argument to the method call.

You can see an example of this in action in the create and edit views generated by scaffolding. As part of form validation, these views highlight the problematic field by surrounding the offender with a red box.

You achieve this through the hasErrors tags, which will evaluate if a particular bean field has any validation errors and will set a CSS class, the name of which is the last argument on the surrounding div element if the field contains errors (see Listing 5-16).

Listing 5-16. *Field Validation Example*

```
<div class="${hasErrors(bean:album,field:'title','errors')}">
</div>
```

These are just a few examples. As you'll soon see, you can create your own tags that can be invoked in the same manner. First, however, let's take a tour through the tags already available to you, starting with linking.

Linking Tags

With all the controllers and actions that end up being created, remembering the URL patterns to link to them may become a bit challenging. Also, depending upon the environment you deploy to, the context path of your application could change. So how can you make sure you are always linking to the right place in a consistent manner? Luckily, Grails provides a number of tags to handle linking in an elegant way, the first of which is the aptly named <g:link>.

The Link Tag

The <g:link> tag will essentially create a simple HTML anchor tag based on the supplied attributes, which include the following:

- controller: the controller name to link to

- action: the action name to link to

- id: the identifier to append to the end of the URI

- mapping: the name of the URL mapping to use

- params: any parameters to pass as a map

One of either the controller or the action attribute is required. If the controller attribute is specified but no action attribute is specified, the tag will link to the default action of the controller. If, on the other hand, an action attribute is specified but no controller attribute is specified, the *currently executing* controller will be linked to.

Beyond the previous attributes, the <g:link> tag also supports all attributes that the regular HTML anchor tag supports, which can be added as required.

It's time for some examples. Using <g:link> is pretty simple and intuitive, and of course the values of the attributes could just as well be expressions of the ${...} kind if dynamic linking is required (see Listing 5-17).

Listing 5-17. *Basic Linking with <g:link>*

```
<g:link controller="album" action="list">list Albums</g:link>
<g:link action="show"  id="1">Show album with id K/g:link>
```

Of interest may be the params attribute, which takes a map of request parameters to pass via the link. In fact, the current request parameters can even be passed from one action to the other by using this attribute in combination with the params object, which you'll recall is an instance of java.util.Map, as shown in Listing 5-18.

Listing 5-18. *Using Parameters with <g:link>*

```
<g:link controller="album"
        action="list"
        params="[max:10,order:'title']">Show first ten ordered by Title</g:link>
<g:link action="create"
        params="${params}">Pass parameters from this action to next</g:link>
```

The first example uses the params attribute in conjunction with a map of parameters and provides your first exposure to another feature of GSP tags: attributes can be specified as maps with the [key:value] syntax. This allows for composite attribute values and minimizes the need for messy nested tags.

Finally, the second example demonstrates what was mentioned previously. Instead of specifying a map explicitly, you provide a reference to the params object via the ${...} expression syntax, which then allows parameters to be passed from the current page to the linked page. Next you'll see how to create links to other resources.

▪ **Note** The linking tags in Grails automatically rewrite the links based on the URL mappings you have defined. URL mappings will be covered in more detail in Chapter 6.

The createLink and resource Tags

The <g:createLink> tag has already been seen in action and so probably needs less of an introduction. Simply put, if it's not clear from the examples, <g:createLink> takes the same arguments as the <g:link> tag, except that it produces just the textual link and not an HTML anchor tag. In fact, the <g:link> tag actually delegates to <g:createLink> when creating its href attribute.

So what is this useful for? You could use it within a regular anchor tag or possibly as a value for a JavaScript variable, as Listing 5-19 shows.

Listing 5-19. *Examples of createLink*

```
<a href="${createLink(action:'list')}">List Albums</a>
<script type="text/javascript">
    var listAlbumsLink = "${createLink(action:'list')}";
</script>
```

Another tag, similar in both name and usage to <g:createLink>, is the <g:resource> tag, which allows convenient linking to resources within the web application's context path.

This tag is most commonly used for linking to images and style sheets and, again, can be seen in action in the views generated by scaffolding:

```
<link rel="stylesheet"
      href="${resource(dir:'css',file:'main.css')}"></link>
```

As is apparent from the previous examples and in Listing 5-19, both tags tend to be used via method calls as opposed to markup, because the values produced by them are usually nested within attributes of other tags.

Now that linking has been covered, let's look at another common activity: creating forms so that users can enter data to be captured by server-side code. In the following section, you'll see how Grails makes this easier.

■ **Note** The `resource` tag effectively replaces the `createLinkTo` tag. The `createLinkTo` tag is still included in Grails 2 but is deprecated in favor of the resource tag. The resource tag provides more flexibility, some of which will be discussed in Chapter 12.

Creating Forms and Fields

A form is most commonly a collection of fields that a user populates with data, although occasionally you find forms that consist entirely of hidden fields and no user interaction whatsoever. Nevertheless, how this is achieved depends on the type of field; in other words, the user's interaction depends on whether it is a text field, a drop-down select, or a radio button.

Clearly, certain fields map nicely onto existing Java (and hence Groovy) types. Check boxes are great for Boolean values, text fields are good for strings, and selects are good when you have strings that can be contained only within a certain list of values (such as enums in Java 5).

To this end, most Java web frameworks provide some mechanism to make form elements (or fields) interoperate smoothly with Java types, Grails being no different. Before you get too deeply involved in looking at the different kinds of fields, let's take care of the basics by looking at how Grails helps in defining forms.

The form Tag

Let's build on what you have seen in linking by starting with the `<g:form>` tag, which is equivalent to the standard HTML `<form>` tag, except that it allows the same arguments as those shown with the `<g:link>` tag to allow easy submission to a specific controller or action or both, as shown in Listing 5-20.

Listing 5-20. An Example Form Tag from grails-app/views/user/register.gsp

```
<g:form action="register" name="registerForm">
    ...
</g:form>
```

By default, the `<g:form>` tag uses the POST method for form submissions; that is, the previous example is roughly equivalent to the HTML definition (minus the closing tag):

```
<form action="/gTunes/user/register" method="POST" name="registerForm">
    ...
</form>
```

As an alternative to Listing 5-20, you can define the `<g:form>` tag using a single `url` attribute that uses the `key:value` map syntax to define the controller and action combination (see Listing 5-21).

Listing 5-21. A <g:form> Tag with url Attribute

```
<g:form url="[controller:'user', action:'register']">
   ...
</g:form>
```

Of course, a form is of little use without some fields, the first of which to be discussed is the *text field*. In HTML, most fields are handled by the <input> tag, which has a type attribute to change its behavior and appearance. The downside of this approach is that it is not clear what its purpose is from simply looking at the tag.

Grails provides a number of wrapper tags that encapsulate the different types of HTML inputs into more meaningful tags.

The textField Tag

First up is the <g:textField> tag. Unsurprisingly, it handles entry of textual values. The <g:textField> tag takes a name attribute, representing the name of the parameter to send as part of the form submission, along with the associated value attribute, as shown in Listing 5-22.

Listing 5-22. Example <g:textField> Usage

```
<g:form action="register" name="registerForm">
...
   <g:textField name="login" value="${user?.login}"></g:textField>
   ...
</g:form>
```

The previous <g:textField> definition will result in HTML input such as the following:

```
<input type="text" name="login" value="A Login Name" />
```

Check Boxes and Radio Buttons

Check boxes are often used as a representation of Boolean values from a domain model. Unfortunately, many frameworks place a lot of burden on the developer both to render check boxes in their correct state and to handle the server-side processing as to whether the boxes are checked.

Grails, on the other hand, provides a <g:checkBox> tag that accepts a Boolean value attribute and will render the tag in its correct state. In addition, Grails transparently handles check box processing through its automatic type conversion and data binding facility (discussed in Chapter 7), as shown in Listing 5-23.

Listing 5-23. Example <g:checkBox> Tag

```
<g:checkBox name="aBooleanValue" value="${true}" />
```

Closely related to check boxes are radio buttons, which are used in groups, because they represent a one-from-many interaction. For example, two radio buttons must each be given the same name to be placed in the same group, and only one button can be selected at a time.

Grails has a <g:radio> tag that provides a convenient way to define radio buttons and also to calculate that one has been checked.

In Listing 5-24, two radio buttons are defined in the same group. The one that has been checked is calculated using the hypothetical someValue variable.

Listing 5-24. Example <g:radio> Tags

```
<p>
<g:radio name="myGroup" value="1" checked="${someValue == 1}" /> Radio 1 </p>
<p>
<g:radio name="myGroup" value="2" checked="${someValue == 2}" /> Radio 2 </p>
```

Handling Lists of Values

When dealing with enumerated values (those that can be only a specific set of values), it is often useful to constrain what the user can enter by presenting an HTML select box as opposed to a free text-entry field.

To make creating selects much simpler, Grails provides a `<g:select>` tag that accepts a list or range of values via a `from` attribute. The currently selected value can be set with the value attribute.

The example in Listing 5-25 creates a select to choose a genre.

Listing 5-25. Example <g:select> Usage

```
<g:select name="genre"
        from="${['Rock', 'Blues', 'Jazz']}"
        value="${album.genre}" />
```

The following is the resulting HTML select, given an album with a genre of Rock:

```
<select name="genre">
  <option value="Rock" selected="selected">Rock</option>
  <option value="Blues">Blues</option>
  <option value="Jazz">Jazz</option>
</select>
```

Clearly, going just by the two examples, using the `<g:select>` tag can save writing a few lines of code. Its usefulness extends further, thanks to two additional attributes that allow `<g:select>` to be used in combination with object graphs and relationships.

The first is the `optionKey` attribute, which allows customization of the value attribute within each option tag of an HTML select. It may seem a little odd that an `optionKey` attribute customizes an attribute called value, but if you think of each `<option>` element as a key/value pair, it begins to make sense. The `optionValue` attribute, on the other hand, allows customization of the value that appears within the body of each option tag.

Using these two in combination, for example, allows you to create a select from a list of domain object instances, as shown in Listing 5-26.

Listing 5-26. Using <g:select> on a List of Domain Objects

```
<g:select name="album.id" from="${Album.list()}"
        optionKey="id" optionValue="title"/>
```

The previous example takes a list of albums and creates an HTML select where the value attribute within the option tag is the id of the Album and the value within the body of each option is the title property of each Album. The result will resemble the following:

```
<select name="album.id">
  <option value="1">Undertow</option>
  ...
</select>
```

In addition to the general-purpose <g:select> tag, Grails provides a few others that may come in handy. The <g:currencySelect>, <g:localeSelect>, and <g:timeZoneSelect> tags are convenience tags for working with java.util.Currency, java.util.Locale and java.util.TimeZone instances, respectively.

Unlike the <g:select> tag, each of these takes only two attributes: a name attribute for the name of the select and a value attribute, which takes an instance of one of the aforementioned classes, as shown in Listing 5-27.

Listing 5-27. *Currency, Locale, and Time Zone Selects*

```
<%-- Sets the currency to the currency of the Locale within the request --%>
<g:currencySelect
        name="myCurrency"
        value="${ Currency.getInstance(request.locale) }" />
<%-- Sets the locale to the locale of the request --%>
<g:localeSelect name="myLocale" value="${ request.locale }" />
<%-- Sets value to default time zone --%>
<g:timeZoneSelect name="myTimeZone" value="${ TimeZone.getDefault() }" />
```

Working with Dates

Dates can be represented in a number of ways, from drop-down selects to advanced JavaScript calendars. One of the more common ways, because of its nonreliance on JavaScript, is use of a combination of HTML select boxes to specify date and time, with each select representing a time unit: year, month, day, minute, hour, and second.

Grails provides support for creating such fields (and automatically performs type conversion onto date instances) using the <g:datePicker> tag (see Listing 5-28).

Listing 5-28. *A Basic Date Picker*

```
<g:datePicker name="myDate" value="${new Date()}" />
```

At its most basic level, the <g:datePicker> tag takes a name attribute and a value attribute as a java.util.Date instance. In the previous example, it creates a <g:datePicker> for the current time, which consists of selects for the year, month, day, minute, hour, *and* second.

Clearly, it is not always useful to have that level of precision, so the <g:datePicker> tag provides the aptly named precision attribute for changing how many selects it renders. For example, to render only the year, month, and day selects, the following will suffice:

```
<g:datePicker name="myDate" value="${new Date()}" precision="day" />
```

All in all, Grails puts quite a few tools in your toolbox for simplifying the creation of forms. Given that forms allow users to enter data, often in a free-form fashion, implementing form handling is often one of the most challenging and error-prone activities in web application development.

To ensure data integrity, form validation is necessary. It can be achieved on the client side using JavaScript. However, client-side validation should only ever be seen as a usability enhancement, not a replacement for server-side validation. Luckily, Grails provides solid support for performing validation with specialized validation and error-handling tags.

Simplifying Forms with the Fields Plug-in

Creating and maintaining complicated forms with a lot of input fields can be tedious and often involves a lot of copy-and-paste code. A form for inputting all of the fields related to creating a Person object may be pretty much exactly the same as the form for inputting all of the fields related to an Account object, except that the input fields would have different names. Consider a Person domain class that has firstName, lastName, and age properties. A form to help create a person might include code like that shown in Listing 5-29.

Listing 5-29. Form for Creating a Person

```
<div class="fieldcontain">
    <label for="age">
        <g:message code="person.age.label"
                default="Age" />
        <span class="required-indicator">*</span>
    </label>
    <g:field type="number"
            name="age"
            required=""
            value="${personInstance.age}"/>
</div>

<div class="fieldcontain">
    <label for="firstName">
        <g:message code="person.firstName.label"
                default="First Name" />

    </label>
    <g:textField name="firstName"
                value="${personInstance?.firstName}"/>
</div>

<div class="fieldcontain">
    <label for="lastName">
        <g:message code="person.lastName.label"
                default="Last Name" />

    </label>
    <g:textField name="lastName"
                value="${personInstance?.lastName}"/>
</div>
```

If you wanted to create a form for creating an Account object that had bankName, accountType, and balance properties, you might copy and paste that code and then go through the code and replace property names. Of course, managing all of that boilerplate code is not ideal.

The fields plug-in provides tools to help eliminate all that boilerplate. As an example, the fields plug-in provides a GSP tag named all, which will render input fields for every property of a bean. The code in Listing 5-29 could be replaced with the following:

```
<f:all bean="personInstance"/>
```

Which would you rather write and maintain?

The fields plug-in provides a good bit more functionality than just the all tag. See http://grails.org/plugin/fields for more information on the plug-in.

Validation and Error Handling

Since you learned how to apply constraints to your domain model in Chapter 3, clearly it becomes useful at some point to display validation errors in the view when they occur. Of course, you could use scriptlets to iterate over the errors of a domain object and output them explicitly, but that's work that Grails can do for you. Just to recap how validation works, take a look at the state diagram shown in Figure 5-1.

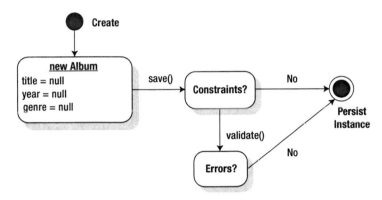

Figure 5-1. Validation state diagram

The hasErrors Tag

Since errors do occur, it is often useful to display information conditionally. To this end, Grails provides a <g:hasErrors> tag that supports the following attributes:

- bean: a bean instance to inspect for errors

- field: the name of the field to check for errors

- model: an alternative to specifying a bean; an entire model (map) can be checked

You'll recall that you have already seen the <g:hasErrors> tag used as a method, but it is also equally applicable as a tag. Interestingly, if no attributes are specified whatsoever, the tag will scan the entire request scope for beans and check each object found for errors. Since the <g:hasErrors> tag is often used in conjunction with <g:eachError>, we'll cover that next, followed by an example.

The eachError Tag

If a bean instance does have errors, it is useful to iterate over them and display each in turn. This can be done simply with the <g:eachError> tag, which takes attributes identical to those expected by the <g:hasErrors> tag.

Listing 5-30 demonstrates how to use the hasErrors and eachError tags to generate a list of error messages for an Album instance.

Listing 5-30. Displaying Errors

```
<g:hasErrors bean="${album}">
        <ul class="errors">
        <g:eachError bean="${album}">
              <li>${it.defaultMessage}</li>
          </g:eachError>
    </ul>
</g:hasErrors>
```

In this instance, `<g:hasErrors>` checks whether there are any errors in the first place, and if there are, it creates an HTML list. These errors are then iterated over via the `<g:eachError>` tag, which creates the list bullets using the *default message*. The default messages for validation errors can be found in the grails-app/i18n/message.properties message bundle.

If a list is all that is required, Grails makes it even easier to display errors via the `<g:renderErrors>` tag, which encapsulates everything you've just seen. Essentially, it takes the same arguments as the `<g:eachError>` tag, as well as an optional as attribute, which allows you to specify what to render the errors as. Listing 5-29 shows how to render the errors as a simple HTML list:

```
<g:renderErrors bean="${album}" as="list"  />
```

As noted previously, the examples shown so far use the default message. Clearly, the default message is not always what is desired, and it is often useful to provide specific messages for each property within a domain class. This is where the `<g:message>` tag comes into play, with support from Grails for internationalization (i18n). Internationalization is covered in detail in Chapter 7.

Paginating Views

Rendering lists of data in a web application is a common thing to do. Grails provides an easy-to-use mechanism for retrieving data from the database (GORM) and simple mechanisms for rendering the data (GSPs and GSP tags).

Web applications often serve as a front end to a database that may contain large volumes of data. The application may need to provide mechanisms for the user to manage navigating through all the data. For example, the gTunes application may contain thousands of artists, albums, and songs. A page that lists all the albums may be overwhelming and difficult for the user to work with (see Figure 5-2).

Figure 5-2. A long list of albums

Figure 5-2 represents what a user who requested a list of all the albums in the system that belong to the Rock genre might see. This very long page includes several hundred albums. An argument could be made that too much data is displayed on a single page. What if there were thousands of albums? Hundreds of thousands of albums? Clearly, it would not make sense to present all those albums to the user on a single page.

The gTunes application needs to be smart about presenting manageable lists of data to the user. Instead of displaying hundreds or thousands of albums in a single list, maybe the application should display only five or ten. If the application displays only five or ten albums on the page, then the application also needs to provide a mechanism for the user to navigate around the larger virtual list to view the rest of the albums five or ten at a time. Figure 5-3 represents a much more manageable interface.

Genre: Rock

Artist	Album	Year
Genesis	Live Over Europe 2007	2007
Genesis	Nursery Cryme	1971
Genesis	Seconds Out	1977
Genesis	Selling England By The Pound	1973
Genesis	The Genesis of Genesis	1969
Genesis	The Lamb Lies Down On Broadway	1974
Genesis	Three Sides Live	1982
Genesis	Trespass	1970
Genesis	Turn It On Again [Tour Edition]	1999
Genesis	We Can't Dance	1991

Previous 1 .. 19 20 21 22 23 **24** 25 26 27 28 .. 86 Next

Back to Store

© gTunes 2012

Figure 5-3. *A paginated list of albums*

The list in Figure 5-3 includes only ten albums. The view provides mechanisms for navigating over the larger virtual list, which includes all the albums in this genre. This approach yields a much better user experience, especially for scenarios where the user may be overwhelmed with large sets of data.

Since some complexity is involved in generating pagination controls like these, the application needs to do several things: (1) retrieve smaller amounts of data from the database for each view; (2) provide support for requesting the batch of records that fall immediately before or immediately after the current batch; (3) provide a mechanism for jumping straight to an area of the list, as opposed to navigating through the larger list a single page at a time; (4) know the total number of records in the larger list. All these things normally involve writing a lot of code.

The good news is that Grails provides a really simple mechanism for managing all that. That mechanism is a GSP tag called `paginate`. The `paginate` tag manages a lot of the tedious work that would otherwise be required in order to provide UI elements for navigating over large lists of data.

The GSP responsible for rendering this list is in `grails-app/views/store/genre.gsp`. That page includes the markup shown in Listing 5-31.

Listing 5-31. *The genre.gsp <h1>Online Store</h1>*

```
<h1>Online Store</h1>

<h2>Genre: ${genre.encodeAsHTML()}</h2>
<table border="0" class="albumsTable">
  <tr>
    <th>Artist</th>
    <th>Album</th>
    <th>Year</th>
  </tr>
  <g:each var="album" in="${albums}">
    <tr>
```

124

```
            <td>${album.artist.name}</td>
        <td><g:link action="show"
                    controller="album"
                    id="${album.id}">${album.title}</g:link>
        </td>
            <td>${album.year}</td>
    </tr>
  </g:each>

</table>
<div class="paginateButtons">
  <g:paginate controller="store"
                action="genre"
                params="[name:genre]"
              total="${totalAlbums}" />
</div>
```

The markup represented there renders an HTML table containing a header row and a row for each of the elements in the albums collection. Notice the use of the paginate tag at the bottom of Listing 5-30. That is all the code required in the GSP to render the pagination controls. The paginate tag takes care of all the tedious work involved in generating the "Previous" and "Next" links, all of the links that support jumping to a particular page, and all of the appropriate request parameters associated with each of those links. All is handled by this single call to a GSP tag. The whole thing could barely be simpler!

The paginate tag is generating a number of links. The controller and action parameters tell the paginate tag where each of those links should submit. In this particular case, all the links submit to the genre action in the StoreController. If all the links reference the same controller action, you might wonder how the application knows the difference between the user clicking one link as opposed to another. The answer has to do with the fact that the paginate tag tacks a number of request parameters on the end of each link; those request parameters are used by the controller action. For example, the "7" link points to the URL /store/genre?offset=60&max=10&name=Rock. The "8" link points to the URL /store/genre?offset=70&max=10&name=Rock. Notice that those links each include the same value for the max and name parameters, but they include a different value for the offset parameter. That offset parameter is an important part of the request, because through it the controller will know what page of data should be returned when the user clicks one of those links. Let's take a look at the relevant controller action.

Listing 5-32 includes the code that is in the genre action in the StoreController.

Listing 5-32. The genre Action

```
def genre() {
    def max = Math.min(params.int('max') ?: 10, 100)
    def offset = params.int('offset') ?: 0

    def total = Album.countByGenre(params.name)
    def albumList = Album.withCriteria {
          eq 'genre', params.name
      projections {
        artist {
          order 'name'
        }
      }
      maxResults max
```

```
        firstResult offset
    }
        return [albums:albumList,
                    totalAlbums:total,
                    genre:params.name]
    }
```

■ **Note**   The query whose code is in Listing 5-32 uses the Hibernate Criteria API, whose general behavior will be described next. The Criteria API is discussed in detail in the "Criteria Queries" section of Chapter 10.

The name request parameter is used in both of the previous queries. The first query is necessary to count the number of albums in the database that belong to a certain genre. The second query actually retrieves a list of albums. That second query does not retrieve all the albums that belong to a certain genre but only a subset of at most ten of those albums.

For example, imagine there is a list of 1,000 albums, and each of them has an index associated with it starting with 0 and running through 999. When a request is sent to the /store/genre?offset=60&max=10&name=Rock URL, the call to the Album.withCriteria(...) method will return ten of those albums, starting with the Album at index 60. The max parameter represents the maximum number of albums that should be returned.

Notice that the first line in the genre action assigns a default value of 10 to max if no max request parameter is found. The int method on the params object accepts a string parameter, which represents the name of a request parameter. If the request parameter exists, its value will be converted to an int and returned. If the request parameter does not exist or if it cannot be converted to an int, then the method returns null. If a max request parameter is found and the value is greater than 100, the system is falling back to a max of 10. Displaying more than 100 albums per page would defeat the purpose of having the pagination support in place.

The offset parameter represents the point in the larger list at which this list of ten should begin. If no offset request parameter is supplied, the system defaults the value to 0, or the beginning of the list.

The map of data being returned by the genre action includes not only the list of albums but also values for totalAlbums and genre, each of which is used in genre.gsp as a parameter to the paginate tag. All of this needs to be kept in sync as part of the interaction between the controller action and the GSP.

The paginate tag supports a number of arguments. Table 5-2 lists those arguments.

Table 5-2. Arguments Supported by the paginate Tag

Argument	Description
total	Total number of elements in the larger list
controller	Name of the controller to link to
action	Name of the action to invoke
params	Map of request parameters
offset	Offset to be used if params.offset is not specified
max	Maximum number of elements per page
prev	Text for the "Previous" link
next	Text for the "Next" link
id	ID to use in links
maxsteps	Number of steps displayed for pagination (the default is 10)

All of the parameters supported by the paginate tag are optional except for the total parameter.

The default scaffolded list views in a Grails application include support for paginating the list and defining a simple domain class, like the Car class shown in Listing 5-33.

Listing 5-33. *A Car Domain Class*

```
package com.demo

class Car {
    String make
    String model
}
```

Generate scaffolding for the Car class, and you will see that the default list action in the CarController and the default grails-app/view/car/list.gsp include support for paginating the list of cars. Listing 5-34 shows the relevant part of the GSP.

Listing 5-34. *grails-app/view/car/list.gsp*

```
<div id="list-car" class="content scaffold-list" role="main">
    <h1><g:message code="default.list.label" args="[entityName]" /></h1>
    <g:if test="${flash.message}">
    <div class="message" role="status">${flash.message}</div>
    </g:if>
    <table>
        <thead>
            <tr>
                <g:sortableColumn property="make" title="${message(code: 'car.make.
label', default: 'Make')}" />
                <g:sortableColumn property="model" title="${message(code: 'car.model.
label', default: 'Model')}" />
            </tr>
        </thead>
        <tbody>
        <g:each in="${carInstanceList}" status="i" var="carInstance">
            <tr class="${(i % 2) == 0 ? 'even' : 'odd'}">

                <td><g:link action="show" id="${carInstance.id}">${fieldValue(bean:
carInstance, field: "make")}</g:link></td>

                <td>${fieldValue(bean: carInstance, field: "model")}</td>

            </tr>
        </g:each>
        </tbody>
    </table>
    <div class="pagination">
        <g:paginate total="${carInstanceTotal}" />
    </div>
</div>
```

The only attribute specified in this call to the paginate tag is the required total attribute. Notice that in this case the value of the total attribute is simply the total number of cars in the database. This is a little bit different from the example shown earlier, where the value of the total attribute was not necessarily that of the whole number of albums in the database but was the number of albums in the database that belong to a particular genre.

Listing 5-35 shows the list action in the CarController.

Listing 5-35. Pagination Support in the CarController

```
class CarController {

    def list(Integer max) {
        params.max = Math.min(max ?: 10, 100)
        [carInstanceList: Car.list(params), carInstanceTotal: Car.count()]
    }

    ...
}
```

The default list action in the CarController will assign a value of 10 to the max request parameter if a value is not supplied.

The application may take control over the order of the cars, using any number of techniques supported by GORM. The simplest solution for this particular case is including the order clause in the dynamic method, as shown in Listing 5-36.

Listing 5-36. Ordering Cars by Model Class CarController {

```
class CarController {

    def list(Integer max) {
        params.max = Math.min(max ?: 10, 100)
        [carInstanceList: Car.listOrderByModel(params),
         carInstanceTotal: Car.count()]
    }

    ...
}
```

With all of that in place, if the database includes more than ten cars, then the pagination support in the view will kick in, as shown in Figure 5-4.

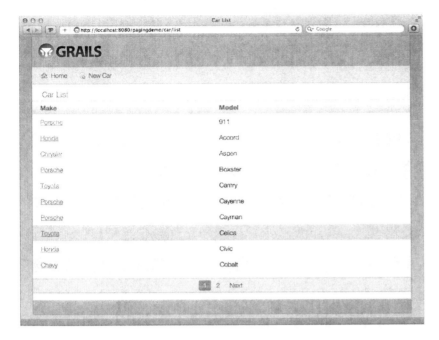

Figure 5-4. Paginating a list of cars

Rendering GSP Templates

A GSP template is a special GSP file that contains only a fragment of a page. A GSP template can contain markup that is rendered from various places in an application. In such a case, the template would facilitate reuse. A template can be extracted from a page to simplify the containing page by breaking it down into smaller, more manageable pieces. Whatever the reason for isolating part of a page into a reusable template, Grails provides a really simple mechanism for rendering the template.

A template can contain just about anything that might appear in a normal GSP. One thing that makes a template special is its file name. GSP templates must be defined in a file whose name begins with an underscore. For example, a template that represents a list of albums might be defined in grails-app/views/album/_albumList.gsp.

The render tag can be used in a GSP to render a GSP template. This tag accepts an attribute, template, that represents the name of the template to be rendered. For example, to render the template in the grails-app/views/album/_albumList.gsp file, you would specify /album/albumList as the value of the template attribute when calling the render tag, as shown in Listing 5-37.

Listing 5-37. Rendering the albumList Template

```
<div id="artists">
<g:render template="/artist/artistList"/>
</div>
```

Notice that the template file name contains an underscore but the name of the template does not.

Rendering a template in a GSP is very much like taking the contents of the GSP template and putting them inline in the containing GSP in place of calling the render tag.

Figure 5-5 shows an updated version of the gTunes application.

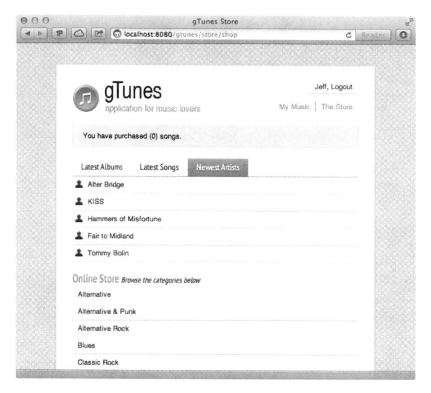

Figure 5-5. *Updated gTunes*

Notice the three tabs across the top of the screen representing the latest albums, latest songs, and newest artists. The markup required to generate the contents of each tab would clutter the GSP. Rather than embed the markup for those tabs in the views/store/shop.gsp file, you can pull it all out into a series of templates and render them from shop.gsp. Using templates to handle this will yield an application easier to maintain than one with monolithic unmodular GSPs.

Listing 5-38 shows what those templates might look like.

Listing 5-38. *GSP Templates for the Top Five Lists*

```
<!-- grails-app/views/artist/_artistList.gsp -->
<ul class="list">
    <g:each in="${artists?}" var="artist">
        <li class="icon">
            <g:link controller="store" action="shop">
                <g:img dir="images/icons" file="artist.png" />
                ${artist?.name}
            </g:link>
        </li>
    </g:each>
</ul>


<!-- grails-app/views/album/_albumList.gsp -->
```

```
<ul class="list">
    <g:each in="${albums?}" var="album">
        <li class="icon">
            <g:link controller="album" action="show" id="${album?.id}">
                <g:img dir="images/icons" file="album.png" />
                ${album.title}
            </g:link>
        </li>
    </g:each>
</ul>

<!-- grails-app/views/song/_songList.gsp -->
<ul class="list">
    <g:each in="${songs?}" var="song">
        <li class="icon">
            <g:link controller="store" action="shop">
                <g:img dir="images/icons" file="song.png" />
                ${song.title}
            </g:link>
        </li>
    </g:each>
</ul>
```

■ **Note**   These are very simple templates that render unordered lists of strings. In Chapter 8 you will develop these templates to contain some really slick Ajax-driven behavior. At that point, the value of knowing how to isolate markup into templates will be even greater.

Notice that each template is iterating over a different collection (artists, albums, songs). Those collections are data that must be passed into the template when the template is rendered. The way to pass data into a GSP template is to specify an attribute, model, when calling the render tag. The value of the model attribute should be a map containing all the data being passed in to the template. Listing 5-39 shows the templates being rendered from the grails-app/views/store/shop.gsp and the appropriate data being passed to each.

Listing 5-39. Rendering Templates from shop.gsp

```
<div id="top5Panel" class="top5Panel">
  <ul id="tabs" class="tabs clearfix">
    <li class="selected"><a href="#albums">Latest Albums</a></li>
    <li><a href="#songs">Latest Songs</a></li>
    <li><a href="#artists">Newest Artists</a></li>
  </ul>

  <div id="albums" class="top5Item">
    <g:render template="/album/albumList"
              model="[albums: top5Albums]"></g:render>
  </div>
```

```
    <div id="songs" class="top5Item hide">
      <g:render template="/song/songList"
                model="[songs: top5Songs]"></g:render>
    </div>

    <div id="artists" class="top5Item list hide">
      <g:render template="/artist/artistList"
                model="[artists: top5Artists]"></g:render>
    </div>
</div>
```

The templates rendered here are /album/albumList, /song/songList, and /artist/ artistList. Each is a fully qualified reference to a template. When a template name is fully qualified, the root refers to the grails-app/views/ directory; so /artist/artistList refers to the template defined in the grails-app/views/artist/_artistList.gsp file. Template references may be defined with a relative path as well. Relative template paths are paths that do not begin with a forward slash.

For example, if instead of referring to /artist/artistList, the shop.gsp referred to the relative artistList template, then Grails would look for the template in the same directory where shop.gsp lives. Relative references can also include a directory structure. If the artistList template were defined in grails-app/views/store/myTemplates/_artistList.gsp, then the grails-app/views/store/shop.gsp page could refer to the template as myTemplates/artistList, since the myTemplates directory is in the same one as shop.gsp.

Each of the calls to the earlier render tag includes a map of data being passed as the model attribute. For shop.gsp to have that data, the controller action that rendered shop.gsp needs to supply those values. In this case, the controller action is the shop action in StoreController, as shown in Listing 5-40.

Listing 5-40. The shop Action in StoreController

```
package com.gtunes

class StoreController {

  def shop() {
    def genreList =
      new DetachedCriteria(Album).distinct('genre').list()
    [top5Albums:  Album.list(max:5, sort:"dateCreated", order:"desc"),
     top5Songs:   Song.list(max:5, sort:"dateCreated", order:"desc"),
     top5Artists: Artist.list(max:5, sort:"dateCreated", order:"desc"),
     genres:  genreList.sort()]
  }

  // ...
}
```

Notice that the controller action is returning values for albums, songs, and artists. The values are lists containing the five most recently created albums, songs, and artists.

These templates have been defined to render these "Top 5" lists in the shop.gsp, but they are reusable templates that can be used anywhere that the application needs to render lists of albums, artists, or songs. It is commonplace for web applications to render the same pieces of information on a lot of pages. When you see the same elements showing up in multiple places, consider pulling that markup out of your GSPs and putting it in a reusable template.

Creating Custom Tags

Custom tags in JSP constitute a wonderfully powerful feature. They provide the ability to cleanly separate concerns between the view and controller logic. In MVC terms, they can be thought of as view helpers. Unfortunately, for all their wonderful attributes, they are tremendously complicated to develop. The reasons for this are understandable, because JSP tags attempt to account for every possible tag creation scenario, including the following:

- simple tags that have attributes only but no body
- body tags that have both attributes and a body
- tags that have a parent-child relationship
- nested tags and a complete API for finding tag ancestors

The implication, however, is that the API for creating JSP custom tags is robust, to say the least. To compound matters, additional information is required about the tag in a tag library descriptor (TLD) file that is loaded on application startup. This makes tags difficult to reload without a server restart, because the application server utilizes this file to configure the tag library. As you can imagine, all this is not very agile; rather, it is a complete contradiction to the code-by-convention approach.

From a user's perspective, developers rarely go to the effort of creating tags themselves, and typically the ones used tend to be those provided by the frameworks and specifications, such as JSTL. This is rather a shame, because the concept is sound, though the implementation is not.

So what can Grails and, more specifically, GSP provide to make creating tags simpler? Clearly, supporting every tag type under the sun would result in a complicated API, much like that in JSP. In reality, the most commonly used tags can be broken down into three categories:

- *Simple tags*: tags that have attributes but no body
- *Logical tags*: those that have a body that executes conditionally
- *Iterative tags*: tags that loop and execute the body of the tag one or more times

You will find that the majority of tags you come across fall into one of these categories. Since Grails is all about making the common cases simple, creating a simplified API for these tag types seems only logical. The question is, why create a new API at all? This is where Groovy and the power of closures start to shine.

Creating a Tag Library

Having already seen quite a few Grails tags throughout this discussion, you may well have already browsed the source and become familiar with what a Grails tag is all about. Whatever the case, it is important to understand how to create a tag library from scratch.

It is generally good practice to place tags inside a library that encapsulates their general function, much as a package does in Java.

A *tag library* is quite simply a class that ends with the convention TagLib in the class name and resides snugly in the grails-app/taglib directory. Like the other Grails artifacts you've seen, a convenience target exists for creating tag libraries. To create a new tag library for the gTunes application, you can run the grails create-tag-lib target (see Listing 5-41).

Listing 5-41. Creating the Gtunes Tag Library $ grails $ `grails create-taglib`

```
$ grails create-tag-lib com.gtunes.Gtunes
| Created file grails-app/taglib/com/gtunes/GtunesTagLib.groovy
| Created file test/unit/com/gtunes/GtunesTagLibTests.groovy
```

To see how to go about making a tag library, in the next section you'll look at a basic tag. In Chapter 8 you'll see how to write a custom tag library, one that will add some snazzy functionality to the gTunes application for rendering album cover art.

Custom Tag Basics

First, let's look at the basics. A tag is essentially a closure property that takes two arguments: the tag attributes as a `java.util.Map` and the body of the tag as a closure (see Listing 5-42).

Listing 5-42. An Example Tag

```
package com.gtunes

class GtunesTagLib {

    def repeat = { attrs, body ->
        // retrieve the 'times' attribute and convert it to an int
        int n = attrs.int('times')

        // render the body 'n' times, passing a 1 based
        // counter into the body each time
        n?.times { counter ->
            out << body(counter + 1)
        }
    }
}
```

This example defines a tag called `repeat`, which looks for an attribute called `times`, which it attempts to convert to an integer; it then uses Groovy's built-in `times` method to execute the body multiple times.

As mentioned previously, the body is a closure and therefore can be invoked like a method. In addition, you pass the number of the current iteration, as the variable `counter`, to the body as the first argument to the closure call. Why is this useful? It means that the number is available as the default `it` argument in the tag's body. As an example, let's try the new tag in a GSP view, as in Listing 5-43. Note that the name of the tag in the markup matches the property name defined in the library shown in Listing 5-42.

Listing 5-43. Using the repeat Tag

```
<g:repeat times="3">
  Hello number ${it}
</g:repeat>
```

As you can see, the tag uses the default `it` argument to reference the value passed when the tag calls the body closure. The resulting output will be the following:

```
Hello number 1
Hello number 2
Hello number 3
```

All the tags that are bundled with Grails are defined in the g namespace. By default, all your own custom tags are also put in the g namespace. To avoid naming conflicts with built-in tags and with tags that may be installed into a project as part of a plug-in, you should define a namespace for your own tag libraries. Defining a namespace for a tag library is as simple as declaring a static property called namespace in the taglib class and assigning that property a String value, as shown in Listing 5-44.

Listing 5-44. Defining a Custom Namespace for a Tag Library class GtunesTagLib {

```
package com.gtunes

class GtunesTagLib {

    static namespace = 'gt'

    def repeat = { attrs, body ->
        // retrieve the 'times' attribute and convert it to an int
        int n = attrs.int('times')

        // render the body n times, passing a 1 based
        // counter into the body each time
        n.times { counter ->
            out << body(counter + 1)
        }
    }
}
```

With that namespace property in place, all the tags defined in the GTunesTagLib are now in the gt namespace. Instead of referring to <g:repeat/>, GSPs should now refer to <gt:repeat/>.

Not only are Grails tags amazingly concise as compared with their JSP brethren, but it is important to note that all changes to tags can be reloaded at runtime, just as with controllers. With no need to configure tag library descriptors or restart servers, Grails tags become a far more interesting and agile proposition.

Testing a Custom Tag

As is true for most of your code in a Grails application, the code in custom tag libraries should be tested. Testing a tag library can be tricky. The test needs a way to invoke a tag, provide parameters, provide a body, and inspect the effect of invoking the tag. Fortunately, Grails provides a really slick mechanism for managing all of that. Unit tests for custom tag libraries should use the @TestFor annotation to specify which tag library is being tested. Listing 5-45 contains a unit test for the GtunesTagLib class defined earlier.

Listing 5-45. Testing GtunesTagLib

```
// test/unit/com/gtunes/GtunesTagLibTests.groovy
package com.gtunes
```

```
import grails.test.mixin.*
import org.junit.*

@TestFor(GtunesTagLib)
class GtunesTagLibTests {

    void testRepeatTag() {
        // define a snippet of markup to evaluate
        def template = '<gt:repeat times="3">Number ${it}<br/></gt:repeat>'

        // evaluate the snippet
        def result = applyTemplate(template)

        // make sure the result contains what we expect
        def expected = 'Number 1<br/>Number 2<br/>Number 3<br/>'
        assert expected == result
    }
}
```

The testRepeatTag() method here renders a block of markup that invokes the repeat tag. The way to do this is to pass a string, representing the markup to be evaluated, as an argument to the applyTemplate method. The applyTemplate method returns a string that represents the result of evaluating the string that was passed as an argument. The assertion at the bottom of the test method checks that the expected result was rendered.

If the string being evaluated is dynamically driven by a model, the model may be passed as a second argument to the applyTemplate method. Listing 5-46 shows an example of a model supplied to the applyTemplate method.

Listing 5-46. *Testing GtunesTagLib with a Model*

```
// test/unit/com/gtunes/GtunesTagLibTests.groovy
package com.gtunes

import grails.test.mixin.*
import org.junit.*

@TestFor(GtunesTagLib)
class GtunesTagLibTests {


    void testRepeatTagWithAModel() {
        // define a snippet of markup to evaluate
        def template =
          '<gt:repeat times="${someNumber}">Number ${it}<br/></gt:repeat>'

        // evaluate the snippet
        def result = applyTemplate(template, [someNumber: 2])

        // make sure the result contains what we expect
        def expected = 'Number 1<br/>Number 2<br/>'
        assert expected == result
```

```
        // evaluate the snippet with a different model
        result = applyTemplate(template, [someNumber: 4])

        // make sure the result contains what we expect
        expected = 'Number 1<br/>Number 2<br/>Number 3<br/>Number 4<br/>'
        assert expected == result
    }
}
```

Summary

In this chapter you learned about the advanced view technology in Grails, about GSP, and about the array of powerful tags that come packaged with it. You also learned how to build and test your own GSP tags, and you further extended your knowledge of Groovy mocking in the process. In short, a lot of ground was covered, and you should now have a clear idea of how powerful GSP is. What with GPath, an expression language, and dynamic tag libraries, GSP has a lot to offer in terms of increasing your productivity and enjoyment.

CHAPTER 6

■ ■ ■

Mapping URLs

Grails provides working URL mappings right out of the box. The default URL mapping configuration is yet one more place that the Grails framework leverages the powerful idea of convention over configuration to lessen the burden put on the application developer. Sometimes, though, you will want to deviate from the convention and define your own custom mappings. For example, you may want to create more descriptive and human-readable URLs. Grails gives you the ability to easily define these custom URL mappings.

Defining application-specific URL mappings is something that comes up all the time while building web applications. The technique for configuring URL mappings in Grails is really powerful while remaining very simple to work with. Like a lot of configuration options in a Grails application, configuring custom URL mappings involves writing a little bit of Groovy code, and that's it. In particular, no XML configuration files are involved. This chapter will describe the flexible URL mapping system provided by Grails and demonstrate how to manage both forward and reverse URL lookups, how to map requests to controller actions or views, and how to map exceptions to controller actions and views, as well as demonstrating how to test all of these actions.

Understanding the Default URL Mapping

The default URL mapping configuration in a Grails app is simple. The first part of the URL corresponds to the name of a controller, and the second, optional part of the URL corresponds to the name of an action defined in that controller. For example, the /store/index URL will map to the index action in the StoreController. Specifying the action name is optional, so if the action name is left out of the URL, then the default action for the specified controller will be executed. Default controller actions are described in detail in the "Setting the Default Action" section of Chapter 4. Finally, the last piece of the URL is another optional element that represents the value of a request parameter named id. For example, the /album/show/42 URL will map to the show action in the AlbumController with a request parameter named id that has a value of 42.

The definition of the default mapping is in grails-app/conf/UrlMappings.groovy. Listing 6-1 shows what UrlMappings.groovy looks like by default.

Listing 6-1. *Default grails-app/conf/UrlMappings.groovy*

```
class UrlMappings {
    static mappings = {
        "/$controller/$action?/$id?"{
            constraints {
                // apply constraints here
```

```
        }
      }
      "500"(view:'/error')
    }
}
```

The key to this mapping is the string "/$controller/$action?/$id?". Notice that the $action and $id elements are both followed by a question mark. The question mark indicates an optional piece of the URL. The $controller element has no question mark, so it is a required piece of the URL. A mapping can define any number of optional elements. If a mapping does contain any optional elements, they must all appear at the end of the pattern.

■ **Note**   The constraints block in the default mapping is empty. The constraints block is optional and will be discussed in the "Applying Constraints to URL Mappings" section later in this chapter. The mapping that begins with "500" will be discussed later in the "Mapping HTTP Response Codes" section.

Including Static Text in a URL Mapping

In the default mapping, each of the elements in the URL is a variable. Variable elements are prefixed with a $ sign. A URL mapping can contain static elements as well. A static element in a URL mapping is simply text that must be part of the URL in order for a particular mapping to apply. See Listing 6-2 for an example of a mapping that contains static text.

Listing 6-2. Including Static Text in a Mapping

```
class UrlMappings { static mappings = {
    "/showAlbum/$controller/$action?/$id?" {
        constraints {
            // apply constraints here
        }
    }
}
```

This mapping will match URLs such as /showAlbum/album/show/42 and /showAlbum/album/list but will not match a URL such as /album/show/42 since that one does not begin with /showAlbum.

Removing the Controller and Action Names from the URL

The controller and action names do not need to be part of the URL. These special elements can be eliminated from the URL pattern and specified as properties of the mapping. As shown previously, the default mapping supports a URL such as /album/show/42, which will map to the show action in the AlbumController. An application can choose to support a URL such as /showAlbum/42 to access that same controller action. The code in Listing 6-3 includes a mapping to support this.

Listing 6-3. Specifying the Controller and Action as Properties of the Mapping

```
class UrlMappings {
    static mappings = {
        "/showAlbum/$id" {
            controller = 'album'
            action = 'show'
        }
        // ...
    }
}
```

The mapping engine in Grails provides support for an alternative syntax to express the same mapping. Which technique is chosen is a matter of personal preference. Listing 6-4 shows the alternative syntax.

Listing 6-4. Specifying the Controller and Action as Parameters to the Mapping

```
class UrlMappings {
    static mappings = {
        "/showAlbum/$id"(controller:'album', action:'show')
        // ...
    }
}
```

Embedding Parameters in a Mapping

Of course, Grails supports request parameters using the standard HTTP request parameter notation. A URL such as /showArtist?artistName=Rush will work if there is a mapping like that shown in Listing 6-5.

Listing 6-5. A Mapping for the /showArtist URL

```
class UrlMappings {
    static mappings = {
        "/showArtist"(controller:'artist', action:'show')
        // ...
    }
}
```

Accessing /showArtist?artistName=Rush would map to the show action in the ArtistController, and a request parameter named artistName would be populated with the value Rush. Notice that the artistName parameter is not represented anywhere in the mapping. This is because the mapping applies to the /showArtist URL, and therefore any arbitrary parameters can be passed to that URL without affecting the mapping.

Although this approach works, it has its drawbacks. One drawback is that the URL is just ugly, and it would continue to get uglier as more request parameters were introduced.

The Grails URL mapping engine provides a much slicker solution to support custom URLs that have request parameters embedded in the URL. Instead of /showArtist?artistName=Rush, let's support a URL such as /showArtist/Rush. The mapping in Listing 6-6 works perfectly for this.

Listing 6-6. Embedding a Request Parameter in the URL

```
class UrlMappings {
    static mappings = {
        "/showArtist/$artistName"(controller:'artist', action:'show')
        // ...
    }
}
```

With this mapping, URLs such as /showArtist/Tool and /showArtist/Cream will be mapped to the show action in the ArtistController with a request parameter named artistName, and the value of that parameter will be whatever is in the last part of the URL; in the previous examples, these were the Tool and Cream values. The action in the AlbumController would have access to the request parameter and could use the parameter in whatever way is appropriate. See Listing 6-7.

Listing 6-7. Accessing a Request Parameter in the Controller Action

```
class ArtistController {
    def show() {
        def artist = Artist.findByName(params.artistName)
        // do whatever is appropriate with the artist...
    }
}
```

A little snag that must be dealt with here is that the artist names may include characters that are not valid in a URL. One technique that might be used to get around the snag is to URL-encode the parameters. This technique would support accessing a band named Led Zeppelin with a URL such as /showArtist/Led%20Zeppelin. Notice that the space in the name has been replaced with %20. Yuck! Let's make an application decision here and say that we'll encode artist names by replacing spaces with underscores. This will lead to a friendlier-looking URL: /showArtist/ Led_Zeppelin. The URL mapping doesn't really care about the value of the parameter, so it does not need to be changed to support it. However, the controller action will need to be updated, since the underscores in the query parameter must be replaced with spaces. Listing 6-8 represents an updating of the code in Listing 6-7 to deal with the underscores.

Listing 6-8. Decoding the Request Parameter to Replace Underscores with Spaces

```
class ArtistController {
    def show() {
        def nameToSearchFor = params.artistName.replaceAll('_', ' ')
        def artist = Artist.findByName(nameToSearchFor)
        // do whatever is appropriate with the artist...
    }
}
```

▪ **Note** This encoding/decoding problem exists even if the request parameter is not embedded in the URL. For example, something like /showArtist?artistName=Led%20Zeppelin or /showArtist?artistName=Led_ Zeppelin would be necessary to deal with the space in the parameter value.

Specifying Additional Parameters

In addition to embedding parameters in the URL, arbitrary request parameters may be specified as properties of a particular mapping that never show up in the URL. Listing 6-9 includes an example.

Listing 6-9. Specifying Additional Request Parameters

```
class UrlMappings {
  static mappings = {
    "/showArtist/$artistName"(controller:'artist', action:'show') {
      format = 'simple'
    }

    "/showArtistDetail/$artistName"(controller:'artist', action:'show') {
      format = 'detailed'
    }
    // ...
  }
}
```

With this mapping in place, a request to the URL /showArtist/Pink_Floyd would map to the show action in the ArtistController, and the request would include parameters named artistName and format with the values Pink_Floyd and simple, respectively. A request to the URL /showArtistDetail/Pink_Floyd would map to the same action and controller, but the format request parameter would have a value of detailed.

Mapping to a View

Sometimes you might want a certain URL pattern to map directly to a view. This is useful when the view does not require any data to be passed in and no controller action is required. In such a case, you can define a URL mapping that is associated with a view rather than with a controller action. The syntax is the same as mapping to an action except that a value must be specified for the view property instead of the action property. Listing 6-10 demonstrates how to do this.

Listing 6-10. Mapping to a View

```
class UrlMappings { static mappings = {
"/"(view:'/welcome')
// ... } }
```

This mapping will handle all requests to the root of the application (/) by rendering the GSP at grails-app/views/welcome.gsp. The mapping engine also allows a mapping to specify a view that belongs to a particular controller. For example, Listing 6-11 demonstrates how to map the /find URL to grails-app/views/search/query.gsp.

Listing 6-11. Mapping to a View for a Particular Controller

```
class UrlMappings { static mappings = {
"/find"(view:'query', controller:'search')
// ... } }
```

Remember that no controller action is being executed for this mapping. The controller is being specified only so the framework can locate the appropriate GSP.

Applying Constraints to URL Mappings

The URL mapping engine provides a really powerful mechanism for applying constraints to variables embedded in a URL mapping. The constraints are similar those applied to domain objects. See the "Validating Domain Classes" section in Chapter 3 for information about domain constraints. Applying constraints to variables in a URL mapping can greatly simplify the job of weeding out certain kinds of invalid data that would otherwise have to be dealt with in an imperative manner in a controller or service.

Consider a blogging application written in Grails. A typical format for a URL in a blogging system might be something like /grailsblogs/2009/01/15/new_grails_release. To support a URL like that, you might define a mapping as is done in Listing 6-12.

Listing 6-12. A Typical Blog-Type URL Mapping

```
class UrlMappings {
    static mappings = {
        "/grailsblogs/$year/$month/$day/$entry_name?" {
            controller = 'blog'
            action = 'display'
            constraints {
                // apply constraints here
            }
        }
        // ...
    }
}
```

With such a mapping in place, the URL /grailsblogs/2009/01/15/new_grails_release would map to the display action in the BlogController with request parameters named year, month, day, and entry_name and the values 2009, 01, 15, and new_grails_release, respectively.

A problem with this mapping is that it will match not only a URL such as /grailsblogs/2009/01/15/ new_grails_release but also a URL such as /grailsblogs/grails/rocks/big/time. In this case, the controller action would receive the value grails for the year, rocks for the month, and so on. Dealing with a scenario like this would complicate the logic in the controller. A better way to manage it is to apply constraints to the mapping that would let the framework know that grails is not a valid match for the year parameter in the mapping, for example. The constraints specified in Listing 6-13 use regular expressions to limit the year, month, and day parameters to match only those values that include the right number of digits and only digits.

Listing 6-13. Applying Constraints to Mapping Parameters

```
class UrlMappings {
    static mappings = {
        "/grailsblogs/$year/$month/$day/$entry_name?" {
            controller = 'blog'
            action = 'display'
            constraints {
                year matches: /[0-9]{4}/
                month matches: /[0-9]{2}/
```

```
            day matches: /[0-9]{2}/
        }
    }

    // ...
}
}
```

As is the case with domain-class constraints, mapping parameters may have as many constraints applied to them as necessary. All the constraints must pass in order for the mapping to apply.

▨ **Note** There is a small syntactical difference between the way constraints are specified in a URL mapping and how they are specified in a domain class. In a domain class, a constraints property is defined and assigned a value that is a closure. In a URL mapping, you are calling a method named constraints and passing a closure as an argument. This is why no equals sign is needed between constraints and the closure in a URL mapping but is needed between constraints and the closure in a domain class.

Including Wildcards in a Mapping

You've seen how a mapping may contain static text as well as any number of variable parameters (optional and required), and you've also seen how constraints may be applied to variable parameters. One more aid to flexibility that you can use in a mapping definition is a wildcard. Wildcards represent placeholders in a mapping pattern that may be matched by anything but do not represent information that will be passed as request parameters. Wildcards in a mapping definition are represented by an asterisk (*). Listing 6-14 includes a mapping with a wildcard in it.

Listing 6-14. A Wildcard in a Mapping

```
class UrlMappings {
    static mappings = {
        "/images/*.jpg"(controller:'image')

        // ...
    }
}
```

This mapping will handle any request for a file under the /images/ directory that ends with the .jpg extension. For example, this mapping will handle /images/header.jpg and /images/ footer.jpg, but it will not match requests for .jpg files that may exist in some subdirectory under the /images/ directory. For example, a request for something like /images/photos/president.jpg would not match. A double wildcard can be used to match any number of subdirectories. Listing 6-15 shows a double wildcard mapping.

Listing 6-15. A Double Wildcard in a Mapping

```
class UrlMappings {
    static mappings = {
        "/images/**.jpg"(controller:'image')
        // ...
    }
}
```

This mapping will match requests for things such as /images/header.jpg and /images/footer.jpg as well as things such as /images/photos/president.jpg.

For some situations, it may be desirable for the value that matched the wildcard to be passed to the controller as a request parameter. This is achieved by prepending a variable to the wildcard in the mapping. See Listing 6-16.

Listing 6-16. A Double Wildcard with a Variable in a Mapping

```
class UrlMappings {
    static mappings = {
        "/images/$pathToFile**.jpg"(controller:'image')
        // ...
    }
}
```

In this case, the pathToFile request parameter would represent the part of the URL that matched the wildcard. For example, a request for /images/photos/president.jpg would result in the pathToFile request parameter having a value of photos/president.

Mapping to HTTP Request Methods

A URL mapping can be configured to map to different actions based on the HTTP request method.[1] This can be useful when building a system that supports RESTful APIs. For example, if a GET request is made to the URL /artist/The_Beatles, then the controller may respond by generating a page that displays details about the Beatles. If a DELETE request is made to the same URL, the controller may respond by attempting to delete the Beatles and all of the band's associated data (albums and so on). An application could deal with all these requests in the same controller action by interrogating the request and reacting differently based on the HTTP request method. Listing 6-17 shows what this might look like in the ArtistController.

Listing 6-17. Inspecting the HTTP Request Method in a Controller Action

```
class ArtistController {
  def actionName() {
    if(request.method == "GET") {
      // handle the GET
    } else if(request.method == "PUT") {
      // handle the PUT
    } else if(request.method == "POST") {
      // handle the POST
    } else if(request.method == "DELETE") {
```

---

1 See http://www.w3.org/Protocols/rfc2616/rfc2616-sec9.html for definitions of all the HTTP request methods.

```
        // handle the DELETE
        }
        // ...
    }
}
```

This is tedious code and would likely be repeated in many places in your application. A better idea is to configure a URL mapping that matches this URL and maps the request to different controller actions based on the HTTP request method. See Listing 6-18 for an example.

Listing 6-18. *Mapping to HTTP Request Methods*

```
class UrlMappings {
    static mappings = {
        "/artist/$artistName" {
            controller = 'artist'
            action = [GET: 'show',
                      PUT: 'update',
                      POST: 'save',
                      DELETE: 'delete']
        }

        // ...
    }
}
```

Note that the value assigned to the action property is, not the name of an action, but a map. The keys in the map correspond to the names of HTTP request methods, and the values associated with the keys represent the name of the action that should be invoked for that particular request method. If the mapping is going to map those standard four HTTP request methods to those particular action names, then an alternative, more concise syntax for expressing the same mapping may be used, as shown in Listing 6-19.

Listing 6-19. *Mapping to HTTP Request Methods*

```
class UrlMappings {
    static mappings = {
        "/artist/$artistName"(resource: "artist")
        // ...
    }
}
```

Mapping HTTP Response Codes

URL mappings may be defined for specific HTTP response codes. The default mapping includes a mapping for the 500 response code (Internal Error).[2] This mapping renders the /error view for any internal error. This view is located at grails-app/views/error.gsp. This GSP renders stack information that may be useful during development and debugging. Listing 6-20 represents the default error.gsp page.

---

2 See http://www.w3.org/Protocols/rfc2616/rfc2616-sec10.html for definitions of all the HTTP response codes.

Listing 6-20. The Default grails-app/views/error.gsp Page

```
<body>
  <h1>Grails Runtime Exception</h1>
  <h2>Error Details</h2>
  <div class="message">
    <strong>Message:</strong> ${exception.message?.encodeAsHTML()} <br />
    <strong>Caused by:</strong> ${exception.cause?.message?.encodeAsHTML()} <br />
    <strong>Class:</strong> ${exception.className} <br />
    <strong>At Line:</strong> [${exception.lineNumber}] <br />
    <strong>Code Snippet:</strong><br />
    <div class="snippet">
      <g:each var="cs" in="${exception.codeSnippet}">
        ${cs?.encodeAsHTML()}<br />
      </g:each>
    </div>
  </div>
  <h2>Stack Trace</h2>
  <div class="stack">
    <pre>
      <g:each in="${exception.stackTraceLines}">
        ${it.encodeAsHTML()}<br/>
      </g:each>
    </pre>
  </div>
</body>
```

You can add your own mappings for specific response codes. For example, if you want to map every request for something that cannot be found to the default action in the StoreController, you can do so. You can also map specific exception types to actions or views. Such custom mappings are shown in Listing 6-21.

Listing 6-21. Custom Mapping for All 404 Response Codes

```
class UrlMappings {
    static mappings = {
        // 404s should be handled by the default
        //action in the store controller
        "404"(controller:'store')

        // IllegalArgumentExceptions should be handled by the
        // illegalArgument action in the errors controller
        "500"(controller: "errors", action: "illegalArgument",
              exception: IllegalArgumentException)

        // NullPointerException should be handled by the
        // nullPointer action in the errors controller
        "500"(controller: "errors", action: "nullPointer",
              exception: NullPointerException)

        // MyException should be handled by the
        // customException action in the errors controller
```

```
    "500"(controller: "errors", action: "customException",
            exception: MyException)

    // all other exceptions should be handled by
    // the /errors/serverError view
    "500"(view: "/errors/serverError")

    // ...
  }
}
```

Taking Advantage of Reverse URL Mapping

You have seen how to support URLs such as /showArtist/Pink_Floyd instead of URLs such as /artist/
show/42. The support seen so far relates to handling a request to a URL. The other end of that interaction is
equally important. That is, you need a slick mechanism for generating links, one that takes advantage of
custom URL mappings. Fortunately, that mechanism is built into Grails and is as easy to work with as the
mapping mechanisms already seen.

The <g:link> GSP tag that is bundled with Grails is useful for generating links to certain controllers
and actions. See Listing 6-22 for a common use of the link tag.

Listing 6-22. The Link Tag

```
<td>
  <g:link action='show'
          controller='artist'
          id="${artist.id}">${artist.name}
  </g:link>
</td>
```

This tag will generate a link like <a href="/artist/show/42">Pink Floyd</a>. That link to /artist/
show/42 is ugly. You would definitely prefer /showArtist/Pink_Floyd. The good news is that it is easy to get
the link tag to generate a link like the latter. You just tell the link tag what controller and action you want to
link to and supply all the necessary parameters that the custom mapping calls for. For example, see the
custom mapping in Listing 6-23.

Listing 6-23. A Mapping for the /showArtist/ URL

```
class UrlMappings {
    static mappings = {
        "/showArtist/$artistName"(controller:'artist', action:'show')
        // ...
    }
}
```

The link tag will generate a link that takes advantage of this mapping whenever a request is made for a
link to the show action in the ArtistController and the artistName parameter is supplied. In a GSP, that
would look something like the code in Listing 6-24.

Listing 6-24. Reverse URL Mapping Using the Link Tag

```
<td>
  <g:link action='show'
          controller='artist'
          params="[artistName:${artist.name.replaceAll(' ', '_')}">
    ${artist.name}
  </g:link>
</td>
```

Named URL Mappings

There may be scenarios where multiple URL mappings match a given request for a reverse mapping and the framework won't necessarily know which mapping to apply. Named URL mappings solve this problem by allowing a mapping to have a name associated with it and then referring to that name when requesting a reverse URL mapping lookup. The framework can then use the name to unambiguously associate the reverse mapping request to a specific URL mapping. Listing 6-25 defines a URL mapping with the name artistDetails.

Listing 6-25. A Named URL Mapping

```
class UrlMappings {
  static mappings = {
    name artistDetails: "/showArtist/$artistName" {
      controller = "artist"
      action = "show"
    }
  }
}
```

The link tag supports an optional attribute named mapping, which may be used to specify the name of the mapping that should be used for this lookup. Listing 6-26 demonstrates this technique.

Listing 6-26. Specifying a Named URL mapping with the Link Tag

```
<g:link mapping="artistDetails"
        params="[artistName:${artist.name.replaceAll(' ', '_')}">
    ${artist.name}
</g:link>
```

Notice that there is no need to specify the controller or action name. The framework will locate the mapping named "artistDetails" and will find the corresponding controller and action names as part of the named URL mapping definition.

As an alternative to specifying the name of the URL mapping as the value of the mapping attribute on the link tag, Grails supports invoking a tag in the link namespace whose name matches the mapping name. When using this approach, parameters may be specified as attributes to the tag. Listing 6-27 shows an example which generates the same link as the code in Listing 6-26.

Listing 6-27. Using the Link Namespace

```
<link:artistDetails artistName="${artist.name.replaceAll(' ', '_')}">
    ${artist.name}
</link:artistDetails>
```

The code in Listing 6-27 is a good bit cleaner than the corresponding code in Listing 6-26.

Defining Multiple URL Mappings Classes

When an application defines a lot of custom URL mappings, the UrlMappings class may get long enough to warrant breaking the mappings up into several mappings classes. Several small, focused mappings classes will be easier to write and maintain than one monolithic class. To introduce new mappings classes, simply define classes under grails-app/conf/ with a name that ends with UrlMappings. The structure of those classes should be exactly the same as the default UrlMappings class. Listing 6-28 shows a custom mappings class that would contain Artist-related mappings.

Listing 6-28. A URL Mappings Class for Artist Mappings

```
class ArtistUrlMappings {
    static mappings = {
        "/showArtist/$artistName" (controller:'artist', action:'display')
    }
}
```

Testing URL Mappings

As with most other aspects of your application, you are going to want to write automated tests for custom URL mappings to assert that the application does in fact respond to requests in the way you intended. Grails provides a really slick mechanism for writing those tests. The simplest way to test URL mappings is to create a unit test for the URL mapping class that can be used to test custom mappings.

Listing 6-29 shows a simple mapping to support URLs like /showArtist/Jeff_Beck. A request to a URL like that should map to the display action in the ArtistController.

Listing 6-29. A Custom URL Mapping

```
class UrlMappings {
    static mappings = {
        "/showArtist/$artistName" (controller:'artist', action:'display')
        // ...
    }
}
```

The assertForwardUrlMapping method can be used to assert that a request to a URL like /showArtist/Jeff_Beck is sent to the appropriate controller action. The code in Listing 6-30 demonstrates what this test might look like.

Listing 6-30. Unit-Testing a URL Mapping

```
@TestFor(ArtistUrlMappings)
@Mock(com.gtunes.ArtistController)
class ArtistUrlMappingsTests {

    void testShowArtistUrlMapping() {
        // assert that /showArtist/Jeff_Beck is handled by the
        // display action in the artist controller
```

151

```
        assertForwardUrlMapping('/showArtist/Jeff_Beck',
                                controller: 'artist', action: 'display')
    }
}
```

Note that it is important to mock any controllers relevant to the URL mappings that are tested. That is accomplished by applying the Mock annotation to the test class and passing the corresponding URL mapping class as an argument. In Listing 6-30 that is the ArtistController. The mapping defined in Listing 6-29 includes an embedded variable, artistName. There is a simple mechanism for asserting that such mapping variables are being assigned the correct value: just pass a closure as the last argument to the assertForwardUrlMapping method, and in the closure assign values to properties with names that are consistent with the embedded variable names. See Listing 6-31 for an example. This test will assert not only that the request maps to the display action in the ArtistController but also that the artistName request parameter is being populated with the correct value.

Listing 6-31. Testing URL Mapping Variables

```
@TestFor(ArtistUrlMappings)
@Mock(com.gtunes.ArtistController)
class ArtistUrlMappingsTests {

    void testShowArtistUrlMapping() {
        // assert that /showArtist/Jeff_Beck is handled by the
        // display action in the artist controller and a request
        // parameter named artistName exists with the value Jeff_Beck
        assertForwardUrlMapping('/showArtist/Jeff_Beck',
                                controller: 'artist', action: 'display') {
            artistName = 'Jeff_Beck'
        }
    }
}
```

Listing 6-32 demonstrates a similar approach to testing whether reverse URL mapping is behaving as expected. Note that the assert method is called assertReverseUrlMapping this time.

Listing 6-32. Testing Reverse URL Mapping

```
@TestFor(ArtistUrlMappings)
@Mock(com.gtunes.ArtistController)
class ArtistUrlMappingsTests {
    void testShowArtistReverseUrlMapping() {
        // assert that when a reverse url lookup is done for the
        // display action in the artist controller with a request
        // parameter named artistName with value Jeff_Beck, then
        // the generated url is /showArtist/Jeff_Beck
        assertReverseUrlMapping('/showArtist/Jeff_Beck',
                                controller: 'artist', action: 'display') {
            artistName = 'Jeff_Beck'
        }
    }
}
```

Often it is the case that you want to test both forward and reverse URL mapping. One way to do so is to use the assertForwardUrlMapping method in addition to using the assertReverseUrlMapping method. Although this combination will get the job done, it involves more work than you need to do. Using the assertUrlMapping method will assert that both forward and reverse URL mapping are working, and if either of them fail, the test will fail. See Listing 6-33 for an example.

Listing 6-33. Testing Both Forward and Reverse URL Mapping

```
@TestFor(ArtistUrlMappings)
@Mock(com.gtunes.ArtistController)
class ArtistUrlMappingsTests {
    void testForwardAndReverseUrlMapping() {
        assertUrlMapping('/showArtist/Jeff_Beck',
                                controller: 'artist', action: 'display') {
            artistName = 'Jeff_Beck'
        }
    }
}
```

Summary

The URL mapping engine provided by Grails is very flexible. Nearly any URL pattern that you might want to map to a particular controller action can easily be configured simply by writing a small amount of Groovy code in UrlMappings.groovy. The framework provides a lot of mechanisms that enable you to spend less time configuring the framework and more time solving business problems in your application. The URL mapping engine is one more example of this. Custom URL mappings are simple to write and simple to test.

CHAPTER 7

■ ■ ■

Internationalization

One of the great things about web applications is that they are really easy to distribute to a lot of people. When deploying web applications to a broad audience, often the applications need to adapt and behave differently under certain circumstances. For example, when a request from Spain is made to a web application, the application may want to display messages to the user in Spanish, but the same application will want to render messages in English if the request comes from New York. The adaptations made by the application may involve more complexity than simply displaying different versions of text. An application may need to impose different business rules based on the origin of a particular request.

Grails provides a number of mechanisms for dealing with the internationalization and localization of a web application. In this chapter, we will explore those mechanisms, and you will see that internationalizing a web application does not have to be terribly difficult.

Localizing Messages

When deploying a Grails application to a broad audience, you may want the application to display messages in the user's preferred language. One way of providing this capability is to have a separate version of the application for each language you want to target. That approach has lots of problems. Maintaining all those different versions and trying to keep them all in sync would be an awful lot of work. A much better idea is to have a single version of the application that is flexible enough to display messages in various languages using localized messages.

To support localized messages in your Grails application, you should be defining all user messages in a properties file. In other words, user messages should not be hard-coded in GSP pages, GSP templates, or anywhere else. Having messages in a properties file allows you to maintain all of them all in a single place. It also lets you take advantage of the localization capabilities provided by Grails.

Defining User Messages

When a Grails app is created, the project includes a number of localized property files in the grails-app/i18n/ directory. Figure 7-1 shows the contents of the grails-app/i18n/ directory.

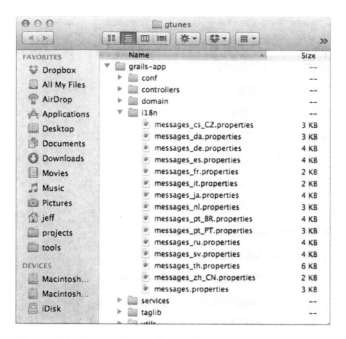

Figure 7-1. The grails-app/i18n/ directory

The messages.properties file in the grails-app/i18n/ directory contains default validation messages in English. These messages are used when validation fails in a domain class or command object. You can add your own application messages to this file. In addition to the default messages.properties file, this directory has several other properties files that contain the same messages in other languages. For example, "es" is the language code for Spanish, so messages_es.properties contains validation messages in Spanish.

■ **Note** The naming convention for the messages files follows the standard convention used by the java.util. ResourceBundle class. For more information, see the documentation for java.util. ResourceBundle and java.util. Locale: http://java.sun.com/j2se/1.5.0/docs/api/.

Property files are plain text files, which contain name-value pairs. Listing 7-1 represents a simple properties file.

Listing 7-1. A Simple Property File

```
# messages.properties
app.name=gTunes
book.title=The Definitive Guide To Grails
favorite.language=Groovy
favorite.framework=Grails
```

Retrieving Message Values

In a standard Java or Groovy program, you would use the `java.util.ResourceBundle` class to retrieve values from a properties file. Listing 7-2 demonstrates how you would retrieve and print the value of the `app.name` property.

***Listing 7-2.** Using java.util.ResourceBundle*

```
// JavaMessages.java
import java.util.ResourceBundle;

public class JavaMessages {

    public static void main(String[] args) {
        ResourceBundle bundle = ResourceBundle.getBundle("messages");
        String appName = bundle.getString("app.name");
        System.out.println("application name is " + appName);
    }
}

// GroovyMessages.groovy
def messages = ResourceBundle.getBundle('messages')
def appName = messages.getString('app.name')
println "application name is ${appName}"
```

The `java.util.ResourceBundle` class takes care of loading the properties file and providing an API to retrieve the values of properties defined in the file. Grails provides a GSP tag called `message` that will retrieve property values from the messages files in the `grails-app/i18n/` directory. For the simplest case, only the code attribute must be specified when calling the `message` tag. The code attribute tells the `message` tag which property value should be retrieved. For example, if a property named gtunes.welcome is defined in `grails-app/i18n/messages.properties`, the value of that property may be rendered in a GSP using code like that shown in Listing 7-3.

***Listing 7-3.** Using the message Tag*

```
<body>
...
<g:message code="gtunes.welcome"/>
... </body>
```

By default, Grails will decide which version of the property file to use based on the locale of the current web request. Thus, you won't often need to do anything special in your application code with respect to localization. If you define your message properties in several language-specific versions of the properties files under `grails-app/i18n/`, then Grails will use the appropriate file based on the client's locale.

Figure 7-2 represents the gTunes home page in English.

Figure 7-2. gTunes in English

There are several user messages represented in Figure 7-2. For example, on the left side of the screen is a navigation area, which includes the "My Music" and "The Store" links. The labels for those links will include different text when the application is accessed from different locales. The best way to deal with that is to define those messages as properties and render the messages in the GSP with the message tag. Listing 7-4 shows how those properties might be defined in grails-app/i18n/messages.properties.

Listing 7-4. User Messages in grails-app/i18n/messages.properties

```
gtunes.my.music=My Music
gtunes.the.store=The Store ...
```

With those properties defined, a GSP can render those values using the message tag, as shown in Listing 7-5.

Listing 7-5. Rendering Property Values from a GSP

```
<div id="navButtons">
  <ul>
    <li><a href="#"><g:message code="gtunes.my.music"/></a></li>
    <li><g:link controller="store" action="shop">
          <g:message code="gtunes.the.store"/>
        </g:link>
    </li>
  </ul>
</div>
```

With that code in place, you may add corresponding properties to as many of the other messages files as you like. To support a Spanish version of the site, add corresponding properties to grails-app/i18n/ messages_es.properties, as shown in Listing 7-6.

Listing 7-6. *User Messages in grails-app/i18n/messages_es.properties*

```
gtunes.my.music=Mi Musica
gtunes.the.store=La Tienda
```

A simple way to test your Grails application's localization is to include a request parameter named lang and assign it a valid language code, such as "es" for Spanish (http://localhost:8080/ gTunes/ ?lang=es). Figure 7-3 shows a Spanish version of the application.

Figure 7-3. *gTunes in Spanish*

Using URL Mappings for Internationalization

As shown previously, a request parameter named lang will tell the framework to use a specific language code while processing this request. One way to specify the request parameter is to include it in the request URL, as in http://localhost:8080/gTunes/?lang=es. Another way to specify the request parameter is by defining a custom URL mapping, as shown in Listing 7-7.

Listing 7-7. A URL Mapping for Localization

```
class UrlMappings {
  static mappings = {
    "/store/$lang"(controller:'store')

    // ...
  }
}
```

The mapping in Listing 7-7 will map all requests to a URL such as `http://localhost:8080/gTunes/en/` or `http://localhost:8080/gTunes/es/`, where "en" and "es" could be any valid language code.

Using Parameterized Messages

Often a user message may consist of more than simple static text. The message may need to include some data that is not known until runtime. For example, gTunes displays a message that lets users know how many songs they have purchased. The message reads something like this: "You have purchased (97) songs." The "97" part of that message is a piece of information that isn't known until runtime.

Using java.text.MessageFormat

Java includes a class called `java.text.MessageFormat`. One of the things that `java.text.MessageFormat` is useful for is supporting parameterized messages, such as the one described earlier, in a language-neutral way. A parameterized message may contain any number of parameters, and the parameters are represented with numbers surrounded by curly braces in the value of the message. Listing 7-8 shows how the "You have purchased (97) songs." message might be represented in `grails-app/i18n/messages.properties`.

Listing 7-8. Defining a Parameterized Message

```
# messages.properties
gtunes.purchased.songs=You have purchased ({0}) songs.
...
```

The value of the `gtunes.purchased.songs` message has one parameter in it. As is almost always the case in Java and Groovy, the `java.text.MessageFormat` class uses a zero-based index; {0} in the message is a placeholder for the value of the first parameter. If the message had multiple parameters, they would be represented in the value of the message with placeholders like {0}, {1}, {2}, and so on.

The code in Listing 7-9 shows how `java.text.MessageFormat` might be used from a Java program.

Listing 7-9. Using MessageFormat to Populate a Parameterized Message with Java

```
// JavaMessages.java
import java.util.ResourceBundle;
import java.text.MessageFormat;

public class JavaMessages {

    public static void main(String[] args) {
        ResourceBundle bundle = ResourceBundle.getBundle("messages");
```

```
        String songsPurchased = bundle.getString("gtunes.purchased.songs");
        String message = MessageFormat.format(songsPurchased, 97);
        System.out.println("message: " + message);
    }
}
```

Listing 7-10 shows a Groovy script that does the same thing.

Listing 7-10. Using MessageFormat to Populate a Parameterized Message with Groovy

```
import java.text.MessageFormat

def bundle = ResourceBundle.getBundle('messages')
def songsPurchased = bundle.getString('gtunes.purchased.songs')
def message = MessageFormat.format(songsPurchased, 97)

println "message: ${message}"
```

Using the message Tag for Parameterized Messages

Grails allows for parameterized messages to be used without the need for you, the application developer, to deal directly with the java.text.MessageFormat class. The message tag supports an optional parameter named args, and if that parameter is assigned a value, its value will be treated as a list of parameters that need to be applied to the message. Listing 7-11 shows how to pass arguments to the message tag.

Listing 7-11. Using the message Tag to Populate a Parameterized Message

```
<div>
<g:message code="gtunes.purchased.songs" args="[97]"/>
</div>
```

Of course, for this or a similar message, you will probably not want to hard-code the parameter value in a GSP like that. More likely, you will want that value to be dynamic. The code in Listing 7-12 is passing a parameter to the message to be applied to the gtunes.purchased. songs message. If the currently logged in user has purchased any songs, then the value of the parameter will be the number of songs he or she has purchased; otherwise, the value of the parameter will be 0.

Listing 7-12. Using the message Tag to Populate a Parameterized Message Dynamically

```
<div> <g:message code="gtunes.purchased.songs"
args="[session.user.purchasedSongs?.size() ?: 0]"/> </div>
```

■ **Note** Note the use of the so-called Elvis operator (?:) in the previous code. The Elvis operator is a shorthand version of Java ternary operator where the return value for the true condition is the same as the expression being evaluated. For example, the following expressions accomplish the same thing:

```
size = session.user.purchasedSongs?.size() ? session.user.purchasedSongs?.size() : 0 size =
session.user.purchasedSongs?.size() ?: 0
```

Using Parameterized Messages for Validation

Notice that the default `grails-app/i18n/messages.properties` file contains a number of messages by default. These messages are there to support the mechanism that is built in to Grails for validating domain classes and command objects. Listing 7-13 shows a domain class that contains some constraints.

Listing 7-13. *A Domain Class with Constraints*

```
class Person {
    String firstName
    String lastName
    Integer age

    static constraints = {
        firstName size: 2..30, blank: false
        lastName size: 2..30, blank: false
        age min: 0
    }
}
```

These constraints are in place to make sure that the firstName and lastName properties are at least 2 characters, no more than 30 characters, and not blank. You might think that specifying a minimum length of 2 would take care of the blank scenario, but that is not the case. A firstName that is simply three spaces would satisfy the length constraint but not the blank constraint. The age property also is constrained: it may never have a negative value. If an instance of the Person class is created that does not satisfy all of those constraints, then a call to the validate() method on that instance would return false. Likewise, a call to save() on the instance would fail.

The default scaffolded views for a domain class contain code to display any validation errors. Listing 7-14 shows a piece of the default grails-app/views/person/create.gsp.

Listing 7-14. *create.gsp Containing Code to Render Validation Errors*

```
<h1><g:message code="default.create.label" args="[entityName]" /></h1>
<g:if test="${flash.message}">
<div class="message" role="status">${flash.message}</div>
</g:if>
<g:hasErrors bean="${personInstance}">
<ul class="errors" role="alert">
    <g:eachError bean="${personInstance}" var="error">
    <li <g:if test="${error in org.springframework.validation.FieldError}">data-field-
id="${error.field}"</g:if>><g:message error="${error}"/></li>
    </g:eachError>
</ul>
</g:hasErrors>
```

The hasErrors tag will render its body only if personInstance has errors. If personInstance does have errors, then the renderErrors tag will render a list of all those errors, and that rendering process is using the validation messages defined in grails-app/i18n/messages.properties.

Figure 7-4 shows what the user might see when attempting to create a Person in the user interface with no firstName, no lastName, and a negative age.

Figure 7-4. *Validation messages in the user interface*

The error messages you see there are all defined in `grails-app/i18n/messages.properties` as parameterized messages, as shown in Listing 7-15.

Listing 7-15. *Default Validation Messages*

```
default.invalid.min.message=\
  Property [{0}] of class [{1}] with value [{2}] is less than minimum value [{3}]
default.blank.message=Property [{0}] of class [{1}] cannot be blank
...
```

You may modify the values of these messages to suit your application. For example, if the `default.blank.message` property was given a value of `{0}` is a required field, then the user would be shown error messages like those in Figure 7-5.

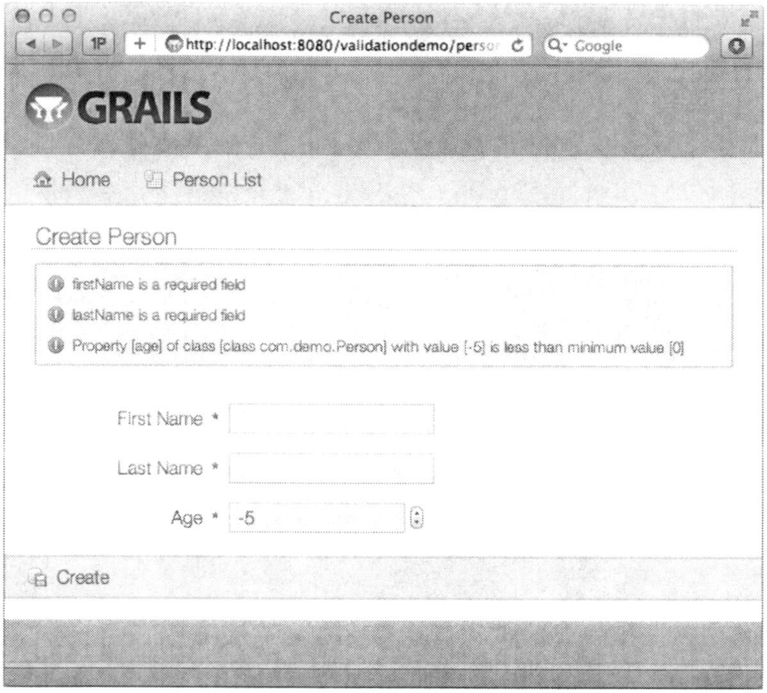

Figure 7-5. Custom validation messages in the user interface

Changing the default validation message in this manner is useful when the validation message applies to all usages of a particular validator. Often it will be necessary to provide a custom message for a validator as it relates to a specific property in a specific class. For example, the min constraint might be applied to the age property in the Person class, and the same constraint might be applied to the balance property in the Account class. Describing a constraint violation for those two scenarios requires two separate messages. If a person's age is a negative number, it would of course not make sense to display "Account is not allowed to be overdrawn" or a similar message. Likewise, the message displayed when an account has a negative balance would be different from the message displayed when a person has a negative age. To help deal with such situations, the framework supports the association of validation messages not only with a particular constraint but also with a particular property in a particular class. Listing 7-16 shows examples of messages with specific properties.

Listing 7-16. Property-Specific Validation Messages

```
person.age.min.notmet=A person may not have a negative age
account.balance.min.notmet=Account is not allowed to be overdrawn
```

Each of the framework-provided validators that support error messages has a specific error code pattern or patterns; they are used to define error messages for that validator, messages that are related to specific properties in specific classes. Those error codes are listed in Table 7-1.

Table 7-1. Custom error codes

Validator	Error Code(s)
blank	className.propertyName.blank
creditCard	className.propertyName.creditCard.invalid
email	className.propertyName.email.invalid
inList	className.propertyName.not.inList
min	className.propertyName.min.notmet
minSize	className.propertyName.minSize.notmet
matches	className.propertyName.matches.invalid
max	className.propertyName.max.exceeded
maxSize	className.propertyName.maxSize.exceeded
notEqual	className.propertyName.notEqual
nullable	className.propertyName.nullable
range	className.propertyName.range.toosmall className.propertyName.range.toobig
size	className.propertyName.size.toosmall className.propertyName.size.toobig
unique	className.propertyName.unique
url	className.propertyName.url.invalid

Using messageSource

The message tag is easy and sensible to use when a user message needs to be retrieved from messages.
properties and the message is going to be rendered in a GSP. However, sometimes an application may

need to retrieve the value of a user message and do something with it other than render the value in a GSP. For example, the message could be used in an e-mail message. In fact, the message could be used for any number of things, and not all of them involve rendering text in a GSP.

Grails provides a bean named messageSource that can be injected into any Grails artefact, including controllers, taglibs, other beans, and so on. The messageSource bean is an instance of the org.springframework.context.MessageSource interface provided by the Spring Framework. This interface defines three overloaded versions of the getMessage method for retrieving messages from the source. Listing 7-17 shows the signatures of these methods.[1]

■ **Note** Throughout the source code and documentation of Grails, the word artefact is used to refer to a Groovy file that fulfills a certain concept (such as a controller, tag library, or domain class). Since it is spelled using the British English spelling of artefact (as opposed to artifact), we will be using that spelling throughout the book to maintain consistency with the APIs.

Listing 7-17. The MessageSource Interface

```
String getMessage(String code, Object[] args, Locale locale)
String getMessage(String code, Object[] args, String defaultMessage, Locale locale)
String getMessage(MessageSourceResolvable resolvable, Locale locale)
```

Since the messageSource bean participates in Grails's dependency autowiring process, all you need to do to get a reference to the bean is declare a property named messageSource in your Grails artefact. The code in Listing 7-18 shows how to use the messageSource bean in a service.

Listing 7-18. Using messageSource in a Service

```
package com.gtunes

class StoreService {

    def messageSource

    def someServiceMethod() {
        def msg = messageSource.getMessage('gtunes.my.music', null, null)
        // ...
    }
    ...
}
```

Note that the second and third arguments are null. The second argument is an Object[], which would be used to pass parameters to a parameterized message. The third argument is a java.util.Locale, which may be specified to retrieve a message for any Locale other than the default Locale for this request. For example, Listing 7-19 demonstrates retrieving a message in Italian.

Listing 7-19. Using messageSource and Specifying a Locale

```
package com.gtunes
```

---

1 See http://static.springsource.org/spring/docs/3.1.x/javadoc-api/ for complete documentation of the MessageSource interface and related classes.

```
class StoreService {

    def messageSource

    def someServiceMethod() {
        def msg = messageSource.getMessage('gtunes.my.music',
                                            null,
                                            Locale.ITALIAN)
        // ...
    }
    ...
}
```

From within a Controller or TagLib artefact, a simpler way to retrieve messages is to invoke the message GSP tag as a method on the special g namespace variable available in those artefacts, as shown in Listing 7-20

Listing 7-20. *Invoking g.message() from a Controller*

```
package com.gtunes

class StoreController {

    def index() {
        def msg = g.message(code:'gtunes.my.music')
        // …
    }
}
```

■ **Note** The code in Listing 7-20 is effectively invoking the message tag, which is defined in the g namespace. There isn't really anything special about accessing the message tag, however. All tag libraries are accessible using the very same technique.

Summary

Internationalization is an important aspect of building widely distributed applications. Grails provides a number of mechanisms that make the process much easier than it might otherwise be. All the message property files in a Grails application are located in the same place. Thus, an application developer does not need to tell Grails where to look for these files. What's more, as a Grails developer moves from one Grails project to the next, he or she knows exactly where to look for the property files because they are always in the same place. This is the practical working power of coding by convention. Also, retrieving messages from a property file is a snap in a Grails application. The message tag is very easy to access and use from GSP pages and GSP templates. The messageSource bean is easily accessible from wherever the application may need it. All of these enhancements are built on top of proven and well-understood Java-platform tools, including java.text. MessageFormat and org.springframework.context.MessageSource.

CHAPTER 8

Ajax

Ajax is a really important piece of the modern web application story. The technology was originally developed by Microsoft to power a web-based version of its Outlook e-mail software. Microsoft implemented Ajax as an ActiveX control that could be used by its browser, Internet Explorer, and be called from JavaScript to perform asynchronous browser requests.

The advantage of the approach is that the browser doesn't have to refresh the entire page to interact with the server, thus allowing the development of applications that bear a closer resemblance to their desktop counterparts. Since then, browsers other than Internet Explorer have standardized on a native JavaScript object called XMLHttpRequest, which has largely the same API as Microsoft's ActiveX control.

Writing Ajax Code

Writing JavaScript code can become rather repetitive and tedious. Fortunately, there are Ajax frameworks that encapsulate much of this logic, ranging from the simple to the comprehensive. Efforts are underway to standardize on a JavaScript library, but as is always the case with any collaborative effort, the process could be long and painful and is likely never to satisfy everyone.

By default, Grails ships with the jQuery. Through the Grails plug-in system, you can add support for alternative libraries that supply the underlying implementation of the Ajax tags in Grails.

Before you delve into the world of Ajax, you should revisit the gTunes application, since you'll be enhancing the gTunes application by adding a range of Ajax-powered features that improve the user experience:

- the ability to log in asynchronously

- a new feature that allows you to search and filter songs within your library and the store using Ajax-powered search fields

- finally, a slicker way of displaying albums and songs, including album art

So before getting too carried away, let's move on to the guts of the chapter by improving the gTunes application interface, Ajax style.

Ajax in Action

Let's start with a simple example. Grails provides a set of tags that simplify the creation of such Ajax-capable components as links, forms, and text fields. For example, to create an HTML anchor tag that, when clicked, executes an Ajax call, you can use the `<g:remoteLink>` tag. These tags, included in Grails since very early versions, are still included, but for most cases the provided tags are not optimal. The tags were developed before jQuery and similar libraries developed to a point where writing the JavaScript really became the right thing to do. The examples shown here will show how to use jQuery to accomplish the same tasks that the Ajax-enabled tags provide. Let's try a "Hello World"–style example using jQuery. First update StoreController by adding the action shown in Listing 8-1.

Listing 8-1. An Action That Renders the Date and Time

```
def showTime() {
    render "The time is ${new Date()}"
}
```

The showTime action in Listing 8-1 uses the render method, introduced in Chapter 4, to render a plain-text response to the client that contains the current date and time, trivially obtained through Java's java.util.Date class. That was simple enough; now open the index.gsp file located in the grails-app/views/store directory. In order to write your own Ajax in the page, you need to tell Grails which Ajax library to use. You can do this through the `<g:javascript>` tag, which needs to go in the `<head>` section of your index.gsp file, as shown in Listing 8-2.

Listing 8-2. Using the jQuery Library

```
<g:javascript library="jquery" />
```

In this case, you are telling Grails to use the jQuery library for Ajax. As a side effect, Grails will import all the necessary jQuery dependencies into the page, so you're ready to go. Now, within the body of the index.gsp page, add the code shown in Listing 8-3, which uses jQuery's api.

Listing 8-3. Using the jQuery Ajax Function

```
<g:link action="showTime" elementId="timeLink">Show the time!</g:link>
<div id="time">
</div>
<r:script>
    $('#timeLink').click(function() {
        $('#time').load(this.href); return false;
    });
</r:script>
```

What this does is add an HTML anchor tag (with the text "Show the time!") to the page, which when clicked will execute an asynchronous request to the showTime action of the StoreController. The jQuery code will be executed when the link is clicked. That code will will initiate an Ajax request to the showTime action and will use the response to update the DOM in the browser. In this case, you've provided an HTML `<div>` element with an id of time just below the anchor tag. That div will be updated with the response of this Ajax call. It is important that the JavaScript function return false in order to prevent the browser from actually following the link. Following the link is not necessary as the Ajax call is going to accomplish the desired behavior here.

Notice that the JavaScript code is all wrapped in the `<r:script>` tag provided by the resources plug-in. By using the script tag, the JavaScript will always be loaded last on the page, thus optimizing page loading time.

With that, you have completed a trivial example of Ajax-enabling your application. Try clicking the link to see what happens. Note that the current date and time gets placed into the <div> each time you click the link! Figure 8-1 shows an example of this behavior.

Figure 8-1. A Simple Ajax call example

Changing Your Ajax Provider

As it stands, you are using jQuery as the underlying library for the Ajax code. Indeed, jQuery is the default JavaScript library for Grails applications because it's a really powerful library—but what if you wanted to use a different library? With Grails it's very easy to swap to a different implementation via its plug-in system. For example, say you wanted to use the Prototype plug-in instead of jQuery. Simply modify BuildConfig.groovy to include a dependency on the plug-in:

```
// grails-app/conf/BuildConfig.groovy
grails.project.dependency.resolution = {

    ...

    plugins {
        runtime ":prototype:1.0"
        ...
    }
}
```

Now modify the <g:javascript> tag, changing the value of the library attribute to prototype:

```
<g:javascript library="prototype" />
```

In order for that to work, the jQuery JavaScript code would need to be rewritten to use the Prototype API. In addition to Prototype, there are plug-ins for Dojo, Ext-JS, and Yahoo UI. The Grails plug-ins page (http://grails.org/Plugins) provides the latest up-to-date information on the available plug-ins. While Grails makes it easy for you to specify which JavaScript library you would like to use, swapping different implementations in and out can be tedious work, as most of the JavaScript in the application will be dependent on a particular JavaScript implementation.

Asynchronous Form Submission

Now that you have had a chance to explore a trivial example, let's try something a little more challenging. When building Ajax applications, it is often useful to submit a form and its data to the server asynchronously. Currently, the login process of the gTunes application uses a regular form submission, but wouldn't it be useful if users could log in without a refresh?

The login form now contained within the grails-app/views/layouts/main.gsp layout submits using a regular form. In other words, form submission is synchronous; it doesn't occur in a background process, as an Ajax request would. The jQuery library makes it fairly easy to create a form that will submit an Ajax request.

However, before you write the jQuery code that is necessary to implement the new Ajax enabled form, let's move the code that renders the login form into its own GSP template. (The importance of doing this will become clear later.) Now create a new file, grails-app/views/user/_loginForm.gsp, which will form the basis of the template, and then cut and paste the code from the layout, so that the template looks like Listing 8-4.

Listing 8-4. The Login Template

```
<p class="legend">Log in to your gTunes account</p>
<g:form name="loginForm" url="[controller:'user',action:'login']" class="form">
    <div class="input">
        <g:textField required="true"
                     placeholder="Username"
                     name="login"
                     value="${fieldValue(bean:loginCmd, field:'login')}" />
        <g:hasErrors  bean="${loginCmd}" field="login">
        <p class="error"><g:fieldError bean="${loginCmd}" field="login" /></p>
        </g:hasErrors>
    </div>
    <div class="input">
        <g:passwordField required="true"
                     placeholder="Password"
                     name="password" />
        <g:hasErrors  bean="${loginCmd}" field="password">
        <p class="error">
            <g:fieldError bean="${loginCmd}" field="password" />
        </p>
        </g:hasErrors>
    </div>
    <div class="submit">
        <input type="submit" value="Login" class="btn" />
    </div>
</g:form>
```

Now create one more template to render the loginForm template and also render some of the markup related to creating a new account. It makes sense to group all of this markup together because the two sections (create new account and login) will always be rendered next to each other. Create a file called grails-app/views/user/_loginBox.gsp that looks like Listing 8-5.

Listing 8-5. The loginBox Template

```
<div class="left">
    <h1>Need an account?</h1>
    <p class="legend"><g:link controller="user" action="register">Signup now</g:link> to start
your own personal Music collection!</p>
    <g:link controller="user" action="register" class="btn">Signup now</g:link>
</div>
<div class="right" id="loginBox">
    <h1>Already a member?</h1>
    <g:render template="/user/loginForm"/>
</div>
```

Now within the grails-app/views/store/index.gsp layout, use the <g:render> tag to render the template, as shown in Listing 8-6.

Listing 8-6. Using the Tag to Display the Login Form

```
<g:render template="/user/loginBox"/>
```

With that done, it is time to write some jQuery code that will initiate the Ajax call and will handle the response. That code should be defined in grails-app/views/store/index.gsp. See Listing 8-7.

Listing 8-7. Ajax Login Code

```
<r:script>
$(function() {
    $('#loginForm').ajaxForm(function(result) {
        $('#loginBox').html(result);
    });
});
</r:script>
```

That code depends on the jQuery Form Plug-in from https://github.com/malsup/form. Note that is not a Grails plug-in. Download the jquery.form.js file from that repository and put it in the web-app/js/ directory. Once the file is in place, edit grails-app/conf/ApplicationResources.groovy to look like Listing 8-8.

Listing 8-8. Add jQuery Form Code to ApplicationResources.groovy

```
// grails-app/conf/ApplicationResources.groovy
modules = {
    application {
        resource url:'js/application.js'
        resource url:'js/jquery.form.js'
    }
}
```

The `ApplicationResources.groovy` file is a configuration file read by the resources plug-in. The resources plug-in helps optimize the management of static resources like JavaScript files used by your application. The code in Listing 8-8 defines a group of static resources, called a module, which contains the two JavaScript files mentioned there. The `r:script` tag from Listing 8-7 is also provided by the resources plug-in. One of the benefits of wrapping that JavaScript code in the `r:script` tag is that the resources plug-in will make sure that the JavaScript is loaded at the bottom of the rendered page, which is beneficial for optimizing page load times. The resources plug-in is discussed in more detail in Chapter 12. For now, just configure the files as described and things should work just fine.

The `ajaxForm` function from Listing 8-7 will submit an Ajax request to the login controller action and use the response to update the `loginBox` element in the DOM. No change is required to any of the input fields or the Submit button. Now if you refresh the page and try to log in, a surprising thing will happen. Surprisingly, you get the contents of the entire page placed within the `loginBox` <div>! This happens because you updated the client code but paid no attention to the server logic, which is still displaying the entire view. To correct this problem, you need to revisit the server-side code to render only a snippet of HTML instead of the entire page.

Just in case you don't recall the code in question, Listing 8-9 shows what the current code for the `login` action of the `UserController` looks like.

Listing 8-9. The Current login Action Code

```
def login(LoginCommand cmd) {
    if(request.method == 'POST') {
        if(!cmd.hasErrors()) {
            session.user = cmd.getUser()
            redirect(controller:'store')
        }
        else {
            render(view:'/store/index', model:[loginCmd:cmd])
        }
    }
    else {
        render(view:'/store/index')
    }
}
```

At the moment, the code in Listing 8-9 renders the entire `grails-app/views/store/ index.gsp` view, but you actually want only the login form displayed again (on login failure) or a welcome message displayed if the user successfully logs in. Let's refactor the code to achieve this goal; Listing 8-10 shows the result.

Listing 8-10. Handing an Ajax Login Request

```
def login(LoginCommand cmd) {
    if(request.method == 'POST') {
        if(!cmd.hasErrors()) {
            session.user = cmd.getUser()
            render template: '/user/welcomeMessage'
        }
        else {
            render template: 'loginBox', model: [loginCmd: cmd]
        }
```

```
    }
    else {
        render template: 'loginBox'
    }
}
```

You could, of course, take this further and deal with both Ajax and regular requests, but for the moment that isn't a requirement. As you can see from the code in Listing 8-10, what you're doing is using the template argument of the render method instead of the view argument, which allows you to reuse the _loginForm.gsp template. In addition, you'll need to create a grails-app/views/user/_welcomeMessage.gsp template to deal with a successful login, the contents of which you can see in Listing 8-11.

Listing 8-11. The _welcomeMessage.gsp Template

```
<header id="header">
    <h1 id="logo"><a href="${createLink(uri: '/')}">gTune</a></h1>
    <g:if test="${session?.user}">
        <div id="quickaccess"><a href="#">${session?.user?.firstName}</a>, <g:link
controller="user" action="logout">Logout</g:link></div>
        <nav id="navigation" class="clearfix">
            <ul>
                <li class="separator"><g:link controller="user" action="music">My
Music</g:link></li>
                <li><g:link controller="store" action="shop">The Store</g:link></li>
            </ul>
        </nav>
    </g:if>
</header>
<div id="message notice">
    <div style="margin-top:20px">
        Welcome back
        <span id="userFirstName">${session?.user?.firstName}!</span>
        <br><br>

        You have purchased
        (${session.user.purchasedSongs?.size() ?: 0}) songs.
        <br>
    </div>
</div>
```

The last bit of work is modify the main Sitemesh layout to take advantage of the newly created welcomeMessage template, as shown in Listing 8-12.

Listing 8-12. Updated Main Sitemesh Layout

```
<body class="application">

    <div id="container">
        <div id="spinner" class="spinner" style="display:none;">
            <img src="${createLinkTo(dir:'images',file:'spinner.gif')}" alt="Spinner" />
        </div>
        <div id="main">
```

```
            <g:if test="${session?.user}">
                <g:render template="/user/welcomeMessage"/>
            </g:if>
            <g:layoutBody />
            <g:javascript library="application"/>
        </div>

        <footer id="footer">
            © gTunes 2012
        </footer>
    </div>
    <r:layoutResources />
</body>
```

Fun with Ajax Remote Linking

In an earlier example you implemented a bit of functionality that displayed the current time when the anchor tag was clicked (not exactly groundbreaking stuff, we know). Let's correct this by looking at a more advanced example.

In Chapter 5, you created a few panels for the right side of the gTunes store; they displayed the newest additions to the gTunes library for songs, albums, and artists, respectively. As a refresher, Listing 8-13 shows the code in question from the grails-app/views/store/shop.gsp file.

Listing 8-13. The Latest Content Panel

```
<div id="top5Panel" class="top5Panel">
    <h2>Latest Albums</h2>
    <div id="albums" class="top5Item">
        <g:render template="/album/albumList"
                model="[albums: top5Albums]" />
    </div>
    <h2>Latest Songs</h2>
    <div id="songs" class="top5Item">
        <g:render template="/song/songList" model="[songs: top5Songs]" />
    </div>
    <h2>Newest Artists</h2>
    <div id="artists" class="top5Item">
    <g:render template="/artist/artistList"
            model="[artists: top5Artists]" />
    </div>
</div>
```

Each of these uses a specific template to render a simple HTML unordered list for each category. It would be nice if the list items, instead of being plain text, consisted of HTML links that used Ajax to display details about the Album, Song, or Artist in question.

Let's start with Album. If you recall from the domain model, an Album has a title, release year, genre, artist, and a list of Songs that apply to that album. To begin with, create a template that can render that information. Listing 8-14 shows the grails-app/views/album/_album.gsp template.

Listing 8-14. Implementing the _album.gsp Template

```
<div id="album${album.id}" class="album">
    <div class="albumDetails">
                <div class="artistName">${artist.name}</div>
                <div class="albumTitle">${album.title}</div>
                <div class="albumInfo">
            Genre: ${album.genre ?: 'Other'}<br>
                Year: ${album.year}
                </div>
        <div class="albumTracks">
            <ol>
                <g:each in="${album.songs?}" var="song">
                    <li>${song.title}</li>
                </g:each>
            </ol>
                </div>
        <div class="albumLinks">
    </div>
</div>
```

Now that you have a template, you can alter the `grails-app/views/album/_albumList.gsp` template to use jQuery to call a controller action, `display`, on the `AlbumController` for each item in the list. Listing 8-15 shows (in bold) the changes made to the `_albumList.gsp` template.

Listing 8-15. Updating _albumList.gsp to use jQuery links

```
<ul>
    <g:each in="${albums?}" var="album">
        <li><g:link update="musicPanel"
                    controller="album"
                    action="display"
                    id="${album.id}"
                    elementId=="albumLink${album.id}">${album.title}</g:link></li>
        <r:script>
            $('#albumLink${album.id}').click(function() {
                $('#musicPanel').load(this.href);
                return false;
            });
        </r:script>
    </g:each>
</ul>
```

Once again you see that the JavaScript code is wrapped in the `r:script` tag, which causes all of the JavaScript to be loaded at the end of the page for performance reasons. If a page includes several uses of the `r:script` tag, all that code is merged into a single script tag at the bottom of the page.

Notice how you can use the `update` attribute to specify that you want the contents of the response to be placed into an HTML `<div>` that has a DOM ID with the value `musicPanel`. If you refresh the page at this point and try the links, you'll notice that the Ajax part of the picture is working already! The downside is that since there is no display action in the `AlbumController` at this point, you get a 404 "Page not found" error from the server.

Let's correct that by opening AlbumController and implementing the display action. Listing 8-16 shows the code, which simply obtains the Album instance using the id parameter from the params object and then uses it to render the _album.gsp template developed in Listing 8-14.

Listing 8-16. *The display Action of AlbumController*

```
def display() {
    def album = Album.get(params.id)
    if(album) {
        def artist = album.artist
        render(template:"album", model:[artist:artist, album:album])
    } else {
        render "Album not found."
    }
}
```

By adding a bit of CSS magic to enhance the look of the _album.gsp template, all of a sudden you have album details being obtained via Ajax and rendered to the view. Figure 8-2 shows the result of your hard work.

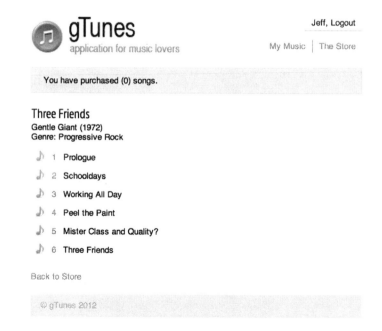

Figure 8-2. *Displaying albums using Ajax*

Sadly, even with the CSS enhancements, Album details are looking a bit bland with all that text. Wouldn't it be nice to be able to display the album art for each album? Where there is a will, there is a way—luckily, Apple has come to the rescue here by providing a REST-based web service that lets developers look up album art from its massive pool of assets. The service is available at http://itunes.

apple.com/search. Open that URL in a web browser and you should see a response that looks something like this:

```
{
 "resultCount":0,
 "results": []
}
```

That doesn't look very interesting. Certainly it doesn't look like anything that will help you display album artwork in gTunes. What is shown there is the JSON response to our request. The problem is that we didn't really request anything useful, and so we didn't *get* anything useful. Let's make it a little more interesting by including some request parameters. Try http://itunes.apple.com/search?media=music&entity=album&attribute=albumTerm&term=Church+Of+Broken+Glass. That URL includes several request parameters.

Event Name	Description	Value
media	the media type to search for	music
entity	the type of results you want returned	album
attribute	the attribute you want to search for	albumTerm
term	the URL-encoded search criteria	Church+Of+Broken+Glass

To summarize, the request URL above is searching for music for an album titled *Church of Broken Glass*. That request should yield a response that looks something like this:

```
{
 "resultCount":1,
 "results": [
{"wrapperType":"collection", "collectionType":"Album", "artistId":80907270,
"collectionId":293455812, "amgArtistId":512604, "artistName":"Hammers of Misfortune",
"collectionName":"Church of Broken Glass", "collectionCensoredName":"Church of Broken Glass",
"artistViewUrl":"https://itunes.apple.com/us/artist/hammers-of-misfortune/id80907270?uo=4",
"collectionViewUrl":"https://itunes.apple.com/us/album/church-of-broken-glass/id293455812?uo=4",
"artworkUrl60":"http://a397.phobos.apple.com/us/r30/Music/98/da/c2/mzi.wvlbbglb.60x60-50.jpg",
"artworkUrl100":"http://a862.phobos.apple.com/us/r30/Music/98/da/c2/mzi.wvlbbglb.100x100-75.
jpg", "collectionPrice":9.99, "collectionExplicitness":"notExplicit", "trackCount":5,
"copyright":" 2008 Hammers of Misfortune", "country":"USA", "currency":"USD",
"releaseDate":"2008-09-30T07:00:00Z", "primaryGenreName":"Rock"}]
}
```

That response includes a lot of information—more than we need—but we can ignore most of it and pull out just what we do need: the value of the artworkUrl100 attribute—http://a862.phobos.apple.com/us/r30/Music/98/da/c2/mzi.wvlbbglb.100x100-75.jpg, in this case. That value represents a URL to the corresponding album artwork.

The API supports a lot of other search options, but those listed above are all you need to satisfy our requirements. More complete documentation of the search service is available at www.apple.com/itunes/affiliates/resources/documentation/itunes-store-web-service-search-api.html.

With that done, it is time to create your first tag library. You'll create an AlbumArtTagLib that deals with obtaining album art from Amazon. To do this, start by running the create-tag-lib command:

```
grails> create-tag-lib com.gtunes.AlbumArt
| Created file grails-app/taglib/com/gtunes/AlbumArtTagLib.groovy
| Created file test/unit/com/gtunes/AlbumArtTagLibTests.groovy
grails>
```

The create-tag-lib command will create a new empty AlbumArtTagLib that resembles Listing 8-17.

Listing 8-17. The AlbumArtTagLib Template

```
package com.gtunes
class AlbumArtTagLib {
}
```

The tag library is going to provide a custom GSP tag which will invoke the REST web service to retrieve the album artwork URL and then output an img tag which points to that URL. There is a Grails plug-in named rest-client-builder; it provides a RestBuilder class that makes it very easy to invoke a REST service and deal with the response. To use the plug-in, we need to add code to BuildConfig.groovy to express a dependency on the plug-in.

```
// grails-app/conf/BuildConfig.groovy

grails.project.dependency.resolution = {

    ...

    plugins {
        compile ":rest-client-builder:1.0.2"
        ...
    }
}
```

Using the RestBuilder class provided by the rest-client-builder plug-in is quite simple. (The plug-in's full documentation is at http://grails.org/plugin/rest-client-builder; we'll cover the basics here.) The RestBuilder class has an instance method, named get, which accepts a String argument; that argument should be a URL that points to the service you want to invoke. The method returns a response that will have a json property, a Grails JSONObject that represents an unordered collection of name/value pairs parsed out of the JSON response. Listing 8-18 shows a simple usage.

Listing 8-18. Using the RestClient

```
def restBuilder = new RestBuilder()
def url = "http://someserver.com/someService"
def response = restBuilder.get(url)
def json = response.json
def someAttributeValue = json.someAttribute
```

Our tag will need to use the RestBuilder to invoke the service to retrieve the album artwork URL and pull the artworkUrl100 value out of the response. Listing 8-19 shows a complete working version of the tag.

Listing 8-19. *The AlbumArtTagLib*

```
package com.gtunes

import grails.plugins.rest.client.RestBuilder

class AlbumArtTagLib {

  static final DEFAULT_ALBUM_ART_IMAGE =  "/images/no-album-art.gif"

  static namespace = "music"

  def albumArt =  { attrs, body ->
    def artistName = attrs.remove('artist')?.toString()
    def albumTitle = attrs.remove('album')?.toString()
    def width = attrs.int('width', 100)
    attrs.remove('width')
    def albumArt = DEFAULT_ALBUM_ART_IMAGE
    if(artistName && albumTitle) {
      try {
        def restBuilder = new RestBuilder()
        def url = "http://itunes.apple.com/search?term=${albumTitle.encodeAsURL()}&media=music&e
ntity=album&attribute=albumTerm"
        def response = restBuilder.get(url)
        def json = response.json
        // retrieve the list of search results
        def records = json.results

        // find the record that has the correct
        // artist name and album title, note that
        // the service will return records that are
        // not an exact match
        def matchingRecord = records.find { r ->
          r.artistName == artistName && r.collectionName == albumTitle
        }
        albumArt = matchingRecord?.artworkUrl100 ?: DEFAULT_ALBUM_ART_IMAGE
      } catch (Exception e) {
        log.error "Problem retrieving artwork: ${e.message}", e
      }
    }
    if(albumArt.startsWith("/")) albumArt = "${request.contextPath}${albumArt}"
    out << "<img width=\"$width\" src=\"${albumArt}\" border=\"0\""
    out << attrs.collect { attributeName, attributeValue ->
      " ${attributeName}=\"${attributeValue.encodeAsHTML()}\""
    }.join(' ')
    out << "></img>"
  }
}
```

Note that having all of this logic inside a GSP tag is not ideal. This will be refactored later in Chapter 10, but for now this code will suffice.

Listing 8-20 shows a unit test for the AlbumArtTagLib.

Listing 8-20. The AlbumArtTagLibTests

```
package com.gtunes

import grails.plugins.rest.client.RestBuilder

import grails.test.mixin.*
import org.junit.*

@TestFor(AlbumArtTagLib)
class AlbumArtTagLibTests {

  void testNoAlbumSpecified() {
    assert applyTemplate('<music:albumArt artist="Tool" />') == """<img width="100"
src="${AlbumArtTagLib.DEFAULT_ALBUM_ART_IMAGE}" border="0"></img>"""
  }

  void testNoArtistSpecified() {
    assert applyTemplate('<music:albumArt album="Lateralus" />') == """<img width="100"
src="${AlbumArtTagLib.DEFAULT_ALBUM_ART_IMAGE}" border="0"></img>"""
    }

  void testGoodResult() {
    def artworkClient = new groovy.mock.interceptor.MockFor(RestBuilder)
    artworkClient.demand.get { String s ->
      def results = []
      results << [artistName: 'Thin Lizzy',
                  collectionName: 'Jailbreak',
                  artworkUrl100: 'http://somesite/jailbreak.jpg']
      results << [artistName: 'Tool',
                  collectionName: 'Lateralus',
                  artworkUrl100: 'http://somesite/lateralus.jpg']
      [json: [results: results]]
      }
    artworkClient.use {
      assert applyTemplate('<music:albumArt artist="Tool" album="Lateralus" />') == '<img
width="100" src="http://somesite/lateralus.jpg" border="0"></img>'
  }
}

  void testSpecifyingImageWidth() {
    def artworkClient = new groovy.mock.interceptor.MockFor(RestBuilder)
    artworkClient.demand.get { String s ->
      def results = []
      results << [artistName: 'Thin Lizzy',
                  collectionName: 'Jailbreak',
                  artworkUrl100: 'http://somesite/jailbreak.jpg']
      results << [artistName: 'Tool',
                  collectionName: 'Lateralus',
```

```
                    artworkUrl100: 'http://somesite/lateralus.jpg']
        [json: [results: results]]
    }
    artworkClient.use {
      assert applyTemplate('<music:albumArt artist="Tool" album="Lateralus" width="50"/>') ==
'<img width="50" src="http://somesite/lateralus.jpg" border="0"></img>'
    }
  }
}
```

Finally, to put all the pieces together, you need to change the grails-app/views/ album/_album.gsp template so that it can leverage the newly created <music:albumArt> tag. Listing 8-21 shows the amendments to _album.gsp in bold.

Listing 8-21. *Adding Album Art to the _album.gsp Template*

```
<div id="album${album.id}" class="album"> <div class="albumArt">
    <music:albumArt artist="${artist}" album="${album}" />
</div> ... </div>
```

After further CSS trickery, Figure 8-3 shows what the new album art integration looks like. Much better!

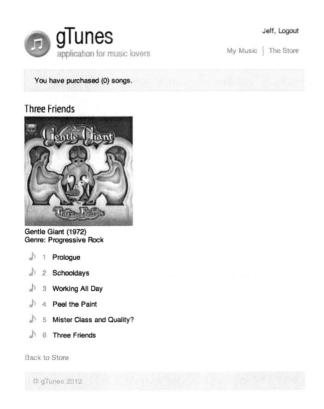

Figure 8-3. *The album.gsp template with integrated album art*

Adding Effects and Animation

What's been achieved so far is pretty neat, but it would be useful to spice it up with a few effects. Say you want albums to fade in when you click the "Latest Album" links; the first thing to do is to make sure albums are hidden to begin with. To do so, open the grails-app/views/ album/_album.gsp template, and ensure the main HTML <div> has its style attribute set to display:none, as in Listing 8-22.

Listing 8-22. Hiding the Album

```
<div id="album${album.id}" class="album" style="display:none;">
... </div>
```

Now you can use jQuery's fadeIn capability to execute the effect. Try adding the following to the bottom of album.gsp:

```
<g:javascript>
    $('#album${album.id}').fadeIn('slow');
</g:javascript>
```

This executes the fade-in effect of the jQuery library. Now whenever one of the "Latest Album" links is clicked, the album fades in nicely. Most notable Ajax libraries—many of which offer Grails plug-ins—feature similar capabilities. Make sure you explore what is available in your Ajax library of choice!

Ajax-Enabled Form Fields

That previous section was quite an adventure, wasn't it? You're not done with Ajax yet. In this section, you'll learn how you can enable Ajax on form fields such as text inputs.

This is often useful if you're implementing features such as autocomplete or an instant search capability like Spotlight on Mac OS X. In fact, search is exactly what you're going to aim to achieve in this section. Sure, it is useful to be able to click the latest additions to the music library, but it is critical that users of gTunes can search the back catalog of songs and albums.

Luckily, jQuery can be used to help implement the search feature. As a start, open the grails-app/views/store/shop.gsp view. In this file you need to define a text field to accept search input and write some jQuery code that will respond to input by invoking the search action, as shown in Listing 8-23.

Listing 8-23. Using the <g:remoteField> Tag

```
<div id="searchBox">
    <h1>Instant Search</h1>
    <g:textField id="searchField" name="searchField"/>
    <div id="searchResults" name="musicPanel"></div>
</div>
<r:script>
$("#searchField").keyup(function() {
    $("#searchResults").load("${createLink(action: 'search')}?q="+this.value);
});
</r:script>
```

Here, you have set up a text field that has a keyup event listener associated with it; it sends a request to the search action of the StoreController.

Instant Search

Figure 8-4. The gTunes instance search box

If you refresh the page and start typing, you'll see that the field is already sending remote requests, although you're getting 404 errors in the page rather than anything useful. At this point, it is worth considering how to implement a search. You could, of course, use Hibernate queries, but Hibernate is not really designed to be used as a search engine, and designing your own search query language would be a pain.

The Grails plug-in system comes to the rescue once again! One of the most popular plug-ins currently available for Grails is the Searchable plug-in, which builds on Compass (`http://www.compass-project.org/`) and Lucene (`http://lucene.apache.org/`).

■ **Note** This example will demonstrate the most basic capabilities of the searchable plug-in. The full documentation is available at `http://grails.org/plugin/searchable`.

As usual, installing Searchable is a trivial matter. Add the dependency to `BuildConfig.groovy`:

```
// grails-app/conf/BuildConfig.groovy
grails.project.dependency.resolution = {

    ...

    plugins {
        runtime ":searchable:0.6.4"
        ...
    }
}
```

The Searchable plug-in integrates with Grails by providing the ability to expose Grails domain classes as searchable entities. At a simple level, it is possible to add search capabilities by adding the following line to the domain class you want to search:

```
static searchable = true
```

However, it is typically the case that you want to search only a subset of the properties of the domain class. This is, of course, perfectly possible with Searchable, and in fact it defines an entire DSL for mapping between your classes and the search index (a topic beyond the scope of this book).

In this case, you'll want to search on an album or song's genre and title and on an artist's name. Listing 8-24 shows how to enable these searches using Searchable.

Listing 8-24. Enabling Search on the gTunes Domain

```
class Song {
    static searchable = [only: ['genre', 'title']]
    ...
}
```

```
class Album {
    static searchable = [only: ['genre', 'title']]
    ...
}
class Artist {
    static searchable = [only: ['name']]
    ...
}
```

Simple enough. Next, let's implement the search action of the StoreController. Like GORM, Searchable provides a bunch of new methods on domain classes that support searching, including the following:

- search: returns a search result object containing a subset of objects matching the query

- searchTop: returns the first result object matching the query

- searchEvery: returns all result objects matching the query

- countHits: returns the number of hits for a query

- termFreqs: returns term frequencies for the terms in the index (advanced)

For full data on what each method does and how it behaves, refer to the searchable documentation mentioned above. For your needs, you're going to use the search method to formulate the search results. Listing 8-25 shows the implementation of the search action of the StoreController using Searchable APIs.

Listing 8-25. Using Searchable to Enable Search

```
def search(String q) {
    def searchResults = [:]
    if(q) {
        searchResults.artistResults = trySearch { Artist.search("*${q}*", [max: 10]) }
        searchResults.albumResults = trySearch { Album.search("*${q}*", [max: 10]) }
        searchResults.songResults = trySearch { Song.search("*${q}*", [max: 10]) }
    }
    render template: 'searchResults', model: searchResults
}

private trySearch(Closure callable) {
    try {
        return callable()
    } catch (Exception e) {
        log.debug "Search Error: ${e.message}", e
        return []
    }
}
```

The code is pretty simple. It obtains the q parameter representing the query and, if it isn't blank, builds a model that contains search results for albums, artists, and songs. One interesting aspect of this code is the trySearch method, which demonstrates a compelling use of Groovy closures to deal with exceptions. Since an exception will likely be the result of an error in the search syntax, it is preferable to log that error and return an empty result than throw the error back to the user.

Once the search results have been formulated within a searchResults variable, the code renders a _
searchResults.gsp template, passing the searchResults as the model. As Listing 8-26 demonstrates, the
grails-app/views/store/_searchResults.gsp template is trivial; it simply reuses such existing templates
as _albumList.gsp and _artistList.gsp to display results.

Listing 8-26. The _searchResults.gsp Template

```
<div id="searchResults" class="searchResults">
  <g:if test="${albumResults?.results}">
    <div id="albumResults" class="resultsPane">
      <h2>Album Search Results</h2>
      <g:render template="/album/albumList"
                model="[albums:albumResults.results]">
      </g:render>
    </div>
  </g:if>
  <g:if test="${artistResults?.results}">
    <div id="artistResults" class="resultsPane">
      <h2>Artist Search Results</h2>
      <g:render template="/artist/artistList"
                model="[artists:artistResults.results]">
      </g:render>
    </div>
  </g:if>
  <g:if test="${songResults?.results}">
    <div id="songResults" class="resultsPane">
      <h2>Song Search Results</h2>
      <g:render template="/song/songList"
                model="[songs:songResults.results]">
      </g:render>
    </div>
  </g:if>
</div>
```

Having called on your CSS prowess once more, you now have nicely formulated search results
appearing, and even better, because they're using the same <g:remoteLink> tag as the "Latest Albums" lists
on the right of the screen, they're Ajax-enabled right out of the box. Simply by clicking one of the search
results, you get an Album's details pulled in via Ajax! Figure 8-5 shows the use of the search box and
demonstrates how wildcard capabilities using the asterisk (*) character are supported thanks to the
Searchable plug-in.

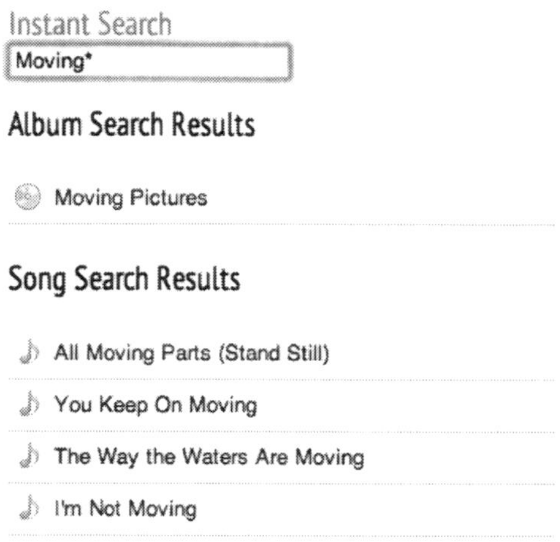

Instant Search

Moving*

Album Search Results

Moving Pictures

Song Search Results

All Moving Parts (Stand Still)

You Keep On Moving

The Way the Waters Are Moving

I'm Not Moving

Figure 8-5. *Instant search results using <g:remoteField> and Searchable*

A Note on Ajax and Performance

It is important to note the impact that using Ajax has on an application's performance. Given the number of small snippets of code that get rendered, it will come as little surprise that badly designed Ajax applications have to deal with a significantly larger number of requests. What you have seen so far in this chapter is a naive approach to Ajax development. You have waved the Ajax magic wand over your application with little consideration of the performance implications.

Nevertheless, it is not too late to take some of these things into account. You can use several techniques to reduce the number of requests an Ajax application performs before you start throwing more hardware at the problem.

Remember that an Ajax call is a remote network call and therefore expensive. Things such as the Data Transfer Object (DTO) are applicable in the Ajax world. Fundamentally, the DTO pattern serves as a mechanism for batching operations into a single call and passing enough state to the server for several operations to be executed at once. This pattern can be equally effective in Ajax, given that it is better to do one call that transmits a lot of information than a dozen small ones.

Another popular technique is to move more complexity onto the client. Given that Ajax clients, in general, occupy a single physical page, a fair amount of state can be kept on the client via caching. Caching is probably the most important technique in Ajax development and, where possible, should be exploited to optimize communications with the server.

Whichever technique you use, it will pay dividends in the long run, and the server infrastructure guys will love you for it. The users of your application will also appreciate its faster response times and interactivity.

Summary

In this chapter, you learned about the extensive range of adaptive Ajax tags that Grails offers and how to apply them to give your gTunes application a more usable interactive interface. On this particular journey, you also explored advanced Grails development, learning a lot more about how controllers, templates, and the render method function in combination.

In the past few chapters, you've been very much involved with the web layer of Grails in the shape of controllers, GSP, tag libraries, and Ajax. However, everything you have looked at so far has used completely stateless communication. In the next chapter, you'll look at how Grails supports web flows for rich conversations that span multiple pages.

CHAPTER 9

GORM

As you may have garnered from this book's table of contents, the persistence layer of Grails is a critical part of the picture. In Chapter 3 you were given a surface-level understanding of what domain classes are and how they map onto the underlying database. In this chapter you'll plunge headfirst into the inner workings of GORM.

As a starting point, you'll learn about the basic persistence operations involved in reading and writing objects from a database. After going through the basics, you'll then be taken through the semantics of GORM, including as many corner cases and surprises as we're able to fit into a single chapter.

Persistence Basics

Fortunately, we won't be spending long on the foundations, since you've already been exposed to the basics of GORM. Nevertheless, as a recap, let's take a look at the basic read operations provided by GORM.

Reading Objects

Each domain class is automatically enhanced with a number of methods that allow you to query for domain instances. The simplest of these is the get method, which takes the identifier of a domain class and returns either an instance or null if no instance was found in the database. Listing 9-1 shows a simple example, highlighted in bold, from the AlbumController you've already developed.

Listing 9-1. Using the get Method

```
class AlbumController {
    def show() {
        def album = Album.get(params.id)
        if(album) {
        }
    }
}
```

In addition to the simple get method, there is also a getAll method, which can take several identifiers and return a List of instances. You can specify the identifiers as a List or using varargs; for example:

```
def albums = Album.getAll(1,2,3)
```

When using the get method, the object is loaded from the database in a modifiable state. In other words, you can make changes to the object, which then get persisted to the database. If you want to load an object in a read-only state, you can use the read method instead:

```
def album = Album.read(params.id)
```

In this case, the Album instance returned cannot be modified. Any changes you make to the object will not be persisted. There is also a performance benefit because Hibernate does not have to keep track of which properties have changed (dirty checking).

Listing, Sorting, and Counting

A common way to retrieve items from a database is to simply list them. Clearly, it is not always desirable to list every instance, and the order in which they are returned is often important. GORM provides a list() method, which takes a number of named arguments, including max, offset, sort, and order, to customize the results, the definitions of which are listed here:

- max: the maximum number of instances to return

- offset: the offset relative to 0 of the first result to return

- sort: the property name to sort by

- order: the order of the results, either asc or desc for ascending and descending order, respectively

In addition to list(), often used in combination with it, is the count() method, which counts the total number of instances in the database. To demonstrate these, let's look at some examples of their usage (see Listing 9-2).

Listing 9-2. Using the list() Method

```
// get all the albums;  careful,  there might be many!
def allAlbums = Album.list()
// get the ten most recently created albums
def topTen = Album.list(max:10,  sort:'dateCreated',  order:'desc')
// get the total number of albums
def totalAlbums = Album.count()
```

As you can imagine, it is fairly simple to use the list() method to perform the pagination of results by customizing the offset argument. In addition, there is a set of listOrderBy* methods that are variations on the list() method.

The listOrderBy* methods provide an example where each method uses the properties on the class itself in the method signatures. They are unique to each domain class, but it is just a matter of understanding the convention to use them. Listing 9-3 is an example that lists all Album instances, ordered by the dateCreated property, simply by invoking the listOrderByDateCreated() method.

Listing 9-3. Using listOrderBy

```
// all albums ordered by creation date
def allByDate = Album.listOrderByDateCreated()
```

Using standard bean conventions, the property name, starting with a capital letter, is appended to the end of the method signature. You'll see more examples of this later in the chapter when we cover dynamic finders, including a variation of the count method.

Saving, Updating, and Deleting

As you've seen already, objects can be persisted by calling the save() method. For example, the code in Listing 9-4 demonstrates how to persist an instance of the Album class, assuming it validates successfully.

Listing 9-4. Saving an Instance

```
def album = new Album(params)
album.save()
```

We'll have more to say about how GORM persists objects to the database in "The Semantics of GORM," later in this chapter. For now, all you need to know is that at some point the underlying Hibernate engine will execute an SQL INSERT to persist the Album instance to the database. Updating objects is strikingly similar; doing so involves calling the same save() method on an existing persistent instance, as shown in Listing 9-5.

Listing 9-5. Updating an Instance

```
def album = Album.get(1)
album.title = "The Changed Title"
album.save()
```

When the save() method is called, Hibernate automatically works out whether it should issue an SQL INSERT or an SQL UPDATE. Occasionally, on certain older databases, Hibernate may get this decision wrong and issue an UPDATE when it should be doing an INSERT. You can get around this by passing an explicit insert argument to the save() method:

```
album.save(insert:true)
```

As for deleting objects, this is done with the delete() method:

```
album.delete()
```

That's the simple stuff. Next you'll be looking in more detail at associations in GORM and how those work.

Associations

Chapter 3 already provided some detail on GORM associations in their different incarnations, but there is a lot more to the associations that GORM supports. In a typical one-to-many association such as the songs property of the Album class, the type is a java.util.Set. If you recall, the semantics of Set as defined by javadoc don't allow duplicates and have no order. However, you may want an association to have a particular order.

One option is to use a SortedSet, which requires you to implement the Comparable interface for any item placed into the SortedSet. For example, Listing 9-6 shows how to sort tracks by the trackNumber property.

Listing 9-6. Using SortedSet to Sort Associations

```
class Album {
    ...
    SortedSet songs
}
```

```
class Song implements Comparable {
    ...
    int compareTo(o) {
        if(this.trackNumber > o.trackNumber) {
            return 1
        } else if(this.trackNumber < o.trackNumber) {
            return -1
        }
        return 0
    }
}
```

Alternatively, you can specify the sort order declaratively, using the mapping property introduced in Chapter 3. For example, if you want to sort Song instances by track number for all queries, you can do so with the sort method:

```
class Song {
    ...
    static mapping = {
        sort "trackNumber"
    }
}
```

You may not want to sort by the trackNumber property for every query or association, in which case you can apply sorting to the songs association of the Album class only:

```
static mapping = {
    songs sort: "trackNumber"
}
```

Another way to change the way sorting is done is to use a different collection type, such as java.util. List. Unlike a Set, a List allows duplicates and retains the order in which objects are placed into the List. To support List associations, Hibernate uses a special index column that contains the index of each item in the List. Listing 9-7 shows an example of using a List for the songs association.

Listing 9-7. Using a List Association

```
class Album {
    ...
    List songs
}
```

Set associations have no concept of order, but with a List you can index into a specific entry; for example:

```
println album.songs[0]
```

GORM also supports associations being stored in a Hibernate Bag. A Bag is not necessarily ordered and doesn't have to guarantee uniqueness; for those reasons, it may be more performant for a lot of situations. To use a Bag, declare the property—like the List declared in Listing 9-7—but use the type java. util.Collection instead of java.util.List.

Finally, GORM also supports Map associations where the key is a String. Simply change the type from List to Map in the example in Listing 9-7 and use a String instead of an Integer to access entries. For both List and Map collection types, Grails creates an index column. In the case of a List, the index column holds a numeric value that signifies its position in the List, while for a Map the index column holds the Map key.

Relationship Management Methods

As well as giving you the ability to map associations to the database, GORM also automatically provides you with methods to manage those associations. The addTo* and removeFrom* dynamic methods allow you to add and remove entries from an association. Additionally, both methods return the instance they are called on, thus allowing you to chain method calls. Listing 9-8 shows an example of using the addToSongs method of the Album class.

Listing 9-8. Using Relationship Management Methods

```
new Album(title:"Odelay",
        artist:beck,
        year:1996)
        .addToSongs(title:"Devil's Haircut",
                    artist:beck, duration:342343)
        .addToSongs(title:"Hotwax", artist:beck, duration:490583)
        ...
        .save()
```

As you see from the example, you can pass just the Song values as named parameters to the addToSongs method; GORM will automatically instantiate a new instance and add it to the songs association. Alternatively, if you already have a Song instance, you can simply pass that into the addToSongs method.

Transitive Persistence

Whenever you save, update, or delete an instance in GORM, the operation can cascade to any associated objects. The default cascade behavior in GORM is dictated by the belongsTo property first discussed in Chapter 3. For example, if the Song class belongsTo the Album class, then whenever an Album instance is deleted, all of the associated Song instances are deleted too. If there is no belongsTo definition in an association, then saves and updates cascade, but deletes don't.

If you need more control over the cascading behavior, you can customize it, using the cascade method of the mapping block, as shown in Listing 9-9.

Listing 9-9. Customizing the Cascading Behavior

```
class Album {
    ...
    static mapping = {
        songs cascade:'save-udpate'
    }
}
```

A special cascade style, delete-orphan, exists in case you want a child object deleted if it is removed from an association but not deleted explicitly.

▓ **Tip** For information on available cascade options, see the related section in the Hibernate documentation: http://docs.jboss.org/hibernate/core/3.6/reference/en-US/html/objectstate. html#objectstate-transitive.

Querying

Pretty much every nontrivial application will need to query persistent data. With the underlying storage medium of choice being the database, the typical way to achieve this historically has been with SQL. Relational database systems, with their tables and columns, are significantly different enough from Java objects that abstracting data access has been a long-term struggle for many an ORM vendor.

Hibernate provides an elegant enough Java API for querying objects stored in a database, but GORM moves up to the next level by completely abstracting the bulk of data access logic. Don't expect to see many dependencies on the org.hibernate package in your codebase, because GORM nicely abstracts the details of interaction with Hibernate. In the next few sections, we'll cover the different ways you can query with GORM, from dynamic finders to criteria GORM.

Note that while relational database systems are the most common type of database for Grails applications, there are numerous so-called NoSQL databases gaining popularity and GORM has great support for dealing with many of these. MongoDB is one of the more popular. See http://grails.org/plugin/mongodb for more information about using GORM with MongoDB.

Dynamic Finders

Dynamic finders are among the most powerful concepts of GORM; as with the previously mentioned listOrderBy* method, they use the property names of the class to perform queries. However, they are even more flexible than this, because they allow logical queries such as And, Or, and Not to form so-called method expressions. There can be hundreds of combinations for any given class, but, again, they're fairly simple to remember if you know the convention. Let's look at an example of the findBy* method first (see Figure 9-1), which locates a unique instance for the specified method expression.

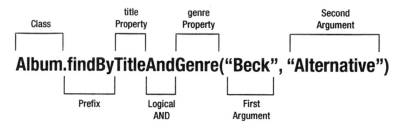

Figure 9-1. *Basic dynamic finder syntax*

The diagram uses the title and genre properties to look up an Album instance. There is a logical And expression in the middle to ensure both values need to be equal in the query. This could be replaced with a logical Or to look up an Album that either has a title of Beck or has a genre of Alternative.

We have, however, only brushed on what is possible with dynamic finders and method expressions. Dynamic finders support a wide range of expressions that allow GreaterThan, LessThan, Like, and Between queries, to name just a few, simply by appending an additional expression on the end of the property name. Listing 9-10 shows some of these in action.

Listing 9-10. Dynamic Finders in Action

```
// retrieve an album where the title contains 'Shake'
def album = Album.findByTitleLike('%Shake%')

// get an album created in last 10 days
def today = new Date()
def last10Days = Album.findByDateCreatedBetween(today-10,today)

// first album that is not 'Rock'
def somethingElse = Album.findByGenreNotEqual('Rock')
```

Table 9-1 illustrates all the possible expressions that can be appended, the number of arguments they expect, and an example of each in action.

Table 9-1. Available Dynamic Finder Method Expressions

Expression	Arguments	Example
Between	2	Album.findByDateCreatedBetween(today-10,today)
Equals	1	Album.findByTitleEquals('Aha Shake Heartbreak')
GreaterThan	1	Album.findByDateCreatedGreaterThan(lastMonth)
GreaterThanOrEqual	1	Album.findByDateCreatedGreaterThanOrEqual(lastMonth)
Ilike	1	Album.findByTitleIlike('shake')
InList	1	Album.findByTitleInList(['Aha Shake Heartbreak', 'Odelay'])
IsNull	0	Album.findByGenreIsNull()
IsNotNull	0	Album.findByGenreIsNotNull()
LessThan	1	Album.findByDateCreatedLessThan(lastMonth)
LessThanOrEqual	1	Album.findByDateCreatedLessThanOrEqual(lastMonth)
Like	1	Album.findByTitleLike('Shake')
NotEqual	1	Album.findByTitleNotEqual('Odelay')
Rlike	1	Album.findByTitleRlike(/F.*/)

The findBy* method has two cousins that accept the same method expressions you've already seen. The first is findAllBy*, which retrieves all the instances that match the method expression as a java.util. List. Finally, there is the countBy* method, which returns the total number of instances found by the method expression as an integer. It is worth opening up the Grails console, by typing grails console in a command window, and playing with these methods to experiment with the different combinations and discover just how easy they are to use.

You'll find that GORM's dynamic finders pretty much eliminate the need for a Data Access Object (DAO) layer, which you typically need in Java applications. Remember those? No? OK, well, the process is something like this:

1. Define an interface for the data access logic. The signatures will look strikingly like the dynamic finder methods you've seen so far.

2. Implement the interface using a Java class.

3. Use Spring (or your IoC container of choice) to wire in dependencies, such as the data source or Hibernate Session.

If you think about it, data access logic is extremely repetitive and heavily violates the DRY principles Grails is founded on. Luckily, with GORM and its dynamic finders, you can forget the DAO.

In the next section, you'll explore how Grails makes criteria more accessible via concise builder syntax.

Criteria Queries

Possibly one of the most powerful mechanisms for querying utilizes criteria. Criteria use a builder syntax for creating queries using Groovy's builder support. A builder in Groovy is essentially a hierarchy of method calls and closures; it is perfect for "building" treelike structures such as XML documents or a graphical user interface (GUI). Builders are also good candidates for constructing queries, particularly dynamic queries, which are often constructed with the horrifically error-prone StringBuffer.

The Hibernate Criteria API is meant to reduce the risk of errors by providing a programmatic way to construct "criteria" queries. However, Groovy's expressive syntax and powerful metaprogramming support has taken this to a new level of conciseness. Let's start by looking at basic usage patterns of criteria, after which we can move on to some more advanced examples.

Before you can perform a criteria query, you need a criteria instance for the class you want to query. To facilitate this, GORM provides a createCriteria static method on each domain class. Once you have acquired the criteria instance, one of four methods can be invoked, each of which expects a closure argument:

- get: locates a unique instance for the query

- list: returns a list of instances for the query

- scroll: returns a ScrollableResults instance for the query

- count: returns the total results as an integer for the query

The most common use case involves the list() method on the criteria instance to perform the query, as shown in Listing 9-11.

Listing 9-11. A Simple Criteria Query

```
def c = Album.createCriteria()
def results = c.list {
    eq('genre', 'Alternative')
    between('dateCreated', new Date()-30, new Date())
}
```

The previous example lists all the Album instances with a genre of Alternative created in the past 30 days. The nested method calls within the closure block translate into method calls on Hibernate's org. hibernate.criterion.Restrictions class, the API for which is too long to list here. Nevertheless, the eq and between methods shown here are just two of many for performing all the typical queries found in query languages such as SQL and HQL.

It is worth taking a look at the API on the Hibernate web site (http://docs.jboss.org/hibernate/core/3.6/javadocs/org/hibernate/criterion/Restrictions.html) to see what is available and to get a better understanding of the power that is at your fingertips. Of course, you can build queries similar to those in Listing 9-11 with dynamic finder methods. What you haven't really explored is the power of closures and building the query up dynamically.

Consider for the moment that a closure is just a block of code; it can be assigned to a variable. Also, consider that a closure can reference variables within its enclosing scope. Put the two together, and you have a pretty powerful mechanism for reusing dynamically constructed queries.

As an example, say you have a map whose keys define the property names to be queried, and the values define the value, such as the params object provided by Grails controllers. A query could easily be built up from this map and assigned to a variable. Listing 9-12 provides an example of this concept in action.

Listing 9-12. Dynamic Querying with Criteria

```
1 def today = new Date()
2 def queryMap =   [ genre: 'Alternative', dateCreated: [today-10,today]   ]
3 def query = {
4     // go through the query map
5     queryMap.each { key, value ->
6         // if we have a list assume a between query
7         if(value instanceof List) {
8             // use the spread operator to invoke
9             between(key, *value)
10        }
11        else {
12            like(key,value)
13        }
14    }
15 }
16
17 // create a criteria instance
18 def criteria = Album.createCriteria()
19
20 // count the results
21 println( criteria.count(query) )
22
23 // reuse again to get a unique result
24 println( criteria.get(query) )
25
26 // reuse again to list all
27 criteria.list(query).each { println it }
28
29 // use scrollable results
30 def scrollable = criteria.scroll(query)
31 def next = scrollable.next()
32 while(next) {
33     println(scrollable.getString('title'))
34     next = scrollable.next()
35 }
```

That fairly long example includes some fairly advanced concepts. To simplify understanding it, we've included line numbers, and we'll go through them one at a time. The first two lines in the following code define a date instance from the current time and a map using Groovy's map syntax that will dictate which properties you're going to query. The map's keys are the property names to query, and the values define the value to query by.

```
1 def today = new Date()
2 def queryMap =   [ genre: 'Alternative', dateCreated: [today-10,today]   ]
```

■ **Tip**   In Listing 9-12, to calculate the date range to be the past ten days, we took a `java.util.Date` instance and subtracted ten from it. This is an example of Groovy's operator overloading feature used to simplify date operations.

On line 3 a closure is assigned to the query variable, which will be used in conjunction with the criteria. The closure's closing bracket is on line 15, but some important stuff is going on in the body of the closure:

```
3   def query = {
        ...
15 }
```

First, a built-in GDK method called each is used to loop over each entry in the Map. Essentially, the method iterates through each element in the map and passes the key and value to the passed closure as arguments.

```
5    queryMap.each { key, value ->
             ...
14   }
```

Next up, the familiar instanceof operator is used to check whether the value passed is a List. If the value passed *is* a List, you can invoke the between method to pass the key and the value. The value is split into two arguments using Groovy's * spread operator:

```
7      if(value instanceof List) {
8          // use the spread operator to invoke
9          between(key, *value)
10     }
11     else {
12         like(key,value)
13     }
```

The * spread operator's job is to split apart a List or an array and pass the separated values to the target. In this case, the between method—which actually takes three arguments, not two—is correctly called, with the first element of the list being the second argument and with the second element being the third argument.

Now let's start to look at how the query, in the form of a closure, works with a criteria instance as a reusable code block. As usual, of course, you have to create the criteria instance, which is accomplished on line 18:

```
18 def criteria = Album.createCriteria()
```

The various methods of the criteria instance are then utilized using the same closure:

```
21 println( criteria.count(query) )
24 println( criteria.get(query) )
27 criteria.list(query).each { println it }
```

The first, on line 21, counts all the results for the query; the next prints out a unique result (if there is one), and the last lists all the results for the query and then iterates through them, with the already encountered **each** method printing each one to standard out.

One more usage, on line 30, uses the scroll method on criteria. This returns an instance of the Hibernate class called `org.hibernate.ScrollableResults`, which has a similar interface to a JDBC java.

`sql.ResultSet` and shares many of the same methods. One major difference, however, is that the columns of results are indexed from 0 and not 1, as in JDBC.

Querying Associations with Criteria

Often it is useful to execute a query that uses the state of an association as its criterion. So far, you have performed queries against only a single class and not its associations. So how do you go about querying an association?

The Grails criteria builder allows querying associations by using a nested criteria method call whose name matches the property name. The closure argument passed to the method contains nested criteria calls that relate to the association and not the criteria class. Say that you want to find all albums that contain the word *Shake*. The criteria shown in Listing 9-13 will do this.

Listing 9-13. *Querying Associations with Criteria*

```
def criteria = Album.withCriteria {
    songs {
        ilike('title', '%Shake%')
    }
}
```

This is a fairly trivial example, but all the criteria you've seen so far can be nested within the nested songs method call in the code listing. Combine this with how criteria can be built up from logical code blocks, and it results in a pretty powerful mechanism for querying associations.

▓ **Tip** You can also combine association criteria, as shown in Listing 9-13, with regular criteria on the class itself.

Querying with Projections

Projections allow the results of criteria queries to be customized in some way. For example, you may want to count only the number of results, as opposed to retrieving each one. In other words, they are equivalent to SQL functions such as `count`, `distinct`, and `sum`.

With criteria queries, you can specify a `projections` method call that takes a closure and provides support for these types of queries. Instead of criteria, however, the method calls within it map to another Hibernate class, named `org.hibernate.criterion.Projections`.

Let's adapt the example in Listing 9-14 by adding a projection that results in counting the distinct `Album` titles in the `Alternative` genre.

Listing 9-14. *Querying with Projections*

```
def criteria = Album.createCriteria()
def count = criteria.get {
    projections {
        countDistinct('name')
    }
    songs {
        eq('genre', 'Alternative')
    }
```

```
}
```

Detached Criteria Queries

Criteria queries, as described in the previous section, are associated with the current Hibernate session (see the section "The Semantics of GORM" for more information on the session). In practice, this means that you can use criteria queries only with the current session, and they cannot be reused across sessions. Attempting to execute a criteria query created with a different session, which potentially is no longer present, will lead to an exception.

In order to facilitate the creation of shared, potentially global, criteria queries that can be reused across the application, Grails 2.0 and above introduced the notion of a detached criteria query. Represented by the grails.gorm.DetachedCriteria class, detached criteria queries are composable, immutable query objects that do not hold an underlying connection to the database. They can be created as global variables or class properties and reused across the application as needed.

Creating Detached Criteria Queries

To create an instance of the DetachedCriteria class, simply import the necessary package and pass the target class to the constructor, as shown in Listing 9-15.

Listing 9-15. Creating a DetachedCriteria instance

```
import grails.gorm.*

def query = new DetachedCriteria(Album)
```

Once you have a reference to the DetachedCriteria instance, you can use the build method to apply regular criteria-style query logic (see Listing 9-16).

Listing 9-16. Building a DetachedCriteria query

```
def newQuery = query.build {
    like('title', '%Shake%')
}
```

Listing 9-16 demonstrates an important aspect of build method: the original query is not mutated; instead, a copy is returned with the criteria applied to the copy. Most operations on the DetachedCriteria instance do not mutate the actual instance. Instead, they return a copy; hence, assigning the return value of the build method to a new variable is required.

Executing Detached Criteria Queries

Once you have constructed the query you wish to execute, there are a number of ways to do so. In fact, the DetachedCriteria API is very similar to the GORM API on domain classes and supports all of the typical operations, including the list, get, and count methods. You can even execute dynamic finders on the DetachedCriteria instance itself! Listing 9-17 shows a few examples of the kinds of queries you can execute on a DetachedCriteria instance.

Listing 9-17. Executing a DetachedCriteria query

```
def list = query.list() // all results
def only10 = query.list(max:10) // pagination
def album = query.get() // one result
int total = query.count() // number of results
boolean alreadyExists = query.exists() // check for existence
def rockAlbums = query.findAllByGenre('Rock') // dynamic finders
def punkAlbums = query.list { // combine with other criteria
    like('genre', 'Punk')
}
```

As you can see from Listing 9-17, the DetachedCriteria API is extremely feature-rich, with a range of ways to execute and compose queries.

Lazy Evaluation of Detached Criteria

In order to increase the performance of your Grails applications, one of the first places to optimize tends to be the queries the application is executing.

Minimizing the network traffic caused by executing SQL queries on a remote database system can significantly improve response times of your applications. It is fairly common when building an application that logic resides in the view to conditionally display data retrieved from the database.

It would be fairly wasteful if a query were executed to obtain some data for the database only to be omitted from view rendering by logic in the view. An interesting use of detached criteria is lazy evaluation, which basically means that the query is executed only until use of the detached criteria.

The DetachedCriteria class implements the java.lang.Iterable interface; as a result, it can be used as a collection-type object. As an example, take the following controller action from Listing 9-18.

Listing 9-18. Lazy DetachedCriteria queries

```
def showAlbums() {
    def rockAlbums = new DetachedCriteria(Album).build {
        eq('genre', 'Rock')
    }

    [rockAlbums: rockAlbums]
}
```

The action builds a DetachedCriteria instance called rockAlbums that is returned as the actual model for the view. The view itself can then iterate over the DetachedCriteria instance as if it were a collection of results, as shown in Listing 9-19.

Listing 9-19. Iterating over DetachedCriteria in the View

```
<g:each in="${rockAlbums}" var="album">
    <p>${album.title}</p>
</g:each>
```

The actual query execution will occur only upon iterating over the DetachedCriteria instance; in other words, the query is lazily evaluated. Your view could contain conditional logic that disabled rendering of the query results, without incurring the cost of the query itself.

Batch Updates and Deletes with Detached Criteria

Batch updating and deleting of data is fairly common in modern applications but not something to be done lightly. The Grails framework tends to shy away from providing easy-use methods that perform potentially destructive operations.

However, if you do need to perform batch updates or deletes, then detached criteria are a great way to achieve that. Essentially, the DetachedCriteria API provides two methods, called deleteAll and updateAll, that allow, respectively, deleting and updating all objects that match the query.

As an example, if you have a particular aversion to reggae music, this can be easily remedied with the batch delete operation from Listing 9-20.

Listing 9-20. Batch Deleting with DetachedCriteria

```
def query = new DetachedCriteria(Album).build {
    eq "genre", "Reggae"
}
int deleteCount = query.deleteAll()
```

As you can see from the example in Listing 9-20, the deleteAll method returns the number of entities that were deleted by the operation.

The updateAll method differs slightly in that it takes a map representing the properties and values you wish to update. Listing 9-21 presents an example.

Listing 9-21. Batch Updating with DetachedCriteria

```
def query = new DetachedCriteria(Album).build {
    eq "genre", "Reggae"
}
int updateCount = query.updateAll(genre: "Rock")
```

Where Queries

Building on the DetachedCriteria API discussed in the previous section, where queries (named as such after the where method, which is the main entry point to the API) provide a way to build compile-time-checked, concise queries using syntax familiar to all Groovy developers.

Groovy's collections API provides numerous "finder" methods that operate on collections and take closure filter results. An example, using Groovy's findAll method, can be seen in Listing 9-22.

Listing 9-22. Groovy Collection API findAll Method

```
def list = albums.findAll { it.genre == "Rock" }
```

The Grails where queries are modeled after this API, whereby you use native Groovy operators such as ==, >, <, and the like, to construct the query.

Where Query Basics

The where method accepts a closure, and within the body of the closure you can use native Groovy operators to construct a DetachedCriteria instance. Listing 9-23 presents a basic example.

Listing 9-23. A Simple where Query

```
def query = Album.where { genre == "Rock" }
def results = query.list()
```

Unlike regular criteria queries, if you misspell the property name, in this case genre, you will receive a compile-time error. The returned object is a DetachedCriteria instance; from there, all the features of the DetachedCriteria API apply (lazy evaluation, dynamic finders, query composition, and so on).

In contrast to Groovy's finder methods, the closure passed to the where method is *not* used to filter results from a collection. Instead the closure is translated under the covers into an appropriate SQL query (or in the case of alternative datastores like MongoDB, whatever native query API is required).

If you wish to execute the query and obtain the results immediately, there are two methods, called find and findAll, that can be used. Listing 9-24 shows these latter two methods in action.

Listing 9-24. Using findAll and find Queries for Eager Querying

```
def rockAlbums = Album.findAll { genre == "Rock" }
def undertow = Album.find { title == "Undertow" }
```

Understanding Where Query Operators

In general the native Groovy operators map quite nicely onto their SQL equivalents when the query is executed. Table 9-2 provides examples of the various supported Groovy operators, what they map to in the SQL world, and an example of use.

Table 9-2. Available Where Query Operators

Operator	SQL	Example
==	=	Album.where { genre == "Rock" }
!=	!= or <>	Album.where { genre != "Rock" }
>	>	Album.where { dateCreated > lastMonth }
>=	>=	Album.where { dateCreated >= lastMonth }
<	<	Album.where { dateCreated < lastMonth }
<=	<=	Album.where { dateCreated <= lastMonth }
in	IN	Album.where { genre in ["Rock", "Punk"] }
==~	LIKE	Album.where { genre ==~ "Ro%" }
=~	ILIKE	Album.where { genre =~ "ro%" }
in 0..1	BETWEEN	Album.where { dateCreated in (lastYear..lastMonth) }
== null	IS NULL	Album.where { genre == null }
!= null	IS NOT NULL	Album.where { genre != null }

A few of the above examples warrant further explanation. Notably, Groovy's matching operator ==~ is mapped onto LIKE, while Groovy's find operator =~ is mapped onto the equivalent of the ILIKE operator (case-insensitive like) in Postgres. Other databases that don't have an ILIKE operator tend to use functions to convert the text to upper or lower case during comparison.

Also, notice that Groovy ranges are used to construct SQL BETWEEN queries to obtain results within between two given values.

Groovy's regular logical operators can be used to construct conjunctions, disjunctions, and even negations. Listing 9-25 presents an example that combines multiple logical operators.

Listing 9-25. Where Queries and Conjunctions/Disjunctions

```
def lastWeek = new Date() - 7
def rockAlbums = Album.where {
    genre == "Rock" && dateCreated > lastWeek && !artist.name == "Pink"
}
```

The previous example also introduced another capability of where queries, which is the ability to query associations via the dot operator. The query in Listing 9-25 queries the name property of the artist association!

Querying Associations with Where Queries

As mentioned in the previous section, using the dot operator you can query both single-ended and collection-type associations. However, if you need to query multiple properties of a given association, it could end up being very repetitive to use the dot operator over and over. For example, consider the code in Listing 9-26.

Listing 9-26. Using the dot operator to query associations

```
def query = Song.where {
    album.title ==~ "A%" && album.dateCreated > new Date() - 7
}
```

The code in Listing 9-24 queries two properties of the album association: title and dateCreated. Notice that the repetitive nature of using the dot operator as the name of the association is used twice, one for each property. A more concise way to write this query can be seen in Listing 9-27.

Listing 9-27. Grouping Association Criterion

```
def query = Song.where {
    genre == "Rock" &&
      album { title ==~ "A%" && dateCreated > new Date() - 7 }
}
```

As you can see from Listing 9-25, you can use a closure after the name of the association to group related criteria and avoid repeating the association name. Also, note that you can combine association criteria with top-level criteria related to the class being queried.

In the case of collection types, used to model one-to-many and many-to-many associations, where queries provide a few additional features designed to allow querying the size of a collection.

In general if you use the size() function on a collection and combine it with a regular Groovy comparison operator, such as == or >, you can constrain the size of the collection returned by a query. Listing 9-28 presents a simple example that limits the number of songs an album can contain.

Listing 9-28. *Querying collection sizes*

```
def shortAlbums = Album.where {
    songs.size() < 10
}
```

Note that, as mentioned previously, the closure code is never actually executed in this form, but instead translated into an SQL query at runtime. So although it may seem like we are invoking the `size()` method on the actual collection here, what we are actually doing is simply telling Grails that the query results should be limited by the `size()` of the collection. Under the covers Grails will do the right thing and produce an appropriate SQL query to be executed.

Subqueries and Functions

One advanced aspect of where queries is the use of subqueries. As of the time of writing, they can be used only on the right-hand side of any Boolean expression. Consider Listing 9-29.

Listing 9-29. *Using Subqueries*

```
def longSongs = Song.where {
    duration > avg(duration)
}
```

The query in Listing 9-29 returns all the songs whose duration is greater than the average. This is achieved by using the avg subquery on the right-hand side of the expression. A more elaborate example is seen in Listing 9-30.

Listing 9-30. *Using More Elaborate Subqueries*

```
def longRockSongs = Song.where {
    genre == "Rock" && duration > avg(duration).of { genre == "Rock" }
}
```

In this case the avg subquery is used to find all the rock songs whose duration is longer than the average rock song. To achieve this query, the of function is used on the result of the avg function. The of function takes a closure, which can contain further Boolean expressions. Table 9-3 provides a comprehensive list of the available subqueries.

Table 9-3. *Available Subqueries*

Subquery	Description
avg	the average of all values
sum	the sum of all values
max	the maximum value
min	the minimum value
count	the count of all values
property	a list of all properties

The property subquery deserves a special mention; it differs in that instead of returning a single value, as is the case with the avg subquery, the property subquery instead returns a list of values. Listing 9-31 presents an example of using the property subquery.

Listing 9-31. Using a property Subquery

```
def query = Song.where {
    duration < property(duration)
}
```

The query in Listing 9-31 differs significantly from the query previously seen in Listing 9-27 in that it compares the duration to the duration of *all* other properties. Since this is unlikely to be very efficient, the property subquery is generally used in combination with the of function to constrain the number of properties compared. An example of this can be seen in Listing 9-32.

Listing 9-32. Using a property Subquery with the of Function

```
def query = Song.where {
    duration < property(duration).of { genre == "Rock" }
}
```

As you have probably noted from the various examples, the property name being queried should always be on the left-hand side of a Boolean expression. There are, however, some additional functions that can be applied to the property being queried. Table 9-4 lists these functions.

Table 9-4. Available Functions

Function	Description
second	the second of a date property
minute	the minute of a date property
hour	the hour of a date property
day	the day of the month of a date property
month	the month of a date property
year	the year of a date property
lower	converts a string property to lower case
upper	converts a string property to upper case
length	the length of a string property
trim	trims a string property

The functions in Table 9-4 can, as of the time of writing, only be used on the left-hand side of an expression. In other words, they should surround the property name. Listing 9-33 gives an example that obtains all albums from 2012.

Listing 9-33. Using Functions on a Property

```
def query = Album.where {
    year(dateCreated) == 2012
}
```

Query by Example

An alternative to criteria queries is to pass an instance of the class you're looking for to the find or findAll method. This is an interesting option when used in conjunction with Groovy's additional implicit constructor for JavaBeans, as shown in Listing 9-34.

Listing 9-34. *Query by Example*

```
def album = Album.find( new Album(title:'Odelay') )
```

As you can see from Listing 9-15, the find method uses the properties set on the passed Album instance to formulate a query. Querying by example is a little limiting, because you don't have access to some of the more advanced expressions such as Like, Between, and GreaterThan when passing in the example. It is, however, another useful addition to your toolbox.

HQL and SQL

Another way to perform queries is via the Hibernate Query Language (HQL), which is a flexible object-oriented alternative to SQL. A full discussion of HQL is beyond the scope of this book; however, the Hibernate documentation does cover it splendidly (http://docs.jboss.org/hibernate/core/3.6/reference/en-US/html/queryhql.html). We will look at some basic examples of how GORM supports HQL via more built-in methods.

Those who know SQL should not find it hard to adapt to HQL, because the syntactic differences are minimal. GORM provides three methods for working with HQL queries: find, findAll, and executeQuery. Each method, when passed a string, will assume it's an HQL query. The example in Listing 9-35 presents the most basic case combined with findAll.

Listing 9-35. *HQL via the findAll Method*

```
// query for all albums
def allAlbums = Album.findAll('from com.g2one.gtunes.Album')
```

In addition, JDBC-style IN parameters (queries with question mark [?] placeholders) are supported by passing a list as the second argument. Thanks to Groovy's concise syntax for expressing lists, the result is very readable, as presented in Listing 9-36.

Listing 9-36. *HQL with Positional Parameters*

```
// query for an Album by title def album = Album.find(
'from Album as a where a.title = ?', ['Odelay'])
```

If positional parameters aren't your preferred option, you can also use named parameters, using the syntax shown in Listing 9-37.

Listing 9-37. *HQL with Named Parameters*

```
// query for an Album by title
def album = Album.find('from Album as a where a.title = :theTitle',
                       [theTitle:'Odelay'])
```

Notice how you use the colon character directly before the named parameter :theTitle. Then instead of passing a list as the final argument to the find method, you pass a map where the keys in the map match the named parameters in the query.

The methods find and findAll assume the query is a query specific to the Album class and will validate that this is so. It is possible, however, to execute other HQL queries via the executeQuery method, as shown in Listing 9-38.

Listing 9-38. *HQL via executeQuery*

```
// get all the songs
def songs = Album.executeQuery('select elements(b.songs) from Album as a')
```

Clearly, there is a lot to learn about HQL, since it is possible to perform more advanced queries using joins, aggregate functions, and subqueries. Luckily, the documentation on the Hibernate web site is an excellent overview of what is possible and can help you on your way.

Pagination

Whichever way you query, a typically useful thing to be able to do is paginate through a set of results. You've already learned that the list() method supports arguments such as max and offset that allow you to perform pagination. For example, to obtain the first ten results, you can use the following:

```
def results = Album.list(max:10)
```

To obtain the following ten, you can use the offset argument:

```
def results = Album.list(max:10, offset:10)
```

While we're on the topic of querying, you'll be happy to know that the same arguments can be used to paginate queries. For example, when using dynamic finders, you can pass a map as the last argument, which specifies the max and offset arguments:

```
def results = Album.findAllByGenre("Alternative", [max:10, offset:20])
```

In fact, you can use any parameter covered in the previous "Listing, Sorting, and Counting" section, such as sort and order:

```
def results = Album.findAllByGenre("Alternative", [sort:'dateCreated',
order:'desc'])
```

In the view, you can take advantage of the <g:paginate> tag that renders "Previous" and "Next" links, as well as linked numbers to jump to a specific set of results à la Google. In its simplest form, the <g:paginate> tag requires only the total number of records:

```
<g:paginate total="${Album.count()}" />
```

This example assumes you want to paginate the current controller action. If you don't, you can customize the controller that is actually performing the pagination using the same attributes accepted by the <g:link> tag, such as controller and action:

```
<g:paginate controller="album" action="list" total="${Album.count()}" />
```

You can change the default "Previous" and "Next" links using the prev and next attributes, respectively:

```
<g:paginate prev="Back" next="Forward" total="${Album.count()}" />
```

If internationalization (i18n) is a requirement, you can use the <g:message> tag, called as a *method*, to pull the text to appear from message bundles:

```
<g:paginate prev="${message(code:'back.button.text')}"
            next="${message(code:'next.button.text')}"
            total="${Album.count()}" />
```

■ **Tip**   If you're interested in the mechanics of i18n support in Grails, take a look at Chapter 7, which covers the details of message bundles and switching locales.

Configuring GORM

GORM has a number of attributes that you may want to configure. Pretty much all the options available in Hibernate are also available in GORM. One of the most fundamental things you're likely to want to achieve is to enable some form of SQL logging so that you can debug performance issues and optimize queries.

SQL Logging

If you're purely interested in monitoring the amount of SQL traffic hitting the database, then a good option to use is the logSql setting in the grails-app/conf/DataSource.groovy file:

```
dataSource {
    ...
    logSql = true
}
```

With this enabled, every SQL statement issued by Hibernate will be printed to the console. The disadvantage of the logSql setting is that you get to see only the prepared statements printed to the console and not the actual values that are being inserted. If you need to see the values, then set up a special log4j logger in grails-app/conf/Config.groovy as follows:

```
log4j = {
    ...
    logger {
        trace "org.hibernate.SQL", "org.hibernate.type"
    }
}
```

Specifying a Custom Dialect

Hibernate has, over the years, been heavily optimized for each individual database that it supports. To support different database types, Hibernate models the concept of a *dialect*. For each database it supports, there is a dialect class that knows how to communicate with that database.

There are even different dialects for different database versions. For example, for Oracle, there are three dialect classes: Oracle8iDialect, Oracle9iDialect, and Oracle10gDialect. Normally, the dialect to use is automatically detected from the database JDBC metadata. However, certain older database drivers do not support JDBC metadata, in which case you may have to specify the dialect explicitly. To do so, you can use the dialect setting of the grails-app/conf/DataSource.groovy file. As an example, if you use the InnoDB storage engine for MySQL, you'll want to use the MySQL5InnoDBDialect class, as shown in Listing 9-39.

Listing 9-39. Customizing the Hibernate Dialect

```
dataSource {
    ...
    dialect = org.hibernate.dialect.MySQL5InnoDBDialect
}
```

Other Hibernate Properties

The logSql and dialect settings of the DataSource.groovy file demonstrated in the previous two sections are actually just shortcuts for the hibernate.show_sql and hibernate.dialect properties of the Hibernate SessionFactory. If you're more comfortable using Hibernate's configuration model, then you can do so within a hibernate block in DataSource.groovy. In fact, you'll note that the Hibernate second-level cache (discussed later in the "Caching" section) is already preconfigured in this manner, as shown in Listing 9-40.

Listing 9-40. Regular Hibernate Configuration

```
hibernate {
    cache.use_second_level_cache=true
    cache.use_query_cache=false
    cache.provider_class=
        'net.sf.ehcache.hibernate.EhCacheRegionFactory '
}
```

You can configure all manner of things if you're not satisfied with the defaults set up by Grails. For example, to change your database's default transaction isolation level, you could use the hibernate. connection.isolation property:

```
hibernate {
    hibernate.connection.isolation=4
}
```

In this example, we've changed the isolation level to Connection.TRANSACTION_REPEATABLE_READ. Refer to the java.sql.Connection class for the other isolation levels.

■ **Tip** For the other configuration options available, see the Hibernate reference material: http://docs.jboss. org/hibernate/core/3.6/reference/en-US/html/session-configuration.html.

Within an application it may be that there are a lot of domain classes that have common configuration settings. For example, it may be the case that you want versioning turned off for all domain classes across the entire application. You can do this by specifying "version false" in the mapping block of every domain class, but having to specify that in every domain class is tedious and leads to errors. Fortunately, mapping settings like that can be configured globally in Config.groovy. See Listing 9-41 for an example.

Listing 9-41. Global GORM mapping Settings

```
grails.gorm.default.mapping = {
    // These will become default mapping settings for
    // all domain classes.  These settings may be overridden
    // in the mapping block of any domain class.
    version false
```

```
    autoTimestamp false
}
```

Similarly, global constraints may be defined in Config.groovy (see Listing 9-42).

Listing 9-42. Global GORM Constraints

```
grails.gorm.default.constraints = {
    nullable true
    blank false
    size 1..20
}
```

The Semantics of GORM

As you have discovered, using GORM is pretty easy. It's so easy, in fact, that you may be lulled into a false sense of security and think that you never have to look at a database again. However, when working with any ORM tool, it is absolutely critical to understand how and what the ORM tool is doing.

■ **Tip** Since GORM is built on Hibernate, it may well be worth investing in a book specifically targeting Hibernate. Still, we'll do our best to cover the key aspects here.

If you start using an ORM tool without understanding its semantics, you will almost certainly run into issues with the performance and behavior of your application. ORM tools are often referred to as an example of a leaky abstraction (see http://www.joelonsoftware.com/articles/LeakyAbstractions.html) because they attempt to isolate you from the complexities of the underlying database. Unfortunately, to follow the analogy, the abstraction leaks quite frequently if you're not aware of features such as lazy and eager fetching, locking strategies, and caching.

This section will provide some clarity on these quirks to ensure that you don't use GORM with the expectation that it will solve world hunger. GORM is often compared, understandably, to ActiveRecord in Rails. Unfortunately, users with Rails experience who adopt Grails are in for a few surprises because the tools are really quite different. One of the primary differences is that GORM has the concept of a persistence context, or *session*.

The Hibernate Session

Hibernate, like the Java Persistence API, models the concept of a persistence session using the org.hibernate.Session class. The Session class is essentially a container that holds references to all known instances of persistent classes—domain classes in Grails. In the Hibernate view of the world, you think in terms of objects and delegate responsibility to Hibernate to ensure that the state of the objects is *synchronized* to the database.

The synchronization process is triggered by calling the flush() method on the Session object. At this point, you may be wondering how all of this relates to Grails, given that you saw no mention of a Session object in Chapter 4. Essentially, GORM manipulates the Session object transparently on your behalf.

It is quite possible to build an entire Grails application without ever interacting directly with the Hibernate Session object. However, for developers who are not used to the session model, there may be a few surprises along the way. As an example, consider the code in Listing 9-43.

213

Listing 9-43. Multiple Reads Return the Same Object

```
def album1 = Album.get(1)
def album2 = Album.get(1)
assertFalse album1.is(album2)
```

The code in Listing 9-1 shows a little gotcha for developers not used to the session model. The first call to the get method retrieves an instance of the Album class by executing an SQL SELECT statement under the covers—no surprises there. However, the second call to the get method doesn't execute any SQL at all, and in fact, the assertion on the last lines fails.

■ **Note**   In the example in Listing 9-43, the final assertFalse statement uses Groovy's is method because == in Groovy is equivalent to calling the equals(Object) method in Java.

In other words, the Session object appears to act like a cache; in fact, it is one. The Session object is Hibernate's first-level cache. Another area where this is apparent is when saving an object. Consider the code in Listing 9-44.

Listing 9-44. Saving a Domain Class in Grails

```
def album = new Album(...)
album.save()
```

Now, assuming the Album instance validates, you may think from the code in Listing 9-2 that GORM will execute an SQL INSERT statement when the save() method is called. However, this is not necessarily the case, and in fact it depends greatly on the underlying database. GORM by default uses Hibernate's native identity generation strategy, which attempts to select the most appropriate way to generate the id of an object. For example, in Oracle, Hibernate will opt to use a sequence generator to supply the identifier, while in MySQL the identity strategy will be used. The identity generation strategy relies on the database to supply the identity.

Since an identifier must be assigned by the time the save() method completes, if a sequence is used, no INSERT is needed because Hibernate can simply increment the sequence in memory. The actual INSERT can then occur later when the Session is flushed. However, in the case of the identity strategy, an INSERT *is* needed since the database needs to generate the identifier. Nevertheless, the example serves to demonstrate that it is the Session that is responsible for synchronizing the object's state to the database, not the object itself.

Essentially, Hibernate implements the strategy known as *transactional write-behind*. Any changes made to persistent objects are not necessarily persisted when you make them or even when you call the save() method. The advantage of this approach is that Hibernate can heavily optimize and batch up the SQL to be executed, hence minimizing network traffic. In addition, the time for which database locks (discussed in more detail in the "Locking Strategies" section) are held is greatly reduced by this model.

Session Management and Flushing

You may be worried at this point that you're losing some kind of control by allowing Hibernate to take responsibility for persisting objects on your behalf. Fortunately, GORM provides you with the ability to control session flushing implicitly by passing in a flush argument to the save() or delete() method, as shown in Listing 9-45.

Listing 9-45. Manually Flushing the Session

```
def album = new Album(...)
album.save(flush:true)
```

In contrast to the example in Listing 9-23, the code in Listing 9-24 will persist the object but also call flush() on the underlying Session object. However, it is important to note that since the Session deals with all persistent instances, other changes may be flushed in addition to the object that is saved. Listing 9-46 illustrates an example of this behavior.

Listing 9-46. The Effects of Flushing

```
def album1 = Album.get(1)
album1.title = "The Changed Title"
album1.save()
def album2 = new Album(..)
album2.save(flush:true)
```

The example in Listing 9-25 demonstrates the impact of passing the flush argument to the second save() method. You may expect that an SQL UPDATE would be executed when save() is called on album1, and then an INSERT would occur when save() is called on album2. However, the actual behavior is that both the UPDATE and the INSERT occur on the call to save() on album2, since the flush:true argument passed forces the underlying Session object to synchronize changes with the database.

You may be wondering at this point how the code in the listings you've seen so far can possibly use the same Session instance and where this Session came from in the first place. Basically, when a request comes into a Grails application, directly before a controller action executes, Grails will transparently bind a new Hibernate Session to the current thread. The Session is then looked up by GORM's dynamic methods, such as get in Listing 9-8. When a controller action finishes executing, if no exceptions are thrown, the Session is flushed, which synchronizes the state of the Session with the database by executing any necessary SQL. These changes are then committed to the database.

However, that is not the end of the story. The Session is not closed but instead placed in read-only mode prior to view rendering and remains open until view rendering completes. The reason for this is that if the session were closed, any persistent instances contained within it would become detached. The result is that if there were any noninitialized associations, the infamous org.hibernate. LazyInitializationException would occur. Ouch! Of course, we'll be saying more about LazyInitializationException and ways to avoid the exception, including in-depth coverage of detached objects later in the chapter.

To elaborate, the reason for placing the Session into read-only mode during view rendering is to avoid any unnecessary flushing of the Session during the view-rendering process. Your views really shouldn't be modifying database state, after all! So that is how the standard Session life cycle works in Grails.

Obtaining the Session

As mentioned previously, the Session is basically a cache of persistent instances. Like any cache, the more objects it has within it, the more memory it's going to consume. A common mistake when using GORM is to query for a large number of objects without periodically clearing the Session. If you do so, your Session will get bigger and bigger, and eventually you may either cause your application's performance to suffer or, worse, run out of memory.

In these kinds of scenarios, it is wise to manage the state of your Session manually. Before you can do so, however, you need a reference to the Session object itself. You can achieve this in two ways. The first involves the use of dependency injection to get hold of a reference to the Hibernate SessionFactory object.

The `SessionFactory` has a method, called `currentSession()`, that you can use to obtain the `Session` bound to the current thread. To use dependency injection, simply declare a local field called `sessionFactory` in a controller, tag library, or service, as shown in Listing 9-47.

Listing 9-47. Using Dependency Injection to Obtain the Hibernate Session

```
def sessionFactory
...
def index() {
    def session = sessionFactory.currentSession()
}
```

As an alternative, you could use the `withSession` method that is available on any domain class. The `withSession` method accepts a closure. The first argument to the closure is the `Session` object; hence, you can code as in Listing 9-48.

Listing 9-48. Using the withSession Method

```
def index() {
    Album.withSession { session ->
        ...
    }
}
```

Let's return to the problem at hand. To avoid memory issues when using GORM with a large amount of data (note this applies to raw Hibernate too), you need to call the `clear()` method on the `Session` object periodically so that the contents of the `Session` are cleared. The result is that the instances within the `Session` become candidates for garbage collection, which frees up memory. Listing 9-49 shows an example that demonstrates the pattern.

Listing 9-49. Managing the Hibernate Session

```
1    def index() {
2        Album.withSession { session ->
3            def allAlbums = Album.list()
4            for(album in allAlbums) {
5                def songs = Song.findAllByAlbum(album)
6                // do something with the songs
7                ...
8                session.clear()
9            }
10       }
11   }
```

The example in Listing 9-49 is rather contrived, but it serves to demonstrate effective `Session` management when dealing with a large number of objects. On line 2, a reference to the `Session` is obtained using the `withSession` method:

```
2  Album.withSession { session ->
       ...
10 }
```

Then, on line 3, a query is used to get a list of all the albums in the system, which could be big in itself, and then iterate over each one:

```
3 def allAlbums = Album.list()
4 for(album in allAlbums) {
    ...
9 }
```

Critically, on line 5, a dynamic finder queries for all the Song instances for the current Album:

```
5    def songs = Song.findAllByAlbum(album)
```

Now, each time the findAllByAlbum method is executed, more and more persistent instances are being accumulated in the Session. Memory consumption may at some point become an issue depending on how much data is in the system at the time. To prevent this, the session is cleared on line 8:

```
8    session.clear()
```

Clearing the Session with the clear() method is not the only way to remove objects from Hibernate's grasp. If you have a single object, you can also call the discard() method. You could even use the *. operator to discard entire collections of objects using this technique:

```
songs*.discard()
```

The advantage of this approach is that although the clear() method removes all persistent instances from the Session, using discard() removes only the instances you no longer need. This can help in certain circumstances because you may end up with a LazyInitializationException because removing the objects from the Session results in them being detached (a subject we'll discuss in more detail in the "Detached Objects" section).

Automatic Session Flushing

Another common gotcha is that by default GORM is configured to flush the session automatically when one of the following occurs:

- whenever a query is run;
- directly after a controller action completes, if no exceptions are thrown;
- directly before a transaction is committed.

This has a number of implications that you need to consider. Take, for example, the code in Listing 9-50.

Listing 9-50. The Implications of Automatic Session Flushing

```
1 def album = Album.get(1)
2 album.title = "Change It"
3 def otherAlbums = Album.findAllWhereTitleLike("%Change%")
4
5 assert otherAlbums.contains(album)
```

You may think that because you never called save() on the album there is no way it could possibly have been persisted to the database, right? Wrong. As soon as you load the album instance, it immediately becomes a "managed" object as far as Hibernate is concerned. Since Hibernate is by default configured to flush the session when a query runs, the Session is flushed on line 3 when the findAllWhereTitleLike method is called and the Album instance is persisted. The Hibernate Session caches changes and pushes them to the database only at the latest possible moment. In the case of automatic flushing, this is at the end of a transaction or before a query runs that might be affected by the cached changes.

You may consider the behavior of automatic flushing to be a little odd, but if you think about it, it depends very much on your expectations. If the object weren't flushed to the database, then the change made to it on line 2 would not be reflected in the results. That may not be what you're expecting either! Let's consider another example where automatic flushing may present a few surprises. Take a look at the code in Listing 9-51.

Listing 9-51. Another Implication of Automatic Session Flushing

```
def album = Album.get(1)
album.title = "Change It"
```

In Listing 9-16, an instance of the Album class is looked up and the title is changed, but the save() method is never called. You may expect that since save() was never called, the Album instance will not be persisted to the database. However, you'd be wrong again. Hibernate does automatic dirty checking and flushes any changes to the persistent instances contained within the Session.

It is our recommendation that you should *always* call the save() method when persisting objects. The save() method will call the Grails validation mechanism and mark the object as read-only, including any associations of the object, if a validation error occurs. If you were never planning to save the object in the first place, then you may want to consider using the read method instead of the get method, which returns the object in a read-only state:

```
def album = Album.read(1)
```

If all of this is too dreadful to contemplate and you prefer to have full control over how and when the Session is flushed, then you may want to consider changing the default FlushMode used by specifying the hibernate.flush.mode setting in DataSource.groovy:

```
hibernate.flush.mode="manual"
```

The possible values of the hibernate.flush.mode setting are summarized as follows:

- manual: Flush only when you say so! In other words, only flush the session when the flush:true argument is passed to save() or delete(). The downside with a manual flush mode is that you may receive stale data from queries, and you must always pass the flush:true argument to the save() or delete() method.

- commit: Flush only when the transaction is committed (see the next section).

- auto: Flush when the transaction is committed and before a query is run.

Nevertheless, assuming you stick with the default auto setting, the save() method might not, excuse the pun, save you in the case of the code from Listing 9-15. Remember in this case the Session is automatically flushed before the query is run. This problem brings us nicely onto the topic of transactions in GORM.

Transactions in GORM

First things first—it is important to emphasize that *all* communication between Hibernate and the database runs within the context of a database transaction regardless of whether you are explicit about the transaction demarcation boundaries. The Session itself is lazy in that it only ever initiates a database transaction at the last possible moment.

Consider the code in Listing 9-15 again. When the code is run, a Session has already been opened and bound to the current thread. However, a transaction is initiated only on first communication with the database, which happens within the call to get on line 1.

At this point, the Session is associated with a JDBC Connection object. The autoCommit property of the Connection object is set to false, which initiates a transaction. The Connection will then be released only once the Session is closed. Hence, as you can see, there is never really a circumstance where Grails operates without an active transaction, since the same Session is shared across the entire request.

Given that there is a transaction anyway, you would think that if something went wrong, any problems would be rolled back. However, without specific transaction boundaries and if the Session is flushed, any changes are permanently committed to the database.

This is a particular problem if the flush is beyond your control (for instance, the result of a query). Then those changes will be permanently persisted to the database. The result may be the rather painful one of having your database left in an inconsistent state. To help you understand, let's look at another illustrative example, as shown in Listing 9-52.

Listing 9-52. *Updates Gone Wrong*

```
def save() {
    def album = Album.get(params.id)
    album.title = "Changed Title"
    album.save(flush:true)
    // something goes wrong
    throw new Exception("Ruh Roh!")
}
```

The example in Listing 9-52 shows a common problem. In the first three lines of the **save** action, an instance of the Album class is obtained using the get method, the title is updated, and the save() method is called and passes the flush argument to ensure updates are synchronized with the database. Then later in the code, something goes wrong, and an exception is thrown. Unfortunately, if you were expecting previous updates to the Album instance to be rolled back, you're out of luck. The changes have already been persisted when the Session was flushed! You can correct this in two ways; the first is to move the logic into a transactional service. Services are the subject of Chapter 10, so we'll be showing the latter option, which is to use programmatic transactions. Listing 9-53 shows the code updated to use the withTransaction method to demarcate the transactional boundaries.

Listing 9-53. *Using the withTransaction Method*

```
def save() {
    Album.withTransaction {
        def album = Album.get(params.id)
        album.title = "Changed Title"
        album.save(flush:true)
        ...
        // something goes wrong
        throw new Exception("Ruh Roh!")
    }
}
```

Grails uses Spring's PlatformTransactionManager abstraction layer under the covers. In this case, if an exception is thrown, all changes made within the scope of the transaction will be rolled back as expected. The first argument to the withTransaction method is a Spring TransactionStatus object, which also allows you to programmatically roll back the transaction by calling the setRollbackOnly() method, as shown in Listing 9-54.

Listing 9-54. Programmatically Rolling Back a Transaction

```
def save() {
    Album.withTransaction { status ->
        def album = Album.get(params.id)
        album.title = "Changed Title"
        album.save(flush:true)
        ...
        // something goes wrong
        if(hasSomethingGoneWrong()) {
            status.setRollbackOnly()
        }
    }
}
```

Note that you need only one withTransaction declaration. If you were to nest withTransaction declarations within each other, then the same transaction would simply be propagated from one withTransaction block to the next. The same is true of transactional services. In addition, if you have a JDBC 3.0–compliant database, then you can leverage savepoints, which allow you to roll back to a particular point rather than roll back the entire transaction. Listing 9-55 shows an example that rolls back any changes made after the Album instance was saved.

Listing 9-55. Using Savepoints in Grails

```
def save() {
    Album.withTransaction { status ->
        def album = Album.get(params.id)
        album.title = "Changed Title"
        album.save(flush:true)
        def savepoint = status.createSavepoint()
        ...
        // something goes wrong
        if(hasSomethingGoneWrong()) {
            status.rollbackToSavepoint(savepoint)
            // do something else
            ...
        }
    }
}
```

With transactions out of the way, let's revisit a topic that has been touched on at various points throughout this chapter: detached objects.

Detached Objects

The Hibernate Session is critically important to understand the nature of detached objects. Remember, the Session keeps track of all persistent instances and acts like a cache, returning instances that already exist in the Session rather than hitting the database again. As you can imagine, each object goes through an implicit life cycle, a topic we'll be looking at first.

The Persistence Life Cycle

Before an object has been saved, it is said to be transient. Transient objects are just like regular Java objects and have no notion of persistence. Once you call the save() method, the object is in a persistent state. Persistent objects have an assigned identifier and may have enhanced capabilities such as the ability to lazily load associations. If the object is discarded by calling the discard() method or if the Session has been cleared, it is said to be in a *detached* state. In other words, each persistent object is associated with a single Session, and if the object is no longer managed by the Session, it has been detached from the Session.

Figure 9-2 shows a state diagram describing the persistence life cycle and the various states an object can go through. As the diagram notes, another way an object can become detached is if the Session itself is closed. If you recall, we mentioned that a new Session is bound for each Grails request. When the request completes, the Session is closed. Any objects that are still around, for example, held within the HttpSession, are now in a detached state.

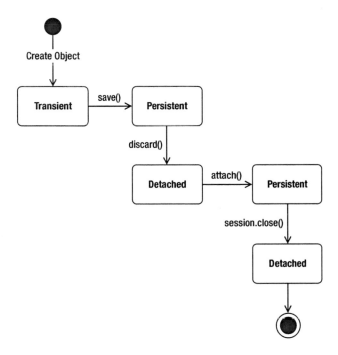

Figure 9-2. *The persistence life cycle*

What is the implication of being in a detached state? For one, if a detached object that is stored in the HttpSession has any noninitialized associations, then you will get a LazyInitializationException.

Reattaching Detached Objects

Given that it is probably undesirable to experience a LazyInitializationException, you can eliminate this problem by reassociating a detached object with the Session bound to the current thread by calling the attach() method, for example:

```
album.attach()
```

Note that if an object already exists in the Session with the same identifier, then you'll get an org.hibernate.NonUniqueObjectException. To get around this, you may want to check whether the object is already attached by using the isAttached() method:

```
if(!album.isAttached()) {
album.attach() }
```

Since we're on the subject of equality and detached objects, it's important to bring up the notion of object equality here. If you decide you want to use detached objects extensively, then it is almost certain that you will need to consider implementing equals and hashCode for all of your domain classes that are detached. Why? Well, if you consider the code in Listing 9-56, you'll soon see why.

Listing 9-56. Object Equality and Hibernate

```
def album1 = Album.get(1)
album.discard()
def album2 = Album.get(1)
assert album1 == album2 // This assertion will fail
```

The default implementation of equals and hashCode in Java uses object equality to compare instances. The problem is that when an instance becomes detached, Hibernate loses all knowledge of it. As the code in Listing 9-35 demonstrates, loading two instances with the same identifier once one has become detached results in you having two different instances. This can cause problems when placing these objects into collections. Remember, a Set uses hashCode to work out whether an object is a duplicate, but the two Album instances will return two different hash codes even though they share the same database identifier!

To get around this problem, you could use the database identifier, but this is not recommended, because a transient object that then becomes persistent will return different hash codes over time. This breaks the contract defined by the hashCode method, which states that the hashCode implementation must return the same integer for the lifetime of the object. The recommended approach is to use Groovy's equals and hashcode AST transformation to generate appropriate equals and hashcode methods. Marking a class with the @EqualsAndHashCode annotation will trigger this transformation. See http://groovy.codehaus.org/api/groovy/transform/EqualsAndHashCode.html for more information on the annotation. Listing 9-57 shows an example implementation.

Listing 9-57. Implementing equals and hashCode

```
@groovy.transform.EqualsAndHashCode
class Album {
    ...
}
```

An important thing to remember is that you need to implement equals and hashCode only if you are:

- using detached instances extensively;
- placing the detached instances into data structures, like the Set and Map collection types, that use hashing algorithms to establish equality.

The subject of equality brings us nicely onto another potential stumbling block. Say you have a detached Album instance held somewhere like in the HttpSession and you also have another Album instance that is logically equal (they share the same identifier) to the instance in the HttpSession. What do you do? Well, you could just discard the instance in the HttpSession:

```
def index() {
```

```
    def album = session.album
    if(album.isAttached()) {
        album = Album.get(album.id)
        session.album = album
    }
}
```

However, what if the detached album in the HttpSession has changes? What if it represents the most up-to-date copy and not the one already loaded by Hibernate? In this case, you need to consider merging.

Merging Changes

To merge the state of one, potentially detached, object into another, you need to use the static merge method. The merge method accepts an instance, loads a persistent instance of the same logical object if it doesn't already exist in the Session, and then merges the state of the passed instance into the loaded persistent one. Once this is done, the merge method then returns a new instance containing the merged state. Listing 9-58 presents an example of using the merge method.

Listing 9-58. Using the merge Method

```
def index() {
    def album = session.album
    album = Album.merge(album)
    render album.title
}
```

Performance Tuning GORM

The previous section on the semantics of GORM showed how the underlying Hibernate engine optimizes database access using a cache (the Session). There are, however, various ways to optimize the performance of your queries. In the next few sections, we'll be covering the different ways to tune GORM, allowing you to get the best out of the technology. You may want to enable SQL logging by setting logSql to true in DataSource.groovy, as explained in the previous section on configuring GORM.

Eager vs. Lazy Associations

Associations in GORM are lazy by default. What does this mean? Well, say you looked up a load of Album instances using the static list() method:

```
def albums = Album.list()
```

To obtain all the Album instances, underneath the surface Hibernate will execute a single SQL SELECT statement to obtain the underlying rows. As you already know, each Album has an Artist that is accessible via the artist association. Now say you need to iterate over each song and print the Artist name, as shown in Listing 9-59.

Listing 9-59. Iterating over Lazy Associations

```
def albums = Album.list()
for(album in albums) {
```

```
    println album.artist.name
}
```

The example in Listing 9-59 demonstrates what is commonly known as the *N+1* problem. Since the artist association is lazy, Hibernate will execute another SQL SELECT statement (N statements) for each associated artist to add to the single statement to retrieve the original list of albums. Clearly, if the result set returned from the Album association is large, you have a big problem. Each SQL statement executed results in interprocess communication, which drags down the performance of your application. Listing 9-60 shows the typical output you would get from the Hibernate SQL logging, shortened for brevity.

Listing 9-60. Hibernate SQL Logging Output Using Lazy Associations

```
Hibernate:
    select
        this_.id as id0_0_,
        this_.version as version0_0_,
        this_.artist_id as artist3_0_0_,
            ...
        from
        album this_
Hibernate:
    select
            artist0_.id as id8_0_,
            ...
        from
            artist artist0_
        where
            artist0_.id=?
Hibernate:
    select
            artist0_.id as id8_0_,
        ...
        from
            artist artist0_
        where
            artist0_.id=?
...
```

A knee-jerk reaction to this problem would be to make every association eager. An eager association uses an SQL JOIN so that all Artist associations are populated whenever you query for Album instances. Listing 9-61 shows you can use the mapping property to configure an association as eager by default.

Listing 9-61. Configuring an Eager Association

```
class Album {
    ...
    static mapping = {
        artist fetch:'join'
    }
}
```

However, this may not be optimal either, because you may well run into a situation where you pull your entire database into memory! Lazy associations are definitely the most sensible default here. If you're merely after the identifier of each associated artist, then it is possible to retrieve the identifier without needing to do an additional SELECT. All you need to do is refer to the association name plus the suffix Id:

```
def albums = Album.list()
for(album in albums) {
    println album.artistId // get the artist id
}
```

However, as the example in Listing 9-38 demonstrates, there are certain examples where a join query is desirable. You could modify the code as shown in Listing 9-62 to use the fetch argument.

Listing 9-62. Using the fetch Argument to Obtain Results Eagerly

```
def albums = Album.list(fetch:[artist:'join'])
for(album in albums) {
    println album.artist.name
}
```

If you run the code in Listing 9-41, instead of N+1 SELECT statements, you get a single SELECT that uses an SQL INNER JOIN to obtain the data for all artists too. Listing 9-63 shows the output from the Hibernate SQL logging for this query.

Listing 9-63. Hibernate SQL Logging Output Using Eager Association

```
select
    this_.id as id0_1_,
    this_.version as version0_1_,
        this_.artist_id as artist3_0_1_,
        this_.date_created as date4_0_1_,
        this_.genre as genre0_1_,
        this_.last_updated as last6_0_1_,
        this_.price as price0_1_,
        this_.title as title0_1_,
    this_.year as year0_1_,
    artist2_.id as id8_0_,
        artist2_.version as version8_0_,
        artist2_.date_created as date3_8_0_,
        artist2_.last_updated as last4_8_0_,
        artist2_.name as name8_0_
from
    album this_
inner join
    artist artist2_
        on this_.artist_id=artist2_.id
```

Of course, the static list() method is not the only case where you require a join query to optimize performance. Luckily, dynamic finders, criteria, and HQL can all be used to perform a join. Using a dynamic finder, you can use the fetch parameter by passing a map as the last argument:

```
def albums = Album.findAllByGenre("Alternative", [fetch:[artist:'join']])
```

Using criteria queries you can use the join method:

```
def albums = Album.withCriteria {
    ...
    join 'artist'
}
```

Finally, with HQL you can use a similar syntax to SQL by specifying the inner join in the query:

```
def albums = Album.findAll("from Album as a inner join a.artist as artist")
```

Batch Fetching

As you discovered in the previous section, using join queries can solve the N+1 problem by reducing multiple SQL SELECT statements to a single SELECT statement that uses an SQL JOIN. However, join queries too can be expensive, depending on the number of joins and the amount of data being pulled from the database.

As an alternative, you could use batch fetching, which serves as an optimization of the lazy fetching strategy. With batch fetching, instead of pulling in a single result, Hibernate will use a SELECT statement that pulls in a configured number of results. To take advantage of batch fetching, you need to set the batchSize at the class or association level.

As an example, say you had a long Album with 23 songs. Hibernate would execute a single SELECT to get the Album and then 23 extra SELECT statements for each Song. However, if you configured a batchSize of 10 for the Song class, Hibernate would perform only 3 queries in batches of 10, 10, and 3. Listing 9-64 shows how to configure the batchSize using the mapping block of the Song class.

Listing 9-64. Configuring the batchSize at the Class Level

```
class Song {
    ...
    static mapping = {
        batchSize 10
    }
}
```

Alternatively, you can also configure the batchSize on the association. For example, say you loaded 15 Album instances. Hibernate will execute a SELECT every time the songs association of each Album is accessed, resulting in 15 SELECT statements. If you configured a batchSize of 5 on the songs association, you would only get 3 queries. Listing 9-65 shows how to configure the batchSize of the songs association.

Listing 9-65. Configuring the batchSize of an Association

```
class Album {
    ...
    static mapping = {
        songs batchSize:10
    }
}
```

As you can see from this discussion on eager vs. lazy fetching, a large part of optimizing an application's performance lies in reducing the number of calls to the database. Eager fetching is one way to achieve that, but you're still making a trip to the database even if it's only one.

An even better solution is to eliminate the majority of calls to the database by caching the results. In the next section, we'll be looking at different caching techniques you can take advantage of in GORM.

Caching

In the previous "The Semantics of GORM" section, you discovered that the underlying Hibernate engine models the concept of a Session. The Session is also known as the *first-level* cache, because it stores the loaded persistent entities and prevents repeated access to the database for the same object. However, Hibernate also has a number of other caches including the second-level cache and the query cache. In the next section, we'll explain what the second-level cache is and show how it can be used to reduce the chattiness between your application and the database.

The Second-Level Cache

As discussed, as soon as a Hibernate Session is obtained by GORM, you already have an active cache: the first-level cache. Although the first-level cache stores actual persistent instances for the scope of the Session, the second-level cache exists for the whole time that the SessionFactory exists. Remember, the SessionFactory is the object that constructs each Session.

In other words, although a Session is typically scoped for each request, the second-level cache is application scoped. Additionally, the second-level cache stores only the property values and/or foreign keys rather than the persistent instances themselves. As an example, Listing 9-66 shows the conceptual representations of the Album class in the second-level cache.

Listing 9-66. How the Second-Level Cache Stores Data

```
9 -> ["Odelay",1994, "Alternative", 9.99, [34,35,36], 4]
5 -> ["Aha Shake Heartbreak",2004, "Rock", 7.99, [22,23,24], 8]
```

As you can see, the second-level cache stores the data using a map containing multidimensional arrays that represent the data. The reason for doing this is that Hibernate doesn't have to require your classes to implement Serializable or some persistence interface. By storing only the identifiers of associations, it eliminates the chance of the associations becoming stale. The previous explanation is a bit of an oversimplification; however, you don't need to concern yourself too much with the detail. Your main job is to specify a cache provider.

By default, Grails comes preconfigured with Ehcache as the cache provider. You can change the cache configuration in DataSource.groovy by modifying the settings shown in Listing 9-67.

Listing 9-67. Specifying a Cache Provider

```
hibernate {
    cache.use_second_level_cache=true
    cache.use_query_cache=true
    cache.provider_class=
        'net.sf.ehcache.hibernate.EhCacheRegionFactory '
}
```

You can even configure a distributed cache such as Oracle Coherence or Terracotta, but be careful if your application is dependent on data not being stale. Remember, cached results don't necessarily reflect the current state of the data in the database.

Once you have a cache provider configured, you're ready to go. However, by default all persistent classes have no caching enabled. You have to be very explicit about specifying what data you want cached and what the cache policy is for that data.

There are essentially four cache policies available depending on your needs:

- read-only: If your application never needs to modify data after it is created, then use this policy. It is also an effective way to enforce read-only semantics for your objects because Hibernate will throw an exception if you try to modify an instance in a read-only cache. Additionally, this policy is safe even when used in a distributed cache because there is no chance of stale data.

- nonstrict-read-write: If your application rarely modifies data and transactional updates aren't an issue, then a nonstrict-read-write cache may be appropriate. This strategy doesn't guarantee that two transactions won't simultaneously modify a persistent instance. It is mainly recommended for usage in scenarios with frequent reads and only occasional updates.

- read-write: If your application requires users to frequently modify data, then you may want to use a read-write cache. Whenever an object is updated, Hibernate will automatically evict the cached data from the second-level cache. However, there is still a chance of phantom reads (stale data) with this policy, and if transactional behavior is a requirement, you should not use a transactional cache.

- transactional: A transactional cache provides fully transactional behavior with no chance of dirty reads. However, you need to make sure you supply a cache provider that supports this feature, such as JBoss TreeCache.

So how do you use these different cache levels in a Grails application? Essentially, you need to mark each class and/or association you want to cache using the cache method of the mapping block. For example, Listing 9-68 shows how to configure the default read-write cache for the Album class and a read-only cache for the songs association.

Listing 9-68. Specifying a Cache Policy

```
class Album {
    ...
    static mapping {
        cache true
        songs cache:'read-only'
    }
}
```

Now, whenever you query for results, before loading them from the database Hibernate will check whether the record is already present in the second-level cache and, if it is, load it from there. Now let's look at another one of Hibernate's caches: the query cache.

Query Caching

Hibernate, and hence GORM, supports the ability to cache the results of a query. Under some circumstances this is useful but can also be problematic for a lot of situations. Enabling the query cache is a controversial topic and the framework errs on the side of disabling the cache by default. The query cache can be enabled and disabled using the hibernate.cache.use_query_cache setting in DataSource.groovy, as shown in Listing 9-46. For more information on some of the issues with enabling the query cache see http://tech.puredanger.com/2009/07/10/hibernate-query-cache/.

▓ **Note**   The query cache works together with the second-level cache, so unless you specify a caching policy as shown in the previous section, the results of a cached query will not be cached.

By default, even if query caching is enabled not all queries are cached. Like caching of instances, you have to specify explicitly that a query needs caching. To do so, in the list() method you could use the cache argument:

```
def albums = Album.list(cache:true)
```

The same technique can be used with dynamic finders using a map passed as the last argument:

```
def albums = Album.findAllByGenre("Alternative", [cache:true])
```

You can also cache criteria queries using the cache method:

```
def albums = Album.withCriteria {
    ...
    cache true
}
```

That's it for caching; in the next section, we'll cover the impacts of inheritance in ORM mapping.

Inheritance Strategies

As demonstrated in Chapter 3, you can implement inheritance using two different strategies called *table-per-hierarchy* or *table-per-subclass*. With a table-per-hierarchy mapping, one table is shared between the parent and all child classes, while table-per-subclass uses a different table for each subsequent subclass.

If you were going to identify one area of ORM technology that really demonstrates the object vs. relational mismatch, it would be inheritance mapping. If you go for table-per-hierarchy, then you're forced to have not-null constraints on all child columns because they share the same table. The alternative solution, table-per-subclass, could be seen as better since you avoid the need to specify nullable columns as each subclass resides in its own table.

The main disadvantage of table-per-subclass is that in a deep inheritance hierarchy you may end up with an excessive number of JOIN queries to obtain the results from all the parents of a given child. As you can imagine, this can lead to a performance problem if not used with caution; that's why we're covering the topic here.

Our advice is to keep things simple and try to avoid modeling domains with more than three levels of inheritance when using table-per-subclass. Alternatively, if you're happy sticking with table-per-hierarchy, then you're even better off because no JOIN queries at all are required. With that, we end our coverage of performance tuning GORM. In the next section, we'll be covering locking strategies and concurrency.

Locking Strategies

Given that Grails executes within the context of a multithreaded servlet container, concurrency is an issue that you need to consider whenever persisting domain instances. By default, GORM uses optimistic locking with versioning. What this means is that the Hibernate engine does not hold any locks on database rows by performing a SELECT FOR...UPDATE. Instead, Hibernate versions every domain instance.

You may already have noticed that every table generated by GORM contains a **version** column. Whenever a domain instance is saved, the version number contained within the **version** column is incremented. Just before any update to a persistent instance, Hibernate will issue an SQL SELECT to check the current version. If the version number in the table doesn't match the version number of the instance being saved, then an org.hibernate.StaleObjectStateException is thrown; it is wrapped in a Spring org.springframework.dao.OptimisticLockingFailureException and rethrown.

The implication is that if your application is processing updates with a high level of concurrency, you may need to deal with the case when you get a conflicting version. The upside is that since table rows are never locked, performance is much better. So, how do you go about gracefully handling an OptimisticLockingFailureException? Well, this is a domain-specific question. You could, for example, use the merge method to merge the changes back into the database. Alternatively, you could return the error to the user and ask him to perform a manual merge of the changes. It really does depend on the application. Nevertheless, Listing 9-69 shows how to handle an OptimisticLockingFailureException using the merge technique.

Listing 9-69. Dealing with Optimistic Locking Exceptions

```
def update() {
    def album = Album.get(params.id)
    album.properties = params
    try {
        if(album.save(flush:true)) {
            // success
            ...
        } else {
            // validation error
            ...
        }
    }
    catch(OptimisticLockingFailureException e) {
        album = Album.merge(album)
    }
}
```

If you prefer not to use optimistic locking, either because you're mapping to a legacy database or because you just don't like it, then you can disable optimistic locking using the version method inside the mapping closure of a domain class:

```
static mapping = {
    version false
}
```

If you're not expecting a heavy load on your site, then an alternative may be to use pessimistic locking. Unlike optimistic locking, pessimistic locking will perform SELECT FOR...UPDATE on the underlying table row, which will block any other threads' access to the same row until the update is committed. As you can imagine, this will have an impact on the performance of your application. To use pessimistic locking, you need to call the static lock() method, passing the identifier of the instance to obtain a lock. Listing 9-70 shows an example of using pessimistic locking with the lock method.

Listing 9-70. Using the lock Method to Obtain a Pessimistic Lock

```
def update() {
    def album = Album.lock(params.id)
    ...
}
```

If you have a reference to an existing persistent instance, then you can call the lock() instance method, which upgrades to a pessimistic lock. Listing 9-71 shows how to use the lock instance method.

Listing 9-71. *Using the lock Instance Method to Upgrade to a Pessimistic Lock*

```
def update() {
    def album = Album.get(params.Id)
    album.lock() // lock the Instance
}
```

Note that you need to be careful when using the lock instance method because you still get an OptimisticLockingFailureException if another thread has updated the row in the time it takes to get the instance and call lock() on it! With locks out of the way, let's move on to looking at GORM's support for events.

Events Auto Time Stamping

GORM has a number of built-in hooks you can take advantage of to hook into persistence events. Each event is defined as a closure property in the domain class itself. The events available are as follows:

- onLoad/beforeLoad: fired when an object is loaded from the database

- beforeInsert: fired before an object is initially persisted to the database

- beforeValidate: fired before an object is validated

- beforeUpdate: fired before an object is updated in the database

- beforeDelete: fired before an object is deleted from the database

- afterInsert: fired after an object has been persisted to the database

- afterUpdate: fired after an object has been updated in the database

- afterDelete: fired after an object has been deleted from the database

These events are useful for performing tasks such as audit logging and tracking. For example, you could have another domain class that models an AuditLogEvent that gets persisted every time an instance gets accessed or saved. Listing 9-72 shows this concept in action.

Listing 9-72. *Using GORM Events*

```
class Album {
    ...
    def onLoad() {
        new AuditLogEvent(type:"read", data:title).save()
    }
    def beforeSave() {
        new AuditLogEvent(type:"save", data:title).save()
    }

    def beforeValidate() {
        // run before validation happens
    }
```

```
    def beforeValidate(List propertiesBeingValidated) {
        // run before validation happens and propertiesBeingValidated
        // is a List containing the names of all of the properties which
        // are about to be validated.
    }
}
```

GORM also supports automatic time stamps. Essentially, if you provide a property called dateCreated or one called lastUpdated, GORM will automatically populate the values for it every time an instance is saved or updated. In fact, you've already been using this feature, since the Album class has lastUpdated and dateCreated properties. However, if you prefer to manage these properties manually, you can disable automatic time stamping using the autoTimestamp method of the mapping block, as shown in Listing 9-73.

Listing 9-73. Disable Auto Time Stamping

```
class Album {
    ...
    static mapping = {
        autoTimestamp false
    }
}
```

Summary

You've now reached the end of this tour of GORM. As you've discovered, thanks in large part to Hibernate, GORM is a fully featured dynamic ORM tool that blurs the lines between objects and the database. From dynamic finders to criteria, there is a plethora of options for your querying needs. However, it's not all clever tricks; GORM provides solutions to such harder problems as eager fetching and optimistic locking.

Possibly the most important aspect of this chapter is the knowledge you have gained on the semantics of GORM. By understanding the ORM tool you are using, you'll find there are fewer surprises along the way, and you'll become a more effective developer. Although GORM pretty much eliminates the need for data access layers such as those you typically find in pure Java applications, it doesn't remove the need for a structured way to group units of logic. In the next chapter, we'll be looking at Grails services that provide exactly this. Don't go away!

CHAPTER 10

Services

A common pattern in the development of enterprise software is the so-called service layer that encapsulates a set of business operations. With Java web development, it is generally considered good practice to provide layers of abstraction and reduce coupling between the layers within an MVC application.

The service layer provides a way to centralize application behavior into an API that can be utilized by controllers or other services. Many good reasons exist for encapsulating logic into a service layer, but the following are the main drivers:

- You need to centralize business logic into a service API.

- The use cases within your application operate on multiple domain objects and model complex business operations that are best not mixed in with controller logic.

- Certain use cases and business processes are best encapsulated outside a domain object and within an API.

If your requirements fall into one of these categories, creating a service is probably what you want to do. Services themselves often have multiple dependencies; for example, a common activity for a service is to interact with the persistence layer, whether that is straight JDBC or an ORM system, such as Hibernate.

Clearly, whichever system you use, you are potentially dependent on a data source, a session factory, or maybe just another service. Configuring these dependencies in a loosely coupled way has been one of the main challenges facing early adopters of the Java EE technology.

Like many other software development challenges, this problem is solved by a software design pattern—in this case, one called Inversion of Control (IoC), or dependency injection. A project such as Spring implements this pattern by providing an IoC container.

Grails uses Spring to configure itself internally, and it is this foundation that Grails builds on to provide services by convention. Let's jump straight into looking at what Grails services are and how to create a basic service.

Understanding Service Basics

Services, like other Grails artefacts, follow a convention and don't extend any base class. For example, say that you decide to move logic related to retrieving album artwork out of the AlbumArtTagLib and into a service; to do so, you would need to create a class called AlbumArtService, located in the grails-app/services/ directory.

Unsurprisingly, there is a Grails target that allows you to conveniently create services. Building on what was just mentioned, to create the `AlbumArtService`, you can execute the `create-service` target, which will prompt you to enter the name of the service, as demonstrated in Listing 10-1.

Listing 10-1. Running the create-service Target

```
grails> create-service com.gtunes.AlbumArt
| Created file grails-app/services/com/gtunes/AlbumArtService.groovy
| Created file test/unit/com/gtunes/AlbumArtServiceTests.groovy
```

This will create the `AlbumArtService` class automatically and put it in the right place. The result will resemble something like Listing 10-2.

Listing 10-2. grails-app/services/com/gtunes/AlbumArtService.groovy

```
package com.gtunes
class AlbumArtService {
    def serviceMethod() {
    }
}
```

The service contains one method, which is just a placeholder for a real method.

Services and Dependency Injection

It is important to note that services are singletons by default, which means there is only ever one instance of a service. So how do you go about getting a reference to a service within a controller, for example? Well, as part of its dependency injection support, Spring has a concept called *autowiring* that allows dependencies to automatically be injected by name or type.

Grails services can be injected by name into a controller. For example, simply by creating a property with the name `albumArtService` within the `AlbumArtTagLib`, the `AlbumArtService` instance will automatically be available to the taglib. Listing 10-3 demonstrates how this is done.

Listing 10-3. Injecting a Service Instance into a Controller

```
class AlbumArtTagLib {
    AlbumArtService albumArtService
    ...
}
```

▓ **Note** The `albumArtService` property is statically typed in Listing 10-3. The property can be dynamically typed, and injection will work in the same way.

The convention used for the name of the property is basically the property name representation of the class name. In other words, it is the class name with the first letter set in lowercase type, following the JavaBean convention for property names. You can then invoke methods on the singleton `AlbumArtService` instance, even though you have done nothing to explicitly look it up or initialize it. The underlying Spring IoC container handles all of this automatically.

You can use the same convention to inject services into other services, hence allowing your services to interact within one another.

It is important that you let Grails inject service instances for you. You should never instantiate instances of service classes directly. Later in this chapter, when we discuss transactions, you will see that there is some special magic going on when Grails is allowed to inject service instances for you. You will get none of those benefits if you create service instances yourself.

Now that you've been shown the basics of services, let's see an example of implementing a service.

Services in Action

The AlbumArtTagLib in the gTunes application already contains quite a bit of logic and complexity. Pulling that logic out of the taglib and into a service is a good idea.

In general, you should strive to keep your Grails controllers and taglibs tight and concise. You should not let a lot of business complexity evolve in a controller or a taglib. When much complexity starts to evolve in a controller or a taglib, that should be a red flag to you. You should then consider refactoring to pull out a lot of that complexity. Much of it will fit perfectly into a service or multiple services.

Let's take a look at the taglib code that is a good candidate for some refactoring. Listing 10-4 shows the current state of the AlbumArtTagLib.

Listing 10-4. *The AlbumArtTagLib Class*

```
package com.gtunes

import grails.plugins.rest.client.RestBuilder

class AlbumArtTagLib {

  static final DEFAULT_ALBUM_ART_IMAGE =  "/images/no-album-art.gif"

  static namespace = "music"

  def albumArt =  { attrs, body ->
    def artistName = attrs.remove('artist')?.toString()
    def albumTitle = attrs.remove('album')?.toString()
    def width = attrs.int('width', 100)
    attrs.remove('width')
    def albumArt = DEFAULT_ALBUM_ART_IMAGE
    if(artistName && albumTitle) {
      try {
        def restBuilder = new RestBuilder()
        def url = "http://itunes.apple.com/search?term=${albumTitle.encodeAsURL()}&media=music&e
ntity=album&attribute=albumTerm"
        def response = restBuilder.get(url)
        def json = response.json
        def records = json.results
        def matchingRecord = records.find { r ->
          r.artistName == artistName && r.collectionName == albumTitle
        }
        albumArt = matchingRecord?.artworkUrl100 ?: DEFAULT_ALBUM_ART_IMAGE
      } catch (Exception e) {
        log.error "Problem retrieving artwork: ${e.message}", e
      }
```

```
    }
    if(albumArt.startsWith("/")) albumArt = "${request.contextPath}${albumArt}"
    out << "<img width=\"$width\" src=\"${albumArt}\" border=\"0\""
    out << attrs.collect { attributeName, attributeValue ->
      " ${attributeName}=\"${attributeValue.encodeAsHTML()}\""
    }.join(' ')
    out << "></img>"
  }
}
```

You should pull most of this code out of the taglib and put it into a service.

Defining a Service

The code that is being refactored out of the StoreController should be put into a service called
AlbumArtService. The AlbumArtService class should be defined in the grails-app/services/com/gtunes/
directory. That refactoring would yield an AlbumArtService like the one shown in Listing 10-5.

Listing 10-5. The getAlbumArt Method in the AlbumArtService

```
package com.gtunes

import grails.plugins.rest.client.RestBuilder

class AlbumArtService {

  static transactional = false

  static final DEFAULT_ALBUM_ART_IMAGE =  "/images/no-album-art.gif"

  String artworkRequestUrl =
  'http://itunes.apple.com/search?media=music&entity=album&attribute=albumTerm'

  def getAlbumArt(String artist, String album) {
    def imageUrl = DEFAULT_ALBUM_ART_IMAGE
    if(artist && album) {
      try {
        def restBuilder = new RestBuilder()
        def urlWithAlbumParam =
          "${artworkRequestUrl}&term=${album.encodeAsURL()}"
        def response = restBuilder.get(urlWithAlbumParam)
        def json = response.json
        def records = json.results
        def matchingRecord = records.find { r ->
          r.artistName == artist && r.collectionName == album
        }
        imageUrl = matchingRecord?.artworkUrl100 ?: DEFAULT_ALBUM_ART_IMAGE
      } catch (Exception e) {
        log.error "Problem retrieving artwork: ${e.message}", e
      }
    }
  }
```

```
    imageUrl
  }
}
```

Configuring Service Bean Properties

The AlbumArtService contains a property named artworkRequestUrl, which is a string that points to a RESTful web service for retrieving album artwork. The value could be hard-coded into the AlbumArtService, but a better idea may be to externalize the definition of that property value into a configuration file. You can use a technique called *property override configuration* to specify the value of this property in grails-app/conf/Config.groovy. Every service in Grails translates into a Spring bean. The name of the bean is formulated from the class name using bean conventions. Hence, the bean name for AlbumArtService will be albumArtService. You can set properties on the albumArtService bean from Config. groovy by using the beans block, as shown in Listing 10-6.

Listing 10-6. *Configuring Beans Using Config.groovy*

```
beans {
  albumArtService {
    artworkRequestUrl =
  'http://itunes.apple.com/search?media=music&entity=album&attribute=albumTerm'
  }
}
```

One advantage of this approach is that thanks to the features offered by Config.groovy, you can easily specify per-environment values rather than hard-coding the value into the AlbumArtService class. With that configuration code in place, the hard-coded value may be removed from the AlbumArtService class. The property still needs to be declared as a field in the class but should not be assigned a value. The framework will take care of initializing the property with the value specified in Config.groovy.

Caching Service Methods

The getAlbumArt method in the AlbumArtService class is functional at the moment but could use some improvement. One problem with the current implementation is that it is inefficient. Every time the method is called, requests are being made to a remote service to retrieve a URL for some album art. One thing to do that might help with this is implement some sort of caching mechanism, so when the artwork for a particular album is requested, a request is made to the remote service to get the relevant artwork URL, which then could be cached. So if another request arrives for artwork for that same album, instead of making a call to the remote service, the URL can be retrieved from the local cache—a much more efficient procedure. Writing efficient and reliable caching mechanisms can be complicated. Fortunately, a Grails plug-in does all the hard work for you.

You can install the cache plug-in by adding the appropriate dependency declaration to grails-app/ conf/BuildConfig.groovy, as shown in Listing 10-7.

Listing 10-7. *Declaring a Dependency on the Cache Plug-in*

```
// grails-app/conf/BuildConfig.groovy
grails.project.dependency.resolution = {
    // ...
    plugins {
```

```
        compile ':cache:1.0.0'
        // ...
    }
}
```

With the plug-in installed, you need to tell the plug-in that all calls to the getAlbumArt method in the AlbumArtService class should be cached. The way to do this is to annotate the method with the grails.plugin.cache.Cacheable annotation, as shown in Listing 10-8.

Listing 10-8. Adding Caching Support to the getAlbumArt Method

```
package com.gtunes

// ...
import grails.plugin.cache.Cacheable

class AlbumArtService {

    // ...
    @Cacheable('albumArt')
    def getAlbumArt(String artist, String album) {
        // ...
    }
}
```

Notice that the Cacheable annotation is passing albumArt as an argument. This represents the name of the cache that will be associated with this method. Some caches may be shared across numerous methods, whereas others may be used by only one method. By default the keys for the cache will be the union of all of the arguments that are being passed to the method, which for this case is exactly what is wanted. If the getAlbumArt method is invoked numerous times with the same argument, the calls to the remote service are made only once for each album.

The cache plug-in by default uses a relatively simple in-memory map for storage. For our demo application this is fine, but more demanding caching requirements call for a more sophisticated cache. There are several extensions to the main cache plug-in to support various cache implementations. For example, there is a Redis implementation, an Ehcache implementation, and a Gemfire implementation. When you use these more sophisticated implementations, the basic usage in your application stays the same, but configuration details will vary.

We are using the cache plug-in in the most basic way and taking advantage of only a small part of its capabilities. See http://grails.org/plugin/cache for more information on configuring and using the cache plug-in.

Using a Service

The AlbumArtTagLib can now take advantage of the getAlbumArt method in the AlbumArtService. To do this, the AlbumArtTagLib needs to define the albumArtService property and then invoke the getAlbumArt method on that property, as shown in Listing 10-9.

Listing 10-9. Calling the getAlbumArt Method from the AlbumArtTagLib

```
package com.gtunes

class AlbumArtTagLib {

    static namespace = "music"

    def albumArtService

    def albumArt = { attrs, body ->
        def artist = attrs.remove('artist')?.toString()
        def album = attrs.remove('album')?.toString()
        def width = attrs.remove('width') ?: 200
        if(artist && album) {
            def albumArt = albumArtService.getAlbumArt(artist, album)
            if(albumArt.startsWith("/")) {
                albumArt = "${request.contextPath}${albumArt}"
            }
            out << "<img width=\"$width\" src=\"${albumArt}\" border=\"0\""
            attrs.each { k,v-> out << "$k=\"${v?.encodeAsHTML()}\" "}
            out << "></img>"
        }
    }
}
```

Managing Transactions

As mentioned previously, services often encapsulate business operations that deal with several domain objects. If an exception occurs while executing changes, you may not want any earlier changes to be committed to the database.

Essentially, you want an all-or-nothing approach, also known as a *transaction*. Transactions are essential for maintaining database integrity via their ACID properties, which have probably been covered in every book that has used a relational database. Nevertheless, let's have a quick look at them here. ACID stands for atomicity, consistency, isolation, and durability.

- *atomicity*: This refers to the fact that operations on data within a transaction must be atomic. In other words, all tasks within a transaction will be completed or none at all will be, thus allowing the changes to be rolled back.

- *consistency*: This requires that the database be in a consistent state before and after any operations occur. There is no point attempting to complete a transaction if the database is not in a legal state to begin with, and it would be rather silly if an operation left the database's integrity compromised.

- *isolation*: This refers to how transactions are isolated from all other operations. Essentially, this means other queries or operations should never be exposed to data that are in an intermediate state.

- *durability*: Once a transaction is completed, durability guarantees that the transaction cannot possibly be undone. Thus, even if system failure occurs, the committed transaction cannot at that point be aborted.

Grails services may declare a static property named transactional. When the transactional property is set to true, the methods of the service are configured for transaction demarcation by Spring. What this does is create a Spring proxy that wraps each method call and provides transaction management.

Grails handles the entire automatic runtime configuration for you, leaving you to concentrate on writing the logic within your methods. If the service does not require any transaction management, set the transactional property to false to disable transactions.

Another option is a service's need to impose its own fine-grained control over transaction management. The way to do this is to assign the transactional property a value of false and take responsibility yourself for managing transactions. The static withTransaction method may be called on any domain class; it expects a closure to be passed as an argument. The closure represents the transaction boundary. Listing 10-10 has an example.

Listing 10-10. Using withTransaction in a Service

```
package com.gtunes
class StoreService {
    // turn off automatic transaction management
    static transactional = false
    void someServiceMethod() {
        Album.withTransaction {
            // everything in this closure is happening within a transaction
            // which will be committed when the closure completes
        }
    }
}
```

If the closure that is passed to the withTransaction method throws an exception, the transaction will be rolled back. Otherwise, the transaction is committed.

Taking explicit control over rolling back the transaction is simple to do as well. It turns out that an instance of the org.springframework.transaction.TransactionStatus interface is being passed as an argument to the closure. One of the methods defined by the TransactionStatus interface is setRollbackOnly().[1] Calling the setRollbackOnly() method will ensure that the transaction gets rolled back. Listing 10-11 demonstrates how to take advantage of this.

Listing 10-11. Using the TransactionStatus Argument

```
package com.gtunes
class StoreService {
    // turn off automatic transaction management
    static transactional = false
    void someServiceMethod() {
        Album.withTransaction { tx ->
            // do some work with the database
            // if the transaction needs to be rolled back for
            // any reason,  call setRollbackOnly() on the
            // TransactionStatus argument...
            tx.setRollbackOnly()
        }
    }
}
```

1 You can find the full documentation for the TransactionStatus interface at http://static. springsource.org/spring/docs/3.1.x/javadoc-api/.

Controllers and other Grails artefacts will, of course, need to get hold of a reference to the singleton StoreService. As described earlier in this chapter, the best way to get hold of a reference to a service is to take advantage of the automatic dependency injection provided by Grails.

Scoping Services

You must be careful about storing state in a service. By default all services are scoped as singletons and can be used concurrently by multiple requests. Further, access to service methods is not synchronized. For stateless services, none of that is a problem. If a service must maintain state, it should be scoped to something other than singleton.

Grails supports several scopes for services. Which scope you use will depend on how your application uses the service and what kind of state is maintained in the service. The support scopes are as follows:

- prototype: A new service is created every time it is injected into another class.

- request: A new service will be created per request.

- flash: A new service will be created for the current and next requests only.

- flow: In Web Flow, the service will exist for the scope of the flow.

- conversation: In Web Flow, the service will exist for the scope of the conversation; in other words, a root flow and its subflows.

- session: A service is created for the scope of a user session.

- singleton (default): Only one instance of the service ever exists.

If a service is to be scoped using anything other than singleton, the service must declare a static property, scope, and assign it a value that is one of the support scopes listed earlier. See Listing 10-12.

Listing 10-12. *A request Scoped Service*

```
class SomeUsefulService {
    boolean transactional = true
    // this is a request scoped service
    static scope = 'request'
}
```

Choose the service scope carefully, and make sure your scope is consistent with the application's expectations of the service. Prefer stateless services; for these, the default scope, singleton, is almost always optimum. When a service must maintain state, choose the scope that satisfies the application's requirements.

Testing Services

Since much of your business logic and complexity is encapsulated in services, it is important that these components be tested. As far as tests are concerned, a service is just another class and can be tested as such. The unit testing support provided for services is similar to that provided for other artefact types.

Listing 10-13 shows the default test that was created by the create-service command.

Listing 10-13. Default Service Unit Test Template

```
package com.gtunes



import grails.test.mixin.*
import org.junit.*

/**
 * See the API for {@link grails.test.mixin.services.ServiceUnitTestMixin} for usage
instructions
 */
@TestFor(AlbumArtService)
class AlbumArtServiceTests {

    void testSomething() {
        fail "Implement me"
    }
}
```

To test the AlbumArtService, fill that out using standard Groovy unit-testing techniques. See Listing 10-14.

Listing 10-14. Unit-Testing AlbumArtService

```
package com.gtunes

import grails.plugins.rest.client.RestBuilder
import groovy.mock.interceptor.MockFor
import grails.test.mixin.*
//import org.junit.*

/**
 * See the API for {@link grails.test.mixin.services.ServiceUnitTestMixin} for usage
instructions
 */
@TestFor(AlbumArtService)
class AlbumArtServiceTests {

    void testNullAlbumAndArtist() {
        def result = service.getAlbumArt(null, null)
                                    assert AlbumArtService.DEFAULT_ALBUM_ART_IMAGE == result
    }

    void testGoodResult() {
        mockCodec org.codehaus.groovy.grails.plugins.codecs.URLCodec
        def artworkClient = new groovy.mock.interceptor.MockFor(RestBuilder)
        artworkClient.demand.get { String s ->
            def results = []
            results << [artistName: 'Thin Lizzy',
                    collectionName: 'Jailbreak',
```

```
                        artworkUrl100: 'http://somesite/jailbreak.jpg']
            results << [artistName: 'Tool',
                        collectionName: 'Lateralus',
                        artworkUrl100: 'http://somesite/lateralus.jpg']
            [json: [results: results]]
        }
        def result
        artworkClient.use {
            result = service.getAlbumArt('Tool', 'Lateralus')
        }
        assert 'http://somesite/lateralus.jpg' == result
    }
}
```

Note that the test refers to a property named service, which is provided by the testing framework and is automatically initialized to be an instance of the class under test, in this case the AlbumArtService class.

Exposing Services

The services you write as part of a Grails application contain a large share of the business logic involved in the application. Those services are easily accessed from just about anywhere in the application using the automatic dependency injection built into Grails. It makes sense that a lot of that business logic may be useful to other Grails applications. In fact, it may be useful to applications that aren't Grails applications. The automatic dependency injection works only within the application. There really isn't any way to inject those services into other applications. However, it is possible to access those services from other applications, and Grails makes that really easy to do.

Making a service available to another process is known as *exposing* the service. A number of available Grails plug-ins support exposing services using various remoting technologies. For example, one plug-in greatly simplifies exposing services using the Java Management Extensions (JMX) technology.[2] JMX, part of the Java Platform since the J2SE 5.0 release, provides a really simple mechanism for monitoring and managing resources within an application.

You can install the JMX plug-in by adding the appropriate dependency declaration to grails-app/conf/BuildConfig.groovy, as shown in Listing 10-15.

Listing 10-15. Declaring a Dependency on the JMX Plug-in

```
// grails-app/conf/BuildConfig.groovy
grails.project.dependency.resolution = {
    // ...
    plugins {
        runtime ':jmx:0.7'
        // ...
    }
}
```

Like other remoting plug-ins available for Grails, the JMX plug-in will look in all service classes for a property named expose. The expose property should be a list of Strings, and if the list contains the string jmx, then the plug-in will expose that service using JMX.

---

2   You can find more information about JMX at http://java.sun.com/javase/technologies/core/mntr-mgmt/javamanagement/.

Listing 10-16 shows a service in the gTunes application that has been exposed using JMX.

Listing 10-16. *The StoreService Is Exposed Using JMX*

```
package com.gtunes

class StoreService {

    static transactional = true

    static expose = ['jmx']
    int getNumberOfAlbums() {
        Album.count()
    }
    int getNumberOfAlbumsForGenre(String genre) {
        Album.countByGenre(genre)
    }
}
```

The StoreService contains a single method, getNumberOfAlbums, which returns the number of Album objects currently in the database. The service may contain any number of methods. All of the methods in the service will be exposed as JMX operations.

In terms of code, to expose your services using JMX, you need only include jmx in the value of the expose property. It couldn't be simpler! There is another step that does not involve code. The way to enable remote access to services that have been exposed using JMX is to set the com.sun.management.jmxremote system property when the Grails application starts. A simple way to do this is to assign a value to the JAVA_OPTS environment variable. The value should include -Dcom.sun.management.jmxremote. Note that the property does not need to be assigned a value; it just needs to be set. For example, in a Bash shell, you can interactively set the environment variable using the code shown in Listing 10-17.

Listing 10-17. *Setting JAVA_OPTS in a Bash Shell*

```
export JAVA_OPTS=-Dcom.sun.management.jmxremote
```

In a Windows shell you can use the code shown in Listing 10-18.

Listing 10-18. *Setting JAVA_OPTS in a Windows Shell*

```
set JAVA_OPTS=-Dcom.sun.management.jmxremote
```

The com.sun.management.jmxremote system property must be set when the Grails application starts. If the property is set after the Grails application has started, the application will not be affected.

Versions 5.0 and later of the J2SE include the Java Monitoring and Management Console, known as JConsole. The JConsole application is a GUI tool for interacting with beans that have been exposed using JMX.

With your Grails application up and running, start JConsole by running the jconsole command at a command prompt. The application should open with the dialog box shown in Figure 10-1.

This dialog box allows selection of the agent you want to connect to. Typically you will see just one agent in the list. Find your Grails application in the list, select it, and click the Connect button.

Once you have connected to an agent, the main JConsole window should appear, as shown in Figure 10-2.

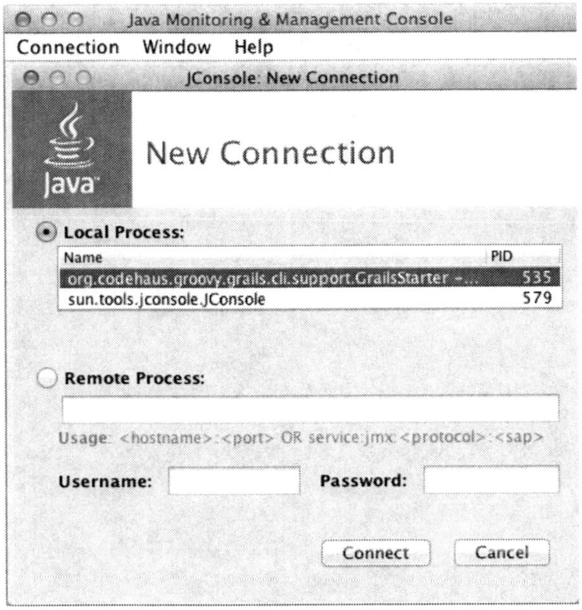

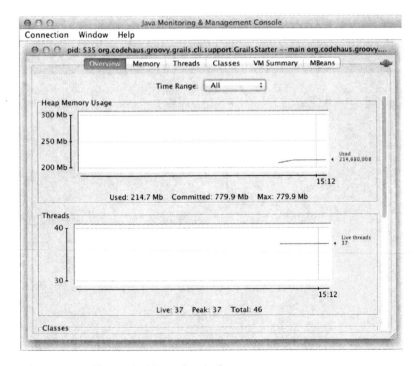

Figure 10-1. *The Connect to Agent dialog box in JConsole*

Figure 10-2. *The main JConsole window*

The main screen displays a lot of information about the Grails process. Click the MBeans tab at the top of the screen to view all the accessible beans. On that screen, you should see a list of all of your JMX-exposed services under the `gtunes/service` folder on the left, as shown in Figure 10-3.

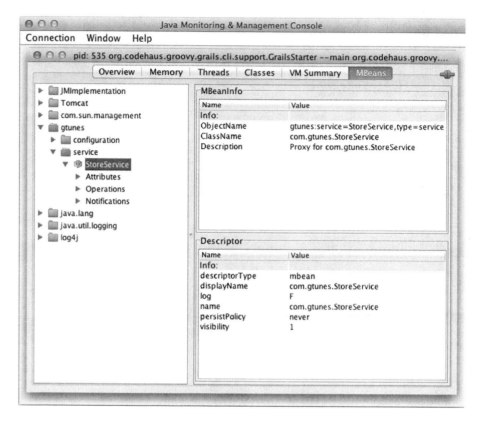

Figure 10-3. *Grails services exposed using JMX*

Expand the Operations folder under StoreService. This will list all the operations that have been exposed by this bean, including all the methods defined in your service, as shown in Figure 10-4.

Notice that for operations that require parameters, JConsole provides a text box, where the value of the parameter is defined. Once that value is filled in, click the button that contains the operation name. The operation will be invoked remotely, and the return value will be displayed.

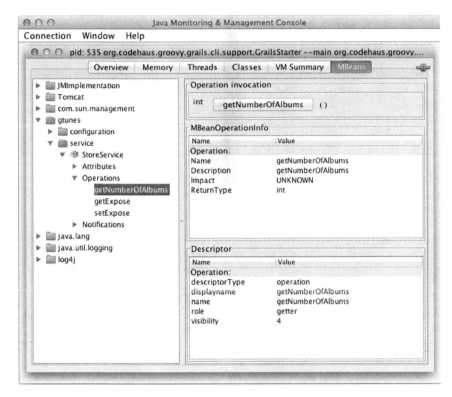

Figure 10-4. JMX operations

The JMX plug-in is one of several Grails plug-ins that support exposing services using various remoting technologies. There is an XML-RPC plug-in, as well as a Remoting plug-in that allows services to be exposed via RMI, Hessian, Burlap, and Spring's HttpInvoker. The Cxf and Axis2 plug-ins each support exposing services via SOAP.

All of the remoting plug-ins use the same expose property in a service class as the trigger for exposing a service using any particular technology. Listing 10-19 shows how you would expose the StoreService using JMX and Axis2.

Listing 10-19. Exposing a Service Using JMX and Axis2

```
package com.gtunes
class StoreService {
    static transactional = true
    static expose = ['jmx', 'axis2']
    int getNumberOfAlbums() {
        Album.count()
    }
    int getNumberOfAlbumsForGenre(String genre) {
        Album.countByGenre(genre)
    }
}
```

Remember that in order for that code to work, you need to have the JMX and Axis2 plug-ins installed.

Exposing Grails services is a great way to allow applications to access business logic inside a Grails application. In fact, you could build a Grails application that is just a service layer. That application might consist of nothing more than domain classes and services that provide access to the data, similar to the StoreService shown earlier. The application would not necessarily need to have any controllers, any views, or anything else.

Summary

Services, important components in almost any nontrivial Grails application, are where much of the application's business logic and complexity belong.

In this chapter, you saw how Grails helps simplify an application by encouraging the isolation of that complexity into services. You learned how you can easily take advantage of the power of Spring's dependency injection capabilities without the burden of having to write configuration files to instrument Spring.

You also saw how transaction management works with respect to Grails services. For most scenarios, the default method-level transaction demarcation is a perfect fit. For scenarios where the application needs more fine-grained control over transactions, Grails provides a really simple mechanism for dealing with them.

With so many options for exposing Grails services, using any number of remoting technologies, you should make a habit of taking advantage of the power and flexibility that Grails services provide. If you do, your applications will be easier to write, easier to understand, easier to maintain, and easier to test.

CHAPTER 11

■ ■ ■

Integration and Dependency Management

So far, a number of the core concepts that underpin Grails have been explored. From controllers to GORM and services, you should now have a pretty good understanding of what makes Grails tick. In this chapter, you'll learn how you can fit Grails into your existing ecosystem. We hope what you'll get from this chapter is a good understanding of how to go about including Grails in your build system, development tools, reporting setup, and server environment.

There is a lot of ground to cover, so let's get started by taking a closer look at configuration in Grails.

Grails and Configuration

Using Convention over Configuration (CoC), Grails significantly reduces the amount of configuration you need to do. Crucially, however, it is convention *over* configuration, not convention instead of configuration. There are still a number of different ways you can configure Grails.

Most configuration can be done using the central configuration mechanism within Grails. The file grails-app/conf/Config.groovy contains many configuration details for the application. You've already seen this file being used at various points throughout the book. In the following sections, we'll look closer at how you use Config.groovy to configure Grails and what configuration options are available to you.

Configuration Basics

The Config.groovy file is a Groovy script similar to a regular Java properties file. You can set its properties using the dot dereference operator:

```
grails.mime.file.extensions = true
```

Since it's a Groovy script, all the type information is retained. So in the previous example a Boolean property called grails.mime.file.extensions is set to true. To access this setting, use the config property of the grailsApplication object available in controllers and views:

```
assert grailsApplication.config.grails.mime.file.extensions == true
```

Besides settings specified on a single line, like the grails.mime.file.extensions setting, Groovy also supports group settings using blocks (see Listing 11-1).

Listing 11-1. Grouping Settings in Config.groovy

```
grails.mime {
    file.extensions = true
    types = [html: 'text/html']
}
```

The example in Listing 11-1 will produce two entries in config: grails.mime.file. extensions and grails.mime.types. You can also configure settings on a per-environment basis. That will be covered next.

Environment-Specific Configuration

As you discovered in Chapter 2, the grails-app/conf/DataSource.groovy file can be configured in an environment-specific way because Grails uses the same mechanism to configure the DataSource as Config. groovy uses for the rest of the application.

Just as with DataSource.groovy, by using Config.groovy you can specify environment-specific settings using the environments block, as shown in Listing 11-2.

Listing 11-2. Environment-Specific Configuration

```
// set per-environment serverURL stem for creating absolute links
environments {
    development {
        grails.serverURL = "http://localhost:8080"
    } production {
        grails.serverURL = "http://www.gtunes.com"
    }
}
```

As Listing 11-2 demonstrates, the environments block can be used to specify a different grails. serverURL setting for production and development environments. The grails.serverURL setting is one of a number of built-in settings that you'll be discovering through the course of this book.

Configuring Logging

Grails uses the popular Log4j (http://logging.apache.org/log4j/) library to configure logging. Traditionally, Log4j has been configured with either a properties file format or XML. Grails, however, provides a specific DSL for configuring logging. Within the Config.groovy script, you can set a property called log4j using a Groovy closure.

Within this closure, you can use the Log4j DSL to configure logging. Listing 11-3 shows the default Log4j configuration in Grails that sets up logging for a bunch of packages internal to Grails.

Listing 11-3. The Default Log4j Configuration

```
// log4j configuration
log4j = {
error 'codehaus.groovy.grails.web.servlet',   // controllers
      'codehaus.groovy.grails.web.pages',    // GSP
      'codehaus.groovy.grails.web.sitemesh',   // layouts
      'codehaus.groovy.grails.web.mapping.filter',  // URL mapping
      'codehaus.groovy.grails.web.mapping',   // URL Mapping
```

```
    'codehaus.groovy.grails.commons',// core / classloading
    'codehaus.groovy.grails.plugins',// plugins
    'codehaus.groovy.grails.orm.hibernate'   // hibernate integration
}
```

As you can see from Listing 11-3, inside the body of the log4j closure, an error method is invoked. It is passed a number of packages as arguments. The error method sets up the specified packages at the error debug level. The following debug levels are available, going from least to most verbose.

- off: no logging at all

- fatal: to log only fatal errors, which are typically errors that would cause an application to abort

- error: to log all errors that occur but still allow the application to continue running

- warn: to log scenarios that could be potentially harmful

- info: to log informational messages that describe the progress of the application

- debug: to log information that is used to debug an application

- trace: the level for even finer-grained events than the debug level

- all: to log all messages that occur

Sources within your own application can also be configured for logging. In Chapter 4 you learned about the log property available in every controller, tag library, or service. The output of this log property by default will use the root logging level of error. However, you can use the name of the class, starting with grails.app, to configure different logging behavior. For example, if you want to see output from all log statements in the UserController and AlbumArtService classes at the debug level, you could use the configuration in Listing 11-4.

Listing 11-4. *Setting the Debug Level*

```
log4j {
    debug   'grails.app.controller.UserController',
            'grails.app.service.AlbumArtService'
}
```

Using sensible defaults, Grails will automatically configure a console appender that logs to standard out while the root logger is set to the error level. You can also create your own custom Log4j appenders. For example, the code in Listing 11-5 sets up an additional file appender that writes the log to a file.

Listing 11-5. *Configuring a File Appender*

```
log4j {
   appenders {
      rollingFile name:"myl_og",
      file:"/var/log/gtunes.log", maxFileSize:"1MB",
      layout:  pattern(conversionPattern:   '%c{2} %m%n')
   }
}
```

The example in Listing 11-5 uses a rollingFile appender, which is an org.apache.log4j. RollingFileAppender instance internally. Each named argument is a property of the org.apache.log4j.

RollingFileAppender class, so to understand the configuration options, you just have to look at the Log4j APIs. The following is a list of the available Log4j appenders.

- jdbc: The org.apache.log4j.jdbc.DDBCAppender logs to a database connection.

- null: The org.apache.log4j.varia.NullAppender does nothing!

- console: The org.apache.log4j.ConsoleAppender logs to standard out.

- file: This is an org.apache.log4j.FileAppender that logs to a single file.

- rollingFile: This is an org.apache.log4j.RollingFileAppender that logs to a file that gets automatically backed up and re-created when a maximum size is hit.

You can also use the Log4j API yourself to create an appender programmatically and then simply call the appender method, passing your appender, to add your own appender. Notice also that Listing 11-5 uses the pattern method to define the layout property of the appender. This translates into an org.apache. log4j.PatternLayout instance. You can use a number of other layout styles, including the following:

- xml:: An org.apache.log4j.xml.XMLLayout instance that outputs the log file in XML format.

- html: An org.apache.log4j.HTMLLayout instance that outputs the logs in HTML.

- simple: An org.apache.log4j.SimpleLayout instance that outputs to a preconfigured text format.

- pattern: An org.apache.log4j.PatternLayout instance that allows you to configure the output from Log4j. See the javadoc API for details.

Once you have an appender, you have to tell Log4j which packages need to be logged to that appender. Listing 11-6 shows an example of logging Hibernate output to the rollingFile appender, defined earlier at the trace level.

Listing 11-6. *Using an Appender*

```
log4j {
    ...
    trace myLog:"org.hibernate"
    debug myLog:["org.codehaus.groovy.grails.web.mapping.filter",
                 "org.codehaus.groovy.grails.web.mapping"]
}
```

Notice that you reference the appender by the name given to it using the name argument. Finally, there is one special logger for stack traces, which we'll discuss in the next section.

Stack Trace Filtering

Whenever an exception is thrown in Grails, the exception's stack trace will be filtered of all Groovy and Grails internals before it is logged. This is very useful because it allows you to narrow the problem down to how it relates to your code. Otherwise, with all the internal layers of Grails exposed, you could be sifting through a rather large stack trace.

Normally, when an exception is thrown in development, you can work out from the filtered trace what the problem is. On a rare occasion, you may want to inspect the full nonfiltered stack trace. Grails, by default, sets up a special logger to which it will log the full stack trace. This logger writes to a file called stacktrace.log in the root of your project.

However, you can quite easily override this default behavior to provide your own custom logger for unfiltered stack traces. Listing 11-7 shows an example configuration that logs all unfiltered stack traces to a rolling file appender.

Listing 11-7. Logging Unfiltered Traces

```
log4j {
appenders {
  rollingFile name:"stacktraceLog",
              file:"/var/log/unfiltered-stacktraces.log",
              maxFileSize:"1MB",
              layout: pattern(conversionPattern: '%c{2} %m%n')
}
error stacktraceLog:"StackTrace"
```

You can also disable this functionality completely by passing the grails.full.stacktrace argument at the command line of your container or as an argument to the run-app command:

```
grails -Dgrails.full.stacktrace=true run-app
```

Externalized Configuration

During deployment, the Config.groovy file is compiled into a class and packaged into the WAR. Although this has its advantages, you may want to keep all configuration outside the main WAR file. For example, say you wanted to allow logging to be configured outside the application; to achieve this, you can use the externalized configuration mechanism in Grails.

Essentially, within Config.groovy you can specify the grails.config.locations setting to contain a list of locations that need to be merged into the main configuration. Taking the logging example, Listing 11-8 shows how to externalize the logging configuration to a file in the USER_HOME directory.

Listing 11-8. Using Externalized Configuration

```
grails.config.locations = ["file:${userHome}/gtunes-logging.groovy"]
```

You can even allow the DataSource to be configured externally using this mechanism. Although DataSource.groovy and Config.groovy are separate files on the file system, Grails merges them into a single logical configuration object. Hence, you can externalize, not just logging or any other configuration, but the DataSource, as shown in Listing 11-9.

Listing 11-9. Externalizing DataSource Configuration

```
grails.config.locations = ["file:${userHome}/.settings/gtunes-logging.groovy",

                           "file:${userHome}/.settings/gtunesdatasource.groovy"]
```

If you prefer, you can also use static properties files in externalized configuration. Just use the extension .properties when referring to the files, and use regular java.util.Properties file semantics for configuration.

Declaring Dependencies

Dependency management for web applications can be tedious and complicated. Fortunately, Grails provides a sophisticated but easy-to-use dependency management system that allows you to express your dependencies in one place, in a declarative way, with minimal configuration. Grails will take it from there. You have already taken advantage of this numerous times up to this point when modifying BuildConfig. groovy to express dependencies on plug-ins.

In this section we will take a closer look at all of the options available in BuildConfig.groovy. Let's start by taking a look at the BuildConfig.groovy file that is in gTunes now. See the code in Listing 11-10.

Listing 11-10. BuildConfig.groovy

```groovy
grails.project.class.dir = "target/classes"
grails.project.test.class.dir = "target/test-classes"
grails.project.test.reports.dir = "target/test-reports"
grails.project.target.level = 1.6
grails.project.source.level = 1.6
//grails.project.war.file = "target/${appName}-${appVersion}.war"

grails.project.dependency.resolution = {
    // inherit Grails' default dependencies
    inherits("global") {
        // uncomment to disable ehcache
        // excludes 'ehcache'
    }
    log "error" // log level of Ivy resolver, either 'error', 'warn', 'info', 'debug' or
'verbose'
    checksums true // Whether to verify checksums on resolve

    repositories {
        inherits true // Whether to inherit repository definitions from plugins
        grailsPlugins()
        grailsHome()
        grailsCentral()
        mavenCentral()

        // uncomment these to enable remote dependency resolution from public Maven repositories
        //mavenLocal()
        //mavenRepo "http://snapshots.repository.codehaus.org"
        //mavenRepo "http://repository.codehaus.org"
        //mavenRepo "http://download.java.net/maven/2/"
        //mavenRepo "http://repository.jboss.com/maven2/"
    }
    dependencies {
        // specify dependencies here under either 'build', 'compile', 'runtime', 'test', or
'provided' scopes, e.g.

        runtime 'mysql:mysql-connector-java:5.1.21'
    }

    plugins {
```

```
    runtime ":hibernate:$grailsVersion"
    runtime ":jquery:1.7.1"
    runtime ":resources:1.1.6"
    runtime ":searchable:0.6.4"
    compile ":cache:1.0.0"
    compile ":rest-client-builder:1.0.2"

    // Uncomment these (or add new ones) to enable additional resources capabilities
    //runtime ":zipped-resources:1.0"
    //runtime ":cached-resources:1.0"
    //runtime ":yui-minify-resources:0.1.4"

    build ":tomcat:$grailsVersion"
    }
}
```

It may look like there is a lot going on there, but don't be intimidated. We will break this down into a few easy-to-deal-with pieces.

The first few lines in the file define a number of properties: grails.project.class.dir, grails. project.test.class.dir, and grails.project.test.reports.dir. These settings tell the Grails build system where to put generated artefacts like class files and test reports. The default values represented there put all of those things in a directory named target. Those values are all relative to the project root directory. If you want to specify a fully qualified path to some other location, that works just as well: grails.project.class.dir='/Development/artefacts/gtunes/classes/'

The next couple of properties are grails.project.target.level and grails.project.source.level, which default to 1.6. Those settings tell the Grails compiler that your source code should be compatible with Java 1.6 and that the compiler should generate 1.6 compatible byte code. If you are deploying to a container that uses Java 1.5, then set the target level accordingly.

So far, none of the foregoing is really about dependency management. They are all configurations that affect the build. The rest of the file is all about dependency management.

The rest of the file is all code defined inside of a closure, which is assigned to the grails.project. dependency.resolution property. Most of that code falls into one of four categories: inherits, repositories, dependencies, and plug-ins (see Listing 11-11).

Listing 11-11. Sections in BuildConfig.groovy

```
grails.project.dependency.resolution = {
    inherits("global") {
        ...
    }
    repositories {
        ...
    }
    dependencies {
        ...
    }
    plugins {
        ...
    }
}
```

Let's examine each of those.

Inheriting Dependencies

The first section is the inherits section. This is where you can specify that you want to inherit dependencies from the framework, which is what most applications are going to want to do. The framework has runtime dependencies on a lot of things, including Spring, SiteMesh, and Hibernate. Since those runtime dependencies need to be available when your application is run, the most common thing to do is to express that you want to inherit those global dependencies from the framework. That is what the default BuildConfig.groovy file expresses by invoking inherits("global").

The inherits method there accepts an optional second parameter, a closure that may be used to further configure what is being inherited. It may be the case that the application wants to inherit all of the global dependencies but for some reason wants to exclude something, maybe multiple things, in particular. The way to do that is by invoking the excludes method inside that closure and passing strings as arguments. Those strings represent the names of dependencies that should be excluded, as shown in Listing 11-12.

Listing 11-12. Excluding Inherited Dependencies

```
inherits("global") {
    excludes "ehcache", "oscache"
}
```

It may be the case that the application wants to inherit all of the global dependencies from the framework but does not want those dependencies to be included in the WAR file when the application is deployed. The most common use case for something like that is when numerous Grails applications are to be deployed to the same container and you would like to avoid having all of those applications bundle their own copies of the same dependencies. The dependencies can be installed into the container (see your container's documentation for details on how to do that); then slimmer WAR files are created for the Grails applications that contain only the dependencies introduced by the applications themselves, not those inherited from the framework. Listing 11-13 shows how to express that those dependencies will be provided by the container with the defaultDependenciesProvided method.

Listing 11-13. Indicating That Default Dependencies Will Be Provided by the Container

```
grails.project.dependency.resolution = {
    defaultDependenciesProvided true
    inherits("global")
}
```

For most of the code in BuildConfig.groovy, order is not important. This is an exception to that rule. It is important that the defaultDependenciesProvided method be invoked before the inherit method; otherwise all of the global dependencies will still be included in the generated WAR file.

Declaring Repositories

Applications will often have dependencies on things that are not provided by Grails. These may include plug-ins and jar files for libraries that your application depends on, such as the MySQL Connector that gTunes is using. Grails needs to know where to find those dependencies, and BuildConfig.groovy allows for the specification of a list of repositories where the dependency resolution system should look for those dependencies. See Listing 11-14.

Listing 11-14. Configuring Repositories

```
grails.project.dependency.resolution = {
    repositories {
        grailsPlugins()
        grailsHome()
        grailsCentral()
        mavenCentral()
        ...
    }
}
```

The repositories section of the file is where you can express which repositories Grails should use for resolving dependencies. The three that are configured by default are grailsPlugins(), grailsHome(), and grailsCentral(). The first, grailsPlugins(), configures a resolver that can find dependencies bundled in the lib/directory of any plug-ins that this project may depend on. The second, grailsHome(), configures a resolver that can find all of the dependencies that are bundled with the framework. The third, grailsCentral(), configures a resolver that can find dependencies in the main public Grails repositories, which is where most Grails plug-ins are deployed. These three are in the file for newly created applications, and most applications will need to leave them there. Some projects may want to augment them with additional repositories, the most common of which is Maven Central; that is the repository that the mavenCentral() method configures, of course. The gTunes application uses mavenCentral() as the place to resolve the MySQL Connector.

For many applications, maybe most, the repositories mentioned are all that will be needed. However, there are cases where you may want Grails to resolve dependencies from some other Maven repository, perhaps one on your enterprise's intranet. There is a simple way to configure those repositories in BuildConfig.groovy; it is done by using the mavenRepo method (see Listing 11-15).

Listing 11-15. Configuring Custom Repositories

```
grails.project.dependency.resolution = {
    repositories {
        // Do not inherit repositories from plug-ins
        inherits false

        mavenRepo  name: 'codehaus', 'http://repository.codehaus.org'
        mavenRepo  'http://myserver.com/repo/'
        ...
    }
}
```

Notice that the codehaus repo is being given a name, which is optional. The name may be useful when evaluating log files. Also notice the call to inherits false, which instructs the dependency resolution system not to inherit repositories from plug-ins installed in the app. This is a very common use case if you want to host your own plug-in repository.

The next section of the file is the dependencies section. That is where you express dependencies on libraries (JAR files), which are not provided by the framework. The gTunes application currently has a dependency on the MySQL Connector (see Listing 11-16).

Listing 11-16. A Runtime Library Dependency

```
grails.project.dependency.resolution = {
    ...
    dependencies {
        // specify dependencies here under either 'build',
        // 'compile', 'runtime', 'test', or 'provided' scopes, e.g.

        runtime 'mysql:mysql-connector-java:5.1.21'
    }
    ...
}
```

Notice that the MySQL Connector library is a runtime dependency. The library will be needed at runtime when the application attempts to connect to the MySQL database, but since no code in the application makes any direct references to MySQL code, there's no need for the library to be available at compile time. Several scopes are supported in addition to runtime (see Table 11-1).

Table 11-1. Dependency Scopes

Scope	Description
build	available to the build system only
compile	available to the application at compile time
runtime	available to the application at runtime but not at compile time
test	available to tests but not the application at runtime
provided	available at development time but not included in the WAR file

The string being passed to the scope method in Listing 11-16 describes the dependency. The syntax is group:name:version, and so in mysql:mysql-connector-java:5.1.21, "mysql" is the group, "mysql-connector-java" is the name, and "5.1.21" is, of course, the version. These terms will be familiar to anyone who has worked with Maven.

An alternative syntax is to specify details of the artefact in the form of named arguments to the scope method (see Listing 11-17).

Listing 11-17. Using Named Arguments to Express a Dependency

```
grails.project.dependency.resolution = {
    ...
    dependencies {
        runtime group: 'mysql'
                name: 'mysql-connector-java'
                version: '5.1.21'
    }
    ...
}
```

Multiple dependencies may be specified in a single call (see Listing 11-18).

Listing 11-18. Specifying Multiple Dependencies at Once

```
grails.project.dependency.resolution = {
    ...
    dependencies {
        // specify dependencies here under either 'build', 'compile', 'runtime', 'test', or
'provided' scopes, e.g.

        runtime 'mysql:mysql-connector-java:5.1.21'
        runtime 'commons-httpclient:commons-httpclient:3.1'

        // or ...

        runtime 'mysql:mysql-connector-java:5.1.21',
                'commons-httpclient:commons-httpclient:3.1'
        // or...

        runtime [[group: 'mysql', name: 'mysql-connector-java', version: '5.1.21'],
                [group: 'commons-httpclient', name: 'commons-httpclient', version: '3.1']]
    }
    ...
}
```

By default, when Grails resolves a dependency, the framework will resolve not only the expressed dependency but also transitive dependencies. This means that if your application expresses a dependency on library A, and library A depends on library B, and library B depends on library C, the system will resolve all of those dependencies. Often this is desirable, as if your application uses A and A depends on B, you probably need B to be there. There are times when you may want to disable transitive dependency resolution. The syntax for doing so is shown in Listing 11-19.

Listing 11-19. Excluding Transitive Dependencies

```
grails.project.dependency.resolution = {
    ...
    dependencies {
        // specify dependencies here under either 'build', 'compile', 'runtime', 'test', or
'provided' scopes, e.g.

        runtime('mysql:mysql-connector-java:5.1.21') {
            transitive = false
        }

        // or...
        runtime group: 'mysql'
                    name: 'mysql-connector-java'
                    version: '5.1.21'
                    transitive: false
        // or, exclude specific dependencies, leaving all other transitive dependencies to be
resolved
        runtime('mysql:mysql-connector-java:5.1.21') {
```

```
        excludes 'xml-apis', 'commons-logging'
    }
  }
  ...
}
```

The last section in the BuildConfig file is the plug-ins section, which you have used numerous times already. This is where you express a dependency on plug-ins the application is going to use. The syntax for expressing plug-in dependencies is very similar to that for expressing library dependencies, as shown above. A noticeable difference is that plug-in dependencies, which do not require a group, default to org. grails.plugins. See Listing 11-20.

Listing 11-20. Specifying Plug-in Dependencies

```
grails.project.dependency.resolution = {
    ...

    plugins {
        runtime ":hibernate:$grailsVersion"
        runtime ":jquery:1.7.1"
        runtime ":resources:1.1.6"
        runtime ":searchable:0.6.4"
        compile ":cache:1.0.0"
        compile ":rest-client-builder:1.0.2"
        build ":tomcat:$grailsVersion"
    }
}
```

Transitive plug-in resolution works very similarly to how transitive library resolution works. If you express a dependency on plug-in A, and plug-in A depends on plug-in B, plug-in B will be resolved. Exclusions are available for plug-in dependencies, just as for library dependencies (see Listing 11-21).

Listing 11-21. Excluding Transitive Plug-in Dependencies

```
grails.project.dependency.resolution = {
    ...

    plugins {
        runtime(':someplugin:1.0') {
            excludes 'pluginA', 'pluginB'
        }
    }
}
```

Understanding the Grails Build System

The Grails build system is powered by the Gant (http://gant.codehaus.org) build tool. Gant is a thin wrapper around Apache Ant (http://ant.apache.org), the ever-popular Java build system. Unlike Ant, which uses an XML format to describe a build, Gant uses a Groovy DSL. The benefit here is that you can easily mix build logic with scripting in Groovy code. Listing 11-22 shows a typical example of a Gant build script.

Listing 11-22. *An Example of a Gant Build Script*

```
targetDir = "build"
target(clean:"Cleans any compiled sources") {
delete(dir:targetDir) }

target(compile:"The compilation task") {
    depends(clean)
    mkdir(dir:"$targetDir/classes")
    javac(srcdir:"src/java",
        destdir:"$targetDir/classes")
}
target(jar:"Creates a DAR file")  {
    jar(destfile:"$targetDir/app.jar",basedir:"$targetDir/classes")
}
target(dist:"The default task") {
    depends(compile, jar)
}
setDefaultTarget ( dist )
```

Notice how the example in Listing 11-10 defines a number of targets by calling the `target` method. These are equivalent to Ant's <target> tag. Also, as you can see, you can specify dependencies between targets using the `depends` method:

```
depends(compile, jar)
```

If you install Gant outside Grails, Gant includes its own command-line interface via the `gant` command. The `gant` command will search for a file called `build.gant`, the same way Ant looks for `build.xml`, and attempts to call it if found. Using the `gant` command, you can call an individual target or chain more than one, as shown here:

```
$ gant clean jar
```

It's at this point that you'll begin to realize the differences between vanilla Gant and Grails. Although Gant behaves much like Ant, Grails wraps Gant in its own `grails` command—the same one you've been using throughout the book. The `grails` command uses conventions within a Grails project to try to automatically figure out which script to execute. For example, when you run the command

```
$ grails create-app
```

Grails will search the following directories for a Gant script called `CreateApp.groovy` to execute:

- `PRODECTHOME/scripts`: The `scripts` directory of the current project.

- `GRAILSHOME/scripts`: The `scripts` directory of the location where you installed Grails.

- `PLUGINS_HOME/*/scripts`: Each installed plug-in's `scripts` directory.

- `USERHOME/.grails/scripts`: The `scripts` directory within the `.grails` directory of the current user's home directory. The location of this is operating system dependent.

If a matching Gant script is found, the `grails` command will execute the *default* target of the Gant script. In contrast to the `gant` command, the `grails` command is optimized for the Grails project layout, for the plug-in system, and for the easy use of passing arguments.

Creating Gant Scripts

To help you understand this better, let's take a look at a simple "Hello World"–style example. Using the create-script command, create a new script called HelloWorld.groovy:

```
grails> create-script HelloWorld
| Created file scripts/HelloWorld.groovy
```

As expected, you'll end up with a new Gant script, HelloWorld.groovy, in the scripts directory of your project. Figure 11-1 shows the script snugly in place.

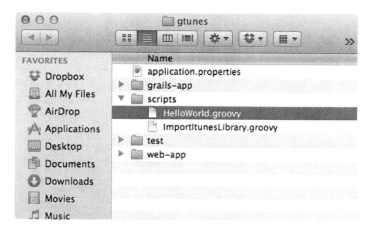

Figure 11-1. The HelloWorld.groovy Gant script

Grails uses lowercase names separated by hyphens—for example, hello-world—when referencing scripts but transforms the name into camelCase for the script name. Listing 11-23 shows the contents of the generated HelloWorld.groovy script from Figure 11-1.

Listing 11-23. The Script Template

```
grailsHome = ant.project.properties."environment.GRAILS_HOME"
includeTargets << grailsScript("_GrailsInit")

target(main: "The description of the script goes here!") {
    // TODO
}
setDefaultTarget(main)
```

As you can see, the template pulls in some existing functionality from a script called _GrailsInit.groovy in the scripts directory of the location where you installed Grails. It then defines a single target, the default target, called main. To complete the "Hello World" example, use a println statement to print a message:

```
includeTargets << grailsScript("_GrailsInit")

target(main: "The description of the script goes here!") {
    println 'Hello World!'
}
```

```
setDefaultTarget(main)
```

To run the hello-world script, just run this command using the grails executable:

```
grails> hello-world
| Environment set to development....
Hello World!
grails>
```

Grails will perform a search of all the directories mentioned previously and find the HelloWorld.
groovy script. Since the main target is the default target, Grails will execute it, and the "Hello World!"
message will be printed.

Of course, having the entire Ant API at your disposal allows you to do a lot more than just print
messages. Ant, along with its plug-ins, provides access to targets that allow you to manipulate the file
system, compile Java or Groovy code, perform XSLT transformations, and do just about anything else you
could dream of from the command line.

▓ **Tip** If you aren't already familiar with the Apache Ant manual (most Java developers are), it may be useful to
take a look at it (http://ant.apache.org/manual/). The manual provides comprehensive information about
what you can do with Ant.

Command-Line Variables

The _GrailsInit.groovy script that was imported by HelloWorld.groovy in Listing 11-11 provides a bunch
of useful variables and targets. Here are some of them.

- grailsVersion: the version of Grails you're using

- grailsEnv: the environment in which Grails is executing

- basedir: a string representing the base directory from which the script is executing

- baseFile: similar to basedir, but a Java. io.File representation

- userHome: the current user's home directory as a string

- pluginsHome: the location where plug-ins are installed

- classesDir: the location to which classes are compiled

The grailsEnv variable deserves special mention. If you recall from Chapter 2, you can tell Grails to
run within the context of development, test, or production environments. To recap, the following
command will execute the run-app command using the production settings:

```
$ grails prod run-app
```

Your scripts can be equally environment-aware using the grailsEnv variable. For example, if you want
a Gant script to run only in the development environment, you can write code like this:

```
if(grailsEnv == 'development')  {
// do something }
```

Some of the other variables, such as the pluginsHome and classesDir variables, are automatically constructed by Grails. By default, Grails stores plug-ins and some compiled resources in your USER_HOME directory under a special path. For example, you can find the gTunes application's plug-in related code in the directory USER_HOME/.grails/2.0.4/projects/gtunes/plugins.

As you can see, Grails takes the Grails version number and the project name to formulate a path within the USER_HOME directory. If you are not happy with this location, then you can tell Grails to use a different path by passing the grails.work.dir argument at the command line:

```
$ grails -Dgrails.work.dir=/tmp run-app
```

In fact, you can pass a whole load of different command-line arguments to customize the different locations that Grails uses.

- grails.work.dir: the base location where all Grails work occurs, including the test and source compilation directories

- grails.project.classes.dir: the location to which project sources are compiled

- grails.project.resource.dir: the location to which project static resources (such as web.xml) are generated

- grails.project.test.class.dir: the location to which test sources are compiled

- grails.plugins.dir: the location where plug-ins are installed

- grails.global.plugins.dir: the location where global plug-ins are installed

Parsing Command-Line Arguments

Unlike raw Gant, the grails command doesn't support chaining of targets; instead, it favors the easy passing of command-line arguments. One useful target to depend on that is provided by the Init.groovy script is the parseArguments target. The parseArguments target will read any command-line arguments and produce a variable called argsMap, containing the values of the arguments in a more accessible form.

For example, say you wanted to enable the HelloWorld.groovy script to be able to print the name of the person to say hello to in either uppercase or lowercase. You could allow the name to be passed as a command-line argument and whether to print in uppercase or not as a command-line flag, as follows:

```
grails> hello-world John
| Environment set to development....
Hello John
grails> hello-world John -uppercase
| Environment set to development.....
HELLO JOHN
grails>
```

Implementing the handling of these is very simple. Listing 11-24 shows an updated HelloWorld.groovy Gant script that gracefully handles these arguments.

Listing 11-24. Handling Command-Line Arguments

```
includeTargets << grailsScript("_GrailsInit")

target(main: "The description of the script goes here!") {
    def message = "Hello ${argsMap.params ? argsMap.params[0] : 'World'}"
    if(argsMap.uppercase) {
```

```
        println message.toUpperCase()
    } else {
        println message
    }
}

setDefaultTarget(main)
```

Notice that command-line flags (the arguments that start with - or --) are placed as Boolean values into the argsMap. The example in Listing 11-12 shows how the -uppercase flag ends up as a Boolean value, with the key uppercase inside the argsMap. You can also have flags with values; for example, if you passed -uppercase=yes, then the value would be a String with the value yes in the argsMap.

All other arguments that are not flags are placed in the params key as a List that retains the order in which they were passed.

Documenting Your Scripts

You may have noticed from the script template in Listing 11-11 that the main target has a placeholder for the description of the target:

```
target(main: "The description of the script goes here!") {
```

You can provide additional information about a target, so that others understand better how to go about using your script, by assigning a value to the USAGE property in the script. For example, to give information about the hello-world script, you could make this modification:

```
includeTargets << grailsScript("_GrailsInit")

target(main: "Prints a Hello message") {
    def message = "Hello ${argsMap.params ? argsMap.params[0] : 'World'}"
    if(argsMap.uppercase) {
        println message.toUpperCase()
    } else {
        println message
    }
}

setDefaultTarget(main)

USAGE = '''
    hello-world [-uppercase] [NAME]

where
    -uppercase = Convert the message to all uppercase
    NAME       = The name of the person to say hello to
'''
```

Then if any other users of your script should need help using the script, they can go to the help command provided by Grails, as shown in Listing 11-25.

Listing 11-25. Getting Help from Gant Scripts

```
grails> help hello-world
| Environment set to development.....

    grails hello-world -- Prints a Hello message

Usage (optionals in square brackets):

    hello-world [-uppercase] [NAME]

where
    -uppercase = Convert the message to all uppercase
    NAME       = The name of the person to say hello to
grails>
```

Reusing More of Grails

The inclusion of the GrailsInit.groovy script in Listing 11-11 is just one example of including an existing Grails script. You can in fact include an array of different scripts that provide different features. For example, say you want to make sure the tests run before your script is executed. You can include the _GrailsTest.groovy script and depend on the allTests target, as shown in Listing 11-26.

Listing 11-26. Executing Tests

```
includeTargets << grailsScript('_GrailsTest')

target(main: "The description of the script goes here!") {
    depends allTests
}

setDefaultTarget main
```

Alternatively, if you want to make sure that the container is up and running, maybe in order to perform some kind of automated functional tests, you can use the RunApp.groovy script. This, the same script used when you type grails run-app at the command line, provides a target called runApp that you can use to load the Tomcat container embedded in Grails. As an extension to this, the next section will look at how to load Grails without even the need for a container.

Bootstrapping Grails from the Command Line

If you need access to the Grails environment from the command line, you can load Grails using the GRAILS_HOME/scripts/Bootstrap.groovy script. This will enable you, for example, to use GORM from the command line for batch processing.

To get started, you need to include the following Bootstrap.groovy script:

```
includeTargets << grailsScript("_GrailsBootstrap")
and then call the bootstrap target:
bootstrap()
```

Once this is done, a number of new variables will be created including the following:

- grailsApp: a reference to the org.codehaus.groovy.grails.commons.
  GrailsApplication class, which allows you to inspect the conventions in a running
  Grails application

- appCtx: the Spring ApplicationContext instance that contains the bean definitions for
  the Grails application, as found at runtime.

- servletContext: a mock implementation of the ServletContext, usable from the
  command line.

- pluginManager: a reference to the org.codehaus.groovy.grails.plugins.
  GrailsPluginManager instance, which allows you to inspect the currently installed
  plug-ins.

The most commonly used of these is the appCtx variable, which allows access to all the beans contained within the Spring ApplicationContext. For example, if you need to obtain the Hibernate SessionFactory and/or SQL DataSource, you can easily do so using the appCtx:

```
DataSource dataSource = appCtx.getBean("dataSource") SessionFactory SessionFactory = appCtx.
getBean("sessionFactory")
```

With the basics out of the way, let's see a couple of examples that show how to use Gant to boost your command-line productivity.

Gant in Action

Printing "Hello World!" to the command window is fun and all, but ultimately it's not very useful. In the following sections, you'll be looking at a couple of real-world Gant scripts. The first is a script that will allow you to quickly deploy to Tomcat.

Automated Deployment to Tomcat

Writing a Tomcat deployment script in Ant is pretty trivial, thanks to the targets that ship with Tomcat (see http://tomcat.apache.org/tomcat-7.0-doc/manager-howto.html). However, before you can start this example, you need to make sure you have Tomcat installed and TOMCAT_HOME set to the location where you installed it. Then run the grails create-script command as follows:

```
$ grails create-script tomcat-deploy
```

With that done, you should have a TomcatDeploy.groovy file in the scripts directory of your project, as shown in Figure 11-2.

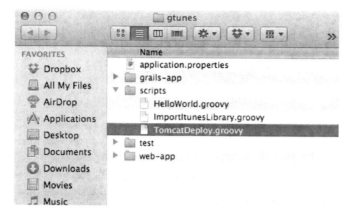

Figure 11-2. The TomcatDeploy.groovy script

The `TomcatDeploy.groovy` script template will look identical to the `HelloWorld.groovy` template you saw earlier. To begin with, you're going to need to figure out the path to the Tomcat installation directory. Inspecting the `TOMCAT_HOME` environment variable can help you achieve this:

```
grailsHome = ant.project.properties."environment.GRAILS_HOME"
tomcatHome = ant.project.properties."environment.TOMCAT_HOME"
```

With knowledge of the Tomcat directory in hand, the next thing to do is include the `War.groovy` script available in `GRAILS_HOME/scripts`. The `_GrailsWar.groovy` template contains targets that allow you to construct a valid WAR file:

```
includeTargets << grailsScript("_GrailsWar")
```

To take advantage of the Tomcat Ant tasks, you have to define them by calling the `taskdef` method. This method relates to the `<taskdef>` target of Ant, so defining Ant tasks in Gant is pretty much identical to doing so in pure Ant—minus the angle brackets:

```
ant.path(id:"tomcat.lib.path") {
    fileset(dir:"${tomcatHome}/server/lib",includes:"*.jar")
}
ant.taskdef(name:"deploy",
            classname:"org.apache.catalina.ant.DeployTask",
            classpathref:"tomcat.lib.path")
```

As you can see, the only tricky part is ensuring that all the JAR files for the `DeployTask` class are placed onto the classpath appropriately using the JAR files available in your Tomcat installation directory. This is done using the `classpathref` named argument and a predefined Ant path called `tomcat.lib.path`.

Moving onto the `main` target of the `TomcatDeploy.groovy` script, you can change it to depend on the `war` target, which will ensure a valid WAR file is constructed before the rest of the code runs:

```
target(main: "Deploys the Grails application to Tomcat") {
    depends war

    ...
}
```

Once that is done, you need to establish the destination to publish the WAR to. You could, for example, accept the destination as the first argument to the command and otherwise default to `localhost`:

```
def dest = argsMap.params ? argsMap.params[0] : "http://localhost:8080/manager"
```

Once that is done, the rest is left to the deploy target supplied by the org.apache.cat-alina.ant. DeployTask class:

```
deploy(war:warName, url:dest,
path:serverContextPath, username:"deployer", password:"secret")
```

The warName and serverContextPath variables are set up by the War.groovy script, which you can reuse here. The deploy target also requires that you pass username and password arguments whenever deploying to Tomcat. Given that you have a running instance of Tomcat locally, if you run the tomcat-deploy target now, you'll probably get a 401 error such as the following:

```
java.io.IOException: Server returned HTTP response code: 401 for URL: http://localhost:8080/
manager/deploy?path=%2FgTunes
```

The reason is that currently Tomcat doesn't have a user called deployer with a password of secret registered with it. To do so, you need to edit the TOMCAT_HOME/conf/tomcat-users.xml file and add a user who has access to the Tomcat manager application, as shown in Listing 11-27.

Listing 11-27. Adding a Tomcat Deployer

```
<?xml version='1.0' encoding='utf-8'?>
<tomcat-users>
   ...
   <user username="deployer" password="secret" roles="standard,manager"/>
</tomcat-users>
```

Once you have added the necessary Tomcat user, when you run the tomcat-deploy script, Grails will successfully deploy your application to Tomcat, as demonstrated in Listing 11-28.

Listing 11-28. Deploying to Tomcat

```
$ grails tomcat-deploy ...
Done creating WAR /Developer/grails-dev/book/dgg/code/ch12/gTunes-0.1.war [deploy] OK - Deployed
application at context path /gTunes
```

You can, of course, take this further and write another tomcat-undeploy script or even combine them into two scripts. Nevertheless, Listing 11-29 shows the full code for the TomcatDeploy.groovy scripts.

Listing 11-29. The TomcatDeploy.groovy Script

```
grailsHome = ant.project.properties."environment.GRAILS_HOME"
tomcatHome = ant.project.properties."environment.TOMCAT_HOME"

includeTargets << grailsScript("War")

ant.path(id:"tomcat.lib.path") {
    fileset(dir:"${tomcatHome}/server/lib",includes:"*.jar")
}
ant.taskdef(name:"deploy",
                classname:"org.apache.catalina.ant.DeployTask",
                classpathref:"tomcat.lib.path")
target(main: "Deploys the Grails application to Tomcat") {
    depends(parseArguments, war)
```

```
        def dest = argsMap.params ? argsMap.params[0] : "http://localhost:8080/manager"

        deploy(war:warName,
               url:dest,
               path:serverContextPath,
               username:"deployer",
               password:"secret")
}
setDefaultTarget(main)
```

Exporting Data to XML

Another fairly common use of command-line scripts is to allow the migration of data. This can be done by performing an SQL dump of the database, but you may want to offer the ability to export all content held in the database as XML, as some web applications such as Atlassian Confluence and JIRA do.

Let's start by considering how you would write an export script that dumped all the relevant data from the gTunes application into a single parsable XML document. First, you'll need to create a new Gant script called export-library-to-xml:

```
grails> create-script ExportLibraryToXml
| Created file scripts/ExportLibraryToXml.groovy
grails>
```

With that done, you're going to need to take advantage of the GRAILS_HOME/scripts/_GrailsBootstrap. groovy script discussed earlier. To do so, simply include _GrailsBootstrap.groovy:

```
includeTargets << grailsScript("_GrailsBootstrap")
```

Inside the main target, you then need to depend on the bootstrap target:

```
depends bootstrap
```

First, using argsMap, you can work out the file to export to by either taking the first argument or creating a name programmatically:

```
        def file = argsMap.params ?
                new File(argsMap.params[0]) :
                new File("./gtunes-data=${System.currentTimeMillis()}.xml")
```

As mentioned previously, the bootstrap target will set up a grailsApp variable that holds a reference to the GrailsApplication instance. This instance can be used to dynamically load classes using the classLoader property. This needs to be done because Gant scripts cannot directly reference the classes in your application, as they can't know whether those classes have been compiled yet. Luckily, obtaining a reference to any class using the classLoader is pretty trivial:

```
def artistClass = grailsApp.classLoader.loadClass('com.gtunes.Artist')
```

Unlike Java, with Groovy you can invoke any static method using a reference to java.lang.Class; hence, you can use regular GORM methods easily even with a dynamically loaded class reference. The first example of this is using the static count() method to figure out how many artists there are:

```
        def artistClass = grailsApp.classLoader.loadClass('com.gtunes.Artist')
        def artistCount = artistClass.count()
```

Now it's time to create the XML. To do so, you're going to use Groovy's StreamingMarkupBuilder class. Listing 11-30 shows how to construct and use StreamingMarkupBuilder.

Listing 11-30. Using StreamingMarkupBuilder to Write to a File

```
new FileWriter(file) << new groovy.xml.StreamingMarkupBuilder().bind {
    music {
        ...
    }
}
```

Builders in Groovy allow you to construct hierarchies of nodes, a concept that fits nicely into the construction of XML. In this case, the music method will become the root element <music> of the XML document. In the next step, you initiate a transaction using the withTransaction method first discussed in Chapter 10.

You use a transaction here so that a common Hibernate Session is shared for the remainder of the code, hence avoiding a LazyInitializationException occurring when accessing uninitialized associations. In Grails, unlike the server environment, the Hibernate Session is not managed for you in scripts, but by using withTransaction, you can circumvent that:

```
artistClass.withTransaction {
    ...
}
```

Along with withTransaction, you're going to take advantage of the withSession method to obtain a reference to the Hibernate Session object used. As discussed in Chapter 10, when reading a large amount of data into the Hibernate Session, you may run out of memory if you don't periodically clear the Session. Since you don't exactly know how much data is in the database, you're going to be doing that here:

```
artistClass.withSession { session ->
    ...
}
```

The next step, if you'll excuse the pun, is to employ the step method, using the previously obtained artistCount variable to perform pagination of records. With this technique, you can obtain, say, ten Artist instances, including associations. You can manipulate them in some way and then clear the Session before loading the next ten. Listing 11-31 shows the code in action.

Listing 11-31. Using the step Method to Paginate Records

```
0.step(artistCount, 10) { offset ->
    def artistList = artistClass.list(offset: offset,
                                      max: 10,
                                      fetch: [albums: 'join'])
    session.clear()
}
```

With a list of Artist instances in hand, now it's just a matter of iterating over each one to create a bunch of <artist> XML elements:

```
for(currentArtist in artistList) {
    artist(name: currentArtist.name) {
        ...
    }
}
```

Finally, you also need to include all the Album instances associated with each Artist and all the Song instances associated with each Album. You can achieve this with a couple more nested loops:

```
for(currentAlbum in currentArtist.albums) {
    album(currentAlbum.properties['title', 'year', 'genre', 'price']) {
        for(currentSong in currentAlbum.songs) {
            song(currentSong.properties['title', 'duration'])
        }
    }
}
```

Notice how you can reference a subset of each Album instance's property values using the subscript operator and a list of property names:

```
currentAlbum.properties['title', 'year', 'genre', 'price']
```

With that, the export-library-to-xml script is complete. Listing 11-32 shows the full code listing for the export-library-to-xml Gant script.

Listing 11-32. The Full export-library-to-xml Code

```
includeTargets << grailsScript("_GrailsBootstrap")

target(main: "Exports the gTunes database to XML") {
  depends bootstrap
  def file = argsMap.params ?
                new File(argsMap.params[0]) :
                new File("./gtunes-data=${System.currentTimeMillis()}.xml")
  def artistClass = grailsApp.classLoader.loadClass('com.gtunes.Artist')
  def artistCount = artistClass.count()
  println "Creating XML for ${artistCount} artists"
  new FileWriter(file) << new groovy.xml.StreamingMarkupBuilder().bind {
    music {
      artistClass.withTransaction {
          artistClass.withSession { session ->
            0.step(artistCount, 10) { offset ->
              def artistList = artistClass.list(offset: offset, max: 10, fetch: [albums:
'join'])
              for(currentArtist in artistList) {
                artist(name: currentArtist.name) {
                  for(currentAlbum in currentArtist.albums) {
                    album(currentAlbum.properties['title', 'year', 'genre', 'price']) {
                      for(currentSong in currentAlbum.songs) {
                        song(currentSong.properties['title', 'duration'])
                      }
                    }
                  }
                }
              }
            }
          session.clear()
        }
      }
    }
  }
}
```

```
    println "Done. Created XML ${file.absolutePath}"
}

setDefaultTarget(main)
```

As you can see from the full code in Listing 11-21, you can also add a couple of `println` statements just to inform the user what is going on. You can now run the `export-library-to-xml` script using the `grails` command, and out will pop an XML document, as shown in Listing 11-33.

Listing 11-33. Running the export-library-to-xml Script

```
$ grails export-library-to-xml
Creating XML for 498 artists
Done. Created XML /Developer/projects/gtunes/gtunes-data=1351863192571.xml
```

As you can see in this example, the script produces a file called `gtunes-data-122224970.xml`. The contents of this file contain the XML built by `StreamingMarkBuilder`. Listing 11-34 shows an example.

Listing 11-34. Example Output XML

```
<?xml version="1.0"?>
<music>
    <artist name="The Killers">
        <album year="2006" title="Sam's Town" price="4.99" genre="Rock">
            <song title="Sam's Town" duration="246099"/>
            <song title="Enterlude" duration="49972"/>
            <song title="When You Were Young" duration="220499"/>
            ...
        </album>
    </artist>
    ...
</music>
```

Continuous Integration with Hudson

Agile and test-driven philosophies have been debated endlessly and are a subject beyond the scope of this book. Nevertheless, if there is one agile practice that would bring immediate benefits to any project, whether "traditional" or agile, it is continuous integration.

Continuous integration involves setting up a server that continuously (either on a schedule or through monitoring for changes) builds the latest code, runs any tests, and produces a snapshot of the code for distribution. The continuous integration server can perform all manner of additional tasks, from producing coverage reports to creating the latest documentation and even sending e-mails or SMS messages to notify of build failures.

This section will demonstrate how to use Hudson, an open source continuous integration server available at `https://hudson.dev.java.net/`. To get started, you need to download the `hudson.war` distribution of Hudson and deploy it to a container, such as Apache Tomcat. Deployment with Tomcat is a simple matter of dropping the WAR into the `TOMCAT_HOME/webapps` directory and firing up Tomcat.

Then you can go to `http://localhost:8080/hudson`, assuming Tomcat is up and running on port 8080, and you'll be presented with the Hudson Dashboard.

The next step is to install the Grails plug-in for Hudson. From the main Dashboard screen, click the "Manage Hudson" link, and then click the "Manage Plugins" link. On the Available tab, select the check box next to the Grails plug-in, and click the "Install" button at the bottom of the page. Once you have installed the plug-in, you'll need to restart Hudson.

Once the Grails plug-in is installed, the next step is to configure your Grails installations in Hudson. The plug-in, which does not come with its own version of Grails, uses a version that must be installed on the system separately from Hudson. The plug-in allows you to configure as many different versions of Grails as you like. This is useful if you are building multiple Grails projects in the same Hudson instance and not all of those Grails projects are built with the same version.

To configure Grails installations in Hudson, click the "Manage Hudson" link on the main Dashboard screen, then click the "Configure System" link. Figure 11-3 shows the part of this screen used to configure your Grails installations.

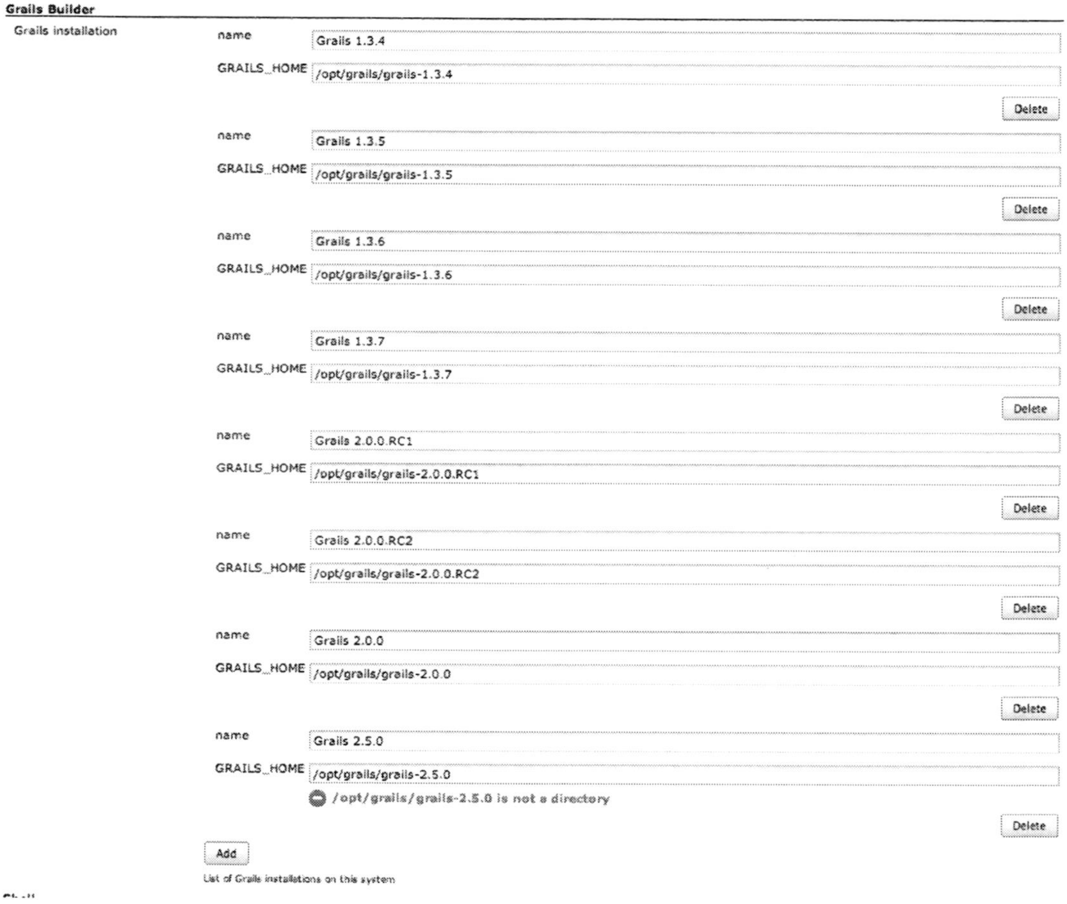

Figure 11-3. *Configuring Grails installations in Hudson*

You can see that each Grails installation has a name and a GRAILS_HOME. The name is simply an identifier that will help you select a particular version of Grails later when configuring jobs. The value of GRAILS_HOME must point to a specific Grails installation directory. Notice that there is validation built in to let you know whether the directory you have entered does not exist. The validation is not activated until you tab out of the text field.

274

Once you have configured all your Grails installations, make sure you scroll all the way to the bottom of the page and click the Save button.

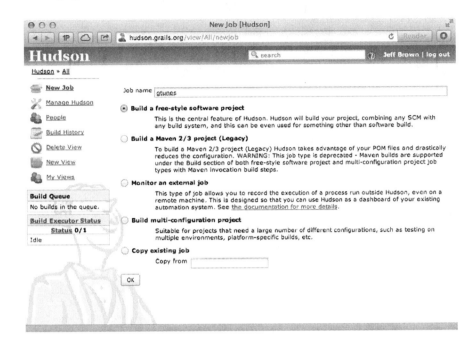

Figure 11-4. Creating a new free-style job

With at least one Grails installation configured in Hudson, you are ready to create a job for a Grails project. You create a job for a Grails project in the same way you would for any other project in Hudson. From the main Dashboard screen, click the "New Job" link. Most often you will be creating a job for a so-called free-style software project, and so you will select that radio button on the form to create a new job (see Figure 11-4).

Once you click the OK button, you will be taken to the page where you configure all the details for how this build will be carried out. This page allows you to define which version control system you are using, paths to the project, a schedule for building the project, and so on. Near the bottom of the page is where you will configure the actual build steps. Once the Grails plug-in is installed, a new build step, "Build With Grails," should show up, as shown in Figure 11-5.

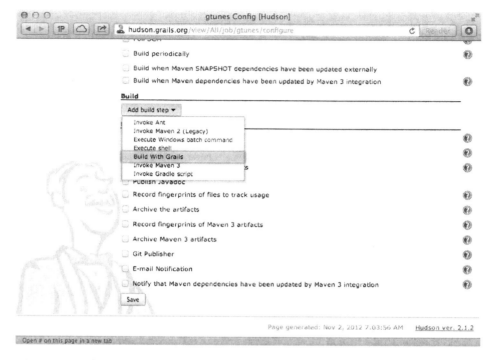

Figure 11-5. *The "Build With Grails" build step*

When you select the "Build With Grails" build step, the page will be updated with a form that lets you configure the Grails build. This will include at a minimum specifying a version of Grails to use and which Grails targets to execute. A typical target to execute is the `test-app` target, but you can configure your job to execute whichever targets make sense. Figure 11-6 shows the details of a Grails build.

The "Grails Installation" drop-down will include all the Grails installations you configured earlier. Select the version of Grails that this job should be built with.

The "Targets" field lets you specify as many targets as you'd like to have executed as part of this build. The targets will be executed in the order specified in this text box. If any arguments are to be passed to a particular target, then the target name and the arguments should be surrounded by double quotes so the plug-in knows to group them as one command.

There are fields for specifying the `grails.work.dir` and `project.work.dir` system properties.

The "Project Base Directory" field will typically be left blank, but it is important if the Grails project is not at the root of the job's working directory. For example, if your Grails project is in your SCM system at a path like `/projects/development/code/grails/gTunes/` and for some reason you need to configure this job to check out everything under `/projects/development/code/ grails/gTunes/`, you will need to specify a value for the "Project Base Directory" field. The problem here is that the job root is `/projects/development/code/grails/gTunes/`; so the plug-in will execute all Grails commands from that directory. Since that isn't the root of the Grails project itself, all the Grails commands will fail. To support this scenario, the "Project Base Directory" field should be given the value `/projects/development/code/grails/gTunes/`; this is a relative path down from the job root directory to the root of the Grails project. With that in place, all Grails commands will be executed from the `/projects/development/ code/grails/gTunes/` directory.

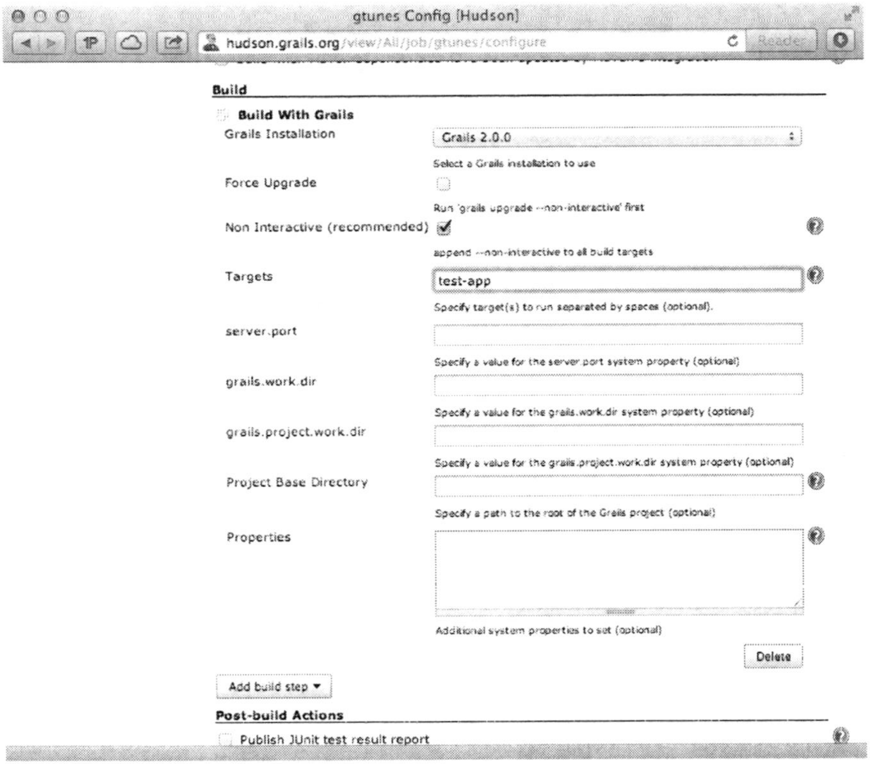

Figure 11-6. Configuring a Grails build

All other aspects of configuring a Grails job in Hudson are no different from what they are for any other type of project.

Adding Support to Your Favorite IDE

Java developers in general have become particularly reliant on the comfort of modern integrated development environments (IDEs), largely because of the strictness of the Java language. From its static typing rules to such quirks as its insistence on semicolons at the end of each line of code, it is hard to write anything in Java without a little nagging from the compiler. Fortunately, modern IDEs such as the Groovy/Grails Tool Suite (GGTS), Eclipse, and IntelliJ IDEA have made life a lot easier. In fact, they've done more than that. With the advent of refactoring tools, Java has become one of the most maintainable languages out there.

The tools in the dynamic language space are in general nowhere near as advanced as those available for Java. On the other hand, many developers create entire applications in TextMate, jEdit, and other simple text editors; they prefer their speed and efficiency to the relative clunkiness and slowness of a robust, richly featured IDE. This is possible because of the simplicity of a framework such as Grails and the relatively forgiving Groovy grammar. It is our view that you can certainly get away with using the simpler tools during the early days of an application's life cycle.

However, as the application grows and enters the maintenance phase, the need for an IDE will also grow—particularly for refactoring and maintenance. Fortunately, although the tooling is much younger, you do have options available to you. We will be covering them in the following sections.

Using The Groovy/Grails Tool Suite (GGTS)

The Groovy/Grails Tool Suite (GGTS) provides the best Eclipse-powered development environment for building Groovy and Grails applications. GGTS provides support for the latest versions of Groovy and Grails and is built on top of the latest Eclipse releases.

GGTS is available from `http://grails.org/products/ggts`. The download includes a double-click installer that simplifies getting the tool installed, up, and running.

Configuring Grails Installations

GGTS ships with the latest version of Grails—that is, the one available when that version of GGTS was created—but you can configure as many different version of Grails in the IDE as you like. This feature is useful when you are upgrading projects from one version of Grails to another and working on multiple projects that do not necessarily use the same versions of Grails.

To configure Grails installations within the IDE, open the application preferences and navigate to Groovy ä Grails as shown in Figure 11-7.

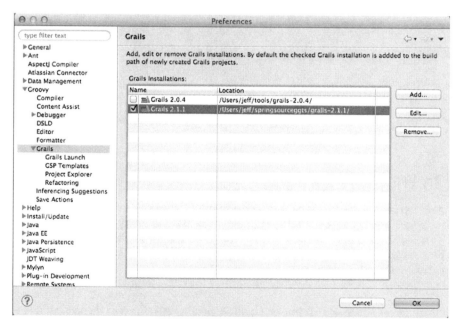

Figure 11-7. Configuring Grails installations

This dialog allows you to configure as many already-installed Grails installations on your system as you like. The check box in the table's far left column allows you to indicate which version should be selected by default when creating a new Grails application from within the IDE.

Importing a Grails Project

Once you have your Grails installation(s) configured, the next step is to import your Grails project. Luckily, Grails automatically creates Eclipse project and classpath files for you when you create the project. So to import the project, select the File ➤ Import menu option, and then select the "Import" option, at which point the dialog box shown in Figure 11-8 will appear.

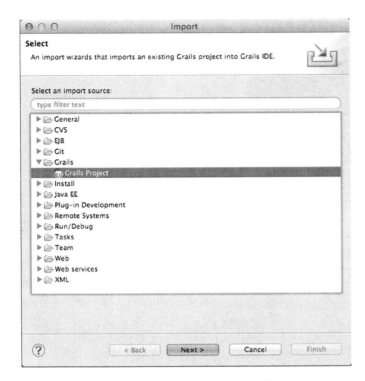

Figure 11-8. Importing a Grails project into GGTS

Select the "Grails Project" option, and click the Next button. Now browse to the root of a Grails project using the Browse button, and click Choose or OK. Once you have chosen the directory where the project is located, GGTS will automatically detect that there are Eclipse project files within the specified root directory and even in subdirectories within the root (see Figure 11-9).

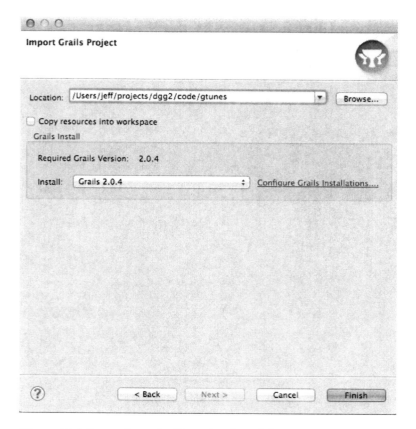

Figure 11-9. Importing a Grails project into Eclipse

Click the Finish button to complete the import. At this point, your project will be configured with the correct source directories and classpath.

Running a Grails Application from GGTS

You can run a Grails application from GGTS by right-clicking on the project and selecting the "Run As" menu. The submenu underneath "Run As" will include a number of options, including "Grails Command (run-app)" (see Figure 11-10).

Figure 11-10. *Running a Grails application from GGTS*

If you want to run the application in the debugger, then instead of selecting the "Run As" menu option, select "Debug As". When running the application in the debugger, you can set breakpoints, watches, and all the other things that Java developers are used to doing in their runtime debuggers.

GGTS gives the workspace a Grails perspective, which provides a smart view over all of the artefacts in a Grails application, among other capabilities. There are wizards for creating artefacts and running arbitrary commands. There is a Grails plug-in manager. GGTS provides a really flexible, really powerful environment for building, testing, and debugging Grails applications, and it is fast becoming the IDE of choice for Grails application developers. For more information on GGTS, see http://grails.org/products/ggts.

Using Spring Tool Suite (STS) and Eclipse

Most developers who want to develop Grails applications in an Eclipse environment opt to use GGTS. GGTS is built on top of Eclipse and provides everything that Eclipse provides, plus a whole bunch of Groovy and Grails support. If for some reason you want to develop a Grails application in an Eclipse environment but do not want to use GGTS, you can install the Groovy and Grails extensions into Eclipse or STS and get the same capabilities—with just a little more work required to piece everything together. You'll find more information on how to do that at www.grails.org/STS+Integration.

IntelliJ IDEA

JetBrains worked closely with the Groovy team when building much of the relevant support in IntelliJ. (You'll learn more about their support for Groovy and Grails and see their documentation at www. jetbrains.com/idea/features/groovy_grails.html.) Figure 11-11 shows IntelliJ IDEA in action.

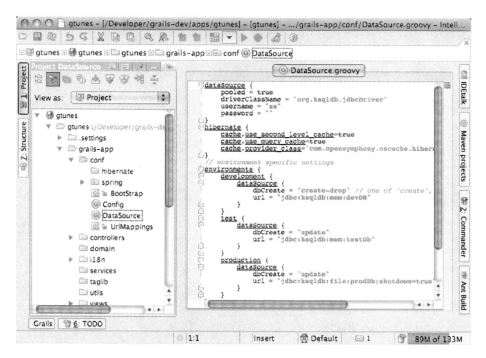

Figure 11-11. IntelliJ IDEA with the Groovy plug-in

NetBeans

Of the open source IDEs available, NetBeans (www.netbeans.org/) provides the most advanced support for Groovy and Grails development. After making NetBeans one of the best Ruby IDEs on the market, Sun began investing in Groovy and Grails support, and with the release of NetBeans 6.5, the results of that investment have really begun to show. Featuring built-in Groovy support, the NetBeans plug-in provides syntax highlighting, code completion, outline views, and menu options to easily access Grails commands. Figure 11-12 shows what the NetBeans Groovy editor looks like.

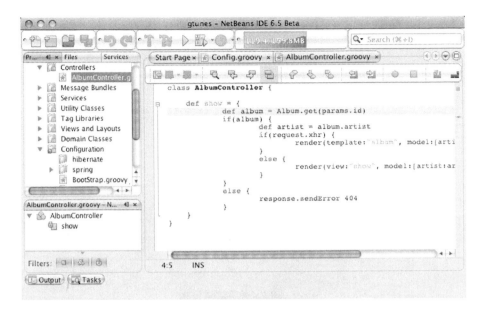

Figure 11-12. NetBeans Groovy/Grails integration

There is a good write-up on what is currently available in NetBeans on the Grails web site: http://www. grails.org/NetBeans+Integration.

Text Editors

There are a number of powerful text editors out there that provide varying levels of support for working with Grails projects. Two of the more popular editors are TextMate and Sublime Text. For information on using TextMate for editing Grails projects, see https://github.com/textmate/groovy-grails.tmbundle. For information on using Sublime Text for editing Grails projects, see https://github.com/osoco/sublimetext-grails.

Remote Debugging with an IDE

You can remote debug Grails by running the grails-debug executable as a substitute for the grails executable.

■ **Tip** The grails-debug executable simply sets up the necessary Java options to start Grails with a remote debugger. You could configure these yourself by setting the JAVA_OPTS environment variable.

The grails-debug executable will start Grails with a debug JVM. The debugger is listening on port 5005, which is the default debugger port for Java. You can then create a remote debug configuration in your IDE. For example, to do this with IntelliJ IDEA, go to the "Debug" menu and click "Edit Configurations". Then click the plus icon (+) at the top left and choose "Remote," which will give you a remote debug configuration, as shown in Figure 11-13.

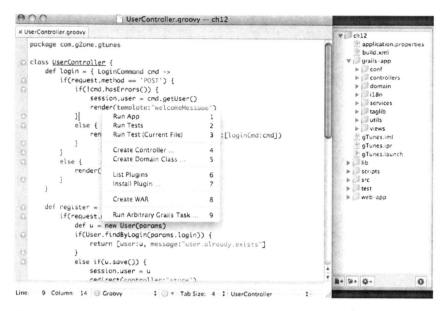

Figure 11-13. An IntelliJ remote debug configuration

You can leave the remaining settings as they are and just click the OK button in the bottom-right corner. With that done, just select the remote debug configuration and hit the Debug button; IntelliJ will connect to the Grails remote server. You can then set breakpoints in your applications sources, and IntelliJ will stop at those points.

If you're willing to be adventurous, you can add the Grails source code to your path and step into the internals of Grails—but we'll leave that decision up to you! With IDEs out of the way, we're now going to talk about how you integrate Grails into the server environment. From mail servers to containers, there is still much to cover, so don't go away.

■ **Note**   As of Grails 2.1, the Grails command line script supports a –debug argument, so instead of grails-debug, you can use grails-debug. In a future version of Grails, the grails-debug.sh and grails-debug.bat scripts will likely be removed.

Integration with E-mail Servers

It has become a frequent use case for web applications to send e-mails. The Simple Mail Transfer Protocol (SMTP) is the enabler for mail delivery and has become pretty much the de facto standard for outgoing e-mail. A number of different server products support SMTP, from Microsoft Exchange Server to the open source Sendmail agent, which is available on most Unix systems.

■ **Note**   The configuration of an SMTP server is beyond the scope of this book; we will show you how to set up Grails to talk to a successfully configured mail server.

You can integrate mail with Grails in several ways. Since Grails is built on Spring, you could use the org.springframework.mail abstraction, which provides a nicer API than JavaMail (http://java.sun.com/products/javamail/). However, that involves a lot of manual configuration, so what we'll be demonstrating is how to integrate the Grails Mail plug-in with your application so as to enable the sending of confirmation e-mails whenever a user registers on gTunes or makes a purchase.

To start, you need to update BuildConfig.groovy to express a dependency on the mail plugin.

```
grails.project.dependency.resolution = {
    ...
    plugins {
        compile ":mail:1.0"
        ...
    }
}
```

The Mail plug-in already comes with JavaMail and its dependencies, so you don't need to install any more libraries or dependencies. It uses sensible defaults and automatically assumes your mail server is running locally on port 25. However, if this is not the case, you can configure it by using some settings in grails-app/conf/Config.groovy. For example, Listing 11-35 shows how you could configure the mail server to send e-mails using a Gmail account instead.

Listing 11-35. *Configuring the Mail Plug-in for Gmail*

```
grails {
    mail {
        host = 'smtp.gmail.com'
        port = 465
        username = 'youraccount@gmail.com'
        password = 'yourpassword'
        props = ['mail.smtp.auth': 'true',
                 'mail.smtp.socketFactory.port': '465',
                 'mail.smtp.socketFactory.class': 'javax.net.ssl.SSLSocketFactory',
                 'mail.smtp.socketFactory.fallback': 'false']
    }
}
```

Notice in Listing 11-35 the use of the props setting, which allows you to configure the properties of the JavaMail framework. However, for our purposes, we'll assume that a mail server running locally is good enough. Returning to the Mail plug-in itself, the main addition is a new method, sendMail, added to all controllers. Listing 11-36 shows an example of its use at its simplest.

Listing 11-36. *Sending a Simple Mail Message with sendMail*

```
sendMail {
    to "john@g2one.com"
    subject "Hello John"
    body "How are you?"
}
```

If you need to access the sendMail method from other places in your application, such as tag libraries and services, the Mail plug-in provides a mailService bean that is available via dependency injection. Simply define a property called mailService in your tag library or service as follows:

```
def mailService
```
The sendMail method can then be called using the mailService instance; for example:
```
mailService.sendMail {
    ...
}
```

In the example in Listing 11-30, a simple string is used for the body of the e-mail. However, it is equally possible to use a GSP view to define the body. That is something you'll be doing to send registration confirmation e-mails to users of the gTunes application. Before you can do so, however, you need to modify the User domain class in order to add a new email property. Listing 11-37 shows the change to the User class.

Listing 11-37. Adding an email Property to the User Class

```
class User {
    String email
    ...
    static constraints = {
        ...
        email email:true, blank:false, unique:true
    }
}
```

As you can see in Listing 11-37, you've also applied a set of constraints to the email property. The email constraint ensures that it is a valid e-mail address, the blank constraint makes sure blank values are not allowed, and the unique constraint ensures that two users can't register with the same e-mail address. With this done, you need to modify the grails-app/views/user/register.gsp view to add a field for the email property to the registration form. Listing 11-38 shows the necessary change to the register.gsp file.

Listing 11-38. Adding a Text Field for the email Property

```
<g:form action="register" name="registerForm">
    ...
    <div class="input clearfix">
        <label for="email">Email <span class="required">*</span></label>
        <g:textField required="true" name="email" value="${user?.email}" />
        <g:hasErrors  bean="${user}" field="email">
            <p class="error"><g:fieldError bean="${user}" field="email" /></p>
        </g:hasErrors>
    </div>

    ...
</g:form>
```

With that done, you now have an e-mail address to send confirmation e-mails to! To send an e-mail, you'll need to modify the register action of the UserController class to use the sendMail method to deliver an e-mail. Listing 11-39 shows the changes to the register action.

Listing 11-39. Sending an E-mail Confirmation

```
def register() {
    ...
    else if(u.save()) {
```

```
            session.user = u
            try {
                sendMail {
                    to u.email
                    subject 'Registration Confirmation'
                    body view: '/emails/confirmRegistration',
                            model: [user: u]
                }
            } catch (Exception e) {
                log.error "Problem sending email ${e.message}", e
            }
            redirect controller:"store"

    }
    ...
}
```

Notice how in Listing 11-33 you can use the view argument of the body method to define the name of the GSP view used to render the e-mail. As you can see, you can also pass a model with the model argument. The code is wrapped in a try/catch block, just in case there is a problem sending the confirmation mail. At the moment, the code simply logs the error, but you could place the message into a queue to be re-sent later using a scheduled job —something you'll be looking at in the next section.

As for the GSP itself, you need to create a new view at the location grails-app/views/emails/confirmRegistration.gsp. The example in Listing 11-39 uses an absolute path to this location. If you don't specify an absolute path, then, as with regular views, the path is assumed to be relative to the current controller. Listing 11-40 shows the confirmRegistration view that renders the e-mail contents.

Listing 11-40. The confirmRegistration View

```
<%@ page contentType="text/plain"%> Dear ${user.firstName} ${user.lastName},
Congratulations! You have registered with gTunes, giving you access to a huge collection of
music.
Your login id is: ${user.login}
You can use the following link to login: <g:createLink controller="store"
absolute="true" />
Kind Regards,
The gTunes Team
```

Note that the code in Listing 11-34 uses a GSP page directive to set the contentType to text/plain. The default contentType is text/html, so if you want to send HTML mail instead, omit this line. With that, you've implemented e-mail confirmation of registration. However, that's not the end of our e-mail adventures; in the next section you'll learn how to send e-mails on a scheduled basis.

Deployment

Moving your application from a development environment onto a production or test server often presents you with a number of choices. The options when deploying Grails are many and varied, and they run the gamut from simple to complex. In the following sections, you'll be looking at different ways of deploying Grails and how to customize the deployment process.

Deploying with Grails

If you're looking for a simple way to manage deployment and aren't too concerned about fine-tuning the details of your container, then deploying with Grails itself is certainly a simple way to go about it. To deploy with Grails, all you need to do is install Grails on the target server and then use the run-war command from the root of the project:

```
$ grails run-war
```

This will start a Tomcat server on port 8080. On this point, you can configure the ubiquitous Apache HTTPD server (http://httpd.apache.org/) to use mod_proxy to relay requests to the Tomcat server. The details of the configuration can be found at the Apache web site, http://tomcat.apache.org/connectors-doc/webserver_howto/apache.html. Alternatively, you could even run Tomcat on port 80, so that it acts as the primary web server:

```
$ grails -Dserver.port=80 run-war
```

As simple as this approach is, many organizations favor a more structured approach to deployment and use that standard Java stalwart, the WAR file.

Deploying to a Container

You learned about creating a WAR file as early as Chapter 2. When thinking about deployment in the Java world, the first thing that usually comes to mind is how to create a WAR. It is one of the strengths of the Java platform that you can take a WAR file and deploy it onto a wide range of containers.

From the commercial 800-pound gorillas like IBM WebSphere and BEA WebLogic to the popular open source containers like Tomcat and JBoss, there are options aplenty. Against the background of all this helpful standardization, it is unfortunate that the way in which you deploy a WAR file is still not standardized.

On something like Tomcat, it's typically just a matter of dropping your WAR file into the TOMCAT_HOME/webapps directory, while on WebSphere there is a fancy GUI wizard that allows you to upload a WAR file via a browser. Nevertheless, there are some important things to consider when deploying to a container. The following is a list of key points to remember when deploying with Grails.

- Make sure that the -server flag is passed to the JVM that runs your container to enable the server VM. Running Grails on the client VM has a negative impact on performance.

- Depending on the number of GSP views you have, you may need to allocate more *permgen* space (the area of memory the JVM uses for dynamically compiled classes). GSP views are compiled at runtime on first load into byte code, so they require permgen space. You can allocate more permgen with the -XX:MaxPermSize=256m flag.

- It is advisable to allocate extra memory to the JVM when running a Grails application. Simple Grails applications have been known to perform well on shared virtual hosting with low memory, but the more you can allocate, the better. For example, to allocate 512 megabytes of heap space, you can use the -Xmx512M flag.

Application Versioning and Metadata

You may have already noticed by now that when you run the grails war command, the generated WAR file has a version number on the end of the file name. You may be wondering where this mysterious version number comes from. Basically, when you create a Grails application, the version number of the application is set to 0.1 in the application's metadata.

You can change the version number by calling the set-version command, as shown in Listing 11-41.

Listing 11-41. *Setting the Application Version Number*

```
grails set-version 0.2
```

Then when you build a new WAR, the version number from Listing 11-41 will be used instead. At runtime you can inspect the application metadata using the grailsApplication object:

```
println grailsApplication.metadata."app.version"
```

or using the <g:meta> tag from a GSP, as shown in Listing 11-42.

Listing 11-42. *Using Application Metadata*

```
Version <g:meta name="app.version"/>
Built with Grails <g:meta name="app.grails.version"/>
```

Customizing the WAR

If you want to customize the way in which the WAR file is produced, you can consider taking advantage of a number of hooks. For example, say you wanted to provide a different base web.xml template in order to include your own custom servlets; you can do so with the grails.config.base.webXml setting in grails-app/conf/Config.groovy:

```
grails.config.base.webXml="file:${userHome}/.settings/my-web.xml"
```

Also, if you need to change the location where the WAR file is generated, you can do so using the grails.war.destFile property:

```
grails.war.destFile = "${tomcatHome}/webapps"
```

If you want to include additional resources in the WAR, you can do so with the grails.war.resources setting, as shown in Listing 11-43.

Listing 11-43. *Using the grails.war.resources Setting to Include Custom Resources*

```
grails.war.resources = { stagingDir ->
// include static resources
  copy(dir:stagingDir) {
   fileset(dir:"/usr/var/www/htdocs")
  }
}
```

Notice how the closure assigned to grails.war.resources gets passed an argument that is the location of the directory where the WAR is being built. You can then use custom copy steps to include whatever extra resources you need. Once you actually have a WAR, you may want to perform some initial population of the database state when the application loads. We'll be covering how to do this in the next section.

Populating the Database with BootStrap Classes

Whenever an application loads for the first time, there may be some initial state that needs to be in place for the application to operate correctly. One way to do this is with BootStrap classes. If you look at the grails-app/conf directory, you may have noticed a class called BootStrap.groovy. Listing 11-44 shows the template for this class.

Listing 11-44. The BootStrap Class

```
class BootStrap {
    def init = {
        servletContext ->
    }
    def destroy = {
    }
}
```

As you can see, there is an init method, which is called when the container first loads, and a destroy method. The destroy method is called on container shutdown. It should be noted, though, that it is not guaranteed to be invoked and hence shouldn't be relied upon for anything critical.

Within the Bootstrap class, you can use GORM to populate the database. Thanks to GORM's usage of fluent APIs[1], it is pretty easy to create an object graph, as Listing 11-45 shows.

Listing 11-45. Populating Data on Application Load

```
def init = {
    def album = new Album(title:"Because of the Times")
    album.addToSongs(title:"Knocked Up").addToSongs(title:"Charmer")
        ...
    new Artist(name:"Kings of Leon") .addToAlbums(album) .save(flush:true)
}
```

If you need to populate per-environment data, use the GrailsUtil class to obtain the environment and perform a switch. See Listing 11-46 for an example.

Listing 11-46. Per-Environment Bootstrapping

```
def init = {
    switch(grails.util.GrailsUtil.environment) {
        case "development":
            // initialize in development here
            break
        case "production":
            // initialize in production here
            break
    }
}
```

---

1 A fluent API is often referred to as method chaining because it involves writing methods that return objects in a manner such that multiple methods can be chained in a sequence. See www.martinfowler.com/bliki/FluentInterface.html for a more complete definition.

Summary

Integrating Grails covers a broad spectrum, as the number of topics covered in this chapter demonstrate. They range from integration with command-line tools to your development environment to the servers you finally deploy onto. Many options are available to you—so many that an entire book on the subject wouldn't be inappropriate. The good news is that many of the deployment options and techniques you use in the Java space are equally applicable to Grails.

Whether it be with a Java EE–compliant container like Tomcat or your favorite build tool, there is typically a way to get Groovy and Grails to work seamlessly in your environment. The next chapter will deal with a whole new subject, one critical to the workings of Grails—the plug-in system. Throughout this book you've already used many of the more prominent plug-ins in Grails.

Now it's time for you to turn into a plug-in creator, to learn how you can modularize your application through the use of plug-ins.

CHAPTER 12

Plug-ins

Up until now, you have been a consumer of the Grails plug-in system at various points throughout the book. Plug-ins are very much a cornerstone of Grails. Grails itself is basically a plug-in runtime with little knowledge beyond how to load and configure an installed set of plug-ins. Most of the core of Grails is implemented as a suite of plug-ins for this runtime.

The Grails plug-in system is very flexible—so much so that it would be quite reasonable to write an entire book on the subject. In this chapter, we aim to summarize the core concepts and demonstrate some common use cases for the plug-in system. However, the full extent of what is achievable with the plug-in system is left to your imagination.

Even if you don't plan to write a plug-in to distribute to the world, we recommend you take the time to read this chapter. Grails plug-ins are not just a way to enhance the functionality of an existing Grails application; they are also an effective way to modularize your code. Later in this chapter, we will demonstrate how you can use plug-ins to split your Grails application into separate maintainable plug-ins that are composed together at runtime.

Plug-in Basics

The core of Grails is a plug-in runtime environment. However, to make it immediately useful, it ships with a default set of plug-ins that you've already learned about, including GORM and the Grails MVC framework. Along with the default plug-ins, Grails ships with a set of commands to automatically discover and install new plug-ins. Let's take a look at these first.

Plug-in Discovery

The Grails plug-in community is a hive of activity; it's one of the most exciting areas of Grails. At the time of writing, more than 850 plug-ins were available from the central repository. Providing a range of functionality from job scheduling to search to reporting engines, all the plug-ins are discoverable through the grails list-plugins command. To run the list-plugins command, simply type "grails list-plugins" in a command window, as shown in Listing 12-1.

Listing 12-1. Running the list-plugins Command

```
$ grails list-plugins
```

What this will do is go off to the Grails central repository and download the latest published plug-in list. The list is then formatted and printed to the console. You can see some typical output from the list-plugins command in Listing 12-2, shortened for brevity.

Listing 12-2. Output from the list-plugins Command

```
$ grails list-plugins
| Downloading: plugins-list.xml

Plugins available in the grailsCentral repository are listed below:
--------------------------------------------------------------
acegi              <0.5.3.2>   --  Acegi Plugin
activemq           <0.4.1>     --  Grails ActiveMQ Plugin
activiti           <5.9>       --  Grails Activiti Plugin - Enabled
activiti-shiro     <0.1.1>     --  This plugin integrates Shiro Security
    ...
```

In the left column, you see the name of the plug-in, and in the middle is its latest released version. Finally, on the right of the output, you see the short description for any given plug-in. If you want to obtain more information about a particular plug-in, use the plugin-info command. Listing 12-3 shows how to obtain more information about the audit-logging plug-in from Listing 12-2.

Listing 12-3. Using the plugin-info Command to Get Detailed Plug-in Information

```
$ grails plugin-info spring-security-core
| Downloading: spring-security-core-1.2.7.3.pom.sha1


--------------------------------------------------------------------------
Information about Grails plugin
--------------------------------------------------------------------------
Name: spring-security-core | Latest release: 1.2.7.3
--------------------------------------------------------------------------
Spring Security Core Plugin
--------------------------------------------------------------------------
Author: Burt Beckwith
--------------------------------------------------------------------------
Author's e-mail: beckwithb@vmware.com
--------------------------------------------------------------------------
Find more info here: http://grails.org/plugin/spring-security-core
--------------------------------------------------------------------------


Spring Security Core plugin


Dependency Definition
--------------------------------------------------------------------------
    :spring-security-core:1.2.7.3
```

```
Required Repositories
--------------------------------------------------------------------------
    http://plugins.grails.org
    http://repo.grails.org/grails/plugins/
    http://repo.grails.org/grails/core/
    http://svn.codehaus.org/grails/trunk/grails-plugins
    http://repo1.maven.org/maven2/

Transitive Dependencies
--------------------------------------------------------------------------
    org.springframework.security:spring-security-core:3.0.7.RELEASE (compile)
    org.springframework.security:spring-security-web:3.0.7.RELEASE (compile)

Transitive Plugins
--------------------------------------------------------------------------

To get info about specific release of plugin 'grails plugin-info [NAME] [VERSION]'

To get list of all plugins type 'grails list-plugins'

To install latest version of plugin type 'grails install-plugin [NAME]'

To install specific version of plugin type 'grails install-plugin [NAME] [VERSION]'
```

For further information, see http://grails.org/plug-ins. As with the plugin-info command, you get more information about the plug-in, including a long description, the author's name, a link to the documentation (http://grails.org/plug-in/spring-security-core), and more.

Plug-in Installation

This brings us to the topic of installing a plug-in into an application. To do so, express a dependency on the plug-in in the grails-app/conf/BuildConfig.groovy file. The code in Listing 12-4 demonstrates how to express a compile-time dependency on version 1.2.7.3 of the spring-security-core plug-in.

Listing 12-4. Installing a Specific Version of a Plug-in with the install-plugin Command

```
grails.project.dependency.resolution = {
    ...
    repositories {
        ...
    }
    plugins {
        compile ':spring-security-core:1.2.7.3'
        ...
    }
    dependencies {
        ...
    }
    ...
}
```

Local Plug-ins

Of course, the plug-ins you create may not necessarily live in the central Grails repository. Grails plug-ins are packaged as simple zip files, and if you download a plug-in zip file from elsewhere, you can install it by simply running the install-plugin command and passing in the location on disk of the plug-in. Listing 12-5 shows how to install a plug-in located in your home directory on a Unix system.

Listing 12-5. Installing a Local Plug-in

```
$ grails install-plugin ~/grails-spring-security-core-1.2.7.3.zip
```

To ease distribution within your team, instead of keeping your plug-ins locally on disk, you could host your plug-ins on a local web server. For that case, the install-plugin command also supports plug-in installation over HTTP. Listing 12-6 shows how to install the spring-security-core plug-in from a private web server over HTTP, bypassing the Grails plug-in autodiscovery mechanism.

Listing 12-6. Installing Plug-ins over HTTP

```
$ grails install-plugin http://plugins.mydomain.com/spring-security-core/spring-security-core-
1.2.7.3.zip
```

Now that you've learned the basics of plug-in discovery and installation, let's move on to how you go about creating a plug-in and demonstrate the basics of plug-in creation and distribution. After that, you'll see how to create some useful plug-ins to enhance and modularize the gTunes sample application.

Creating Plug-ins

Creating plug-ins in Grails is as simple as creating regular applications. All you need to do is run the grails create-plugin command and specify a name for your plug-in. In fact, what you will soon discover is that a Grails plug-in *is* a Grails application. To understand this, create a simple Grails plug-in called simple-cache that can provide caching services to a Grails application. You do this using the create-plugin command, as shown in Listing 12-7.

Listing 12-7. Creating a Plug-in with the create-plugin Command

```
$ grails create-plugin simple-cache
```

The result is what looks like a regular Grails application. You have all the typical resources that make up an application, including a grails-app directory. However, on closer inspection, you'll notice there is a file called SimpleCacheGrailsPlugin.groovy in the root of the project. This file contains a class that represents the *plug-in descriptor*. Figure 12-1 shows the plug-in descriptor residing snugly in the root of the project.

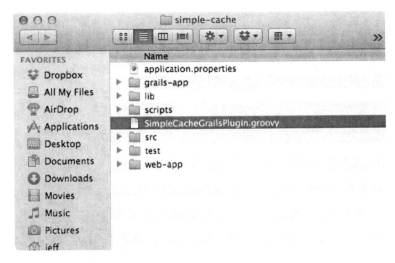

Figure 12-1. The simple-cache plug-in descriptor

Providing Plug-in Metadata

The plug-in descriptor serves a number of purposes. The first and primary purpose is for the plug-in author to provide metadata about the plug-in: the author name, version number, description, and so on. Listing 12-8 shows the SimpleCacheGrailsPlugin class and the placeholder fields used to supply this information.

Listing 12-8. The SimpleCacheGrailsPlugin Plug-in Descriptor

```
class SimpleCacheGrailsPlugin {
    // the plugin version
    def version = "0.1"
    // the version or versions of Grails the plugin is designed for
    def grailsVersion = "2.0 > *"
    // the other plugins this plugin depends on
    def dependsOn = [:]
    // resources that are excluded from plugin packaging
    def pluginExcludes = [
        "grails-app/views/error.gsp"
    ]

    // TODO Fill in these fields
    def title = "Simple Cache Plugin" // Headline display name of the plugin
    def author = "Your name"
    def authorEmail = ""
    def description = '''\
Brief summary/description of the plugin.
'''

    // URL to the plugin's documentation
    def documentation = "http://grails.org/plugin/simple-cache"
```

```
    ...
}
```

Properties such as author, title, and so on, appear in the list-plugins and plugin-info commands when a plug-in is published to a Grails plug-in repository. The following list summarizes the available properties and what they represent:

- author: The name of the plug-in author

- authorEmail: An e-mail contact address for the author

- title: A short title for the plug-in to appear in the right column of the list-plugins command (see Listing 12-2)

- description: A longer, more detailed description that is displayed by the plug-in-info command

- documentation: A link to the location of the documentation for the plug-in

All the properties in this list are optional; however, providing this information will help others understand the purpose of your plug-in. Listing 12-9 shows the simple-cache plug-in's metadata information.

Listing 12-9. The simple-cache Plug-in Descriptor with Metadata Provided

```
class SimpleCacheGrailsPlugin {
    // the plugin version
    def version = "0.1"
    // the version or versions of Grails the plugin is designed for
    def grailsVersion = "2.0 > *"
    // the other plugins this plugin depends on
    def dependsOn = [:]
    // resources that are excluded from plugin packaging
    def pluginExcludes = [
        "grails-app/views/error.gsp"
    ]

    // TODO Fill in these fields
    def title = "Simple Cache Plugin" // Headline display name of the plugin
    def author = "Jeff Brown"
    def authorEmail = "jbrown@vmware.com"
    def description = '''\
A simple demo plugin which provides very simple caching services.
This plugin is for demonstration purposes only.  For serious
caching needs, http://grails.org/plugins/cache is a real solution.
'''

    // URL to the plugin's documentation
    def documentation = http://grails.org/plugin/simple-cache

    ...
}
```

Supplying Application Artefacts

One of the more obvious ways a plug-in can enhance an existing application is by providing a new artefact, such as a controller, tag library, or service.

Because a Grails plug-in is simply a Grails application, supplying an artefact is a simple matter of creating it, just as you would in a regular application. For the simple-cache plug-in, you'll implement a service that provides application-layer caching. To do so, simply use the create-service command from the root of the plug-in:

```
$ grails create-service com.cache.Cache
```

Once completed, you'll end up with a new service at the location grails-app/services/com/cache/CacheService.groovy. Because it's pretty simple to do, you'll also be implementing a little tag library to perform content-level caching. To create the tag library, run the create-tag-lib command:

```
$ grails create-tag-lib com.cache.Cache
```

Note that since a Grails plug-in is simply a Grails application, you can run it just like a Grails application! Just use the grails run-app command, and you're on your way. This has significant benefits for the plug-in developer in that plug-in development is not very different from regular application development. You can run your plug-in like a regular application, and you can also test your plug-in like a regular application using the test-app command. You can even install other plug-ins into a plug-in, something that is critical when developing a plug-in that has dependencies on other plug-ins.

As for the CacheService and the CacheTagLib, we'll get to the implementation details of these later. For the moment, all you need to know is that when you package up your plug-in for distribution, it will provide two new artefacts: a tag library and a service.

Plug-in Hooks

Let's return to the plug-in descriptor. As well as providing metadata about the plug-in, the descriptor also enables you to supply hooks into the plug-in runtime. Each hook is defined as a closure property and allows the plug-in to participate in the various phases of the plug-in life cycle. The hooks are listed here in the order of their execution:

- doWithWebDescriptor: This gets passed the XML for the web.xml file that has been parsed by Groovy's XmlSlurper into a GPathResult. See the "Modifying the Generated WAR Descriptor" section later in the chapter for more information on this one.

- doWithSpring: This allows participation in the runtime configuration of Grails' underlying Spring ApplicationContext. See the "Providing Spring Beans" section for more information.

- doWithDynamicMethods: Executed after the construction of the ApplicationContext, this is the hook that plug-ins should use to provide new behavior to Grails classes. See the "Using Metaprogramming to Enhance Behavior" section later in the chapter for more information.

- doWithApplicationContext: This is executed after the Grails ApplicationContext has been constructed. The ApplicationContext instance is passed to this hook as the first argument.

By default, the simple-cache plug-in you created earlier comes with empty implementations of all of these. If you don't plan to implement any of these hooks, you can simply delete them from the plug-in descriptor. Listing 12-10 shows the various plug-in hooks, just waiting to be implemented.

▨ **Note** If you merely want to use plug-ins to provide application modularity, you can skip to the "Packaging and Distributing a Grails Plug-in" section. The next few sections go into significant detail on how to hook into all aspects of the Grails plug-in system.

Listing 12-10. Plug-in Hooks in the simple-cache Plug-in

```
class SimpleCacheGrailsPlugin {
    def version = 0.1
    ...
    def doWithWebDescriptor = { xml -> }
    def doWithSpring = {}

    def doWithDynamicMethods = { applicationContext -> }

    def doWithApplicationContext = { applicationContext -> }

}
```

Plug-in Variables

A number of implicit variables are available within the context of these hooks that allow you to inspect the conventions within a running Grails application. The following are the available variables and associated descriptions:

- application: An instance of the org.codehaus.groovy.grails.commons. GrailsApplication class; it provides information about the loaded classes and the conventions within them.

- manager: An instance of the org.codehaus. groovy.grails.plugins. GrailsPluginManager class; it allows you to find out what other Grails plug-ins are installed.

- plugin: A reference to the org.codehaus.groovy.grails.plugins.GrailsPlugin class, which allows you to find out various information about the plug-in including its name, version, and dependencies.

The GrailsApplication class is typically the most critical to understand if you plan to implement any hooks that work with the Grails conventions. Essentially, it defines a number of dynamic properties that map to each concept in a Grails application. For example, to obtain a list of the controller classes in a GrailsApplication, you can do this:

```
def controllerClasses = application.controllerClasses
```

Note that when we refer to *classes*, we're not talking about instances of the Java.lang.Class interface but of the org.codehaus.groovy.grails.commons.GrailsClass interface, which defines a number of methods to inspect the conventions within a GrailsApplication for a particular artefact type.

For example, given the CacheService created earlier, Listing 12-11 demonstrates some of the methods of the GrailsClass interface and how they behave.

Listing 12-11. Using the Grails Convention APIs

```
GrailsClass serviceClass =
    application.getServiceClass("com.cache.CacheService")
assert "CacheService" == serviceClass.shortName
assert "Cache" == serviceClass.name
assert "com.cache.CacheService" == serviceClass.fullName
assert "cacheService" == serviceClass.propertyName
assert "cache" == serviceClass.logicalPropertyName
assert "com.cache" == serviceClass.packageName
assert true == serviceClass.getPropertyValue("transactional")
```

You'll notice in Listing 12-11 the use of the getServiceClass method to obtain the CacheService by name. The getServiceClass method is another dynamic method available on the GrailsApplication class. Essentially, for each artefact type, the GrailsApplication class provides dynamic methods to access the artefacts of that type, which are summarized here:

- get*Classes: to obtain a list of all the GrailsClass instances for a particular artefact type, such as with getControllerClasses() or via property access such as controllerClasses.

- get*Class(String name): to obtain a specific GrailsClass instance by name, as in ge tControllerClass("HelloController").

- is*Class(Class theClass): to inquire whether a given Java.lang.Class is a particular artefact type, as in isControllerClass(myClass).

The asterisks in the previous method names are substitutes for the relevant artefact types you are interested in. Table 12-1 summarizes the different artefact types and shows an example of the typical use for each.

Table 12-1. Summary of Existing Artefact Types

Artefact Type	Example
Bootstrap	def bootstrapClasses = application.getBootstrapClasses()
Codec	def codecClasses = application.getCodecClasses()
Controller	def controllerClasses = application.getControllerClasses()
Domain	def domainClasses = application.getDomainClasses()
Filters	def filterClasses = application.getFiltersClasses()
Service	def serviceClasses = application.getServiceClasses()
TagLib	def tagLibClasses = application.getTagLibClasses()
UrlMappings	def urlMappingClasses = application.getUrlMappingsClasses()

The artefact types in Table 12-1 cover existing artefacts, but Grails also lets you add your own artefact types; we'll look at them in the next section.

Custom Artefact Types

Out of the box, Grails ships with a set of features, including controllers, domain classes, and so on. As you saw in the previous section, you can access all aspects of these via the GrailsApplication interface.

However, what if you want to add a new artefact type? Take, for example, the existing Quartz plug-in. Quartz is a job-scheduling API that runs specified tasks on a scheduled basis. For example, you may want to run some code at noon on the last Friday of every month. Quartz aims to address a situation of this kind.

Look at the existing artefact types; none of them models the idea of a job. How can you extend Grails and provide it new knowledge it about what a job is? Fortunately, you can find the answer in the Grails org.codehaus.groovy.grails.commons.ArtefactHandler interface. Listing 12-12 shows the key methods of the ArtefactHandler interface.

Listing 12-12. The ArtefactHandler Interface

```
public interface ArtefactHandler {
    String getType();
    boolean isArtefact(Class aClass);
    GrailsClass newArtefactClass(Class artefactClass);
}
```

The getType() method returns the type of the GrailsClass, which will be one of the values shown in the first column of Table 13-1. The isArtefact(Class) method is responsible for identifying whether a given class is of the current artefact type based on some convention. For example, does the class end with the convention *Controller*? If so, then it's a controller class.

The newArtefactClass(Class) method will create a new GrailsClass instance for the given java.lang. Class. The ArtefactHandler interface has other methods, but most of them are abstracted away from you because when implementing a custom ArtefactHandler, you'll typically extend the org.codehaus.groovy. grails.commons.ArtefactHandlerAdapter class. Look at Listing 12-13, which shows a possible implementation for the Quartz plug-in.

Listing 12-13. An ArtefactHandler for the Quartz Plug-in

```
1 class JobArtefactHandler extends ArtefactHandlerAdapter {
2
3     static final TYPE = "Job"
4
5     JobArtefactHandler() {
6         super(TYPE, GrailsClass, DefaultGrailsClass, TYPE)
7     }
8
9     boolean isArtefactClass(Class clazz) {
10            // class shouldn't be null and shoudd ends with Job suffix
11        if(!super.isArtefactClass(clazz)) return false
12        // and should have an execute method
13            return clazz.methods.find { it.name == 'execute' } != null
14    }
15 }
```

There are a few key things to look at in the JobArtefactHandler in Listing 12-13. First, take a look at the constructor on lines 5 to 7:

```
5     JobArtefactHandler() {
6         super(TYPE, GrailsClass, DefaultGrailsClass, TYPE)
7     }
```

The constructor calls the super implementation, passing four arguments:

- *The artefact type.* In this case, you're using a constant, called TYPE, that has the value Job.

- *The interface to use for the artefact type.* You could extend the GrailsClass interface to provide a more specific interface such as GrailsJobClass.

- *The implementation of the interface for the artefact type.* Grails provides a default implementation in the DefaultGrailsClass, but you could subclass this if you want to provide custom logic within the artefact type.

- *The suffix that the class name should end with for a* Java.lang.Class *to be considered of the artefact type.* The default implementation of the isArtefactClass method in ArtefactHandlerAdapter will perform a check on the passed Java.lang.Class to ensure that the class name ends with the specified suffix. As you can see on line 11 of Listing 12-13, the logic from the superclass isArtefact method is being reused.

The next thing to note about the code in Listing 12-13 is the implementation of the isArtefactClass(Class) method, which checks that the class ends with the appropriate suffix by calling the superclass implementation of isArtefactClass (Class) and whether the class possesses an execute method. You can assert your expectations of the behavior of the JobArtefactHandler by writing a simple unit test (see Listing 12-14).

Listing 12-14. *Testing an ArtefactHandler*

```
class JobArtefactHandlerTests extends GroovyTestCase {
    void testIsArtefact() {
        def handler = new JobArtefactHandler()
        assertTrue handler.isArtefactClass(TestJob)
        assertFalse handler.isArtefactClass(JobArtefactHandlerTests)

        GrailsClass jobClass = handler.newArtefactClass(TestJob)
        assertEquals "TestJob", jobClass.shortName
        assertEquals "Test", jobClass.name
        assertEquals "TestJob", jobClass.fullName
        assertEquals "testJob",jobClass.propertyName
        assertEquals "test",jobClass.logicalPropertyName
        assertEquals "", jobClass.packageName
    }
}
class TestJob {
    def execute() {}
}
```

At this point, there is one thing left to do. You have to tell your plug-in about the ArtefactHandler. Say that you are creating the Quartz plug-in and you have a QuartzGrailsPlugin descriptor. If you add an artefacts property that contains a list of provided artefacts, the plug-in will make Grails aware of the JobArtefactHandler:

```
def artefacts = [new JobArtefactHandlerQ]
```

So once the Quartz plug-in is installed, if there is a class within the grails-app/jobs directory that looks like the one in Listing 12-15, the JobArtefactHandler will approve the class as being a "job."

Listing 12-15. An Example of a Job

```
class SimpleJob {
    def execute() {
        // code to be executed
    }
}
```

An added bonus of going through these steps is that suddenly the GrailsApplication object has become aware of the new artefact type you just added. With this hypothetical Quartz plug-in installed, you can use all the dynamic methods on the GrailsApplication object first shown in Listing 12-11. Listing 12-16 demonstrates a few examples using the SimpleJob from Listing 12-15.

Listing 12-16. Using the GrailsApplication Object to Inspect Jobs

```
def jobClasses = application.getJobClasses()
GrailsClass simpleJobClass = application.getJobClass("SimpleJob")
assert application.isJobClass(SimpleJob)
```

The key thing to learn from this section is that Grails provides you with an *extensible* convention-based API. You are in no way restricted by the existing conventions and can easily start adding your own ideas to the mix. The next section will look at how the idea of Convention over Configuration (CoC) extends to the runtime configuration of Spring.

Providing Spring Beans

The doWithSpring hook allows you to specify new Spring beans to configure at runtime using the Grails BeanBuilder domain-specific language (DSL) for Spring. Grails is built completely on the Spring Framework. Grails has what is known as an ApplicationContext, which is essentially a container provided by Spring that holds one or more beans. By default, each bean is a singleton, meaning there is only one of them in the ApplicationContext.

As you learned in Chapter 10, Grails allows services to be autowired into controllers and tag libraries. This autowire feature is powered by the Spring container and is often referred to as *dependency injection*. An extremely powerful pattern, it allows you to effectively separate out dependencies and the construction of those dependencies. That's the theory. . . now let's take a look at an example.

Earlier, you created a new service in the simple-cache plug-in called CacheService. The CacheService is going to work in conjunction with a cache provider to provide application-layer caching to any user of the simple-cache plug-in. Since it is a little pointless to reinvent the wheel and implement your own homegrown caching implementation, you're going to take advantage of the Ehcache library.

Plug-ins may register beans with the Spring application context by using doWithSpring. Listing 12-17 shows how to define a globalCache bean.

Listing 12-17. Defining Beans in doWithSpring

```
class SimpleCacheGrailsPlugin {
    ...
    def doWithSpring = {
        globalCache(org.springframework.cache.ehcache.EhCacheFactoryBean) {
            timeToLive = 300
        }
    }
}
```

The name of the bean is the name of the method, which in this case is globalCache. The bean class is the first argument, while the closure passed as the last argument allows you to set property values on the bean. In this case, a globalCache bean is configured to expire entries every 5 minutes (300 seconds).

With that done, let's begin implementing the CacheService. First you need to get a reference to the globalCache bean defined by the plug-in. To do this, simply add a property that matches the name of the bean to the CacheService, as shown in Listing 12-18.

Listing 12-18. Obtaining Beans Supplied by doWithSpring

```
import net.sf.ehcache.Ehcache
class CacheService {
    static transactional = false
    Ehcache globalCache
    ...
}
```

The globalCache property is in bold in Listing 12-18. Note that transactions have been disabled for the service by setting static transactional = false, since transactions won't be a requirement for this service.

Now let's implement the caching logic. When implementing caching, the pattern is typically that you look up an object from the cache, and if it doesn't exist, you execute some logic that obtains the data to be cached. Listing 12-19 shows some pseudocode for this pattern.

Listing 12-19. The Caching Pattern

```
def obj = cache.get("myentry")
if(!obj)   {
    obj = ...
    // do some complex task to obtain obj
    cache.put("myentry", obj)
}
return obj
```

However, given that you have the power of closures at your disposal, it makes more sense to take advantage of them to come up with a more elegant solution. Listing 12-20 shows how to implement caching of entire logical blocks using closures.

Listing 12-20. Caching the Return Value of Blocks of Code Using Closures

```
1 import net.sf.ehcache.Ehcache
2 import net.sf.ehcache.Element
3
4 class CacheService {
5    ...
6    def cacheOrReturn(Serializable cacheKey, Closure callable) {
7         def entry = globalCache?.get(cacheKey)?.getValue()
8         if(!entry) {
9              entry = callable.call()
10             globalCache.put new Element(cacheKey, entry)
11         }
12         return entry
13    }
14 }
```

To understand what the code is doing in Listing 12-20, let's step through it line by line. First, on line 7 an entry is obtained from the globalCache bean, which is an instance of the net.sf.ehcache.Ehcache class:

```
7      def entry = globalCache?.get(cacheKey)?.getValue()
```

Notice how you can use Groovy's safe-dereference operator ?. to make sure that a NullPointerException is never thrown when accessing the value, even if the globalCache property is null! The get method of the globalCache instance returns a net.sf.ehcache.Element instance, which has a getValue() method you can call to obtain the cached value. Next on lines 8 and 9 the code checks that the returned value is null, and if it is, the passed closure is invoked, which returns the result that needs to be cached:

```
8          if(!entry) {
9              def entry = callable.call()
```

The return value of the call to the closure is used to place a new cache entry into the cache on line 10:

```
10 globalCache.put new Element(cacheKey, entry)
```

Finally, on line 12 the cache entry is returned regardless of whether it is the cached version:

```
12 return entry
```

With that done, let's see how to implement the CacheTagLib that can take advantage of the CacheService in Listing 12-21.

Listing 12-21. *Adding Content-Level Caching*

```
class CacheTagLib {
    static namespace = "cache"

    CacheService cacheService
    def text = { attrs, body ->
        def cacheKey = attrs.key
        out << cacheService.cacheOrReturn(cacheKey) {
            body()
        }
    }
}
```

Once again, Listing 12-21 shows how to use dependency injection to get hold of a reference to the CacheService in the CacheTagLib. The cacheOrReturn method is then used to cache the body of the tag using the key attribute passed into the text tag. Notice how the CacheTagLib has been placed inside a namespace, a concept you first learned about in Chapter 5.

Users of the simple-cache plug-in can now take advantage of content-level caching simply by surrounding the body of markup code they want to cache with the <cache:text> tag that the CacheTagLib provides. Listing 12-22 shows an example of its usage.

Listing 12-22. *Using the Tag Provided by the simple-cache Plug-in*

```
<cache:text key="myKey">
    This is an expensive body of text!
</cache:text>
```

Dynamic Spring Beans Using Conventions

In the previous section, you implemented the simple-cache plug-in using an Ehcache bean registered in the Spring ApplicationContext. What this example didn't demonstrate, though, is the ability to dynamically create beans on the fly using the conventions in the project.

In the "Custom Artefact Types" section, you explored how to create a plug-in that identified Quartz jobs. In a typical Spring application, you would need to use XML or annotations to configure each individual job using the org.springframework.scheduling.quartz.JobDetailBean class. With a Grails plug-in that knows about conventions, you can do it dynamically at runtime! Listing 12-23 shows this in action in a QuartzGrailsPlugin plug-in descriptor.

Listing 12-23. Dynamically Creating Beans at Runtime

```
1    import org.springframework.scheduling.quartz.*
2
3    class QuartzGrailsPlugin {
4        ...
5        def doWithSpring ={
6            application.jobClasses.each { GrailsClass job ->
7                "${job.propertyName}"(JobDetailBean) {
8                    name = job.name
9                    jobClass = job.getClazz()
10               }
II            }
12           ...
13       }
14 }
```

To better understand the code in Listing 12-23, let's step through it. First, on line 6 the each method is used to iterate over all the artefacts of type Job:

```
6        application.jobClasses.each { GrailsClass job ->
```

Then on line 7, a new bean is dynamically created using Groovy's ability to invoke methods using a String (or a GString) as the method name:

```
7        "${job.propertyName}"(JobDetailBean) {
```

In this case, given the SimpleJob from Listing 12-15, you would end up with a bean called simpleJob in the Spring ApplicationContext that is an instance of the Quartz JobDetail class. The JobDetailBean class is a Spring-provided helper class for creating Quartz JobDetail instances as Spring beans. Finally, on lines 8 and 9, the name of the job and the class of the job are set using properties of the GrailsClass interface:

```
name = job.name
jobClass = job.getClazz()
```

To finish up the Quartz plug-in, you could set up beans within doWithSpring for the Scheduler, using Spring's SchedulerFactoryBean, the triggers, and so on. However, since this serves mainly as a demonstration of what is possible, we recommend you take a look at the excellent existing Quartz plug-in for Grails, which is installable with the following command:

```
$ grails install-plugin quartz
```

Using Metaprogramming to Enhance Behavior

In the previous section, you saw how plug-ins can participate in the configuration of the Spring `ApplicationContext`. Now let's look at another area that plug-ins typically contribute to: the application behavior. Groovy is a fully dynamic language that allows you to completely modify the behavior of a class at runtime through its metaprogramming APIs.

■ **Tip**   If you want a book with significant coverage of Groovy's metaprogramming capabilities, look at *Programming Groovy*, by Venkat Subramaniam (Pragmatic Programmers, 2008).

Like Smalltalk, Ruby, Lisp, and other dynamic languages, Groovy features a (Meta Object Protocol MOP). The key thing to remember is that it is the MOP that decides the behavior of Groovy code at runtime, so code that looks as though it may do one thing at compile time could be made to do something completely different. For each `java.lang.Class` that Groovy knows about, there is an associated `MetaClass`. The `MetaClass` is what dictates how a particular method, constructor, or property behaves at runtime.

Groovy's `MetaClass` allows you to add methods, properties, constructors, and static methods to any class. For example, consider the code in Listing 12-24.

Listing 12-24. Adding New Methods to a Class

```
class Dog {}
Dog.metaClass.bark = { "woof!" }
assert "woof!" == new Dog().bark()
```

Here you have a simple class called `Dog`. Instances of the `Dog` class cannot, as it stands, bark. However, by using the `MetaClass`, you can create a bark method with this expression:

```
Dog.metaClass.bark = { "woof!" }
```

Clearly, this example has only brushed the surface of what is possible. Groovy provides a whole lot of capabilities related to runtime metaprogramming, all of which are available in the context of a Grails application.

Let's look at an example within the context of a Grails plug-in by trying to add the `cacheOrReturn` method to all controllers to eliminate the need to inject the service via Spring first. Listing 12-25 demonstrates how, by simply delegating to the `CacheService`, you can add a `cacheOrReturn` method to all controllers too.

■ **Tip**   If you prefer not to create a plug-in but would still like to do metaprogramming in your Grails application, we recommend you do so within a `Bootstrap` class, a topic covered in Chapter 12.

Listing 12-25. Adding Methods to All Controllers

```
class SimpleCacheGrailsPlugin {
    ...
    def doWithDynamicMethods = { applicationContext ->
        def cacheService = applicationContext.getBean("cacheService")
        application.controllerClasses*.metaClass*.cacheOrReturn = {
            Serializable cacheKey, Closure callable ->
```

```
                cacheService.cacheOrReturn(cacheKey, callable)
        }
    }
}
```

Another important aspect to notice about the code in Listing 12-25 is the use of Groovy's spread dot operator *. to obtain all the MetaClass instances from all the controllerClasses and also the use of a spread assignment to create a cacheOrReturn method for each MetaClass. That's far easier than adding a for or each loop!

Plug-in Events and Application Reloading

As well as the plug-in hooks discussed in the "Plug-in Hooks" section, plug-ins can also participate in a number of events, including application reload events. Grails aims to minimize the number of application restarts required during development time. However, since reloading is typically different for each artefact type, the responsibility to reload is delegated to plug-ins.

A plug-in can essentially listen for three core events: onChange, onConfigChange, and onShutdown. Let's take a look at onChange first, as it is the most common event dealt with by plug-ins. Each individual plug-in can monitor a set of resources. These are defined by a property called watchedResources. For example, as part of Grails core, there is a plug-in that provides support for internationalization (covered in Chapter 7) through the use of message bundles found in the grails-app/i18n directory. The i18n plug-in defines its watchedResources property as follows:

```
def watchedResources = "file:./grails-app/i18n/*.properties"
```

What this says is that the i18n plug-in will monitor all files within the grails-app/i18n directory ending with the file extension .properties.

▓ **Tip** If you're wondering about the file-matching patterns the watchedResources property uses, take a look at Spring's org.springframework.core.io.support.PathMatchingResourcePatternResolver class, as well as the Spring Core IO package in general, which Grails uses under the covers.

Whenever one of the properties files in the grails-app/i18n directory changes, Grails will automatically trigger the onChange event of the plug-in or plug-ins, monitoring the file passing in a change event object. The event object is essentially just a map containing the following entries:

- source: the source of the event, which is either a Spring org.springframework.core.io.Resource instance, representing the file on disk, or the recompiled and changed Java.lang.Class instance, if the watchResources property refers to Groovy classes

- application: a reference to the GrailsApplication instance

- manager: a reference to the GrailsPluginManager instance

- ctx: a reference to the Spring ApplicationContext instance

Typically the most important entry in the event map is the source, which contains a reference to the source of the change. In the case of the i18n plug-in, the source entry would reference a Spring org.springframework.core.io.Resource instance, since the properties files monitored by the i18n plug-in are not Groovy classes. However, if you develop a plug-in where you choose to monitor Groovy classes instead,

Grails will automatically recompile the changed class and place the altered class within the source entry in the event map.

Consider the Quartz plug-in discussed in previous sections. The `watchedResources` definition for that plug-in would look something like this:

```
def watchedResources = "file:./grails-app/jobs/**/*Job.groovy"
```

Whenever one of the Groovy files changes, Grails will recompile the class and pass you a reference to the `java.lang.Class` instance representing the job. However, that is all Grails will do. It's then up to you to make whatever changes you deem necessary to the running application to ensure it is now in the correct state. For example, in the "Dynamic Spring Beans Using Conventions" section, you saw how to dynamically register new `JobDetail` beans for each job class. To implement reloading correctly for the Quartz plug-in, you need to ensure that those beans are replaced with the new class. Listing 12-26 shows a hypothetical implementation that takes the newly recompiled class and registers new beans with the `ApplicationContext`.

Listing 12-26. *Implementing onChange for the Quartz Plug-in*

```
1   class QuartzGrailsPlugin {
2       def watchedResources = "file:./grails-app/jobs/**/*Job.groovy"
3       ...
4
5       def onChange = { event ->
6           Class changedJob = event.source
7           GrailsClass newJobClass = application.addArtefact(changedJob)
8           def newBeans = beans {
9               "${newJobClass.propertyName}"(JobDetailBean) {
10                  name = newJobClass.name
11                  jobClass = newJobClass.getClazz()
12              }
13          }
14          newBeans.registerBeans(applicationContext)
15      }
16 }
```

Although the code is pretty short, it has quite a few new concepts to understand. Let's walk through them starting on line 6, where a reference to the event's source is obtained:

```
6 Class changedJob = event.source
```

With the source in hand, the next thing the onChange event does is register the new `Class` with the `GrailsApplication` instance by calling the `addArtefact` method:

```
7       GrailsClass newJobClass = application.addArtefact(changedJob)
```

The code on line 8 is pretty interesting. Here the implicit beans method is used; it takes a block of code that uses the `BeanBuilder` syntax discussed in the "Providing Spring Beans" section. The beans method returns a `BeanBuilder` instance containing the bean definitions (but not the instantiated beans themselves):

```
8       def newBeans = beans {
```

The code on lines 8 to 13 is essentially the same as that in Listing 12-26; all the code does is create a new `JobDetailBean` bean definition from the new class. Line 14 is far more interesting; it shows how to use the registerBeans method of the BeanBuilder class to register all the bean definitions defined within the BeanBuilder instance with the provided ApplicationContext:

```
14 newBeans.registerBeans(applicationContext)
```

Of course, not all plug-ins will need to register new beans based on an onChange event. This is a requirement only if in the doWithSpring closure you registered beans that require reloading behavior. It may be possible to work with the existing beans to implement effective reloading for a plug-in. For example, the i18n plug-in discussed earlier simply clears the MessageSource cache, forcing it to be rebuilt:

```
def messageSource = applicationContext.getBean("messageSource")
if (messageSource instanceof ReloadableResourceBundleMessageSource) {
    messageSource.clearCache()
}
```

Other than the onChange event, the two other events available are onConfigChange and onShutdown. The onConfigChange event is fired if the Grails global configuration file, found at grails-app/conf/Config.groovy, is changed by the user. In the case of the onConfigChange event handler, the source of the change event is the altered ConfigObject. Often, plug-ins rely on settings found within Config.groovy for configuration. Remember, Grails uses Convention *over* Configuration, which means that conventions are used to ease development, but configuration is still possible if required. Later in this chapter you'll see an example that uses the Grails ConfigObject, which is obtainable using the getConfig() method of the GrailsApplication class.

Finally, the onShutdown event is fired when the shutdown() method of the GrailsPluginManager is called. This happens, for example, when a Grails application is undeployed from a container and the Grails servlet's destroy() method is invoked.

Modifying the Generated WAR Descriptor

As discussed in Chapter 12, the web.xml file Grails uses to integrate with servlet containers is generated programmatically. You saw in Chapter 12 that it is possible to modify the template used to generate web.xml by using the install-templates command. However, it is also possible for plug-ins to modify web.xml programmatically by using the doWithWebDescriptor hook.

Essentially, when the web.xml file is generated, it gets parsed into memory by Groovy's DOMBuilder. This parser creates an in-memory representation of the XML that you can modify. The doWithWebDescriptor hook is passed a reference to the XML as the first argument to the doWithWebDescriptor closure. XmlSlurper allows you to use a builder-like syntax to make modifications to the XML.

As an example, one of the core Grails plug-ins is the URL mappings plug-in, which provides the functionality covered in Chapter 6. The plug-in works by providing a Servlet filter that rewrites requests onto the main Grails servlet. To add this Servlet filter to the mix, the doWithWebDescriptor implementation of the URL mappings plug-in looks something like the code in Listing 12-27.

Listing 12-27. Example doWithWebDescriptor That Adds a New Servlet Filter

```
1  def doWithWebDescriptor = { webXml ->
2      def filters = webXml.filter
3      def lastFilter = filters[filters.size()-1]
4      lastFilter + {
5          filter {
6              'filter-name'('urlMapping')
7              'filter-class'(UrlMappingsFilter.getName())
```

```
8            }
9        }
10       ...
11 }
```

To understand what the code in Listing 12-27 is doing, let's look at it line by line. First, on line 2, a GPath expression is used to get a list of all the existing <filter> elements contained within the web.xml file:

```
def filters = webXml.filter
```

Then, on line 3, a reference to the last <filter> element in the list is obtained:

```
def lastFilter = filters[filters.size()-1]
```

As you can see from the previous two examples, using Groovy's XML APIs is nothing like using a Java XML parser. The XML object parsed by XmlSlurper almost feels like a first-class object, with very little evidence that the underlying data structure is in fact XML. Finally, onlines 4 through 9, the overridden + operator is used to add a new <filter> element directly after the last <filter> element:

```
4 lastFilter + {
5     filter {
6         'filter-name'('urlMapping')
7         'filter-class'(UrlMappingsFilter.getName())
8     }
9 }
```

Notice how in Groovy you can use strings for method names; for instance, you can choose an idiomatic XML element name like <filter-name> as the name of a method. The previous code will append the following equivalent XML snippet to the web.xml document:

```
<filter>
<filter-name>urlMapping</filter-name>
<filter-class>
org.codehaus.groovy.grails.web.mapping.filter.UrlMappingsFilter
</filter-class>
</filter>
```

As you see, Grails makes it pretty easy to participate in the generation of the web.xml file. Although not a common thing to do in a plug-in, it is sometimes useful when you want to integrate legacy servlets, filters, and so on. As mentioned previously, you could have used the grails install-templates command and modified the web.xml template directly, but this technique allows you to create plug-ins that automatically do this configuration for you. Reducing configuration, as well as embracing simplicity, is very much the Grails way, and doWithWebDescriptor is just another example of that.

Packaging and Distributing a Grails Plug-in

Once you are confident that your plug-in is ready for distribution, you can package it using the grails package-plugin command. In the command window, simply type grails package-plugin from the root of your plug-in project, as shown in Listing 12-28.

Listing 12-28. Packaging a Plug-in

```
$ grails package-plugin
  ...

| Plugin packaged grails-simple-cache-0.1.zip
```

As you can see from the output in Listing 12-28, the package-plugin command generates a zip file using the name and version number of your plug-in. In this case, you're packaging the simple-cache plug-in you developed earlier. Figure 12-2 shows an example of the resulting zip file.

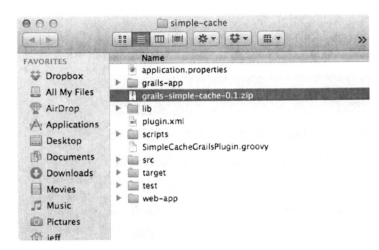

Figure 12-2. The simple-cache plug-in's packaged zip file

Using the steps explained earlier in this chapter in the "Plug-in Installation" section, you can now install the simple-cache plug-in into other applications and make use of the tag library and services it provides.

If you want to distribute your plug-in within the Grails central repository, you first need to obtain a plug-in developer account for the Grails central repository. You can find the steps to do so on the Grails web site at http://grails.org/Creating+Plugins.

Once you have obtained an account, you can publish your plug-in to the Grails central repository by using the publish-plugin command, which is provided by the release plug-in.

```
$ grails publish-plugin
```

The publish-plugin command needs your authorization credentials in order to publish to the repository. Those credentials should be defined in $HOME/.grails/settings.groovy, as shown in Listing 12-29.

Listing 12-29. Plug-in Repository Credentials

```
// ~/.grails/settings.groovy
grails.project.repos.grailsCentral.username = 'your username'
grails.project.repos.grailsCentral.password = 'your password'
```

The publish-plugin command does all the heavy lifting for you in making sure that the appropriate resources have been published in the repository and been tagged appropriately. The publish-plugin command will also generate an updated plug-in list so that your plug-in appears whenever a Grails user types the list-plugins command.

Local Plug-in Repositories

If you want to take advantage of the plug-in distribution and discovery mechanism in Grails on your own local network, you can set up a local plug-in repository. The Grails plug-in repositories are currently backed by a maven-compatible repository. Tools like Nexus and Artifactory can be used to help manage these. Once you have a maven-compatible repository up and running, you need to configure the release plug-in so that it knows about your repository. The way to do that is by defining a property in BuildConfig. groovy for each of the repositories that you want to interact with (see Listing 12-30).

Listing 12-30. Configuring Maven Repositories in BuildConfig.groovy

```
grails.project.repos.myRepo.url = "http://localhost:8081/myRepo"
grails.project.repos.myRepo.type = "maven"
grails.project.repos.myRepo.username = "admin"
grails.project.repos.myRepo.password = "password"
grails.project.repos.myRepo.portal = "grailsCentral"

grails.project.repos.myOtherRepo.url = "http://localhost:8081/myOtherRepo"
grails.project.repos.myOtherRepo.type = "maven"
grails.project.repos.myOtherRepo.username = "admin"
grails.project.repos.myOtherRepo.password = "password"
grails.project.repos.myOtherRepo.portal = "grailsCentral"
```

Now that you have configured the system to know about your own Maven repositories, you can publish to them, as shown in Listing 12-31.

Listing 12-31. Publishing to a Custom Repository

```
grails publish-plugin --repository=myRepo
grails publish-plugin --repository=myOtherRepo
```

The release plug-in also supports publishing to your local Maven cache. This does not require any repository server but instead installs directly to your file system under $HOME/.m2/. The maven-install command will publish a plug-in to the local Maven cache. In order for an application to resolve plug-ins that have been installed to the local Maven cache, mavenLocal() needs to be configured as a repository in BuildConfig.groovy, as shown in Listing 12-32.

Listing 12-32. Configuring the Local Maven Cache As a Repository

```
grails.project.dependency.resolution = {
    ...
    repositories {
        mavenLocal()
        ...
    }
    ...
}
```

With that, we've reached the end of this tour of the plug-in system. You've seen how to take advantage of the plug-in system in many different ways. This section has touched on some ideas for plug-ins, including the simple-cache plug-in and the Quartz plug-in, but the plug-in system is such a critical part of the Grails ecosystem that the lessons learned should be put to further use. In the next section, you'll be applying what you've learned so far to create two new plug-ins for the gTunes application. Along the way, you'll discover how plug-ins in Grails can be used as both a way to extend the functionality of an existing application and a way to effectively modularize your code base.

Plug-ins in Action

You've learned what plug-ins are and the basics of creating plug-ins. Now it is time to put that knowledge to work by developing a couple of plug-ins for the gTunes application. The first one you're going to create is a plug-in that makes the album art service and tag library you developed in Chapter 8 into a reusable plug-in. This is a perfect example of developing a plug-in to add functionality and enhance behavior.

Adding Behavior With Plug-ins

To start with, run the create-plugin command to create the basis of an album-art plug-in: $ grails create-plugin album-art The next step is to move the AlbumArtService.groovy file and the AlbumArtTagLib.groovy file into the newly created plug-in project. Once this is done, your plug-in should be structured like Figure 12-3.

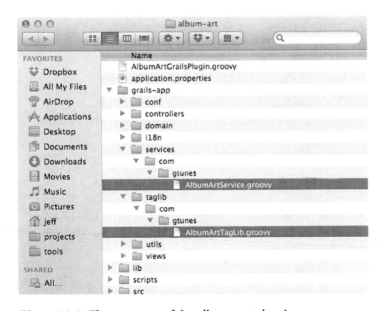

Figure 12-3. The structure of the album-art plug-in

Remember that the AlbumArtService class makes use of the RestBuilder class provided by the rest-client-builder plug-in. The plug-in dependency needs to be expressed in the album-art plug-in's BuildConfig.groovy; once the album-art plug-in is installed in the application, the dependency on rest-client-builder may be removed from the application's BuildConfig.groovy. Also, don't forget to move the two tests that provide coverage for the AlbumArtService and AlbumArtTagLib from the application into the plug-in. As mentioned previously, the great thing about plug-ins is that since they can be developed and tested separately, they are useful for larger projects with multiple developers. With the AlbumArtServiceTests and AlbumArtTagLibTests test cases included in the album-art plug-in, you can now immediately test whether your plug-in is working by running the test-app command.

Once the tests are passed, you can add the plug-in metadata to the plug-in descriptor that describes what this plug-in is all about. Listing 12-33 shows the updated plug-in descriptor with the metadata provided.

Listing 12-33. *Providing Metadata to the album-art Plug-in*

```
class AlbumArtGrailsPlugin {
    def version = 0.1
    def author = "Joe Someone"
    def authorEmail = "joe@company.com"
    def title = "Album art look-up plugin"
    def description = 'A plug-in that provides facilities to look-up album art'
    ...
}
```

To spice things up even further, you're going to do a bit of metaprogramming—first, by adding a getAlbumArt method to all controllers and second by allowing instances of the Album class from the gTunes application to retrieve their art simply by calling a getArt() method. The first case, in Listing 12-34, shows the necessary code, which just gets the AlbumArtService instance and adds a method to all controllers that delegate to the AlbumArtService.

Listing 12-34. *Adding a getAlbumArt Method to All Controllers*

```
class AlbumArtGrailsPlugin {
    ...
    def doWithDynamicMethods = { ctx ->
        def albumArtService = ctx.getBean("albumArtService")
        application.controllerClasses*.metaClass*.getAlbumArt = { String artist, String album ->
            return albumArtService.getAlbumArt(artist, album)
        }
    }
}
```

Adding a getArt() method to the Album class is a little trickier, because the plug-in doesn't know anything about the Album class. So to implement this enhancement, you'll search the GrailsApplication instance for a domain class called Album and, if it exists, add the getArt() method to it. Listing 12-35 shows the modifications to the doWithDynamicMethods plug-in hook.

Listing 12-35. *Adding a getAlbumArt Method to All Controllers*

```
class AlbumArtGrailsPlugin {
  ...
  def doWithDynamicMethods = { ctx ->
    ...
    def albumClass = application.domainClasses.find { it.shortName == 'Album' }
    if(albumClass) {
      albumClass.metaClass.getArt ={->
        albumArtService.getAlbumArt(delegate.artist?.name,
```

```
                delegate.title)
        }
      }
    }
}
```

Notice how within the body of the new getArt method you can use the closure delegate to obtain the artist and title. The delegate property of a closure, when used in this context, is equivalent to referring to this in a regular method. With the code in Listing 12-35 in place, you can now obtain the URL to an Album instance's album art with the code shown in Listing 12-36.

Listing 12-36. Using the getArt() Method to Obtain Album Art

```
def album = Album.get(10)
println "The art for this album is at ${album.art}"
```

Note that, in Groovy, methods that follow bean conventions are accessible via the property access notation, so the expression album.art is equivalent to album.getArt(). And with that, you have completed the album-art plug-in.

Specifying Plug-in Locations on the File System

Several times during this book you have installed plug-ins into the gTunes application, something normally done by expressing a dependency in the plug-ins section of BuildConfig.groovy. This is the most common way to express a dependency on a plug-in but not the only way. An application may express a dependency on a plug-in from anywhere on the file system, even if the plug-in has never been packaged and never been installed into a repository. This is useful for cases where you have the source code for the plug-in and may want to be actively developing the plug-in while developing the application. The way to express a dependency like this is to define a property in BuildConfig.groovy where the property name is of the form grails.plugin.location.<plugin name> and the value assigned to that property is a path to the directory on the file system containing the source for the plug-in project (see Listing 12-37).

Listing 12-37. Installing the album-art Plug-in into gTunes

```
grails.plugin.location.'album-art'='../album-art'
...
grails.project.dependency.resolution = {
    ...
}
```

Note that the value assigned to the property is "../album-art", a relative path; that path is relative to the root directory of the gTunes application. For this to work, the album-art plug-in and the gTunes application directory need to share a parent directory. Also, notice that part of the grails.plugin.location.'album-art' property name is quoted; that is because the name of the plug-in has a hyphen in it. A hyphen is not a valid character for an identifier in Groovy; seeing it, the compiler thinks that you are trying to do subtraction. Groovy offers a simple way around this by quoting the property name that contains the otherwise invalid character—namely, the hyphen.

Now you can start up the gTunes application, and it will behave exactly as before, except it is utilizing the album-art plug-in's functionality instead! One thing to note about the album-art plug-in is that although it provides new functionality in the form of services, tag libraries, and new methods, it does not comprise an entirely self-contained application. We'll look at how you can achieve this in the next section.

Plug-ins for Application Modularity

As well as making it possible to extend the available APIs within a Grails application, plug-ins also provide entire modules of application functionality. Many newcomers dismiss plug-ins as purely for plug-in developers who are willing to jump into the core Grails APIs, but in fact, plug-ins are an extremely effective way to modularize your application. In this section, you'll learn how to create an entire application as a plug-in that can be installed into the gTunes application.

To keep things simple, let's tackle a very commonly demonstrated application in screencasts and presentations around Grails: the blog. Yes, as with any self-respecting modern web application, the gTunes application needs a blog, where the proprietors of the gTunes store can make big announcements about new music, events, and so on. Luckily, a simple blog isn't too complicated; it takes about five minutes to implement in Grails.

The first step is to run the `create-plugin` command to make the blog plug-in:

```
$ grails create-plugin blog
```

This will create the blog plug-in and associated `BlogGrailsPlugin` descriptor. You can populate the descriptor with some plug-in metadata. Listing 12-38 shows a sample blog plug-in descriptor.

Listing 12-38. Adding Metadata to the blog Plug-in

```
class BlogGrailsPlugin {
    def version = 0.1
    def author = "Joe Someone"
    def authorEmail = "joe@company.com"
    def title = "A blogging plugin"
    def description = 'A plugin that provides a blog facility'
    ...
}
```

Now it's time to create a domain class that models a blog post:

```
$ grails create-domain-class com.blog.Post
```

Thinking about the `Post` domain class for a moment, it's going to have the obvious things like a title and a body, as well as a date posted. Putting this into practice, Listing 12-39 shows the `Post` domain class containing the necessary properties.

Listing 12-39. The Post Domain Class Package com.blog

```
class Post {
    String title
    String body
    Date dateCreated
    Date lastUpdated
    static constraints = {
        title blank:false
        body type:"text", blank:false
    }
}
```

Note that the `Post` domain class is using the property names dateCreated and lastUpdated to take advantage of auto time stamping capabilities in Grails that were first discussed in Chapter 9. With an appropriate domain class in place, to help you get started, you can use scaffolding to quickly generate a controller and views for the Post domain class:

```
$ grails generate-all com.blog.Post
```

For this first revision of the blog plug-in, you're going to support the creation of new entries only; hence, you can remove the generated edit, update, and delete actions. In addition, you need to show only the first five posts; therefore, you can use the max parameter to the static list method of the Post class to specify that. Listing 12-40 shows the full code for the PostController.

Listing 12-40. *The PostController for the blog Plug-in*

```
package com.blog

class PostController {

    // only allow the save action to be accessed via a POST request
    static allowedMethods = [save: 'POST']

    def index() {
        redirect(action:list,params:params)
    }

    def list() {
        [ postList: Post.list( max:5) ]
    }

    def create() {
        [post: new Post(params) ]
    }

    def save() {
        def post = new Post()
        post.properties['title', 'body'] = params
        if(!post.hasErrors() && post.save()) {
            flash.message = "Post ${post.id} created"
            redirect(action:list)
        } else {
            render(view:'create',model:[post:post])
        }
    }
}
```

Now let's move onto the views. In the case of the blog plug-in, the list.gsp view is the most important, because it will be responsible for showing each blog entry. However, the default scaffolding in Grails displays the list view as a table, which is not very useful in this case. You can correct that by modifying the list.gsp view to render a _post.gsp template instead. Listing 12-41 shows the updated list.gsp code.

Listing 12-41. The blog Plug-in's list.gsp View

```
<html>
<head>
<meta http-equiv="Content-Type" content="text/html; charset=UTF-8"/> <meta name="layout"
content="${params.layout ?: 'main'}" /> <title>Post List</title>
</head>
<body>
<div class="nav">
<span class="menuButton">
<g:link class="create" action="create">New Post</g:link> </span> </div> <div class="blog">
<h1>${grailsApplication.config.blog.title ?: 'No Title'}</h1>
<g:render plugin="blog"
template="post" var="post"
collection="${postList?.reverse()}" /> </div> </body> </html>
```

There are a few key things to mention about the list.gsp view in Listing 12-41. First, note that when using the <g:render> tag to render a template in a plug-in view, you *must* specify the plug-in that this template belongs to; otherwise, Grails will attempt to resolve the template within the application it is installed into. Second, take note of the usage of the grailsApplication variable to specify the blog title:

```
<h1>${grailsApplication.config.blog.title ?: 'No Title'}</h1>
```

Here the implicit grailsApplication object is used to read a configuration setting from the grails-app/conf/Config.groovy file. If the setting called blog.title is specified in Config.groovy, then the view will use that. Hence, users of this plug-in are able to configure the blog to their needs. An alternative approach to doing this would be to use the <g:message> tag, in which case the plug-in user has to specify the message in the grails-app/i18n/messages.properties file. The choice is up to you.
Finally, take note of the HTML <meta> tag, which dictates what layout the list.gsp uses:

```
<meta name="layout" content="${params.layout ?: 'main'}" />
```

If there is a layout parameter within the params object, this tag will use that parameter for the layout; otherwise, it uses the main layout. The main layout will, of course, resolve to grails-app/views/layouts/main.gsp, but why the decision to allow customization via a parameter? The idea here is that the user of the plug-in can very easily customize the layout of the blog through URL mappings. For example, consider the URL mapping in Listing 12-42.

Listing 12-42. Using a URL Mapping to Customize the blog Plug-in's Layout

```
class BlogUrlMappings {
    static mappings = {
        '/blog'(controller: 'post', action: 'list') {
            layout = 'funky'
        }
    }
}
```

If you add the URL mapping in Listing 12-42 to your grails-app/conf/BlogUrlMappings.groovy file, users can go to the /blog URL and have the list action of the PostController execute, which in turn renders the list.gsp view. However, notice how a property called layout is set inside the body of the closure passed to the URL mapping definition. As you learned in Chapter 6, it is possible to pass parameters in this way. The result is that for the /blog mapping, a layout called grails-app/views/layouts/

funky.gsp will be used instead! This is a pretty powerful pattern because it allows you to apply a different layout simply by applying a new URL mapping to the same controller and action.

As for the _post.gsp template used in the <g:render> method of Listing 12-41, it is pretty simple and just formats each Post instance appropriately. You can see the code for the _post.gsp template in Listing 12-43.

Listing 12-43. *The _post.gsp Template*

```
<div id="post${post.id}" class="blogPost"> <h2>${post.title}</h2> <div class="body">
${post.body} </div>
<div class="desc">
Posted on <g:formatDate date="${post.dateCreated}" format="dd MMMMM yy" /> </div>
</div>
```

With that, you have pretty much completed the list.gsp view. Figure 12-4 shows what the list.gsp view looks like when you run the blog plug-in and head off to the list action of the PostController.

New Post

No Title

Figure 12-4. *The list view of the blog plug-in*

Since the view renders each Post directly in the list.gsp view, the show.gsp view has been made redundant and can be deleted. Also, for the first revision, you're interesting in creating new posts only, so edit.gsp can be deleted, too. You can always add editing later!

Moving on to the create.gsp view, it too could use a little cleaning up. Also, it would be nice to provide a rich text–editing capability for authoring the post. One of the plug-ins available for Grails is the CKEditor plug-in, which adds support for CKEditor (http://ckeditor.com), a rich text–editing component. To install the CKEditor plug-in into the blog plug-in add the corresponding dependency in BuildConfig.groovy, as shown in Listing 12-44.

Listing 12-44. *Add a Dependency to CKEditor*

```
grails.project.dependency.resolution = {

    ...

    plugins {
        runtime ":ckeditor:3.6.3.0"
        ...
    }
}
```

With that done, let's enable CKEditor in _form.gsp by using the <ckeditor:editor> tag provided by the CKEditor plug-in. Listing 12-45 shows the updated _form.gsp file with the usage of the <ckeditor:editor> tag highlighted in bold.

Listing 12-45. Using the CKEditor to Enable Rich Text Editing

```
<%@ page import="com.blog.Post" %>

<div class="fieldcontain ${hasErrors(bean: postInstance, field: 'title', 'error')} ">
    <label for="title">
        <g:message code="post.title.label" default="Title" />
    </label>
    <g:textField name="title" value="${postInstance?.title}" />
</div>

<div class="fieldcontain ${hasErrors(bean: postInstance, field: 'body', 'error')} ">
    <ckeditor:editor name="body" height="300" width="500">
        ${postInstance?.body}
    </ckeditor:editor>
</div>
```

With the <ckeditor:editor> tag, you can specify that you want only a simple toolbar with basic formatting options; otherwise, you'll get a toolbar with almost as many options as a word processor like Microsoft Word. The plug-in documentation at http://grails.org/plug-in/ckeditor covers all of the configuration options. Figure 12-5 shows the create.gsp view, with the <ckeditor:editor> tag doing the job of rendering a rich text–editing component.

Create Post

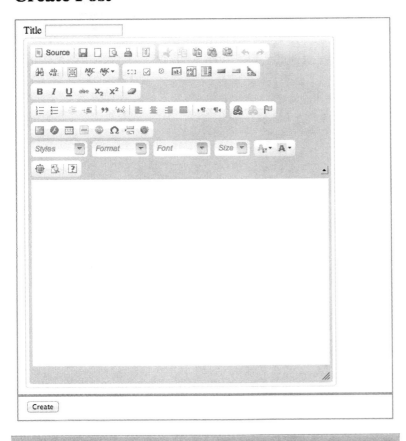

Figure 12-5. Creating a post with CKEditor

Of course, both the list.gsp and create.gsp pages currently look rather uninspiring, but it is up to the application you install the blog plug-in into to provide useful style information via CSS. Speaking of installing the blog plug-in into an application, it is time to do exactly that! In the gTunes BuildConfig. groovy file, express a dependency on the plug-in using the same technique used earlier to express a dependency on the album-art plug-in, as shown in Listing 12-46.

Listing 12-46. Installing the blog Plug-in into gTunes

```
grails.plugin.location.blog='../blog'
...
grails.project.dependency.resolution = {
    ...
}
```

Remember, the blog.title setting allows you to customize the blog title; simply adding the following setting to Config.groovy will do the trick:

```
// configuration for the blog blog.title="The gTunes Weblog"
```

Run the gTunes application using the run-app command, and then navigate to the URL http://localhost:8080/gTunes/post/list. Like magic, you have the blog plug-in running inside the gTunes application exactly as it was before—except that it is now taking advantage of the gTunes application's main layout. Clicking the New Post button will take you to the create.gsp view you developed earlier. Figure 12-6 shows the CKEditor component running within the gTunes application.

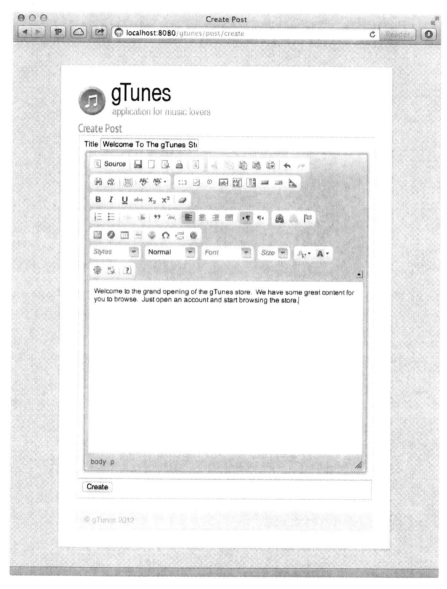

Figure 12-6. *Creating blog posts in the gTunes application*

If you type some content, including a title and body, and then hit the Post button, you'll be able to create new posts on the gTunes application blog, as shown in Figure 12-7.

Figure 12-7. A blog post in the gTunes application

Clearly, this is a very basic blog plug-in at the moment, one with no support for RSS, comments, calendars, archives, and all that jazz. However, as a demonstration of the concept of using plug-ins to separate your application in reusable modules, it's a perfect example. A separate team of developers could happily work on the blog plug-in and gradually integrate its functionality into the primary application over time. You could even create an automated build, as you learned in Chapter 11, to build and test all your plug-ins and install them into your main application for integrating testing. So plug-ins are definitely worth a look, even if you don't intend to become an expert on Grails internals.

Using the Resources Plug-in

The resources plug-in provides a lot of functionality related to managing static resources in your application. This includes things like deferring the inclusion of Javascript files until the end of the document to optimize page load times, preventing resources from being included in the same page multiple times unnecessarily, correcting load order of resources, and others. The plug-in is quite flexible and quite powerful. Here we will take a look at some of the basic functionality provided by the plug-in. Let's start by writing a couple of simple Javascript functions in separate files.

Listing 12-47. web-app/js/hello.js

```
function sayHello() {
    alert('Hello!');
}
```

Listing 12-48. web-app/js/goodbye.js

```
function sayGoodbye() {
    alert('Goodbye!');
}
```

Now let's write a simple GSP page, one that will make use of those Javascript functions.

Listing 12-49. grails-app/views/index.gsp

```
<!doctype html>
<html>
        <head>
                <title>Resources Plugin Demo</title>
         <g:javascript library="jquery"/>
         <g:javascript src="hello.js"/>
         <g:javascript src="goodbye.js"/>
         <r:layoutResources/>
        </head>
        <body>
            <r:script>
            $('#helloLink').click(function() {
                sayHello();
                return false;
            });
            $('#goodbyeLink').click(function() {
                sayGoodbye();
                return false;
            });
            </r:script>
            <p><a id="helloLink" href="hello">Say Hello</a></p>
            <p><a id="goodbyeLink" href="goodbye">Say Goodbye</a></p>
            <r:layoutResources/>
        </body>
</html>
```

When that GSP is rendered, the result will look something like Listing 12-50.

Listing 12-50. A Simple Rendered Page

```
<!doctype html>
<html>
  <head>
    <title>Welcome to Grails</title>
    <script src="/resourcesdemo/js/hello.js" type="text/javascript"></script>
    <script src="/resourcesdemo/js/goodbye.js" type="text/javascript"></script>
    <script src="/resourcesdemo/static/plugins/jquery-1.7.1/js/jquery/jquery-1.7.1.min.js"
type="text/javascript" ></script>
  </head>
  <body>
    <p><a id="helloLink" href="hello">Say Hello</a></p>
    <p><a id="goodbyeLink" href="goodbye">Say Goodbye</a></p>
    <script type="text/javascript">
```

```
    $('#helloLink').click(function() {
      sayHello();
      return false;
    });
    $('#goodbyeLink').click(function() {
      sayGoodbye();
      return false;
    });
  </script>
 </body>
</html>
```

Most of the rendered page is very straightforward and maps closely to what is written in the GSP—and probably maps pretty closely to what you expected. One interesting thing to note is that the Javascript that is embedded into the page, the code that is attaching functions to the "hello" and "goodbye" anchor tags, is rendered at the very bottom of the body, even though the code in the GSP is written at the top of the body. This is our first look at one of the benefits offered by the resources plug-in. Best practice is to put all Javascript at the bottom of the page to improve page load times. The resources plug-in is making that happen. The plug-in is rendering the Javascript at the very bottom of the page. The layoutResources tag, which is invoked at the bottom of the body in the GSP, is what actually does that. Let's move on.

One of the features that the resources plug-in provides is the ability to define "modules," or groups of static resources, that should be loaded together. It may be that you want goodbye.js and hello.js to be kept separate from a coding perspective to make them easier to maintain but you want them always to be loaded together into a page. If that is the case, it may make sense to define those two .js files as part of a module. Then pages that want to make use of the contents of the module don't have to make references to each of the static resources that are contained in the module; instead, they can simply express a dependency on the module.

Now let's edit grails-app/conf/ApplicationResources.groovy. In the file we'll define a new module, "messages," and include both of your .js files in the module. The syntax for this task is shown in Listing 12-51.

Listing 12-51. Defining the messages Module

```
modules = {
    application {
        resource url:'js/application.js'
    }

    // This defines a new module named "messages" and the
    // contents includes 2 js files
    messages {
        resource url: 'js/hello.js'
        resource url: 'js/goodbye.js'
    }
}
```

Now remove references to the .js files from the GSP and replace it with <r:require module="messages"/> to express that this page should include all of the .js files that are part of the messages module. See Listing 12-52.

Listing 12-52. Including a Module

...

```
<head>
    <title>Welcome to Grails</title>
    <g:javascript library="jquery"/>
    <r:require module="messages"/>
    <r:layoutResources/>
</head>
```

...

Now the rendered page will look something like Listing 12-53.

Listing 12-53. The Rendered Page

```
<!doctype html>
<html>
  <head>
    <title>Welcome to Grails</title>
    <script src="/resourcesdemo/static/plugins/jquery-1.7.1/js/jquery/jquery-1.7.1.min.js"
type="text/javascript" ></script>
  </head>
  <body>
    <p><a id="helloLink" href="hello">Say Hello</a></p>
    <p><a id="goodbyeLink" href="goodbye">Say Goodbye</a></p>
    <script src="/resourcesdemo/static/bundle-bundle_messages_defer.js" type="text/javascript"
></script>
    <script type="text/javascript">
      $('#helloLink').click(function() {
        sayHello();
        return false;
      });
      $('#goodbyeLink').click(function() {
        sayGoodbye();
        return false;
      });
    </script>
  </body>
</html>
```

Notice there are no longer references to hello.js and goodbye.js in the page; instead, there is a reference to bundle-bundle_messages_defer.js. If you point your browser at that URL, you will see that the file contains the union of the contents from your hello.js and goodbye.js files. Pretty slick stuff, indeed. Let's take this a little further.

Edit BuildConfig.groovy and add a dependency on the yui-minify-resources plug-in, as shown in Listing 12-54.

Listing 12-54. Depend on the yui-minify-resources Plug-in

```
grails.project.dependency.resolution = {
```

```
...

plugins {
    runtime ":hibernate:$grailsVersion"
    runtime ":jquery:1.7.1"
    runtime ":resources:1.1.6"
    runtime ":yui-minify-resources:0.1.5"

    ...
}
}
```

Including the yui-minify-resources plug-in will allow the resources plug-in to minify all of the Javascript in the messages module. The rendered HTML will now include a reference to a file named bundle-bundle_messages_defer.min.js (note that "min" is part of the file name), and that file will include a minified version of all of the relevant Javascript.

The resources plug-in is capable of a lot more than what has been introduced here, but even the little bit of functionality you've seen is quite valuable. The plug-in document at http://grails.org/plug-in/resources has much more detail on the plug-in's capabilities.

Using the Database Migration Plug-in

So far we haven't dealt much with defining database tables and columns or any kind of DDL. GORM does a great job of helping manage a lot of that. As you have seen, you can define your domain classes, and then let GORM take it from there. If you want to customize the schema that is being generated or if you are mapping your application to an existing schema, you can tweak some of the ORM details, like table names and column names, by writing code in the mapping block of your domain classes. This is all very flexible and very powerful but doesn't take care of everything. For example, it may be that a particular version of your application introduces new domain classes or new properties to existing domain classes; when that happens, you need some way to migrate your schema from one version of your domain model to the next. This is where the database migration plug-in comes into play. The database migration plug-in helps manage the evolution of your database schema from one version of your domain model to the next.

Here's an example scenario. Consider that you have a trivial application which contains a Person domain class, such as that defined in Listing 12-55.

Listing 12-55. The Person Class

```
package migrationdemo

class Person {
    String firstName
    String lastName

    static constraints = {
        firstName blank: false, size: 1..35
        lastName blank: false, size: 1..35
    }
}
```

Your application is fully developed, and you are ready to ship to production. This is a good time to create a snapshot of what your schema looks like. This snapshot will be a base point that may come into play later if your domain model changes. When the model does change, you will want to create a diff between this initial snapshot and the schema that is necessary to support the future model after changes have been made. A way to create this initial snapshot is with the dbm-generate-gorm-changelog command provided by the database migration plug-in. In order to use that, the plug-in must first be installed, as shown in Listing 12-56.

Listing 12-56. Installing the database-migration Plug-in

```
// grails-app/conf/BuildConfig.groovy
grails.project.dependency.resolution = {

    ...

    plugins {
        runtime ":database-migration:1.2"
        ...
    }
}
```

Note that you need to install the plug-in if you are using Grails 2.0.x. As of Grails 2.1 the plug-in is installed by default.

With the plug-in installed you can now execute the dbm-generate-gorm-changelog script.

```
$ grails dbm-generate-gorm-changelog changelog.groovy
| Packaging Grails application.....
| Finished dbm-generate-gorm-changelog
```

This will create grails-app/migrations/changelog.groovy. See Listing 12-57.

Listing 12-57. grails-app/migrations/changelog.groovy

```
databaseChangeLog = {

  changeSet(author: "jeff (generated)", id: "1352303958472-1") {
    createTable(tableName: "person") {
      column(autoIncrement: "true", name: "id", type: "bigint") {
        constraints(nullable: "false", primaryKey: "true",
                    primaryKeyName: "personPK")
      }

      column(name: "version", type: "bigint") {
        constraints(nullable: "false")
      }

      column(name: "first_name", type: "varchar(35)") {
        constraints(nullable: "false")
      }

      column(name: "last_name", type: "varchar(35)") {
        constraints(nullable: "false")
      }
    }
  }
}
```

Obviously that file contains, not SQL, but DSL code for defining your schema. The plug-in can interpret that code and turn it into SQL suitable for execution in the database. The DSL is pretty intuitive. You can probably read through the code and understand pretty much everything that is being expressed there. It is important that you review this code and understand what is being expressed. You should not blindly rely on the generated code. Make sure that it represents what you need before applying this code to your production database. That process should include evaluating not only the DSL code but also the generated SQL. A way to see the corresponding SQL code is by running the dbm-update-sql command, as shown in Listing 12-58.

Listing 12-58. Running dbm-update-sql

```
$ grails dbm-update-sql
| Starting dbm-update-sql for database sa @ jdbc:h2:mem:devDb;MVCC=TRUE;LOCK_TIMEOUT=10000
-- **********************************************************************
-- Update Database Script
-- **********************************************************************
-- Change Log: changelog.groovy
-- Ran at: 11/7/12 8:04 AM
-- Against: SA@jdbc:h2:mem:devDb
-- Liquibase version: 2.0.5
-- **********************************************************************


-- Create Database Lock Table
CREATE TABLE DATABASECHANGELOGLOCK (ID INT NOT NULL, LOCKED BOOLEAN NOT NULL, LOCKGRANTED
TIMESTAMP, LOCKEDBY VARCHAR(255), CONSTRAINT PK_DATABASECHANGELOGLOCK PRIMARY KEY (ID));

INSERT INTO DATABASECHANGELOGLOCK (ID, LOCKED) VALUES (1, FALSE);


-- Lock Database
-- Create Database Change Log Table
CREATE TABLE DATABASECHANGELOG (ID VARCHAR(63) NOT NULL, AUTHOR VARCHAR(63) NOT NULL, FILENAME
VARCHAR(200) NOT NULL, DATEEXECUTED TIMESTAMP NOT NULL, ORDEREXECUTED INT NOT NULL, EXECTYPE
VARCHAR(10) NOT NULL, MD5SUM VARCHAR(35), DESCRIPTION VARCHAR(255), COMMENTS VARCHAR(255), TAG
VARCHAR(255), LIQUIBASE VARCHAR(20), CONSTRAINT PK_DATABASECHANGELOG PRIMARY KEY (ID, AUTHOR,
FILENAME));

-- Changeset changelog.groovy::1352303958472-1::jeff (generated)::(Checksum: 3:cbe21510703560534
c81be19417709dd)
CREATE TABLE person (id BIGINT GENERATED BY DEFAULT AS IDENTITY NOT NULL, version BIGINT NOT
NULL, first_name VARCHAR(35) NOT NULL, last_name VARCHAR(35) NOT NULL, CONSTRAINT personPK
PRIMARY KEY (id));

INSERT INTO DATABASECHANGELOG (AUTHOR, COMMENTS, DATEEXECUTED, DESCRIPTION, EXECTYPE, FILENAME,
ID, LIQUIBASE, MD5SUM, ORDEREXECUTED) VALUES ('jeff (generated)', '', NOW(), 'Create Table',
'EXECUTED', 'changelog.groovy', '1352303958472-1', '2.0.5', '3:cbe21510703560534c81be19417709dd'
, 1);
| Finished dbm-update-sql
```

Once you have reviewed the DSL code and the corresponding SQL and are happy that all is consistent with your requirements, you can have that SQL executed against your production database in a couple of different ways. One is to let the plug-in handle it for you at deployment time. To do that, you need to set the grails.plug-in.databasemigration.updateOnStart config property to true in Config.groovy, as shown in Listing 12-59.

Listing 12-59. Enable Automatic Schema Updating

```
// grails-app/conf/Config.groovy
grails.plugin.databasemigration.updateOnStart = true
```

Note that for your production database you will most likely want to set dbCreate to "none" in grails-app/conf/DataSource.groovy. The migrations plug-in is more controlled and safer way of managing schema migrations. Using Hibernate's schema generation tools by setting dbCreate to something like "create-drop" is useful and efficient for your development environment, but probably not what you want for production.

With updateOnStart set to true, the migration plug-in will make sure that your schema is up to date at deployment time by generating and executing the SQL that corresponds to the latest migration DSL code. Some applications will want to be a little more explicit about this before deployment time. If you want to generate the schema ahead of time and do not want to set updateOnStart to true, a way to do that is with the dbm-update script. The dbm-update script will evaluate the migration DSL, generate the corresponding SQL, and send that SQL to the database for execution. Listing 12-60 shows the syntax for running the dbm-update script against your production dataSource configuration from DataSource.groovy.

Listing 12-60. Update the Production Schema

```
$ grails prod dbm-update
```

Be careful about running anything against your production data source. Make sure that the SQL has been reviewed and that you have appropriate backups in place.

Now that the production schema is consistent with your current domain model, you can create a WAR file and deploy the WAR file to production; everything should be good to go for now. If you ever change your domain model, you will need to generate a new migration script that will adapt your existing schema to account for whatever changes have been made to the domain model. Let's add a couple of new properties to the Person class, as shown in Listing 12-61.

Listing 12-61. Add age and email Properties to the Person Class

```
package migrationdemo

class Person {
    String firstName
    String lastName
    Integer age
    String email

    static constraints = {
        firstName blank: false, size: 1..35
        lastName blank: false, size: 1..35
        email email: true
        age range: 16..66
    }
}
```

If we deployed that code to production, we would have problems, since there are no columns in the person table to account for the age and email properties. The migration plug-in can help migrate the existing schema to support the new properties. The dbm-gorm-diff script will evaluate your current domain model, compare it with your existing schema, and then generate the code necessary to adapt your existing schema to support your current domain model.

```
$ grails dbm-gorm-diff change1.groovy --add
```

The first argument to the dbm-gorm-diff command is the name of the DSL file that will be created—in this case change1.groovy. The --add switch tells the migration plug-in to add an inlude to the root changelog file that references this newly created file. See Listing 12-62.

Listing 12-62. The Contents of change1.groovy

```
databaseChangeLog = {

        changeSet(author: "jeff (generated)", id: "1352305604562-1") {
            addColumn(tableName: "person") {
                column(name: "age", type: "integer") {
                        constraints(nullable: "false")
                }
            }
        }

        changeSet(author: "jeff (generated)", id: "1352305604562-2") {
            addColumn(tableName: "person") {
                column(name: "email", type: "varchar(255)") {
                        constraints(nullable: "false")
                }
            }
        }
}
```

Notice that change1.groovy does not contain information about the entire domain model. The file includes only information related to the differences between the current model and the current schema. In this case it includes change sets related to the email and age properties. Run the dbm-update-sql script again to see the corresponding SQL.

```
$ grails dbm-update-sql
| Starting dbm-update-sql for database sa @ jdbc:h2:devDB;MVCC=TRUE;LOCK_TIMEOUT=10000
-- ******************************************************************
-- Update Database Script
-- ******************************************************************
-- Change Log: changelog.groovy
-- Ran at: 11/7/12 8:36 AM
-- Against: SA@jdbc:h2:devDB
-- Liquibase version: 2.0.5
-- ******************************************************************

-- Lock Database
-- Changeset changelog.groovy::1352303958472-1::jeff (generated)::(Checksum: 3:cbe21510703560534
c81be19417709dd)
```

```
CREATE TABLE person (id BIGINT GENERATED BY DEFAULT AS IDENTITY NOT NULL, version BIGINT NOT
NULL, first_name VARCHAR(35) NOT NULL, last_name VARCHAR(35) NOT NULL, CONSTRAINT personPK
PRIMARY KEY (id));

INSERT INTO DATABASECHANGELOG (AUTHOR, COMMENTS, DATEEXECUTED, DESCRIPTION, EXECTYPE, FILENAME,
ID, LIQUIBASE, MD5SUM, ORDEREXECUTED) VALUES ('jeff (generated)', '', NOW(), 'Create Table',
'EXECUTED', 'changelog.groovy', '1352303958472-1', '2.0.5', '3:cbe21510703560534c81be19417709dd'
, 2);

-- Changeset change1.groovy::1352305604562-1::jeff (generated)::(Checksum:
3:0dce963c7c6e443c64ac983289725133)
ALTER TABLE person ADD age INT NOT NULL;

INSERT INTO DATABASECHANGELOG (AUTHOR, COMMENTS, DATEEXECUTED, DESCRIPTION, EXECTYPE, FILENAME,
ID, LIQUIBASE, MD5SUM, ORDEREXECUTED) VALUES ('jeff (generated)', '', NOW(), 'Add Column',
'EXECUTED', 'change1.groovy', '1352305604562-1', '2.0.5', '3:0dce963c7c6e443c64ac983289725133',
3);

-- Changeset change1.groovy::1352305604562-2::jeff (generated)::(Checksum:
3:d67ce27cffbfbc1c117fc0d3841e9a16)
ALTER TABLE person ADD email VARCHAR(255) NOT NULL;

INSERT INTO DATABASECHANGELOG (AUTHOR, COMMENTS, DATEEXECUTED, DESCRIPTION, EXECTYPE, FILENAME,
ID, LIQUIBASE, MD5SUM, ORDEREXECUTED) VALUES ('jeff (generated)', '', NOW(), 'Add Column',
'EXECUTED', 'change1.groovy', '1352305604562-2', '2.0.5', '3:d67ce27cffbfbc1c117fc0d3841e9a16',
4);

| Finished dbm-update-sql
```

Notice that the generated SQL is altering the person table to add columns for the new properties and is also updating the DATABASECHANGELOG table, which is the table that the migration plug-in uses to keep track of information about migrations that have been run. At this point you have the same options for having the diff applied as when you initially created the schema. You can set the updateOnStart property to true or run the dbm-update script explicitly.

The usage described above is a good introduction to some of the capabilities provided by the plug-in, but the plug-in provides quite a bit more functionality than is described here. See the documentation at http://grails.org/plug-in/database-migration for more details.

Summary

In this chapter, we hope you have learned the power of the Grails plug-in system, not just for plug-ins that provide API enhancements but equally for use cases that provide fully functional application modules, like those you saw in the previous section. Plug-in development is a very broad topic, and this chapter only brushed the surface of what is possible. However, the chapter has given you enough knowledge to investigate developing your own plug-ins.

From the basics of creating and populating plug-in metadata, to the intricacies of developing the plug-in itself, and finally to the packaging and distribution of your plug-ins, this chapter has covered a lot of ground. As you have seen, Grails provides a broad set of functionality out of the box, yet it can be extended without limits through its plug-in system.

Index

CPSIA information can be obtained at www.ICGtesting.com
Printed in the USA
LVOW122143271212

313485LV00002B/2/P